Budget Innovation
in the States

Allen Schick

Budget Innovation
in the States

The Brookings Institution
Washington, D.C.

Library of Congress Cataloging in Publication Data:
Schick, Allen.
　Budget innovation in the States.
　Includes bibliographical references and index.
　1. Budget—United States—States.　2. Program
budgeting—United States—States.　I. Title.
HJ2053.A1S35　1976　　353.9′3′722　　76-161594
ISBN 0-8157-7730-2
ISBN 0-8157-7731-0 pbk.

9 8 7 6

THE BROOKINGS INSTITUTION is an independent organization devoted to nonpartisan research, education, and publication in economics, government, foreign policy, and the social sciences generally. Its principal purposes are to aid in the development of sound public policies and to promote public understanding of issues of national importance.

The Institution was founded on December 8, 1927, to merge the activities of the Institute for Government Research, founded in 1916, the Institute of Economics, founded in 1922, and the Robert Brookings Graduate School of Economics and Government, founded in 1924.

The general administration of the Institution is the responsibility of a Board of Trustees charged with maintaining the independence of the staff and fostering the most favorable conditions for creative research and education. The immediate direction of the policies, program, and staff of the Institution is vested in the President, assisted by an advisory committee of the officers and staff.

In publishing a study, the Institution presents it as a competent treatment of a subject worthy of public consideration. The interpretations and conclusions in such publications are those of the author or authors and do not necessarily reflect the views of the other staff members, officers, or trustees of the Brookings Institution.

Foreword

The techniques of budgeting usually do not make the front pages or the newscasts, not even during those brief periods when public interest is stimulated by the presentation of the executive budget to the legislature. Public attention generally is focused on a few of the more controversial items and on those programs that represent significant changes in government policy. The press and the public may be concerned with why more money is recommended for public assistance or law enforcement, but they rarely seek to ascertain how these decisions were made and what kinds of information were used in determining budget policies. Accordingly, there probably are few public matters that are more opaque for the ordinary citizen than the methods used for determining how much to spend and for what purposes. Yet the policies and programs of every government are very much a product of the procedures it uses for assembling and reviewing the spending requests of its administrative agencies. That much of the business of budgeting is conducted behind the scenes and is enmeshed with complex accounting and administrative procedures does not diminish its importance.

As the public sector has grown in size and scope, there has been increasing concern about the adequacy and effectiveness of the methods used for determining public expenditures. Twice in the postwar period, broad-based attempts have been made to improve the budget machinery of American government—in the 1950s under the aegis of performance budgeting, and in the 1960s as a result of efforts to develop planning-programming-budgeting (PPB) systems. The performance budgeting drive was sparked by a study of federal organization, but it quickly spread to many states and localities, as did the PPB effort, which was launched by the Defense Department in 1961 and applied to other major federal agencies beginning in 1965. The goal of performance budgeting was to inform budget makers more fully concerning the work and services of government agencies. PPB had a significantly broader purpose—to use the budget process for analyzing the objectives and future consequences of public programs, and for evaluating the extent to which programs are achieving their objectives.

In this study, Allen Schick—a research associate in Brookings' Governmental Studies Program—examines the application of these two budget innovations in state governments. He delineates the diverse roots and aims of performance budgeting and PPB and finds that both have been hindered by the difficulty of changing entrenched budget practices and traditions. Yet he also finds that some states are substantially more advanced than others in the development and use of modern budget techniques. He bases his conclusions on a general survey of the states as well as on detailed investigation in selected states.

The author was aided in his research by many state budget officers who willingly responded to questionnaires and interviews. The entire manuscript benefited from careful reading and comment by Carl Akins, Herbert Kaufman, Gilbert Y. Steiner, and several anonymous readers. Successive drafts were typed by Pamela Tennyson and Delores Burton. Virginia C. Haaga edited the manuscript, and Joan C. Culver prepared the index.

The views expressed are those of the author and are not necessarily those of the trustees, officers, or other staff members of the Institution.

KERMIT GORDON
President

April 1971
Washington, D.C.

Contents

1. The Functions of Budgeting   1
The Uses of Budgeting 3
Performance Budgeting and PPB 8
Method of Study 10

2. Tradition and Innovation in Budgeting   14
The Executive Budget Movement 14
The Expansion of Budgetary Control 21
From Control to Management 25
Planning and Budgeting for Public Objectives 31

3. Performance Budgeting in the States   44
Performance Techniques 44
New Patterns of Control 48
The Hybridization of Performance Budgeting 52
The Hybridization Syndrome 54
The Strategy of Hybridization 60
Attitude toward Performance Budgeting 62
Performance Budgeting in Three States 69
Concluding Comment 85

4. The Status of PPB in the States   86
Problems of Assessment 87
Elements of PPB 89
Alternative Approaches to the Implementation of PPB 95
Training for PPB 100
What Has Been Accomplished? 103
Attitudes and Intentions 107
Concluding Comments 115

5. PPB in Five States   117
New York State: From Long-Range Planning to Program Analysis 117
Wisconsin: From Program Budgeting to PPB 128
California: Applying Federal PPB to State Government 138
Pennsylvania: A Systems Approach to PPB 145
Hawaii: Legislature versus Executive 153
Conclusion 163

6. Budgetary Men: Roles and Relationships   164
The Potential for Dissatisfaction 165
The Spenders 169
The Cutters 173
The Gatekeeper 177
The Uprooted 180
Fragmentation and Interdependence of Budget Roles 185
Information Specialization and Budget Roles 188
Changing Budgetary Roles 191

7. Is Budget Innovation Possible?   192
Reason and Politics in Budgeting 193
The Problem of Crosswalking 203
Alternatives to PPB: Systems for Planning and Analysis 211
The Possibility of Budgetary Improvement 216

Index   219

Tables

1. Performance Data in State Budget Documents   56
2. Attitudes of Budget Officers toward Selected Changes in
   Budget Practices   67
3. Attitudes toward PPB   108
4. Desirability and Feasibility of PPB Components   111
5. Attitudes of Budget Officials Concerning the Installation of PPB   114

Budget Innovation
in the States

1

The Functions of Budgeting

On August 25, 1965, President Lyndon B. Johnson called a meeting of his Cabinet to announce the introduction of a planning-programming-budgeting (PPB) system for the federal government. According to the President's announcement, the new system would enable public officials to "(1) identify our national goals with precision and on a continuing basis, (2) choose among those goals the ones that are most urgent, (3) search for alternative means of reaching those goals most effectively at the least cost, (4) inform ourselves not merely on next year's costs, but on the second, and third, and subsequent years' costs of our programs, (5) measure the performance of our programs to insure a dollar's worth of service for each dollar spent."[1] The new system quickly came to be known by its initials, and as it spread through the federal government and to states and localities, PPB was regarded as one of the major administrative innovations of recent times.

States already engaged in budget innovation redirected their efforts toward the PPB concept. Other states were introduced to PPB through federal grants, training programs, visits by teams of federal officials, and professional publications and conferences. Within a few years more than half of the states had been impelled to consider or implement some form of PPB. In terms of the popularization of an idea, therefore, the PPB story must be rated as a great success. However, in terms of actual implementation, the picture is quite different. By mid-1970, PPB was not yet operative in a single state, and only a few

1. Reprinted in U.S. Senate, Committee on Government Operations, *Planning-Programming-Budgeting, Official Documents*, 90 Cong. 1 sess. (1967), p. 1.

states had firm blueprints for future implementation. Moreover, interest in the new system had begun to recede, and in most states its development was no more advanced than it had been a year earlier. One could not identify a single state in which most of the benefits envisaged by the President had been achieved. Budgeting in the states operated as it had for more than half a century—principally as a means for financing the ongoing activities of established bureaucracies, not as an instrument for determining public objectives.

In explaining the mercurial career of PPB, it is important to realize that this is not the first budget innovation to fall short of its mark. Nearly two decades before PPB—in 1949—the Hoover Commission recommended the adoption of performance budgeting, a method of budget decision "based upon functions, activities, and projects."[2] As conceived by the commission, performance budgeting would focus attention

upon the general character and relative importance of the work to be done, or upon the service to be rendered, rather than upon the things to be acquired, such as personal services, supplies, equipment, and so on. These latter objects are, after all, only the means to an end. The all-important thing in budgeting is the work or service to be accomplished, and what that work or service will cost.[3]

Following this recommendation, many states tried to apply performance budgeting[4] to their own budget operations. Yet performance budgeting did not achieve its key objectives; it won only limited acceptance in a limited number of jurisdictions. While the detailed line itemizations were purged from most budget documents, they remained prominent in budget preparation and execution. Activity accounts and work statistics were added, but few states reported or measured accomplishments. Even when the realignments of data and formats called

2. U.S. Commission on the Organization of the Executive Branch of the Government, *Budgeting and Accounting* (Government Printing Office, 1949), p. 8.

3. *Ibid.*

4. Throughout this book, "performance budgeting" refers to the budget reforms that were associated with the Hoover Commission's recommendation and were proposed in many states during the 1950s and early 1960s. Performance budgeting is not used interchangeably with "program budgeting." The latter term is reserved for end-product or objective-oriented classifications, in contrast to performance budgeting, which applies to activity classifications and work measurements. Program budgeting is regarded as one of the components of PPB and, accordingly, is identified with later budget reforms.

Of course, in quotations from other writings, the original usage is retained, whether or not it conforms with this definition.

for by performance budgeting were made, they did not (and could not, it is now generally conceded) produce the anticipated changes in budget practice. Long ago the enthusiasm and confidence that marked performance budgeting's debut turned into doubt and indifference, and it now appears that PPB may follow a similar troubled path.

There are many ways of examining the problems encountered in efforts to change the budget process. In this study the main perspective is on the functions the budget process serves in the administration of public agencies and in the control of public spending. Performance budgeting and PPB were attempts to alter the purposes to which the budget power is put. Even if the implementation strategy is well designed and well executed and the political climate reasonably favorable, both performance budgeting and PPB have to confront the established traditions and uses of the budget process. It is to these functions that one must turn for an understanding of the budgetary events of the past two decades.

The Uses of Budgeting

The budget has many uses and many users. It is a critical component of the political, economic, and bureaucratic processes of all modern governments.

Through more than half a century of practice, budgeting has acquired a variety of administrative functions related to the control of agency spending, the management of public activities, and the determination of governmental objectives. Every budget reform alters the uses to which the budget is put, and it is these uses that are most germane to the success or failure of the reform, the way it is implemented, and the attitudes of those involved in the day-to-day conduct of budgeting.

"Budget reform," Charles Beard wrote during the first period of budget innovation in the early years of this century, "bears the imprint of the age in which it originated."[5] This observation on the course of the executive budget movement is fully applicable to the later chapters in budget history—the performance budgeting and PPB episodes. Each period of budget reform has been associated with a particular concep-

5. Charles A. Beard, "Prefatory Note," in Arnold W. Lahee, "The New York City Budget," *Municipal Research*, Vol. 88 (1917), p. 95.

tion of the budget function. In Beard's period the budget was perceived primarily as an instrument of expenditure *control*; in the performance budgeting era an effort was made to use the budget to achieve efficient *management* of the activities and work of public agencies; and the current PPB movement conceives the budget process as an instrument of policy and program *planning*. Long ago the executive budget reforms became the tradition of American budgeting, focusing on the routines of preparing and executing the budget according to detailed items of expense. Post-World War II proposals have been attempts to dislodge or modify that tradition, to change the informational basis of budgeting, and thereby to alter the uses of the budget process.[6]

Although every budget process includes aspects of control, management, and planning, one function tends to predominate. As a practical matter, these three functions are competitive; emphasis on one diminishes use of the others. Central authorities must be selective in their use of the crowded days and months of the fiscal year. If they use the central budget apparatus to maintain close surveillance over the spending actions of agencies, it is unlikely that they will have the opportunity or the capability to plan or manage through the budget process. The several budget functions require different skills and perspectives and different budgetary roles and relationships. Control, management, and planning also have diverse informational bases. The time frame and degree of aggregation suitable for one function may be inappropriate for another. Similarly, for each function, data have a particular source, distribution, and use.

Control in budgeting is the process of enforcing the limitations and conditions set in the budget and in appropriations, and of securing compliance with the spending restrictions imposed by central authorities. If the budget details the allowances for items of expense, the central budgeters will be required, or at least tempted, to monitor agency actions in order to enforce the limits. If restrictions are imposed on the spending discretion of agencies, the budget power will be used to uphold these restrictions. *Management* involves the use of budgetary authority, at both agency and central levels, to ensure the efficient use of staff and other resources in the conduct of authorized activities.

6. This and subsequent paragraphs are adapted from Allen Schick, "The Road to PPB: The Stages of Budget Reform," *Public Administration Review*, Vol. 26 (December 1966), pp. 243–58.

In management-oriented budgeting, the focus is on agency outputs—what is being done or produced and at what cost, and how that performance compares with budgeted goals. *Planning* refers to the process of determining public objectives and the evaluation of alternative programs. To use the budget for planning, central authorities must have information concerning the purposes and effectiveness of programs. They must also be informed of multiyear spending plans and of the linkage between spending and public benefits.

Thus, if the budget process is dominated by a control orientation, its range of concerns is limited: How can the agencies be held to the expenditure restrictions—both in detail and in the aggregate—that have been established by the legislature and the central executives? What reporting procedures should be used to enforce propriety in expenditure and accuracy in the accounts? What limitations should be placed on agency authority to spend for personnel, equipment, travel, and other items? A management-oriented budget process, on the other hand, is concerned with operation rather than with control, that is, with the efficiency rather than the legality of expenditure. What is the best way to organize for the performance of an authorized activity? What is and what should be the cost of performing a unit of work? What is the maximum productivity derived from a unit of input? And finally, a planning orientation encompasses a broad range of policy concerns. What are the objectives of the government and the missions of its agencies, and how are these expressed in the budget? What criteria should be used for evaluating programs and for computing their costs and benefits? What is the effectiveness of program A compared to program B?

It should be clear that even where one function is dominant, the other two are also served, at least to a limited degree, by the budget process. A control-oriented budget process subordinates management and planning, but does not eliminate them altogther. The crucial issue is the balance among these vital functions at the central levels. What weight does each have in the design and operation of the central budget process? Several indicators provide clues to the orientation of a budget process. Each function emphasizes a different stage of the budget cycle: in a control environment, budget execution often commands a considerable amount of central time, but a management process gives greater significance to the preparation of the budget; and the planning orientation stresses the pre-preparation period—the conduct of policy analysis before the estimates are submitted. Each function has its distinctive budget classification: items of expense in the case of control, activity accounts for management budgeting, and the program categories for planning. A different budget skill is associated with each perspective: accounting is the traditional skill of budget controllers; public administration is the usual background of budget managers; economics and systems analysis is the specialized discipline of budget planners. Both control and management work within the single-year frame of the fiscal year, but planning necessarily has a multiyear dimension.

Every major reform changes the control-management-planning balance. In the first period of budget reform, the main emphasis was on expenditure control. In federal budgeting, this period opened with the passage of the Budget and Accounting Act of 1921 and the establishment of the Bureau of the Budget and was formally terminated with the Hoover Commission report in 1949. However, the decline of the control orientation began during the New Deal era, and, in many respects, the commission's performance budgeting recommendation was a recognition of changes that had been unfolding for more than a decade. In the states and cities, the period of control began earlier, usually with the installation of the jurisdiction's first budget system, and ended later, some years after the federal performance budgeting concept had filtered to the other levels of government. The hallmark of control was the detailed itemization of expenses, by means of which central supervision was maintained over purchasing and hiring practices, and agency spending was closely monitored.

While there is no requirement that governments must pass through a particular sequence of budgetary development, most governments begin with control and its line-item form. Bureaucratic conditions common to modern government, rather than special political circumstances, seem to be the motivating factor. All governments face the problems of preventing financial improprieties and of limiting agency spending to authorized levels. For this reason, government budgeting inevitably "begins with indispensable efforts to promote 'accountability' by preventing public funds from being stolen, used for unauthorized purposes, or spent at uncontrolled rates. . . ."[7]

The management orientation, which marked the second stage of

7. Bertram Gross, "The New Systems Budgeting," *Public Administration Review*, Vol. 29 (March/April 1969), p. 117.

budgeting, is reflected in the movement for performance budgeting and the concomitant redesign of expenditure accounts, the development of work and cost measures, and adjustments in the roles of central budgeters and in their relationships with agencies. The management approach has roots that go back to the beginnings of public administration in the United States, but it was the growth of the administrative state during the 1930s and the subsequent performance budgeting movement that pushed it to the forefront of administrative reform. Inasmuch as there remains a vast amount of unfinished performance budgeting business, the management era has extended into the recent PPB era.

PPB itself represents the third stage of U.S. budgeting, the planning orientation. In this stage, the determination of public objectives and programs becomes the key budget function. Planning also has significant connections with the transitions under the New Deal, but it is directly a product of the modern informational and decisional technologies associated with economics and systems analysis. In ideal form, PPB would centralize the planning function (that is, convert the central budget office into a policy- and program-making group) and delegate first-instance management and control responsibilities to the supervisory and operating levels.

Line-item and performance budgeting are unifunctional; each is concerned with its particular function and neglects the others. The line-item structure effectively serves the control function by providing central budgeters with numerous opportunities and justifications for intervening in agency spending. In this control environment, management and planning are done tacitly, usually in the agencies, but without any direct link to budget choice. There is a covert understanding of the program implications of budget estimates and of the work levels to be supported, but these are not made explicit. In performance budgeting, control and planning are decentralized or dispersed. Management-minded officials tend to delegate away the problem of control, hoping that it will be handled adequately in the agencies. Performance budgeting tried to come to grips with the essential need for new control mechanisms compatible with its management orientation, but without much success.

PPB has a multipurpose perspective. Although it regards planning as the central budget function, it does not ignore the need for control and management and for informational structures oriented to these functions. Accordingly, PPB works within a specialized rather than a homogeneous informational structure, with each function and each budget user assigned appropriate data. The difficulty of operating a multipurpose scheme has been one of the problems confronting PPB.

Performance Budgeting and PPB

Throughout the performance budgeting era, there was persistent confusion over the meaning of performance budgeting and program budgeting, and their relation to each other. Some writers used the terms interchangeably; some regarded program budgeting as a stepping-stone to performance budgeting; and some considered the program budget to be a step beyond the performance budget. The 1949 Hoover Commission preferred the term "performance budget," but its task force used "program budgeting," as did the task force of the second Hoover Commission. The level of confusion escalated with the arrival of PPB, as some writers equated PPB with program budgeting while others tried to distinguish between the two concepts.

The functional distinction between management and planning clarifies the relation between performance budgeting and PPB. Performance budgeting pertains to activities, not to objectives. Its principal thrust is to improve work efficiency by means of activity classifications and work/cost measurements. In line with its management orientation, the Hoover Commission spoke of the work or service to be accomplished as "the all-important thing in budgeting." In a planning framework, however, the all-important thing is not work or service but objectives and benefits. Whereas performance budgeting implicitly regards work and activities as values in themselves, PPB (along with its program budget component) treats them as intermediate processes of converting inputs into public benefits.

The function of a planning-programming-budgeting system is to enable policymakers to evaluate the costs and benefits of alternative expenditure proposals. For this purpose, its primary focus is on expenditure aggregates, and details come into play only as they contribute to an understanding of the total budget or of marginal choices among competing programs. In this analytical approach, the stress is on a systemic grouping of data into categories that facilitate comparisons among alternative expenditure mixes. The basic purpose of the performance budget, however, is to enable administrators to assess the efficiency and the work of the spending agencies. Its method is particularistic—the itemizing of data into discrete work/cost units. While it would be misleading to portray a full-blown PPB system—each jurisdiction will have its own version to suit its limitations and opportunities—it is useful to identify the basic elements and to indicate how they diverge from traditional and performance budgeting. PPB introduces four major changes in budget practice: (1) Budget choices are to be made more explicitly in terms of public objectives rather than in terms of the resources needed to finance agency activities and operations; (2) the multiyear costs and effects of public programs, not just next year's costs, are estimated; (3) formal consideration is given to alternative means of accomplishing public objectives, not merely to the single way justified in the budget estimates; (4) efforts are made to evaluate the benefits or the effectiveness of government expenditures.

Under PPB, the budget is stretched from single- to multiyear length, expenditures are classified into program categories, new procedures for planning and analysis are incorporated into the budget process, and the information system is adjusted to accommodate the expanded functions of budgeting and to link the program, organizational, and budgetary accounts. PPB tries to infuse an analytic disposition into budgeting by bringing economists and other new men into positions of influence, by creating new centers of analytic talent at the top decision-making levels, and by moving the budget process closer to the central planning and program development functions.

The evaluation of programs and the evaluation of performance are two distinct budgetary processes. It would be a mistake to assume that the use of performance techniques presupposes that program budgeting has been undertaken or that it is not possible to collect performance data without program classification.[8] It is possible to devise and apply performance methods without relating them to, or having the use of, larger program aggregates. A cost accountant or

8. Nevertheless, the view gained hold that a program budget is "a transitional type of budget between the orthodox (traditional) character and object budget on the one hand and performance budgeting on the other." Lennox L. Moak and Kathryn W. Killian, *A Manual of Techniques for the Preparation, Consideration, Adoption and Administration of Operating Budgets* (Municipal Finance Officers Association, 1963), p. 11.

work measurement specialist can measure the cost or effort required to perform a routine task without probing into the purpose of the work or its relationship to the program of the organization. Indeed, the compilation of workload statistics and some types of cost data (for example, per capita costs for hospital patients) is a routine practice in many agencies that do not budget on a program basis. Work measurement is only distantly and indirectly related to the process of determining government policy at the higher levels. Program classifications, however, deal with the function or the mission of the organization. They are vitally linked to the making and implementation of policy through the allocation of public resources. Whereas program techniques are directed at the *purpose* of work and at deciding what activities should be authorized, performance techniques generally are concerned with the *process* of work and with determining what methods should be used. The strong tendency toward itemization in performance budgeting thus presents a constant threat to PPB's emphasis on a systemic assessment of alternatives.

Method of Study

This study assesses the full career of performance budgeting and the first years of PPB. Although performance budgeting and PPB have different antecedents and purposes, there is much to be gained in studying them together. Both aim to rationalize budget choice by reorienting the informational structure from inputs to outputs. Each in its own way runs counter to the budget traditions established during the first decades of this century. As administrative innovations, they face common hurdles in persuading people and organizations to change their ways. A retrospect on performance budgeting can alert state officials to some of the problems that might confront PPB. Finally, much confusion can be avoided by comparing the two reforms. The advent of PPB has made it possible to clarify the meaning and intent of performance budgeting and to distinguish it decisively from program budgeting.

PPB strives to be more innovative than was its predecessor. It is appropriate to question whether the more challenging and difficult PPB device can succeed even though the modest performance budgeting effort did not. Is it practicable to require agencies to plan and analyze when they lack reliable data on what they are doing and accomplishing? Can agencies look ahead several years when they do not even look to next year to determine performance goals? Can agency officials think realistically about end-products when they do not even think about products?

Only a few years have passed since the official launching of PPB in 1965. Most states are still searching for the right approach, proceeding through trial and error to some accommodation of the existing and the possible. They can be expected to make substantial modifications in their original intentions as they become better acquainted with this new system. Changes in political and financial circumstances also will affect the development of PPB. It probably will be a decade or more before a complete appraisal can be made. Nevertheless, experience in the first states to use PPB provides an adequate basis for an initial evaluation of its progress and potential.

Material for this study was drawn from two sources: (1) field observations in selected states, including extensive interviews with program and finance officials, administrators and legislators, and individuals at high and middle levels of central and agency operations, (2) a survey of budget practices in all the states based on mail questionnaires, correspondence with state officials, and a review of budget documents and reports. To evaluate performance budgeting and PPB, two separate sets of studies were undertaken. The first field study was made in the early 1960s, during the waning years of performance budgeting but before the official inauguration of PPB. Eight states—Connecticut, Maryland, Massachusetts, New Jersey, New York, Ohio, Pennsylvania, and Rhode Island—were selected on the basis of geographical factors and diversity of performance budgeting experience.[9]

A second round of field studies was conducted in the late 1960s, several years after the emergence of PPB. Six states—Connecticut, Maryland, Pennsylvania, New Jersey, New York, and Rhode Island—were covered again, thereby providing a basis for comparing performance budgeting and PPB in the same states. And to obtain wider geographical representation than had been possible the first time, the

9. Of the eight states, all but Massachusetts had some performance budgeting experience. Connecticut and Maryland were the earliest adapters and had made the most progress, while New Jersey, New York, and Pennsylvania had varied experiences. Ohio used performance budgeting in the 1961–63 biennium but abandoned it subsequently.

sample was expanded. Michigan and Wisconsin were selected from the Midwest; California, Hawaii, Oregon, and Washington from the West, and Arkansas from the South and border regions. Each of these states has had some PPB experience, if only at the early preparation or investigation stage. Collectively, they comprise more than half of the states that had taken some PPB action by 1969.

The sample states do not furnish a cross-section of state politics and administration. All the performance budgeting states are in the Northeast, a section that has been characterized as oriented to traditional budget controls.[10] The states in the PPB sample are larger and more urbanized than the national average, they have higher per capita incomes, and they probably lean to the liberal side on public spending and policy issues.[11] They also tend more to competitive party alignments and to strong governors than does the typical state.[12] They rank significantly above the national norm in the adoption of innovations. According to the innovation scores computed by Jack L. Walker, thirteen of the states included in one or both of the surveys rank among the top sixteen in the country.[13]

It is understandable that the larger, more innovative states also have been the most active in budget reform. These states are more likely to have the will or the resources to redirect their budget systems and are therefore ones to look at in examining the effectiveness and potential of budget reform.

In a study of state budget reform, caution must be used in drawing evidence from other levels of government. Many political and administrative circumstances differentiate the states from the federal and local governments. But, it would be unduly timorous to refrain from all intergovernmental comparisons. In budgeting, as in public admin-

10. This is the view expressed by James W. Martin in "Patterns of State Budgeting" (1960; processed).

11. See Thomas R. Dye, *Politics, Economics, and the Public: Policy Outcomes in the American States* (Rand McNally & Co., 1966).

12. Comparisons among states on the basis of many factors can be found in Herbert Jacob and Kenneth N. Vines (eds.), *Politics in the American States* (Little, Brown & Company, 1965). For a statistical comparison of interparty competition, see p. 65. For a statistical composite of the formal powers of the governors, see p. 229.

13. "The Diffusion of Innovations among the American States," *American Political Science Review*, Vol. 63 (September 1969), p. 883. Among the states in both samples, only Arkansas had a relatively low innovation score. Hawaii was not ranked in the Walker study because it had been a state for little more than a decade.

istration generally, there have always been considerable diffusion and interchange among the several levels of government. The executive budget movement received its initial impetus from the New York Bureau of Municipal Research during the first decade of this century; it was made the focal point of federal administrative reform by President Taft's Commission on Economy and Efficiency in 1912; and it was carried to most of the states between 1915 and 1925. The emulative behavior of the "Little Hoover Commissions," endorsing performance budgeting during the 1950s, also suggests the intergovernmental flow of innovation, as does the PPB parade formed after President Johnson announced his federal decision. Accordingly, the experiences of the national government and the cities are enlisted to aid the study of state budgeting.

2

Tradition and Innovation
in Budgeting

Performance budgeting and PPB challenge the budget traditions established during the first decades of this century. Both confront the same forces that influenced governments to use budgeting for central control of agencies, and neither can succeed unless the earlier traditions are uprooted. This chapter deals with the history of modern budgeting from the formation of the control tradition through the development of performance budgeting and the emergence of PPB.

The Executive Budget Movement

Between 1911 and 1926 significant budget innovations were adopted in all of the states.[1] During this fifteen-year period, century-old appropriation and expenditure practices, grounded in legislative initiative and supremacy in financial affairs, were modified under the impact of the executive budget movement. The following conditions characterized legislative budgeting prior to the institutionalization of executive budget power. (1) No central official was empowered to review or revise departmental estimates, or to make fiscal recommendations to

1. The early history of budget reform is described in several studies. See Fred Wilbur Powell, "The Recent Movement for State Budget Reform, 1911–1917," *Municipal Research*, Vol. 91 (1917); William Franklin Willoughby, *The Movement for Budgetary Reform in the States* (D. Appleton and Company, 1918); Frederick A. Cleveland and Arthur Eugene Buck, *The Budget and Responsible Government* (The Macmillan Company, 1920), pp. 215–330.

14

the legislature; (2) in most states, each department's estimates were submitted separately, often at different times during the legislative session; (3) each agency classified its accounts in its own way; (4) the estimates usually were lacking supporting data and often were presented in lump sums; (5) agency requests were not related to revenue projections or to overall state expenditures; (6) each department bargained with the appropriations committees, and funds were appropriated separately for each department; (7) there was little or no central supervision of department spending.[2]

This fragmented public expenditure process was a product of nineteenth century views of government: limitations on gubernatorial power and tenure, the dispersion of administrative authority among independent boards and commissions, and partisanship in the public service. But early in this century, the old dogmas began to lose favor as reform reached into almost every aspect of government administration. The climb in total expenditures of the states (from $188 million in 1902 to $1.4 billion in 1922), the muckraking exposés of public ineptitude and corruption and the growing influence of public administration and its scientific management ethic stimulated widespread dissatisfaction with established budgetary methods. Procedures that were good enough just a few years earlier were discredited by the new gospel of executive budgeting that spread rapidly across the nation.

Three Conceptions of the Executive Budget

As the focal point of fiscal reform, the executive budget concept was advocated by diverse interests. Each interest viewed the reform in its own way, and each had its own conception of the budget function. The leading spokesmen for executive budgeting (especially Frederick A. Cleveland, Frank J. Goodnow, and William F. Willoughby) emphasized the planning potential of the budget process. Cleveland argued in 1915 that only the chief executive "can think in terms of the institution as a whole"; therefore, he "is the only one who can be made

---

2. Leonard D. White summed up the situation before the introduction of executive budgeting. "In 1910 a typical state agency or institution prepared its own estimates, submitted them directly to the appropriations committee, ultimately received an independent appropriation, and spent its funds without supervision other than that provided by the auditor." Leonard D. White, *Trends in Public Administration* (McGraw-Hill Book Company, 1933), pp. 207–08.

responsible for leadership."[3] In line with this planning perspective, Cleveland and his followers regarded the executive as the principal maker of budget policy. The executive was not to be merely the conveyor of agency estimates to the legislature, but the official who imposed a comprehensive and consistent set of judgments on all government spending. His budget would not be just a compilation of agency requests (with a few additions and deletions) but an authoritative statement of policies and programs. Accordingly the budget should have a special status; the legislature should be able to reduce or delete items but not add to the budget. Otherwise the "wholeness" of the budget would be destroyed because agencies would be encouraged to bypass the executive and negotiate with the legislature to restore budget cuts.

However, this was not the only conception of the budget function. Many reformers viewed the budget as a means of coordinating government activities. The executive budget was a major plank in the campaign for administrative reorganization and in this capacity was allied with efforts to achieve the functional consolidation of agencies, the elimination of independent boards and commissions, the strengthening of the chief executive's appointive and removal powers, and other changes that would bolster the central administrative capability of government. Under this management perspective, the job of the executive would be to standardize and consolidate agency estimates and to ensure that the budget facilitated the efficient conduct of the public business.

A third conception of executive budgeting derived from the quest for central controls to deter wasteful or unlawful administrative behavior. In this connection, the executive budget was associated with the installation of uniform accounting procedures, centralized purchasing, personnel control, and expenditure audits. This version of the executive budget called for the governor to be the chief controller of the state, exercising his authority to protect the public against improper action by agency officials.

The three conceptions of the executive budget had diverse roots. The planning viewpoint had its source in fundamental ideas about the workings of democratic government, the appropriate powers of the

3. Frederick A. Cleveland, "Evolution of the Budget Idea in the United States," *Annals of the American Academy of Political and Social Science*, Vol. 62 (1915), p. 17.

legislative and executive branches, and the means of maintaining accountability to the public. The management approach had close ties with the newly developed field of public administration, while the control posture was promoted by the influential advocates of economy and efficiency. All three conceptions made common cause in the movement for executive budgeting because all were to be served by lodging the budget power in the chief executive. But the planning, management, and control functions diverged sharply when the "budget idea" (as Cleveland called it) became an operational reality. As budget traditions were formed and hardened, the budget became the central instrument for administrative control over spending. In practice it was not feasible to accommodate all budget functions. Control won out because it was in harmony with the preferences of legislators and ranked as the number one need in finance administration.

Role of the Legislators and Governors

The executive budget idea had been conceived by persons who viewed government from an executive perspective, but its implementation had to be authorized by legislators, who had their own views of proper budgetary arrangements. In the minds of its prime movers, budget reform meant executive budgeting. The two were inseparable. Thus Cleveland's dictum: "To be a budget it must be prepared and submitted by a responsible executive."[4] This principle, Fred Powell wrote, was "the dominant force in the recent movement for state budget reform."[5] Yet fewer than half of the state budget systems established during the first wave of reform gave the basic power over budget preparation to the governor. In a majority of states, this authority was vested in an administrative board (comprised of the governor and other state officials) or in an executive-legislative commission.[6] Only after the initial arrangements proved unsatisfactory did these

4. *Ibid.*, p. 16.
5. Powell, "The Recent Movement for State Budget Reform," p. viii.
6. Contemporary writers were not in agreement in their classification of state budget systems. Powell (in 1917) listed twelve states in the executive budget category and sixteen in the legislative budget, administrative board, and mixed executive-legislative categories; Willoughby (in 1918) classified fourteen states in these latter groupings and eleven in executive budgeting; Cleveland and Buck (in 1920) placed twenty-three states in the executive-type category and twenty in the remaining groups.

states adopt the formalities of executive budgeting. Gulick's informative study of the evolution of budgeting in Massachusetts reveals that a succession of increasingly centralized authorities (the auditor, a commission on economy and efficiency, a supervisor of administration) was used before the governor was made the chief budget authority.[7]

It was not easy for state legislatures to yield portions of their power of the purse to the executive. Perhaps more than any other, this power had been regarded as the mark of legislative vitality and independence. It was over this power that the long struggles were waged between Parliament and the Crown in England and between legislature and governor in the colonies. The decisive language of the U.S. Constitution—"No money shall be drawn from the treasury, but in consequence of appropriations made by law"—is echoed in most state constitutions. In nineteenth century practice, this power of appropriations meant that there was no intermediary between the legislature and the spending agencies, no authoritative executive budget that might constrain legislative action. But as it was conceived by the leading reformers, the executive budget would have forced a radical shift in fiscal power from the legislature to the chief executive. Yet legislators could not resist the tide of reform; they too wanted to do something about the incessant rise in public spending, and they were frustrated by the loose financial arrangements that weakened their legal control over spending. They wanted to impose effective control over agency actions, and they perceived that the budget power could be used to curb the personnel and purchasing discretion of administrators. By trading away some of their financial powers, legislators were able to gain budgetary control over expenditures.

Accordingly, legislators turned budget reform to their own purposes, adopting those features that strengthened control over agencies but dropping those that would have expanded the policy role of the governor. De facto, the governor became the control agent of the legislature; his job was to present the budget accounts in a way that facilitated detailed legislative scrutiny of agency requests and enabled the legislature to intervene when it wanted to. The conception of the governor as an active policymaker fell by the wayside, although his potential for this role remained. The governor was interposed between the agencies and the legislature, but agencies continued to submit their

7. See Luther H. Gulick, *Evolution of the Budget in Massachusetts* (The Macmillan Company, 1920).

estimates without prior policy guidance from central authorities. Now, however, the estimates were channeled through a central controller, who checked their accuracy, made sure that spending rules were not violated, and brought aggregate spending into line with available income.

In this deployment of the budget function for control purposes, the governor was a willing ally of the legislature. Governors had been weakened by the growth of autonomy in agency spending, and they welcomed the opportunity to impose central control. Moreover, governors were not prepared to use budgeting for management or planning purposes. They lacked both the staff and the capability to undertake these larger functions. Control had to be the first order of business. Once control was institutionalized, it might be possible to use the budget power for program planning and coordination. But this was for future generations of budget innovators, not for those preoccupied with the priorities of accounting and purchasing. As the proportion of executive budget states increased during the 1920s and 1930s, there was a strengthening of central control over departments. The new budget systems did not conform to Frederick Cleveland's specifications, but they satisfied the public desire for control over spending.

Byproducts of Control

When the first budget systems were established, the older tradition of unfettered agency initiative in the preparation of estimates was not disturbed. Just as they had for a century or more, agencies submitted their estimates without substantive central guidance. What was added, however, was a central review facility, based in a budget office and empowered to cut or modify the agency requests before official legislative action began. Central administrators became budget cutters, a role that was compatible with their control responsibilities. If a planning scheme had been established, it would have called for a different central role, that of determining broad policy guidelines before agency estimates were formulated. As it turned out, however, the control perspective fostered a division of budgetary labor, in which central officials eschewed policy issues and agencies brought on central control because of their unconstrained requests.

The line-item tradition was another byproduct of control. There is overwhelming evidence that the ideologists of executive budgeting favored activity or functional classifications and the subordination of objects of expense. This preference grew out of their vision of the budget as a planning instrument and was consistent with the contemporary drive to organize departments along functional lines. The subordination of items of expense conformed to the prevailing ideas of separation of politics from administration. Thus Frank Goodnow wrote that the legislature "may properly extend its control of appropriations to the point of defining with a considerable degree of particularity the activities for which public moneys shall be expended and the amounts of money which shall be expended for the particular activities. . . ."[8] Concerning appropriations by objects of expense, however, Goodnow held that "it is more than doubtful if it is ever justified . . . except where it is imposed as a limitation of the maximum expenditure which may be incurred."[9] President Taft's Commission on Economy and Efficiency vigorously opposed object-of-expense appropriations and recommended that appropriations be made according to class of work, organization unit, character of expense, and method of financing.[10]

From the perspective of budgetary control, item-of-expense classifications had considerable utility. Such classifications, it was believed, would deter administrators from excessive or improper expenditures and enable central officials (the legislature, the governor, and his budget staff) to maintain close surveillance over department spending. Hence, in varying degrees of itemization, the first expenditure classifications were tied to the myriad items of expense of the agencies. Most state budget laws either mandated the line-item form or specified that the budget was to be itemized (which was understood to mean itemized into objects of expense). On these line-itemizations were built the control routines for preparing and executing the budget.

8. Frank J. Goodnow, "The Limit of Budgetary Control," *Proceedings of the American Political Science Association*, Ninth Annual Meeting, 1913, p. 72.

9. *Ibid.*, p. 73.

10. U.S. President's Commission on Economy and Efficiency, *The Need for a National Budget*, House Doc. No. 854, 1912. "The Legislature having determined the amount to be spent, the person to spend it, and the character of the expenditure, then it is thought that legislative control should cease . . . the executive officer should be made responsible for judgment with respect to contracting and purchasing relations which are to be entered into in the execution of the policies and work provided for." P. 211.

The Expansion of Budgetary Control

Throughout the 1920s and 1930s, the successors to Frederick Cleveland and his coterie of reformers carried the new gospel of budgeting to the state houses and city halls across the nation. But these second generation budgeters were preoccupied with the tasks of refining and diffusing the widely approved control procedures, and they had little appreciation of the ideas and objectives that had inspired the executive budget movement. They did not undertake trial and error experimentation; rather they applied the line-item techniques as given. Budgeting had become a cycle of routines; no longer was it an idea in search of application. A budgeting tradition already was at work, and there was no longer a need to search for one. Budget writers were concerned about forms and formats, and their publications were filled with detailed descriptions of actual and recommended practices. Each edition of the trade journals brought news of fresh additions to the growing list of governments that had climbed aboard the budget bandwagon. Although the techniques of planning and management were retained in A. E. Buck's catalog of "approved" budget practice, this was more a tribute to the author's comprehensiveness than to any serious evaluation of budgetary purposes.[11] The accountants who took command of the budget offices were trained in the methods of control and committed to line-item operations. Technique triumphed over purpose,[12] as budgeters settled into the busywork of maintaining financial accounts according to the prevailing standards of efficiency and accuracy. Charles G. Dawes, the first director of the budget, was able to write of federal budgeting:

The Bureau of the Budget is concerned only with the humbler and routine business of government. Unlike cabinet officers, it is concerned with no question of policy save that of economy and efficiency.[13]

Control would not have gained ascendency if it had not been in step with the mood and needs of the times. The emergence of modern budgeting occurred during an era in which many public and business

11. See Arthur Eugene Buck, *Public Budgeting* (Harper and Brothers, 1929), pp. 181–88.

12. The phrase is taken from Wallace Sayre, "The Triumph of Techniques over Purpose," *Public Administration Review*, Vol. 8 (1948), pp. 134–37.

13. Charles G. Dawes, *The First Year of the Budget of the United States* (Harper and Brothers, 1923), p. ii.

leaders were skeptical of the value of government programs and expenditures. To those who regarded government as a "necessary evil," the job of budgeting was to minimize the evil by holding government spending in check. For this purpose, it made sense to concentrate on central control over inputs. After all, the outputs were deemed of fixed and limited value, and the only question was whether more or less was to be spent to run the government. Accordingly, a budgeter could focus exclusively on the inputs with full confidence that none of the relevant factors had been disregarded. To reduce spending, all that was necessary was to examine each item of input. This attitude was buoyed by the conventional belief that administrators cannot be trusted to manage their operations frugally and competently and by the retrenchment mood of the period.

An output oriented budget process would have offered opportunities for spending and program expansion during a period (the 1920s) when federal revenues, expenditures, and indebtedness declined. (State and local governments did not succeed in retrenching—though the rate of growth was diminished—but this only hardened the belief in the need for more potent central financial controls.)

Control budgeting serviced existing administrative needs. Most governments had to put their purchasing and personnel systems in order and develop basic accounting systems before they could even begin to come to grips with the problems of management performance and program effectiveness. Central officials decided to use the budget power to obtain purchasing and personnel control and to impose accounting standards because they had no other instrument with the same authority and sweep. Accordingly, line-item budgeting became the ubiquitous means of control. (But it would be erroneous to assume that removal of the line items from the budget or appropriations has meant the abandonment of control. Habits and roles can persist long after the generating force has disappeared.)

Line-Item Control

A budgetary process keyed to items of expense fosters central control in many ways. (1) It enables central authorities to control inputs, that is, to control before the expenditure is made or obligated. (2) It provides external control by legislators and central monitors who are not beholden to a particular agency. (3) Line-item controls are especially effective for salaries and purchases, which together account for the bulk of state government spending, perhaps 90 percent or more in some instances. (4) Control is uniform. Each agency is governed by the same accounts and standards. A typewriter in agency A has the same status and is subject to the same rules as a typewriter in agency B. (5) Control is comprehensive. No item escapes central surveillance. Control extends to all the fiscal transactions of government. (6) Control is exact. It can be imposed with pinpoint precision on the class of actions or expenditures that central officials want to control. There is little ambiguity in line-item controls, and little opportunity for agency people to contravene central intentions. There can be no deviation from the schedule of expenditures authorized in the budget. (7) Control is routine. The records upon which control is built are acquired in the ordinary course of activity: purchase specifications, personnel actions, voucher approvals, travel authorizations, etc. There is no need for special intervention to impose control. (8) There are multiple opportunities for control. Central authority can be exercised at many points in the expenditure process and throughout the fiscal year. (9) Both aggregate and detailed control are promoted. Line-item supervision ensures that the expenditure ceilings established by law or administrative fiat will not be breached, but it also permits control to extend down to particular items. And finally, (10) line-item controls establish a basis for budget cutting. To bring the budget into a desired relationship with income, central controllers are able to delete or reduce items until the target is reached.

The development of modern budgeting was accompanied in many governments by major improvements in accounting, personnel, and purchasing practices. Logically, the institutionalization of nonbudgetary controls should have enabled central officials to free budgeting from its control mission. Nevertheless, fiscal control was increased rather than diminished. Once the initial controls were in operation, more controls became self-justifying. The advent of budget control was followed by the creation of a central control agency, the budget bureau. The central budget staffs had a vested interest in the perpetuation and expansion of control. Control agencies, Anthony Downs says, "become advocates of greater control over the operating bureaus they monitor," and "the quantity and detail of reporting required by monitoring bureaus tends to rise steadily over time, regardless of the amount or the nature of the activity being monitored."[14]

14. Anthony Downs, *Inside Bureaucracy* (Little, Brown & Company, 1967), p. 150.

Budget Controls in the Thirties

In addition to increases in the scope and variety of controls, the character of control was modified significantly during the great depression. As income fell sharply below projections, the states were compelled to reduce spending below the amounts authorized by the legislature. Under traditional concepts of budgeting, once funds were voted, agencies had a free hand in determining how much to spend, provided they kept within appropriations. But the depression forced a change in practice. In many states, the governor was empowered by the legislature to withhold funds if the expenditures threatened to exceed income. In some states, the governor was merely authorized to impose an across-the-board percentage cut in expenditures, but in others he was equipped with an array of spending controls. The chief invention was the allotment system, which originally had been conceived for other purposes but now was put to a control use. The agencies' freedom to spend their appropriations without central interference was superseded by gubernatorial power to impound appropriated funds and to control the pace of agency spending.

Thus there was a change in the purpose of budget control. Initially conceived as a means of enforcing legislative intent, it now became the vehicle for imposing executive intent on the agencies in executing the budget. Although the governor once had been the control agent of the legislature, he now was a controller in his own right, having his own incentives for control. The motivation for control no longer came primarily from legislative bodies but rather from the administrators who manned the central apparatus. This new philosophy of executive budget control was expounded in 1932 by Mark Graves, who was at the time director of the New York State Budget.

It is not sufficient, as I see the situation, to attempt to control expenditures entirely through the instrumentality of the appropriation act. . . . I maintain that it is quite as important to control expenditures out of appropriations as it is to exercise great care in making the appropriations in the first instance. . . . It is essential to have vested somewhere authority to restrain the spending agencies; otherwise they are too apt to view the appropriation as a command to spend rather than an allowance to spend.[15]

Several lasting consequences flowed from this unheralded change in budget purpose. First, execution of the budget became the main busi-

15. Mark Graves, "State Expenditure Control," *Proceedings of the National Tax Association*, 1932, pp. 148–49.

ness of the budget office, taking more time and staff than did the preparation process. Execution no longer was focused solely on maintaining agency fidelity to legislative intent, but also on agency subservience to administrative regulations. Second, as chief controllers, the governor and his budget staff were motivated to proliferate controls. In addition to the potent allotment restraints, controls were imposed on procurement, hiring, travel, and other agency actions. Third, as the line items were consolidated into broader groupings or even into lump sums, there was little slackening of central control. The items of expense continued to be prominent in the documents that were used for executive control—the detailed agency estimates and the allotment schedules. Fourth, the second round of budget legislation in the states during the late 1920s and 1930s cemented the shift to executive control in many states as the governor was given broader fiscal powers and budget staffs were established. The agencies grudgingly adhered to the controls, which the budgeters regarded as necessary to protect public funds and to limit spending. This drove out whatever spark of budgetary planning had remained, for there was no opportunity or incentive during the deadline- and routine-filled cycle to address the purpose or work of government.

At the close of the 1930s, the control tradition was firmly entrenched, though its application varied from state to state.[16] Every state required the itemization of expenses in one or more of the basic budget schedules (agency estimates, the budget document, the appropriations act, and the allotment schedule). Some states required itemization in all the schedules, so that the cumulative impact was to focus budgeting on the inputs and on control operations. In none was sustained attention given to agency management and program planning.

From Control to Management

Even during the decades of control budgeting, dissident voices urged a return to the original conceptions of budgeting. In a notable article in 1924, Lent D. Upson argued that

the average city official confronted with the budget finds nothing in it that enables him to determine in a large way the value of the activities that are

---

16. An excellent survey of the status of state budgeting in the late 1930s was compiled by J. Wilner Sundelson, *Budgetary Methods in National and State Governments* (J. B. Lyons Company, 1938).

rendered the public, or in a lesser way the degree of efficiency with which such activities are conducted.[17]

The two budget tasks identified by Upson, determining the efficiency and the value of public activities, delineate the two paths of budget reform represented in the performance budgeting and PPB movements. Like other insightful reformers, Upson envisioned the full scope of budget purposes, but in the subsequent buildup toward performance budgeting the difficult value issues were deferred in favor of efficiency considerations. To remedy the existing deficiencies in budget practice, Upson proposed six modifications in the form and classification of the budget.

A similar position was taken a decade later by Wylie Kilpatrick, who decried "the failure to visualize the problem of expenditure as a whole and to appreciate that more than one category of classification is essential."[18] But the dissenters had little chance of success against the control orientation that dominated budget practice at all levels of government. While there were sporadic attempts to introduce functional budgeting (for instance, Harvey Walker's efforts in Ohio during the 1929–31 biennum), as well as some experimentation with cost and work measurements, there could not be significant changes in budgeting without concomitant changes in government operations and public expenditure policy.

The politico-administrative changes instituted by the New Deal supplied the opportunity for a shift, though some of the budgetary implications were not realized until many years later. No single action caused the innovations; rather the broadening of public purposes and operations impelled changes in the role and uses of budgeting. The steep rise in federal activities and expenditures brought new responsibilities to budgeting and rendered it less suitable for the old ones. With the expansion of government, it became more costly and less productive for central officials to keep track of the myriad items in the budget. The bits and pieces into which expenses were detailed became less and less meaningful, while the public services and activities became more significant. With expansion, the need for executive leader-

17. Lent D. Upson, "Half-Time Budget Methods," *The Annals of the American Academy of Political and Social Science*, Vol. 113 (1924), p. 72.

18. Wylie Kilpatrick, "Classification and Measurement of Public Expenditures," *Annals of the American Academy of Political and Social Science*, Vol. 183 (1936), p. 20.

ship over the growing sprawl of government agencies and activities became more pressing and the lack of reliable methods to appraise administrative performance more noticeable. A stringent control procedure would have slowed down the "pump priming" of the New Deal. Since it was committed to rapid economic and social improvement, the New Deal could not abide the slowdown in program and expenditure expansion that the traditional central controls would have required.

The New Deal and the Budget Process

The growth in activities and expenditures inevitably had an impact on the budget process. The federal government possessed inadequate management and coordinating mechanisms to handle its mushrooming administrative responsibilities. Although the budget apparatus was not the only management instrument available to the President (during the 1930s, he gained new reorganization authority and broader appointive and removal powers), it was among the most effective because it enabled him to influence agency actions and policies directly by withholding or granting funds. No longer was the budget process used primarily to control agency purchases; budgeting became a key decisional process for determining the scope and conduct of public activities. For the first time, there was explicit recognition that government spending means public outputs and services; it no longer made sense to determine the budget by looking only at the inputs. There was a need for new classifications and measurements that identified and appraised the quantity and performance of public services. This change in the use of the budget was spurred by a decisive shift in public opinion. In place of the "limited government" attitude that had served the control orientation, the opening up of new areas of social action fostered broad new ideas of the role and capability of government. As the work and services of public agencies came to be valued, budgeting was redefined as using public resources to produce public services.

The difficulties of, and the opportunities in, managing large bureaucracies to accomplish public purposes moved to the forefront in public administration, displacing older concerns over frugality and propriety in public expenditure. This reorientation of the budget mission was facilitated by improvements in nonbudgetary control. Many of the malpractices that had provoked the use of budgeting for control purposes were curbed as personnel and purchasing reforms were introduced and reliable accounting systems installed. These improvements made it possible to free budgeting from some of the watchdog chores that had been assigned to it. As it moved from accounting to administration, budgeting was joined with other management functions under the popular POSDCORB banner.[19] As the final stage in the POSDCORB process, budgeting became the power center around which the other elements clustered.

The New Deal stirred a critical mass of budgetary changes. The new Keynesian economics (the full implications for the budget process did not emerge until the 1960s) stressed the relationship between public expenditure and the state of the economy. The President's Committee on Administrative Management (1937) castigated the Bureau of the Budget for failing to achieve "maximum possible usefulness and effectiveness as an instrument of administrative management."[20] The committee recommended that the bureau be reorganized and its staff enlarged to serve as the center of administrative management, program coordination, and legislative clearance. With its transfer in 1939 from the Treasury Department to the newly created Executive Office of the President, the bureau started to convert "from routine business to general staff" and became the leading management arm of the federal government.[21] Many of the routine controls were discarded, but the

19. POSDCORB was coined by Luther Gulick to represent the major management activities of chief executives: planning, organizing, staffing, directing, coordinating, reporting, and budgeting. During its heyday, POSDCORB was used as a statement of the elements of public administration. See Luther Gulick, "Notes on the Theory of Organization," in Luther Gulick and L. Urwick (eds.), *Papers on the Science of Administration* (Institute of Public Administration, 1937), pp. 3–45.

20. U.S. President's Committee on Administrative Management, *Report with Special Studies* (Government Printing Office, 1937), p. 16. In his background report for the committee, A. E. Buck was much more critical of the bureau. "The existing staff has become accustomed to a certain routine of duties and has neither the inclination nor the time to do anything beyond this routine. Under such circumstances, it is not possible to develop the functions of the Bureau as they should be, even according to the provisions of present law. Any marked improvement in the staff, therefore, depends mainly upon a general reorganization of the Bureau ... and a complete realinement of its duties and responsibilities." *Ibid.*, p. 142.

21. Norman Pearson, "The Budget Bureau: From Routine Business to General Staff," *Public Administration Review*, Vol. 3 (1943), pp. 126–49. See also Fritz Morstein Marx, "The Bureau of the Budget: Its Evolution and Present Role," *American Political Science Review*, Vol. 39 (1945), pp. 653–89, 869–98.

staff was increased tenfold to handle the new management, clearance, and coordination functions. The bureau was directed

to keep the President informed of the progress of activities by agencies of the Government with respect to work proposed, work actually initiated, and work completed, together with the relative timing of work between the several agencies of the Government; all to the end that the work programs of the several agencies of the executive branch of the Government may be coordinated and that the monies appropriated by the Congress may be expended in the most economical manner possible to prevent overlapping and duplication of effort (Executive Order 8248).

During World War II, the bureau applied its management authority broadly and effectively. By the end of the war, Harold D. Smith, its distinguished director, was able to write: "The main function of the Bureau is to serve as an agent of the President in coordinating operations and in improving the management of the Government."[22]

In the states, budget change was less dramatic and innovative. While the depression forced the federal government to an expansionist role, it had a different effect on the states. Their relatively inelastic tax structures and debt restrictions barred the states from expanding programs to meet the crisis. They had to tighten their belts in order to maintain the required budget balance, and this meant imposing additional central budget controls. Nevertheless, some of the factors that influenced federal budgeting were emerging in the states. There was the same tendency to recruit budget staffs from among public administrators, though the top budget echelons still were dominated by the accountants. Under the impact of secular expenditure growth, objects were consolidated into broader classifications, and brief narrative explanations of agency operations and requests began to appear in the budget documents of some states. The trends toward stronger gubernatorial leadership and administrative integration gained impetus, and the first departments of administration (grouping purchasing, personnel, and some of the POSDCORB functions with budgeting) were created. But not until the Hoover Commission triggered a new round of reorganization efforts was the full thrust of budget reform carried to the states.

Despite the transformation of the budget function, very few changes were made in classification, measurement, and other techniques. Indi-

22. Harold D. Smith, *The Management of Your Government* (McGraw-Hill Book Company), p. 69.

vidual federal agencies (such as the Department of Agriculture and the Tennessee Valley Authority) restructured their budget accounts to reflect the management function, and a few (for example, the Census Bureau, the Forest Service, and the Bureau of Reclamation) applied work measurement techniques to their operations. Various professional associations pushed the development of grading systems to assess administrative performance. The common thread in all these endeavors was confidence that administration could be made scientific by designing objective techniques. The height of the scientific impulse was marked by the publication of *Measuring Municipal Activities: A Survey of Suggested Criteria for Appraising Administration.*[23] In this book, the authors viewed measurements as "practical tools by means of which practical legislators and administrators can meet the practical need of choosing between alternative courses of action." They identified five types of measurement: needs, results, costs, effort, and performance. They acknowledged the difficulties of measuring needs and results (the two categories closely related to PPB-type measurements) and concentrated their attention on the latter three categories, which were combined into a measure of administrative efficiency.

Emergence of Performance Budgeting

The ferment of the 1930s culminated in the performance budgeting recommendation of the Hoover Commission in 1949. The commission coined the name; it did not invent the concept. By giving a new label—performance budgeting—to what long had been known as "activity" or "functional" budgeting,[24] the commission succeeded in creating a feeling of novelty and excitement for the postwar generation of public administrators.

Why did it take so long for the rise of management to influence budget practice? Why the hiatus between the events of the 1930s and the emergence of performance budgeting in the late 1940s? An obvious answer is that World War II interrupted the administrative and bud-

23. Clarence E. Ridley and Herbert A. Simon (2nd ed., Chicago: The International City Managers' Association, 1943).

24. Frederick Mosher recounts that "the story is told in Washington that former President Hoover himself invented the term 'performance budgeting' to lend sales appeal to a different and improved method of federal budgeting." *Program Budgeting: Theory and Practice* (Chicago: Public Administration Service, 1954), p. 78.

getary developments started in the 1930s. The Hoover-type reorganizations meant a resumption of pre-war trends, but they did not represent a revival of the old administrative reform ethic. The war deflected the course of public administration in the United States from science to behavior and from reform to research. Wartime administrators returned to their academic posts disenchanted with the old dogmas and principles and determined to bridge the gulf that had grown between politics and administration. They rejected a simplistic confidence in a science of administration and turned to the complexities of organizational behavior and to the experiences of other societies for an understanding of administrative *Realpolitik*. They abandoned work and cost measurements and no longer gave their best to the reorganization movement. The "1313" organizations lost much of their influence and became spokesmen for professional interests rather than promoters of innovation in government.[25] Reform became the business of the management consulting firms, which sold the latest administrative fashions to bemused clients. In short, the Hooverites tried to impose a prewar outlook on a postwar age. Performance budgeting in the 1950s was the leading product of the reorganization movement, but it had little more than coattails support.

Planning and Budgeting for Public Objectives

In these speeded-up times, the close of one era often is followed by the onset of another. Performance budgeting still was *au courant* in the early 1960s; just a few years later it was surpassed and shunted aside by a new surge of budget reform. The International City Managers' Association informed its membership in 1964 that "the urban management problem of today is more likely to be spelled NAACP than POSDCORB."[26] But the very next year, the first and final elements of POSDCORB were packaged into a new budgetary formula: the Planning-Programming-Budgeting System (PPB). Many states followed the

25. "1313 East 60th Street" in Chicago was the address of many of the public administration groups that either were formed or became prominent in the 1930s. These included the Council of State Governments, the Municipal Finance Officers Association, the Public Administration Service, and the International City Managers' Association.

26. International City Managers' Association, *Long Range Program for Urban Management Research* (1964), p. 21.

federal initiative, and PPB quickly became one of the leading administrative reforms in state government. However, budgeting was not the architect of its own reform. It was preoccupied after World War II, as it had been before, primarily with the procedure for budget preparation and the format of the budget. Budgeters did not show much concern over the uses to which their techniques were put. An interest in budgetary mechanics does not often lead to an examination of budgetary purposes, nor does a preoccupation with routines encourage practitioners to inquire whether their work serves a useful function. The critical mass for change came from three sectors: economics, the new data sciences, and planning.

The Rise of Economics

While PPB is a microanalytic system—for deciding how the shares shall be allocated, not for determining the total size of the budget—its design and application have been promoted by the Keynesian influence on public expenditure policy. Keynesian economics called attention to the opportunities for attaining full employment through government action and thereby brought about a basic restatement of the budget function. In order to achieve the new fiscal objectives, the budget had to cease being only a means of financing public activities and controlling administrative spending and become as well an instrument of government direction of the economy. From the use of fiscal powers to attain economic objectives it was only a few steps to the use of the budget to accomplish fiscal objectives. Nevertheless, because of the entrenched balanced-budget ideology, there was a gap of several decades between the emergence and the still incomplete triumph of the New Economics.

The crucial influence of macroeconomics was that it brought economists into government—new men who were not wedded to traditional administrative uses of the budget—and new perspectives on public policy. The economists brought along their analytic concepts and tools, but they quickly learned that the budget process was not suited for a planning or an analytic role. They had no overall scheme for revamping the budget process; rather their immediate aim was to upgrade the informational and analytic quality of budgeting. They wanted reliable data on the effects of federal spending and on the relation between current spending and future costs and results. To obtain these data, they needed a budget procedure for relating expenditures and programs to objectives and for giving explicit attention to multiyear program costs and benefits. None of these informational needs was being supplied adequately by the existing budget machinery. Accordingly, the new budgeters decided to break new ground. PPB was the product of their search, more a package of desirable features culled from a variety of sources than a systematic structure for choice. Yet PPB quickly came to be regarded as an overarching budget system among reformers who were swayed more by the glamour of systems analysis than by the modest claims and aspirations of the economists who had launched it.

Although the entry of economists into budgeting is a recent development, welfare economists had wrestled for decades with the problems of devising a science of public finance grounded on the principles of marginal utility. They hoped that the marginal analysis of spending alternatives (battleships versus poor relief in Pigou's classic case) would enable governments to adopt a mix of programs that maximized the welfare of their citizens. The quest for a welfare formula led to ingenious methodologies for bypassing the problems of interpersonal comparisons (Pareto rules and compensation schemes, for example). But welfare economics furnished scant guidance to budget-makers, who still were faced with V. O. Key's "basic budgeting problem": "On what basis shall it be decided to allocate x dollars to activity A instead of activity B?"[27] Key rejected the approach offered by welfare economics: "The doctrine of marginal utility, developed most finely in the analysis of the market economy, has a ring of unreality when applied to public expenditures. The most advantageous utilization of public funds resolves itself into a matter of value preferences between ends lacking a common denominator."[28]

Welfare economics has had little influence on public budgeting. It has not been possible to devise an operational formula that accommodates the diverse interests at stake in budgeting. But stripped of their normative overtones, some rudiments of marginal analysis were applied to budgeting during the 1950s. Arthur Smithies suggested that "expenditure proposals should be considered in the light of the objectives they are intended to further, and in general final expenditure

27. V. O. Key, "The Lack of a Budgetary Theory," *American Political Science Review*, Vol. 34 (December 1940), p. 1138.
28. *Ibid.*, p. 1143.

decisions should not be made until all claims on the budget can be considered."[29] Verne Lewis suggested an "alternative budget" scheme predicated on basic economic rules, under which each agency would submit several sets of estimates at stipulated percentages (for example, 90, 100, and 110 percent) of current spending.[30] Some economists worked out sophisticated ways of computing the costs and benefits of comparable activities, such as water resource projects. Roland McKean, one of the pioneers in this field, estimated "that opportunities for quantitative analysis are numerous in activities that account for about three-quarters of current disbursements [1954 budget]."[31] As quantitative analysis was extended to more complex decisional sectors (such as national defense and social-urban programs), cost-effectiveness (rather than cost-benefit) became the predominant mode of analysis. While it is meaningless (or impossible) to put a numerical value on the benefits of national security, it is feasible to compare the performance of alternative weapons systems in terms of specific results—the percentage of attacking missiles intercepted and destroyed, the delivery of ordnance on target, the movement of troops and supplies.

The status of economic analysis was enhanced in the 1960s by the sustained affluence of the period. Confidence in the success of the new economic strategy, combined with optimism about the future fiscal condition and program performance of the federal government, bolstered the standing and influence of economic policymakers. A tax cut had produced higher tax yields, and economists began to consider the policy implications of a prospective fiscal dividend, that is, cumulatively larger increments of uncommitted funds supplied by the existing tax structure. Estimates of the 1965–70 dividend ranged as high as $50 billion, and economists saw the need for new decisional processes for allocating that bounty among possible uses. The traditional budget machinery was appropriate for incremental choice, for deciding how much more to give an ongoing program. But it could not cope adequately with the task of dividing a huge surplus among the private sector (tax cuts), state and local governments (revenue sharing, grants,

29. Arthur Smithies, *The Budgetary Process in the United States* (McGraw-Hill Book Company, 1955), p. 16.

30. Verne B. Lewis, "Toward a Theory of Budgeting," *Public Administration Review*, Vol. 12 (Winter 1952), pp. 42–54.

31. Roland B. McKean, *Efficiency in Government Through Systems Analysis* (John Wiley & Sons, 1958), p. 16. For an itemization of these "opportunities," see Chaps. 13 and 14.

tax credits, etc.), and new programs (the Great Society, guaranteed annual income, and other). Economists and public officials began to talk and act with confidence that hard-core social and human problems could be remedied by the government. For them it was not a question of new programs but of more productive and effective ones. With so many spending and program options open, federal policymakers faced an unusual budget predicament, more complex and opportunistic than could be handled through the established decisional processes. In its new programs, the government was not bound by sunk costs and past commitments; it could fashion programs that met rigorous cost-effectiveness standards. PPB would be the application of economic reasoning to the federal budget and its programs. It would ensure that the fiscal dividend would not be eroded by the uncontrolled expansion of existing programs and also that the new programs would meet public objectives effectively.

But if the times were ready for economics, economics was not fully prepared for its new role. Microeconomics had been elevated to public prominence largely on the coattails of its macro partner. Yet considerably less is understood about the mix of public expenditures than about the aggregates. Compared to the readiness of Keynesian economics in 1936, the economics of public expenditure is woefully underdeveloped. In the macroeconomic revolution, the use of national income statistics preceded the application of the new fiscal concepts. Revision of the macrobudget was among the last changes, implemented after a consensus about economic policy and the government's role had spread to the key fiscal institutions. The order of development has been reversed in the extension of economic analysis to public expenditures. The overhaul of the budget process has been one of the first steps, certainly not the culmination of years of experience. Except for the highest levels of budget making and the specialized analytic staffs, economics is still an alien discipline to most budgeters, romanticized by some and disparaged by others, but rarely used by any.

The situation is not even this far advanced in the states. Although many states have moved to implement PPB, the influence of economics is weak. It has become fashionable for some governors to set up councils of economic advisers and to issue reports on the economy of their state. Nevertheless, economic analysis has not infiltrated the central budget arenas. After all, it is hard for a state to act as if its fiscal condition had an impact on the national economy. The business of preparing a budget is above all else a matter of responding to agency and political pressures. For this job, administrative management skills have been deemed adequate, and there are few central budget staffs that have a significant complement of economists. Program development and review is sporadic and often is stimulated more by federal grant practices than by analytic calculations of costs and benefits.

Application of Data Technology

The joining of economic and quantitative analysis in the setting of government programs gave rise to systems analysis, one of the main analytic methodologies of the new policy sciences. The indebtedness of economics to quantitative analysis is quite straightforward insofar as PPB is concerned, and quantitative analysis itself depends on the new data technologies associated with the computer. Without the range and capacity of the computer, it is doubtful that PPB would be part of the budget scene today. PPB vastly increases and complicates budget making and multiplies the amount of evidence necessary for budget choice. The computer enables budgeters to keep track of the several data subsystems that coexist within PPB, to store and retrieve multiyear and effectiveness statistics, and to compare alternatives. They cannot provide the concepts or do the analysis, but computers elimi-nate much of the manual calculation and data processing. They also open up new ways to perform the control and management functions of budgeting.

During the 1950s, RAND built a reputation as a sophisticated and influential analyst of American defense policy. RAND's studies of Defense expenditures were in terms of systems and cost-effectiveness analysis. Viewed from these novel perspectives, the Defense Depart-ment's budget process was inadequate because it failed to group re-lated elements together or to furnish an analytic basis for trading off program alternatives. David Novick, perhaps the leading exponent of this view, published a number of documents to show how the defense budget could be recast into a program form.[32] Novick was convinced that contemporary budget reform, particularly performance budgeting

32. David Novick, *Efficiency and Economy in Government through New Budgeting and Accounting Procedures* (1954); *A New Approach to the Military Budget* (1956); and *Which Program Do We Mean in "Program Budgeting"?* (1954), all published by the RAND Corporation.

(which, he argued, was wrongly equated by many with program budgeting) was moving in the wrong direction because it focused on activities rather than on objectives. Novick insisted that a program be defined as "the sum of the steps or interdependent activities which enter into the attainment of a specified objective. The program, therefore, is the end objective and is developed or budgeted in terms of all the elements necessary to its execution." But, Novick complained, "this is not the sense in which the government budget now uses the term."[33]

Other RAND personnel devised elaborate statistical applications of economic and systems analysis to Defense policy. The most thorough and extensive of these, *The Economics of Defense in the Nuclear Age,* led to the appointment of Charles Hitch (the senior author) as comptroller of the Defense Department. RAND's concepts were applied vigorously and authoritatively, under Secretary Robert McNamara, to the Defense budget and to weapons systems decisions. Popular and professional media carried many laudatory reports on the McNamara revolution, and PPB received a good share of the credit as one of the main components of the new system. Although there was—and is—a surfeit of propaganda and polemic and a dearth of accurate description of the changes in the Defense Department, the public image of its "success story" accelerated the government-wide adoption of PPB. The PPB systems that have been installed in the civilian agencies and in state and local governments have been patterned on the Defense Department version, or at least on what that version was thought to be.

Rapprochement of Planning and Budgeting

A third spur to the emergence of PPB has been the recent narrowing of the gulf between planning and budgeting. The integration of these central processes appears to be so sensible and natural that their separation often is attributed to some administrative malfunction that can be remedied by organizational changes. Efforts to unite these two vital decisional processes go back to the POSDCORB era and are basic to the rationality and order of public administration. Yet most planning "occurs independently of budgeting and with very little relation to it."[34] In a typical plea for rapprochement, Robert Walker wrote in 1944 of the interdependence of planners and budgeters. The

33. Novick, *Which Program Do We Mean in "Program Budgeting"?* p. 17.
34. Mosher, *Program Budgeting,* pp. 47–48.

former "have the problem of getting plans for the future translated into appropriations"; the latter must consider the future "if they are to make intelligent recommendations on alternative expenditures."[35] This convergence began to materialize in the 1960s as a result of large changes in planning and a few small ones in budgeting.

To understand why and how planning and budgeting are moving closer together, it is necessary to understand why they have been apart. For a long time, planning and budgeting had competing, or disparate, interests. Traditionally each worked with its specialized resources—budgeting with public expenditures, planning with space and physical elements. Budgeting's perspective was the fiscal year; planning necessarily had a multiyear horizon. Budgeting had a retrospective bias, to finance ongoing activities; planning had a prospective intent, to design a future that is purposefully different from what current programs would have produced. Budgeters were preoccupied with the continuing routines of government operation; planners with the processes of change. Planners were mobilizers of public resources; their function was to assemble a package of land (and, recently, money as well) to attain some desired objective. Budgeters were rationers of public resources; their role was to curb the use of public funds. Budgeting was dominated by a sense of scarcity; planning by a sense of opportunity. Budgeters pointed to the cost of doing all that government agencies wanted; planners to the benefits that would accrue if only the money were spent. Budgeting was an escape from tomorrow; planning, an escape from today. Unable to cope with the burgeoning fiscal demands of the future, budgeters confined their sights to the short run, to the difficult job of forging some balance between next year's income and expenses. Budgeters sensed that an explicit regard for future objectives would intensify spending pressures; hence they preferred to muddle through one year at a time. Much traditional planning was a flight to the future in hope of liberation from the burdens and limits of the present.

In sum, budgeting and planning have had radically divergent missions and perspectives: one has been conservative and constraining; the other, innovative and expansionist.

The formidable institutional and work barriers separating planning and budgeting have begun to disintegrate. Planning has been the more

35. "The Relation of Budgeting to Program Planning," *Public Administration Review*, Vol. 4 (1944), p. 99.

innovative, though both have moved beyond their traditional preoccupations. A compartmentalized division of labor no longer exists. In some instances, planners and budgeters have discovered that they are doing many of the same things, that they unknowingly step on each other's toes or duplicate effort, and that consequently some cooperative arrangement and demarcation of responsibilities would be beneficial.

In line with PPB expectations, budgeting and planning have moved toward a common program focus.

On the budgeting side, the moves have not been dramatic, but they have influenced resource allocation procedures. There is a desire for multiyear information and a growing recognition of the program implications of expenditures. In 1956 the Congress passed a law requiring five-year projected cost estimates for new programs, but this has never been enforced. Within the Bureau of the Budget, ten-year projections were developed under Maurice Stans (1959) and five-year projections under David Bell (1961). Many federal agencies, especially the capital-intensive ones, made long-range budget estimates before the advent of PPB. The use of forecasting methods has been motivated by several factors: feelings of futility (particularly among congressmen) over the seemingly uncontrollable growth of federal spending; the lengthening lead time between program design and implementation; the insistence of systems analysts on computing total cost, not just the first year's installment. It would be misleading, however, to imply that there had been much multiyear budgeting before the advent of PPB. The incentive to take it one year at a time, in order to benefit from the foot-in-the-door strategy or to hold future options open, always has been more powerful than the rationalist yearning for awareness of long-range costs.

The transformation of planning and its effects on budgeting have been far reaching. The changes have been debated in the pages of the *Journal of the American Institute of Planning* and are reflected in the revision of school curricula, in the role and work of planning agencies, and in the orientations of planners. The new planning departs from the old in many respects. For example,

1. The goal-setting ethos of planning has been modified to accommodate provisional rather than fixed plans and alternative rather than single statements of objectives. In conventional planning, there could be only one master plan, compared to which all others lacked legitimacy and merit. Once the master plan had been developed, planning

ceased. Increasingly, planning is viewed as "an organizational process of moving toward provisional goals rather than as the delineation of an ideal state to be achieved at some future date."[36]

2. In traditional planning there is little evaluation of results by planners. But analysis and evaluation now are being built into the planning process from the start, and increased use is being made of systems techniques, computer-based statistical procedures, and feedback mechanisms.

3. Conventional planning was confined for the most part to the physical aspects of government activities, such as land-use control and capital construction. Now planning is being applied to the full range of government programs and to the means of coordinating dispersed programs and organizational activities. This is true particularly in areas that are just beginning to be involved in planning, for example, law enforcement, human resources, and health.

4. Planning has become more sensitive to costs—dollar, human, and social. It has come to recognize that different costs produce different outcomes and that the policy function of planners is not to formulate some idealized image of the future but to create workable programs that meet public needs and are realistically alert to costs and other constraints.

This new focus does not pervade the entire planning profession; for every planner who has broadened beyond the traditional physical facilities perspective, there probably are several who continue the old ways. But the new planning clearly is the frontier of the discipline, and it exerts an enormous sway over the planning media and the training and work orientations of those who are beginning their careers. It is especially influential in state governments, where planning traditions are not as firmly entrenched as they are in urban governments, and where a multiplicity of new planning enterprises have been seeded by federal grants and state initiatives.

Since 1961 states have been eligible for "701" comprehensive planning grants from the federal Department of Housing and Urban Development. At first these funds were used to bring the land-use ideology of urban planning to state government. A good deal of effort was spent on aerial mapping, on dividing the state into economic regions, and on compiling economic and demographic data and inventorying

36. Kenneth L. Kraemer, "New Comprehensiveness in City Planning," *Public Administration Review*, Vol. 28 (1968), p. 382.

the state's physical assets. More and more, however, these funds are being used for program planning, the improvement of the organizational caliber and informational resources of the state, and the development of action programs that represent the views and priorities of the governor. State planning also has been promoted by federal grant specifications. More than one hundred categorical grant programs require "state plans" of one sort or another.

The States and Planning

However, the most potent impetus for planning has come from the states themselves. A special committee on state planning of the National Governors' Conference has been conveying the new planning idea to state governors. As viewed by the conference, central planning would cover much of the state's programming and fiscal policymaking apparatus and would inevitably spill over into the normal jurisdiction of the central budget agency. Thus, planning

should be considered as a source of information and a research arm for the decision-makers—the governor and the legislature. It should give to those decision-makers the assistance required in setting goals; it should provide a communication network for state government; it should work to coordinate effort; it should staff the governor's situation-briefing room, and it should develop an early warning system for social and economic crises.[37]

In no state has this comprehensive planning mandate been carried out yet; to attempt it would provoke intense jurisdictional disputes. It also would be too much for the current information and coordination capabilities of even the most advanced states. But in an increasing number of states—large and small alike—the central planning unit (or officer) has been made directly responsible to the governor and has a major role in preparing policy statements and programs. In these states, the thrust toward PPB has been strong, and the budget agency has been pressured to reorient its mission and broaden its perspective.

PPB is thus an outgrowth of transformations in the government's environment and machinery for policymaking. The advances in data technology have been supportive of the trends in economics and planning. By strengthening the relevance and applicability of economics and planning and by broadening the systems perspective of these dis-

37. National Governors' Conference, Committee on State Planning, *A Strategy for Planning* (Chicago, 1967), p. 7.

ciplines, the new data sciences have made them more useful for public policy and program analysis. Although they derive from different analytic and policy traditions, economics and planning have remarkable affinities, at least as they relate to public expenditure decisions. Both are inherently optimizing disciplines; that is, both strive for rational choice in the use of limited resources. Planning is a specialized economizing process; it gives more explicit weight to the future than economics ordinarily does, but it shares the basic concern for the effective achievement of desired ends. When planners have written of the budget process, they often have reported the same defects that have troubled economists; fragmented decision making and failute to relate spending to objectives or to consider alternatives.[38]

The infusion of the economics-planning ethic into budgeting helps to explain why budget innovation was able to advance independently of public administration and contrary to the significant theoretical insights on budget making proffered by Charles Lindblom and Aaron Wildavsky.[39] Public administration has been a minor factor in the emergence of PPB. Whereas all previous budget reforms were part and parcel of the reorganization movement, PPB takes its lead from new sources that are now only beginning to be felt in public administration. Thus, despite the quick popularity of the Lindblom-Wildavsky argument, the advance of PPB was not seriously impeded because it was dependent on classic economics and planning conceptions of rationality rather than on political-administrative theories.

When state governments began to develop their PPB systems, they did not have a clean slate to work with. In most states, interest in PPB was a direct outgrowth of the extension of PPB in 1965 to major federal agencies. Before this time only a few "lead" states (notably New York, California, and Wisconsin) had shown much interest in this type of innovation. The federal action received widespread attention and approbation in professional circles and at meetings of government

38. See Edward C. Banfield, "Congress and the Budget: A Planner's Criticism," *American Political Science Review*, Vol. 43 (1949), pp. 1217–27.

39. Charles E. Lindblom, *The Intelligence of Democracy* (The Free Press, 1965); David Braybrooke and Charles E. Lindblom, *A Strategy of Decision* (The Free Press, 1963); and Aaron Wildavsky, *The Politics of the Budget Process* (Little, Brown & Co., 1964).

Charles L. Schultze attempts to reconcile Lindblom's incrementalist position with PPB's systematic analysis in *The Politics and Economics of Public Spending* (Brookings Institution, 1968).

officials. Federal publicity was backed by concrete efforts to spread PPB to other units of government. The State-Local Finances Project ("the 5-5-5 project") was conceived initially by PPBers in the U.S. Bureau of the Budget as part of a grand scheme to inject planning and analysis into state and local resource allocation processes.[40] While some of its more ambitious aspects were not funded, the project assisted the installation of PPB in five states and in an equal number of cities and counties. The project published a series of instructional documents keyed to the circumstances and capabilities of state and local governments, and it liberally offered high quality advisory services to many state governments. HUD "701" funds have been granted to a number of states, and other federal agencies also have provided moneys for state development of PPB. The Civil Service Commission has opened its PPB courses to state personnel, and many states have conducted their own training programs, drawing heavily on federal perspectives and experiences to convey the doctrine and technique of PPB to thousands of their middle and upper level employees. Perhaps the most direct federal involvement has been the deployment of squads of "Flying Feds" to visit particular states and give on-site advice concerning the installation of PPB.[41]

The federal presence has fostered widespread uniformity in state PPB systems, for though there are numerous important differences in the details of state applications, most have conformed to the federal formula. Many have even adopted the nomenclature and techniques of federal PPB. If the states had explored the various alternatives without prior federal influence, some might have moved in different directions.

40. The State-Local Finances Project was a demonstration effort to test the implementation of PPB in five cities, five counties, and five states. It was formally commenced in July 1967 (though an antecedent project under the same name and direction had been operative several years earlier) and terminated its work in June 1969. The project was funded by a grant from the Ford Foundation with each participating government matching its grant "in kind" or through cash support. The project was directed by Selma Mushkin and a small staff stationed in Washington. More than a dozen useful publications were issued, including a series of PPB instructional notes, reports from the participating jurisdictions, and a final staff report.

41. In 1969 and 1970 the "Flying Feds" visited New Mexico, Tennessee, Colorado, and Wisconsin. This group is composed of federal officials from the Bureau of the Budget, HUD, and other agencies, along with a few consultants. The team spends approximately one week in the state, beginning with intensive interviews with state officials, and ending with presentation of a formal report and briefing of the governor and his staff.

3

Performance Budgeting in the States

Performance budgeting represents above all else a change in budget form. It is anchored in the "conviction that the way in which revenue and expenditure are grouped for decision-making is the most important aspect of budgeting."[1] Its essential, though ambiguous, expectation is that modifications in budget form and technique will generate changes in the roles and decisions of the budget participants. This chapter identifies the main techniques associated with performance budgeting and shows how they have been applied generally in the states as a whole. A closer look is then taken at the performance budgeting experience in a few selected states. Here the status of performance budgeting in the mid-1960s, before the influence of PPB was felt, is considered.

Performance Techniques

Like all other budget approaches, performance budgeting has its distinctive methods. While these have not been described in the literature in any comprehensive way, the main elements can be inferred from the practices of governments and the proposals of reformers. The common components of performance budgeting systems are: (a) activity classifications, (b) performance measurements, and (c) performance reports.

1. Jesse Burkhead, *Government Budgeting* (John Wiley & Sons, 1956), p. viii.

Functional and Activity Classifications

Performance budgeting places considerable emphasis on redesigning expenditure accounts and grouping expenses into functional and activity categories. In performance budgeting terminology, a function refers to "a group of related activities . . . for which a governmental unit is responsible."[2] Public safety, health, and transportation are three of the functions performed by most American governments. Functions are divisible into activities—specific groupings of work and expenditures. For example, the health activities of government include food inspection, the licensing of doctors, and the operation of clinics.

The classification structure used in each government is a product of fiscal, organizational, and political considerations. There is no universal classification scheme; each government is free to devise the system it wants.

Performance categories are artifacts, to be used for particular purposes. Hence the performance classifications reflect the uses for which they are intended and the interests they serve. When an activity is multifunctional, there are as many ways to classify it as there are functions, and the several classifications may be incompatible with one another. Dental care instruction in a school can be classified under the health function or as part of the education budget. Different policy outcomes and interests are involved, and much more is at stake than the classification of funds in the budget. Inasmuch as many activities serve two or more functions, this problem is quite widespread.

Another set of problems pertains to the relationship of the functional classification to the organization structure. Even under performance budgeting, the organization is the basic appropriation and spending unit. There is no exception to the practice of preparing estimates, making appropriations, and controlling spending according to organization categories. The second Hoover Commission recommended that agencies should "synchronize their organization structures, budget classifications, and accounting systems."[3] If this were accomplished, both organizations and budgets would be structured functionally, and

2. This definition of function is taken from Lennox L. Moak and Kathryn W. Killian, *A Manual of Technique for the Preparation, Consideration, Adoption, and Administration of Operating Budgets* (Municipal Finance Officers Association, 1963), p. 15.
3. U.S. Commission on Organization of the Executive Branch of Government, *Budget and Accounting* (June 1955), p. 13.

there would be little reason for deviating from organizational lines in constructing budget accounts.

Budgeters have a range of choices in determining the scope of activity to be included within a particular class of expenditures. They must decide, for example, whether a hospital should (a) constitute a single, identifiable activity, (b) be consolidated into a large medical program, (c) be divided into subactivities, such as dietary services, nursing care, and the like. All three are suitable classifications, but because the activity is the basic control unit, it makes a great deal of difference whether the activity is defined broadly or narrowly. While there are no rules for ascertaining the appropriate scope of an expenditure unit, performance budgeting was pulled in opposite directions by its cost accounting and reorganization heritages. The cost accounting influence led to an expenditure structure keyed to cost (or responsibility) centers, that is, to operating units that have control over costs and can be held accountable for them. Under this scheme, the tendency would be to particularize expenditure into many units in order to maintain direct and effective cost control. The reorganization influence produced a somewhat different structure, geared to the coordinated accomplishment of work rather than to cost control. The activity units would be larger, grouping together all work components serving a common activity.

The actual effects of performance techniques will vary among governments, for it is always as a departure from existing practices that budget innovations take on meaning. The past serves as a benchmark against which reforms are introduced and their purposes defined. If identical performance classifications were installed in two states that previously had divergent systems, the new systems might also be perceived as different. Suppose, for example, that the mental hospital budgets in two states were reclassified into ten activities according to some scheme devised by the American Hospital Association. In State A, the hospital previously was funded in two categories, personal services and other operating expenses. The installation of activity classifications might mean a five-fold increase in expenditure categories and a like increase in central control units. In State B, however, the hospital's budget had been detailed into many items of expense. For this hospital, performance classifications might bring a substantial reduction in the number of control points and new autonomy for the hospital.

Performance Measurements

Performance measurements generally are derivatives of cost accounting and scientific management. From cost accounting there have been adapted methods of measuring the (total or partial) cost of each unit of production or service; from scientific management, techniques for relating units of input (such as labor) to quantities of output. In its application to government, cost accounting is more often used for ascertaining than for controlling costs.

Like scientific management, performance measurements deal with the use of manpower, but at a much more complex level. Whereas a discrete motion (such as "grasp," "hold," or "release") constituted the basic unit in scientific management, performance measurements embrace a complete operation (typing a letter, processing an application, or paving a mile of road).[4] Performance budgeting did not have scientific management's faith in the "one best way" to accomplish a particular task. It shied away from establishing standards of performance, and where standards were set, they usually were keyed to historical rather than to optimal levels of performance.[5]

The basic format of all performance measurements is the relation of inputs to outputs. (This definition excludes workload statistics, which measure work volume but not the cost or effort expended in providing the service or product.) Scientific management and cost accounting provide alternative ways of measuring inputs. The former measures effort; the latter, cost. In both types, outputs are stated in terms of the number of work units produced. Thus the selection of appropriate work units is a crucial step in measuring performance. Work measurement is impracticable or not useful when the output is heterogeneous, of varying quality, or unstable. None of the criteria for work measurement require that the output be an important aspect of the agency's program. Typing a letter and placing a trainee in a job seem to have equivalent rank as units of work.

Performance measurements can be used to bypass objects of expense in budget estimation. Estimates can be computed from carefully

4. U.S. Bureau of the Budget, *A Work Measurement System* (Government Printing Office, 1950).

5. Frank P. Sherwood, "Work Measurement," in *Administrative Use of Performance Budgets* (Municipal Finance Officers Association, 1954), p. 5.

selected work and cost statistics rather than from detailed lists of expenses. For example, the cost of operating a state hospital might be computed by multiplying the projected number of patients and the estimated cost per patient. A similar procedure might be used for estimating the costs of discrete hospital activities; for example, the cost of nursing services or of a recreational program. This form of budget preparation—called "factorial budgeting" by Frederick Mosher —is much more innovative than is a performance budgeting procedure in which the estimates are built from detailed items of expense but are consolidated under functional and activity classifications.[6]

Performance Reports

Reports are a special type of performance measurement, retrospective assessments of what was accomplished with budgeted resources. The performance report can be either an interim-audit or a post-audit of work and costs. It compares the actual cost and accomplishment with what was projected in the budget. Periodic reports issued during the fiscal year might show deviations from the expected performance rates, thereby prodding program managers or budgeters to take corrective action. A report also might lead to a reappraisal of performance targets. Although its focus is past performance, the report can be a useful document for projecting future budget requirements.

New Patterns of Control

No matter how committed a budget process is to its management functions, it cannot ignore the necessities of control. If they do not tend to control properly, budgeters will be compelled to abandon their management focus as the pressures for control intensify. Understandably, performance budgeting gave much more attention to what was wrong with traditional control methods than to how control can be made compatible with management objectives.

In recasting the budget process along management lines, there must be developed and applied substitute methods of control at both the

6. For a description of factorial budgeting in the Department of Defense in the early 1950s, see Frederick C. Mosher, *Program Budgeting: Theory and Practice* (Public Administration Service, 1954), pp. 140–41 and 148–50.

operating and the central levels. The problem boils down to this: how to operate a system that satisfies the requirements of control without driving out management. Budgeters will not abandon their control techniques unless satisfactory alternatives are available. And this means alternatives that serve control as well as the popular management perspective. The major changes in control projected by a performance budgeting system were (1) a loosening of central control over inputs, (2) primary reliance on internal rather than external control, (3) a reduction of itemized detail in the budget and appropriations, (4) a shift from budgetary to other administrative controls, (5) the use of objective measurements, (6) the regular use of post audits and post controls, and (7) control over variances.

1. *Loosening control over inputs.* One immediate aim of performance budgeting was to divest central authorities of first-instance control over inputs, such as personnel, supplies, and equipment. An entire range of departmental actions would be freed of prior central scrutiny. Central officials would intervene only in special circumstances—when there was over-expenditure of funds, a fiscal emergency, evidence of misuse of spending authority—but day-to-day spending decisions would be made by the departments without central clearance. In place of input controls, central authorities would control outputs—the work and activities of the departments.

But output controls are not likely to be as detailed or as specific as input controls because it is much more difficult to monitor what a department does than what it buys. It is relatively simple to operate an accounting system that informs central officials of expenses. These officials have easy and routine access to payroll records, requisitions, travel vouchers, and other expense data. Moreover, control over inputs can be imposed at multiple stages of the spending process—when personnel are to be hired or positions reclassified, before travel is authorized or automobiles traded in, or when contracts are let and equipment purchased. But control of outputs is dependent on the way departments define and report their activities. Because there ordinarily is no uniform method of reporting outputs, departments can construct categories that conceal what they are doing and relieve them of central surveillance. Conventional output reports (such as annual reports) usually are issued long after the fiscal year has ended, much too late to be useful control documents.

2. *Reliance on internal controls.* Performance budgeting stressed

cost consciousness and internal (self) control as a substitute for central surveillance. It challenged the traditional fear that without strong central involvement, departments would abuse their spending authority. Performance budgeters argued that administrators want to be effective and efficient, but they are thwarted by the control system. What department managers need are opportunities and incentives to perform their responsibilities capably and at minimal cost. Released from central interference, spending officials would be encouraged to improve the performance of their agencies. They would become conscious of the costs of doing the job and therefore more willing to develop ways of curbing costs while fulfilling their budgetary responsibilities.

Furthermore, if all participants were governed by objective and rational norms—such as efficiency—the problem of control would diminish. Control would be internalized; that is, it would be based on willing adherence to spending rules that are regarded as legitimate and rational. Under such conditions, top authorities could focus their budget attention on management functions and decentralize control operations to the agencies.

3. *Reduction in budgetary detail.* The cornerstone of control budgeting is the itemization of expense. After appropriations have been voted, the detailed estimates become precise limitations on department spending, and the budget process is geared to safeguarding the details. Even when appropriations are made in lump sums or in aggregates, the administrative details produced as a result of budget preparation and execution are controlling. Thus it is not enough to change the form of appropriation; the administrative side of the budget process must also be divested of its input detail. In terms of budget preparation, this means using such techniques as the factorial estimation procedures described above. The budget office would work with key statistics (such as per capita costs) in projecting spending levels and overseeing agency performance. Input details would be controlled internally, and central authorities would not enforce adherence to detailed statements of expense.

4. *Reliance on nonbudgetary controls.* Many administrative actions have financial implications, and most actions having such implications have been attached in one way or another to the budget process. But budgeting is not the only instrument of administrative control, nor is it always the most appropriate or effective one. Controls can be oper-

ated with only indirect reliance on the budgetary machinery, and in this way they can be more properly earmarked to the class of actions they govern. For example, automobile purchases can be controlled by legislative or administrative policy governing mileage and usage; travel, by regulations applicable to all agencies; personnel actions, by classification and pay schedules; requisitions, by purchasing standards. The use of nonbudgetary controls would free the budget process for management responsibilities.

5. *The use of objective measurements.* The final three controls are elements of the performance reporting system mentioned earlier in this chapter. In the absence of any objective way to appraise departmental performance, central authorities may feel compelled to interpose their own judgments concerning the hiring of new staff and the filling of vacancies, the wisdom of replacing old equipment, or the merits of attending a professional conference.

Performance budgeting gives central authorities measurements of agency performance, thereby removing some of the grounds for central supervision. By measuring costs and outputs and relating them to accepted standards or to planned levels of performance, central budgeters can monitor the efficiency of agency expenditures without concerning themselves with the desirability or propriety of particular expenses.

6. *Shifting from pre-control to post-control.* The decentralization of control does not free departments entirely from central surveillance. Agencies have discretion in spending funds in the performance of authorized activities, but they must report their expenses and accomplishments periodically, usually every month or quarter. The budget agency audits the work and expenditures of the departments, checking actual performance against budget estimates. While pre-control is designed to deter illegal or imprudent expenditures, post-control acts as a check on inefficiency in expenditure.

Post-control uses a reporting procedure that focuses on questions of efficiency: What did the agencies accomplish with their expenditures? Are unit costs in line with expectations? These efficiency issues are at the heart of performance reports.

7. *Control of variances.* Coupled with post-control is another feedback device, the concentration of central oversight on variances from original plans. The examination of variances replaces the blanket scrutiny of every spending action, with selective inspection of excep-

tions and deviations. Obviously variance controls cannot be exercised unless an accurate and current reporting procedure is in use.

The Hybridization of Performance Budgeting

The actual impact of the performance techniques discussed thus far depends on how they are applied in practice. When performance budgeting was introduced, the tacit message of the Hoover Commission and some state reorganization groups was that objects of expense and activities are competing and incompatible bases for budgeting. Hence, the objects must be purged from the central budget process if performance budgeting is to flourish. The Hoover Commission lent weight to this impression by polarizing objects versus activities: "under performance budgeting, attention is centered on the function or activity . . . instead of on lists of employees or authorizations of purchases."[7] The commission relegated items of expense to "supporting schedules" shown in one of the sample performance budgets annexed to its report. Similar impressions were conveyed by some state "Little Hoover Commissions." Connecticut's Commission on State Government Organization (1950) recommended that the budget "be made up on a 'performance' basis . . . rather than by 'objects.' "[8] Maryland's Commission on Administrative Organization of the State (1951) proposed that "the present 'line-item' budget should be discontinued and the so-called 'program budget' should be adopted as the basis for making appropriations."[9]

A close reading of these reports or an understanding of finance administration would have demonstrated that it was neither intended nor feasible to operate a budget system without some prominent use of object data. At the very least, items of expense must continue to be used for essential accounting and administrative routines, such as keeping track of personnel and purchases, disbursing payments, and maintaining fiduciary control over expenditures. But because the initial performance budgeting proposals were cast in either/or terms, they inevitably created the expectation that there would be little or no

7. U.S. Commission on the Organization of the Executive Branch of the Government, *Budgeting and Accounting* (Government Printing Office, 1949), p. 8.
8. Connecticut Commission on State Government Organization, *The Report* (1950), p. 13.
9. *The Maryland Budget System* (November 1951), p. 14.

place for objects in the new budget framework. After a few years of experience, this simplistic view gave way to a more mature conception of performance budgeting, in which the items of expense coexist with the new informational and decisional structures. Near the close of the performance budgeting era, the Public Administration Service characterized the line-item versus performance budgeting argument as "fruitless debate," and it concluded that "various methods of classification serve different purposes, any of which may be useful for specific budgetary needs in a particular government."[10]

Once the clearcut demarcation between itemized and performance budgeting was obliterated, it became exceedingly difficult to appraise the progress or impact of budget reform. For the growing number of hybrid states, the important question was not whether they used line-item or performance methods—they used both—but whether the changes they introduced had any significant effect on budgetary control and management. In the process of hybridization, what features were taken from performance budgeting and what were retained from the traditions of object budgeting? Did the hybrids favor line-item traditions, or were they closer to the expectations of performance budgeting? When object categories are used exclusively, form might be a fairly reliable indicator of practice. But in a hybrid environment, form is not always an adequate guide to practice. There might be a widening gulf between the formal and the real sides of budgeting. Despite the use of performance methods, object controls might remain dominant. As a hybrid, performance budgeting might be more successful in grafting new forms onto traditional procedures than in changing the orientations and work practices of public officials.

Performance budgeting might mean substituting administrative for legislative controls, or it might represent a genuine change in the system of budget control. It depends on how the different kinds of material are used in the "back rooms," not only on how they are arrayed in the public budget document.

Under hybridization, each state had its particular brand of performance budgeting. One prominent observer commented that performance budgeting "is not a destination but a pilgrimage,"[11] implying

10. *Modernizing Government Budget Administration* (Public Administration Service, 1962), p. 45.

11. Catheryn Seckler-Hudson, "Performance Budgeting in Government," *Advanced Management*, Vol. 18 (1953), p. 32.

that every move in the right direction was to be valued. Any sign of change from a pure (object) to a hybrid system, however slight or superficial, was regarded as evidence that the budget process had crossed into performance budgeting territory. Understandably, budget officers tended to overrate the innovations made by their governments. In response to a questionnaire circulated by the National Association of State Budget Officers (NASBO), all but four states reported that budget requests were submitted on a program basis.[12] In another survey, conducted by the Tax Foundation, thirty-eight states were placed in the performance (or program) budget category on the basis of the information in their budget documents.[13] But each state or observer was free to define the key terms in any way it wanted, so that superficial changes in the format of a budget could qualify it as a performance budget.

In sum, hybridization weakened the application, and complicated the study, of performance budgeting. Performance budgeting had no model indicating how the objects and activities were to be related; hence, it was not possible to develop operational guidelines to action and study. Lacking these, performance budgeting constantly was hamstrung by uncertainty about the proper use of objects and about its own status in a hybrid world.

The Hybridization Syndrome

At the time of the first Hoover report in 1949, almost all of the states relied exclusively on object-of-expenditure techniques. Between 1949 and 1965 (when PPB was introduced) there was substantial attrition in the ranks of these states and a marked movement toward hybrid forms. The hybrid states were those that gave explicit and formal consideration to the activities and work of agencies, incorporated elementary performance measurements into their budget estimation procedures, and subordinated (usually timorously) the object-of-expense forms. None of the hybrid states discarded expense itemization altogether, though at least two (Hawaii and Pennsylvania) deleted the objects from their budget

12. *Budgeting by the States* (Council of State Governments, 1967), p. 61, and Table VIII, pp. 63–66.
13. *State Expenditure Controls: An Evaluation* (Tax Foundation, Inc., 1965), p. 29.

documents. The hybrid states did not all depart from tradition—or accept performance budgeting—to the same extent. In some, change was limited to "quickie" adjustments in expenditure classifications; in others, efforts were made to compile work and cost statistics.

Extent of Hybridization

To ascertain the extent of hybridization, the budget documents of all the states except Arkansas and South Dakota were examined. The documents reviewed were the most recent ones available from the 1960–67 period; late enough for the full effects of performance budgeting to have appeared in most of the states, but before the newer wave of PPB reforms had begun to influence state budgeting. Budget documents can show only *what* forms are being used, not *how* they are being used. Nevertheless, these clues are valuable as measures of the formal progress made under performance budgeting.

Although the budget document does not give a complete picture of the formal development of performance budgeting, it reflects priorities among competing forms of information in ways that the estimates do not. Moreover, in their budget documents, state budget officials try to put their best foot forward, to show the innovations they have introduced. These documents receive wide distribution among their peers and often are taken as evidence of the quality of a state's budget operation. The budget documents reflected the zenith in performance budgeting attainment. Their revision was the number one target in almost every state that adopted performance budgeting. The authoritative manual on budget practice issued by the International City Managers' Association counseled,

It is usually neither practical nor desirable to attempt to adopt all the features of performance budgeting overnight. Initially, the emphasis should probably be placed on completely revising the form of the budget document to make it primarily an explanation and justification of the muncipal service program.[14]

All in all, "the budget document reflects more of the budgeteer than he likes to admit."[15] In the case of performance budgeting, it also

14. *Municipal Finance Administration* (5th ed., International City Managers' Association, 1955), p. 62.
15. George W. Mitchell, "Recent Trends in State Budget Practices" (paper presented at annual meeting of the National Association of State Budget Officers, Sept. 12, 1955; processed), p. 1.

Table 1. Performance Data in State Budget Documents

State	Fiscal year(s)	Narra- tives	Activity classifications	Workload data	Cost data
Alabama	1968–69	No	No	No	No
Alaska	1964–65	Yes	Yes	No	No
Arizona	1962–63	No	No	No	No
California	1967–68	Yes	No	Yes	Yes
Colorado	1964–65	Yes	Yes	Yes	Yes
Connecticut	1963–65	Yes	Yes	Yes	Yes
Delaware	1965–67	No	No	No	No
Florida	1967–69	Yes	No	No	No
Georgia	1967–69	Yes	No	No	No
Hawaii	1963–64	Yes	Yes	Yes	No
Idaho	1965–67	No	No	No	No
Illinois	1963–65	Yes	Yes	Yes	No
Indiana	1963–65	Yes	No	No	No
Iowa	1967–69	No	No	No	No
Kansas	1965	Yes	Yes	Yes	Yes
Kentucky	1964	Yes	No	No	No
Louisiana	1966–67	Yes	No	Yes	Yes
Maine	1964–65	No	No	No	No
Maryland	1964	Yes	Yes	Yes	Yes
Massachusetts	1966	Yes	Yes	No	No
Michigan	1967–68	No	No	No	No
Minnesota	1967–69	Yes	No	No	No
Mississippi	1966–68	No	No	No	No
Missouri	1965–66	Yes	Yes	Yes	No
Montana	1967–69	Yes	Yes	No	No
Nebraska	1967–69	No	No	No	No
Nevada	1967–69	Yes	No	No	No
New Hampshire	1965	No	No	No	No
New Jersey	1965–67	Yes	No	Yes	Yes
New Mexico	1967–68	Yes	No	No	No
New York	1965–66	Yes	Yes	Yes	No
North Carolina	1965–67	Yes	Yes	Yes	Yes
North Dakota	1963–65	No	No	No	No
Ohio	1965–67	No	No	No	No
Oklahoma	1966–67	Yes	Yes	Yes	Yes
Oregon	1965–67	Yes	Yes	Yes	No
Pennsylvania	1965–66	Yes	Yes	Yes	No
Rhode Island	1966	Yes	No	Yes	No
South Carolina	1965	No	No	No	No
Tennessee	1965–67	No	No	No	No
Texas	1968–69	Yes	No	No	No
Utah	1967–69	Yes	No	Yes	No
Vermont	1965–67	Yes	Yes	No	No
Virginia	1964–66	No	Yes	No	No
Washington	1961–63	Yes	Yes	Yes	Yes
West Virginia	1967–68	No	No	Yes	No
Wisconsin	1965–67	Yes	Yes	Yes	No
Wyoming	1967–69	No	No	No	No
Total number of yeses		31	19	20	10

Source: State budget documents for the indicated fiscal years.

affords a reasonably accurate measure of what the states tried to do and what they accomplished.

Hybridization is measured in terms of four kinds of changes that were made in state budgets: (1) the inclusion of narrative information in the budget, (2) the development and use of activity classifications, (3) the collection and publication of workload data, and (4) the use of cost statistics. Obviously it has not been possible to avoid subjective judgments, particularly in borderline cases where the use of these techniques has been sporadic or irregular.[16] Table 1 reports the status of these four informational categories in forty-eight states.

The transition from traditional to hybrid budgeting was made in perhaps one-third or one-half of the states, depending on the criteria used. If one measures hybridization in terms of narrative information, more than half of the states would qualify for the hybrid designation. But it probably would be more appropriate to restrict the hybrid label to those states that applied activity classifications or work measurements. Fewer than half the states qualify on these grounds. It is significant, though not unexpected, that as one proceeds from narratives to cost data, the number of states adopting the changes declines sharply. Furthermore, all of the states using cost measurements adopted at least two of the other reforms, thereby confirming the expectation that cost data were the most advanced performance application in the states. It is also worth noting that all but one of the states using workload data also provided narrative statements. This correlation manifests the tendency to introduce both sets of information concurrently in the changeover to hybrid budgeting. On the other hand, many of the states that established activity classifications had no work data in their budgets.

The number of states that adopted none, one, two, three, or all of the changes is shown below:

Number of techniques	Number of states
0	15
1	10
2	6
3	10
4	7

16. Two researchers (the author and his assistant) reviewed the state budget documents separately and compared their findings. In most instances, they came up with identical results. Where they did not, they went back to the documents and argued it out until agreement was obtained.

The largest number (fifteen) failed to take a single formal step, while ten states installed one feature, usually narrative statements. Only seven implemented all of the reforms. On the average, the populous states were more receptive to performance budgeting than were the less populated ones. Regionally, states in the East and the West had a slightly more favorable record than did southern and midwestern states.

Object of Expense in the Hybrid States

To put this hybridization process in proper perspective, it is necessary to study what was left unchanged as well as to look closely at the changes that were made. Object of expense retained a prominent, and in many states a preferred, position in budgeting. Not only were the objects the main instrument of budget control, they also continued to serve as the key elements in the making and review of agency estimates. In virtually all the hybrid states, agencies were still required to itemize their requests by *minor* objects. These details were the focal point of budget preparation—not "building blocks" for estimating costs, but items having their own value for agencies and budgeters. Agencies continued to decide how much to request by reckoning the items they wanted to buy. Budget examiners did not abandon the item-by-item review of the objects requested by the agencies. In many hybrid states, the only significant difference was the consolidation of items under functional and activity groupings.

Attention to the objects also persisted at the legislative stage of budget making. In many states, the detailed departmental estimates were transmitted to key finance committees, and these formed the basis of legislative scrutiny of the governor's budget proposals. In California, Rhode Island, and Maryland—all hybrid states—a detailed personnel supplement accompanied the budget. In New York and New Jersey—also hybrid states—the appropriation acts retained the thorough itemization of expenses characteristic of control-oriented budgeting. Where the object detail in the appropriations was reduced, it was often the result of the vast growth in government expenditures and the gradual attrition of legislative fiscal influence rather than a deliberate attempt to restructure the state's financial control and management procedures.

Where legislative control over objects of expense had been relaxed, central budgeters often imposed administrative control over them.

A wide range of spending actions—filling vacant positions and establishing new ones, equipment purchases and travel authorizations, transfers between objects—were subject to central budget surveillance and control in a majority of the states. Many of the actions could not be taken without prior clearance from the central budget agency. Allotment controls in many states extended down to minor objects and allowed central budgeters to use the budget process for the traditional control mission: cutting down spending, protecting against unauthorized expenditure, and maintaining hiring and purchasing regulation. In no state was there a genuine attempt to establish the pattern of performance controls spelled out earlier in this chapter. Perhaps in some there was a grudging relaxation of central control over inputs, but control over outputs was not developed. The use of performance measurements for checking agency costs and work was not extensive in any state, and in no state was performance auditing taken seriously.

The Innovations

Turning now to the changes that were introduced, the results do not compare favorably with performance budgeting's potential. *Narrative material* was added to bolster agency budget claims and to provide some public information on government activities and expenditures to complement the usual statistical tables. In very few instances were the narratives helpful to budget makers and other "insiders." Sometimes the narrative merely cited the legal status of an agency or activity; sometimes it gave information on organization structure; sometimes it talked a bit about what the agency was doing; sometimes it tried to justify proposed changes in the level of spending. Some carefully prepared narratives (such as Hawaii's and Wisconsin's) provided useful information on what agencies intended to do with their funds. At the other extreme, some narratives offered perfunctory and irrelevant bits of information. Few narratives dealt directly or rigorously with questions of performance. They provided a small amount of additional budgetary information without really affecting the orientation of the budget process.

A second popular innovation—*activity classifications*—served as intermediate categories between the object and organizational levels and supplied an additional way of viewing expenditures without disturbing the old methods. In most instances, the activity classifications were designations for existing organizational units. One state's Bureau of

Environmental Health was renamed the "environmental health activity." Only in rare cases did the activity units cut across organizational lines to provide a unified picture of government activities and programs. As one critic noted, these classifications have "substantially more significance with regard to organization than finance."[17] Like the narratives, the activity classifications created an aura of progressiveness without disturbing the existing budgetary order.

The third change was the compilation and reporting of *workload statistics*. These data resembled the information one regularly finds in the annual reports of government agencies. They give some hint of the volume of government activity, but they fail utterly to relate work to costs or performance. Workload statistics "tell us how much work has been done; but they do not tell us how well it was done, nor whether the particular work undertaken was appropriate to the desired end."[18] Work data, like the previously discussed "innovations" were effective justificatory material for the vast majority of agencies that were able to report annual increases in workload. Because they were comparatively easy to gather, gave strategic support to agency demands for increased funds, and did not infringe on traditional procedures or call the agencies' cost or performance into question, workload data gained considerable acceptance.

Compared to narratives, activity accounts, and work data, *cost statistics* relating the work done to the cost incurred had very limited application. There were scattered efforts to develop cost formulas for selected functions, such as higher education. Most of the cost data assembled in the budget were simple per capita computations (for example, the daily or annual cost of maintaining a patient or inmate in a state institution). Yet even these comparatively routine cost measures were not used extensively in the states.

The Strategy of Hybridization

The hybridization of performance budgeting was engineered to minimize (a) the costs of innovation, (b) departure from prevailing

17. John E. Briggs, *A Refined Program Budget for State Governments* (Center for Technology and Administration, The American University, 1962), p. 8.

18. Clarence E. Ridley and Herbert A. Simon, *Measuring Municipal Activities* (2nd ed., International City Managers' Association, 1943), p. 2.

control practices, and (c) the complexity of the new system. This strategy proceeded along several paths.

1. Reform concentrated on the visible areas of budgeting, notably the form of the budget document. In many states, this was the sole accomplishment. Reform was concerned with the manner of presenting budget information, not with the character of budget decisions. Hence, the critical areas of budget choice were not affected by the superficial changes, though there was an appearance of significant innovation.

2. The greater the incompatibility of a performance technique with traditional control procedures, the less likely were its chances for adoption. Cost data are a case in point. Unlike work statistics, they relate level of work to costs and therefore pose a potential threat to agency requests for increased funds. This explains the paucity of cost applications compared to the popularity of work measures. Even where they were applied, cost data usually were ex post facto derivatives of decisions made on object-of-expense grounds. For instance, after a hospital added up the costs of personnel, supplies, and other objects, the total cost was divided by the projected number of patients to derive per capita costs.

3. New information did not push out the old. The narratives, work data, and activity categories provided additional bits of information to be used alongside the basic organizational-object information.

4. Reform was dominated by an old-wine-in-new-bottles approach. Familiar information was packaged in new ways: organization sub-units were redesignated as activities; workload data were retrieved from neglected reports and given prominence in the budget; agency justifications were refashioned into so-called statements on program and performance. However, there was little search for new informational resources. Only if the data were available from conventional sources were they likely to find a place in the new budgetary scheme.

5. The most innovative and difficult changes were "pretested" in a few agencies, usually hospitals or other institutions. Even if the pretest was successful, rarely was it extended to other areas. Rather, the experiment served to quarantine performance budgeting from regular government operations.

6. Performance budgeting was applied piecemeal, the easier steps first. Some observers regarded this piecemeal advance as a virtue, as evidence of performance budgeting's adaptability to various conditions. Performance budgeting, Jesse Burkhead said, "has one very great ad-

vantage in that it can be introduced in a step-by-step process over a period of years. . . . The techniques developed in the departments and agencies where the task is relatively simple can be adapted to the more difficult areas."[19] Yet through the piecemeal approach, budget officials committed to traditional control budgeting were able to co-opt some of the peripheral features of performance budgeting. Each piecemeal adjustment made traditional budgeting seem to be somewhat more suitable for modern administrative needs. Once the initial changes were made and budgeting reached a respectable level of technical proficiency, the incentive for further reform was curbed. This happened in two of the early performance budgeting states—Maryland and Connecticut—where the hybrids introduced in the 1950s were unchanged more than a decade later.

This was the status of state budget reform at the close of the performance budget era. The advent of PPB, however, was to force a reexamination of budget operations in ways that its predecessor reform could not.

Attitude toward Performance Budgeting

For an innovation to attract support, it must be perceived as relevant to the interests of the participants. The available evidence, culled from interviews with state officials in the 1961–65 period and from an evaluation of state action, indicates that once the initial allure of performance budgeting had worn off, it was viewed with indifference. Performance budgeting was not salient to the interests of budget participants, nor was it regarded as an important reform.

The concept that the Hoover Commission and its progeny injected into the world of budgeting had enough glamour and promise to attract the enthusiastic support of reformers as well as the attention of public administrators. Budget people heard the many testimonials to performance budgeting's virtues, and many were impelled to explore the possibility of applying it in their own states. During the first blush of excitement, performance budgeting was given prime time on conference agendas; it or a cognate theme was a scheduled topic at all

19. Burkhead, *Government Budgeting*, p. 155.

but one of the meetings of the National Association of State Budget Officers between 1951 and 1957.[20] The imitative zeal of numerous "Little Hoover Commissions," and the hortatory appeals of avant garde budgeters effectively shielded performance budgeting from rigorous scrutiny. Performance budgeting's first decade was spent in selling the reform to government officials, and few critical studies appeared in print. But during its later years, there was a distinct decline in enthusiasm and certitude, as articles and conferences turned their attention toward stocktaking themes—"has the theory worked?"—and away from promotional efforts.[21] After 1957, performance budgeting was not a specific topic at any of the State Budget Officers' meetings.

During the budget interviews undertaken for this study, it was necessary to invent for performance budgeting an importance it did not have in the minds of administrators and legislators. Only a few had heard of it; fewer still considered it a matter of importance. Among central budgeters, the level of awareness was higher, but the indifference was very pronounced. "Budgeting is budgeting; how you present it is just another matter" sums up the prevailing attitude.

Why Innovation Faltered

In examining the dearth of interest in performance budgeting, comparison with the earlier executive budget movement is useful. In the "age of reform," discontent and rejection of the status quo were widespread. Reform and reorganization were spurred by the muckraking exposés of public corruption and ineptitude, the growth of the administrative state, and the network of groups organized to support administrative and political improvement. Budget reform contributed to the realization of two key public values—efficiency and accountability. Though executive budgeting benefited from the popularity of other

20. The following topics related to performance budgeting were scheduled at NASBO meetings between 1951 and 1957: "Criteria and standards used to estimate budget allowances for various services" (1951); "Progress on introduction of performance budgeting" (1952); "Comparative costs of performance budgeting in state institutions" (1953); "Relative merits of line-item versus lump sum appropriations" (1954); "Recent trends in state budgeting practices" (1955); "Budget requests, construction, and presentation" (1957).

21. See the symposium "Performance Budgeting: Has the Theory Worked?" in *Public Administration Review*, Vol. 20 (1960), pp. 63–85.

government reforms, it was propelled by its own momentum and support. Executive budgeting satisfied the expressed need for administrative leadership and financial control; in response to this need, the adoption of budget reform was seen as a clear-cut break with the discredited past.

No such upheaval bestirred the public or government officials in the 1950s. A budget system already was in operation, and though there was concern over the rise in public spending, there was little pressure for a radical break with existing practices. The emergence of performance budgeting was primarily a byproduct of the reorganization efforts then under way, not an indigenous response to budget discontent. The ballyhoo accompanying the Hoover reports gave performance budgeting an aura of importance that more than compensated (at the start) for the absence of ferment within budgeting. Performance budgeting rode the coattails of reorganization in Connecticut, Maryland, Pennsylvania, and perhaps a dozen other states. Where performance budgeting proceeded independently of reorganization, as it did in New York State, the type of reform attempted may have reflected the perspectives of budget innovators rather than of reorganizers. Over all, the fate of performance budgeting was tied to reorganization, and as it waned, so also did the impulse for budget reform.[22]

The opportunity for budget reform was limited in the 1950s. The issue was not as urgent as it had been several decades earlier. The budget process was operating reasonably well, and although piecemeal improvements might be adopted, radical changes could not. Thus the strategy that aided the early twentieth century budget drive could not be used to promote performance budgeting. When there is overwhelming discontent with the current course, the prospects for reform are enhanced by portraying it as a complete break with the past. But when there is no strong groundswell for change, emphasis on the difference between the old and the new may diminish the attractiveness of the reform. When they talked and wrote of "radical departures," "new ways of thinking," and "complete reorientations," the proponents of performance budgeting unwittingly conveyed the image of a remote, unrealistic, and needless reform.

The governor had a relatively small stake in performance budgeting

22. For a survey of the results of the flurry of administrative reforms in the early 1950s, see Karl A. Bosworth, "The Politics of Management Improvement in the States," *American Political Science Review,* Vol. 47 (1953), pp. 84–99.

compared to his interest in executive budgeting. State governors stood to gain substantially from their new budget role under the executive budget, and they became vigorous advocates of that innovation. In the drive for performance budgeting, however, the situation was entirely different. Outside the small circle of reformers, no one provided forceful and sustained leadership. None of those involved in budgeting could see advantages to be gained from performance budgeting, and none, therefore, were moved to give it strong support.

Performance budgeting was of marginal utility to the budget participants who followed their routines scarcely cognizant of the need for change. Least affected and least interested were those on the periphery of budget life: legislators, operating officials, and governors. Each of these has a vital stake in budget outcomes and also in the form in which the budget is cast, but none perceived performance budgeting as having a critical influence over form or outcome. All these participants draw some advantage from the use of line items and the lack of explicit programming and planning (as will be explained in Chapter 6), and none of them failed to have his budget interests "satisficed"—that is, fulfilled to a satisfactory minimum—by the existing arrangements. The development of performance budgeting as a hybrid further drained away potential interest. It was hard to get excited about a reform that spent itself in surface changes in budget presentation. Once the small changes in format were made, the impulse for reform withered away. If performance budgeting had been developed in pure form with rigorous work and cost measurements, it might have attracted the loyalty of the minority who wanted a reorientation of the budget process. But as a hybrid, performance budgeting was almost inconsequential.

Performance budgeting meant the elevation of management concerns to central prominence. Yet if one were to rate participant interest in the control, management, and planning functions of budgeting, management would score the lowest. "Who the hell cares how much a pound of laundry costs?" a New York legislator exclaimed when he was shown the detailed statistics produced by his state's performance budget project. Cost accountants and work measurers might be stirred up by cost and work details, but most budget people have other interests. Budgeting can attract intense interest when it is used to control spending or to determine policy objectives, but when it is used to maintain efficiency, few but the efficiency experts are interested.

The Apathy of Budget Officials

The apathy of the budgeters needs to be explained also. The indifference of this group doomed performance budgeting because the responsibility for its implementation usually was lodged in the central budget office. When performance budgeting was launched, state budgeters were swayed by their own incentives to keep up with the times and to do a good job. Yet they never had a vested interest in performance budgeting. As long as it was fashionable, they gave it modest support. But they did not take the decisive action that might have converted performance budgeting from form into practice. Most state budget officers were controllers, trained in the techniques of control, convinced of its virtues, and benefiting from the strict application of control over agency spending. New men entered at the lower levels, too low to influence the basic budgetary orientation. Even those who had management training quickly succumbed to the habits and pressures of budget tradition.

The starting point for many calls for reform of state budgeting in the 1960s was the explosive growth of state spending. In state after state this growth pattern and the depletion of the surpluses accumulated during World War II were taken as conclusive evidence of the need for budget reform. After all, how could a system designed for a $50 million budget be adequate for a $1 billion one? State budgeters reacted to the spending rise by consolidating the items of expense into broad categories to avoid being inundated by masses of detail. For this purpose, the activity classification was a useful level of aggregation between the organization and the items of expense. But the seemingly uncontrollable rise in spending also strengthened their conviction that expenditure controls must be retained. In mail questionnaires, state budget directors were asked, "Do you think that your budget office exercises too much control, just the right amount of control, or too little control over the agencies?" Of the twenty-five directors who responded, two-thirds held that the right amount of control was exercised.[23]

In this questionnaire five innovations connected with performance budgeting were listed. These were (1) using unit cost data, (2) re-

23. When the identical question was asked again in the 1969 questionnaire, the responses were almost the same. Eighteen of the twenty-four budget directors replied that the right amount of control was maintained.

moving control over objects of expense, (3) removing detailed object data from the budget, (4) relaxing controls over transfers between objects of expense, and (5) relaxing personnel controls. The budget officers were asked to rate each of these as (1) useful, (2) hardly makes any difference, or (3) harmful. The replies are reported in Table 2. The attitude of budget officers toward these innovations was quite clear. They regarded unit cost data as useful but were unwilling to trade away object data or to yield budget officer control over transfers.

In one progressive state, the budget director acknowledged that "there is a terrific amount of picayune detailed control over operations," and he spoke of his "sense of futility" in trying to hold down spending by means of such controls. His views were shared by his chief assistants, some of whom urged him to move further along the road to performance budgeting. But the director was constrained by his own doubts, the persistent pressure for budget balance, and the limitations on the size and role of his staff. "This is not a matter of choice; rather it is a matter of necessity," the director explained in justifying the continuing stress of object of expense controls. Lower down in the budget office, the control orientation was dominant. "Budget execution," an examiner remarked, "involves a tremendous amount of attention to details. You control the aggregate by paying attention to details."

Thus the downgrading of the control function in performance budgeting made it less useful to budget officials who did not want, or were unable, to relinquish central control. Under the pressure of expendi-

Table 2. Attitudes of Budget Officers toward Selected Changes in Budget Practices

Change	Useful	No difference	Harmful
Using unit cost data	23	1	1
Removing budget office control over objects of expense	4	2	19
Removing detailed object data from budget	8	2	14
Permitting transfers between objects without budget office approval	0	0	22
Permitting hiring of personnel without budget office approval	6	4	8

Source: Answers to questionnaires mailed to state budget officers, 1965.

ture increases, they were forced to tighten their surveillance over the details. They were preoccupied with efforts to keep the budget in balance, with the spreading uncontrollability of the budget in areas such as intergovernmental finance and higher education, and with the daily strains and routines of budget work. They became less concerned with the procedural refinements of performance budgeting. Some aspects were useful, however. The activity classifications identified the main areas of spending and showed what the money was being spent for; the narrative statements provided a convenient justification for the spending increases; and the work statistics showed that the government was spending more because it was doing more.

State budgeters looked to their peers in other states in setting their own standards and expectations. They adjusted "their criteria [of satisfaction] to the achieved levels of other individuals with whom they compare themselves, and to the levels that are established as norms by relevant reference groups."[24] Peer expectations were satisfied by making a few visible changes in the budget. Other states were using activity classifications and compiling work statistics; these became the signs of progressive budgeting as well as the outside boundaries of change. Beyond these changes, there were no peer expectations to guide or prod the budgeter.

Despite the indifference of budget participants, it was possible to install some of the features of performance budgeting in hybrid form. Actually, indifference facilitated hybrid reforms by giving each of the parties to the budget a capability to implement some changes if it wanted to. If any of the participants abandoned his indifference in favor of reform, he was in a good position to get it adopted, provided the other participants remained neutral. The neutral participants would defer to the reformer's preferences. But indifference also meant that changes were likely to be minimal because substantial reform requires the support (not merely the passive acquiescence) of other participants, and because the more radical the reform, the more likely that it will convert indifference into opposition. In other words, budget reform, like other aspects of administration, operates within a "zone of acceptance."[25] Within this zone, the participants are able to innovate

24. James G. March and Herbert A. Simon, *Organizations* (John Wiley & Sons, 1958), p. 183.
25. The term is taken from Herbert A. Simon, *Administrative Behavior* (2nd ed., The Macmillan Company, 1957), p. 12.

without interference from others in the organization. But the zone has narrow boundaries, and these served as effective constraints on budget reform.

The general trend of performance budgeting in the states supports these propositions. In Connecticut, New Jersey, Ohio (1961–63), and Rhode Island, reform was sponsored by the budget office. In Pennsylvania, the governor and his aides introduced performance budgeting in conjunction with a reorganization of state administration. New York's performance budget project was a joint enterprise of a fiscal study commission, the Health Department, and the Administrative Management unit in the Budget Division. Maryland's performance budget was spurred by the state's reorganization commission, and it received valuable support from legislative leaders who were hamstrung by the detailed itemization of appropriations.

The variety of sources of support for performance budgeting would indicate that any of the participants could get modest reforms if his colleagues were indifferent. But if any opposed performance budgeting, it almost certainly was doomed. In the face of opposition, no one cared enough or was strong enough to carry the fight. In Ohio, opposition from the new leadership in the Department of Finance led to the termination of that state's performance budget. New York's experiment was dropped when the examiners switched from neutrality to opposition. The dogged resistance of the legislature to any relaxation of the subsidiary accounts blocked the development of performance budgeting in Massachusetts.

When most participants are indifferent, the expectation of opposition may be enough to prevent reform. Many budget directors were apprehensive of legislative reaction to performance budgeting, but it was anticipated rather than actual opposition that they feared. Accordingly, they decided against performance budgeting, or in favor of a weak hybrid, rather than risk an adverse legislative reaction. Whether opposition would have developed is another matter, for indifferent budgeters may have preferred to overrate legislative resistance in order to justify their inaction.

Performance Budgeting in Three States

A closer view of the hybridization process can be obtained by an appraisal of the performance budgeting experience in selected states.

Each of the case studies presented below represents a different pattern of accommodation to the reform impulse. Maryland was the prototype; its experiences were copied in many states, though few advanced as far as it did. New York attempted a widely publicized performance budgeting experiment, only to retreat to the general hybridization pattern. Ohio moved to performance budgeting for one biennium, but reversed its direction when a new administration took office.

Maryland: The Performance Budgeting Model

Maryland was the first state to adopt performance budgeting. Before 1950 its budget system was geared to the detailed itemization of expense. The estimates were coded into some forty-eight objects; and this detail was duplicated in the budget and the appropriations bill. As a result, the state had approximately five thousand separate appropriation accounts. Each of these was maintained centrally by the comptroller and the Budget Bureau, and each was a statutory limitation on departmental spending authority. Prior approval by the Budget Bureau and the governor was required for transfers between objects of expense (even within the same institution or program). The commitment to object-control budgeting was reinforced by a provision in the Maryland Constitution "that each budget shall embrace an itemized estimate of the appropriations," which was interpreted by the attorney general to require appropriations by objects.

As was indicated above, in November 1951, the Maryland Commission on Administrative Organization of the State sharply condemned the prevailing budget methods and recommended the adoption of performance budgeting. Pursuant to the commission's report, the state legislature and the voters approved a constitutional amendment providing that the budget and appropriations be classified "in such form and detail as the governor shall determine or may be prescribed by law." The first performance budget (for the 1954 fiscal year) was presented in February 1953, just fifteen months after the commission's report.

The first hint that the new arrangement would be a hybrid came in 1952, when the state legislature spelled out the minimum object of expense detail that was to be included in the budget. Apparently fearful that the shift to performance budgeting would deprive it of object data, the legislature enacted a requirement that the governor submit an itemized listing of expenditures by major objects, as well as "supporting data which shall include the number of officers and employees in each department of the State Government, the number in each job classification, the amounts paid, appropriated and proposed for each classification in each department, and the total amount for salaries in each department."[26] In accord with this requirement, the governor annually submits a *Personnel Detail,* and the budget contains an itemization by major objects (of which there are fourteen) for each activity.

In Maryland's performance budgeting scheme, expenditures were grouped into approximately six hundred work programs, which supplanted objects as the basic units of appropriation. Each work program is "a definite segment of the organized efforts of an agency which is planned and executed as a whole."[27] Work programs conform to administrative boundaries and, except for institutions, usually are coterminous with distinct organizational bureaus and divisions. For each type of institution, a uniform work-program classification was developed. Appropriations were made to agencies by these work units, the comptroller's accounts were kept on this basis, and there were no statutory restrictions on transfers among objects within work programs.

The budget document contained a statement on program and performance for each program. This statement, usually one-third to one-half a page in length, gave a general description of the program, but it did not connect the level of expenditure to the amount of work done. Workload statistics were furnished for more than half of the activity categories; in most instances, these data were not used for cost purposes. Fragmentary cost data were presented for easily measurable institutional services. Some typical examples were: "Cost per patient clothed"; "Daily program cost per capita"; "Annual per capita cost of institutional wearing apparel."

Despite the addition of these types of performance data, objects were scarcely less important than they had been prior to the development of performance budgeting. In the preparation of estimates, each agency still was required to justify its requests by major and minor objects and to submit an itemized listing of personnel and equipment. The *Personnel Detail* and the major object information in the budget

26. Annotated Code of Maryland (1960), Article 15A, Section 17A.
27. Maryland Department of Budget and Procurement, *Instructions for the Preparation and Submission of the Budget* (July 1, 1958), p. 3.

gave the legislature almost as much object of expense information as it had received previously. Although objects were eliminated from the appropriations, agencies were subject to three types of object control, each of which was tightened after performance budgeting had been installed. First, the annual appropriations act authorized the director of the Budget and Procurement "to fix the number and classes of positions or man years of authorized employment for each agency, unit or program thereof."[28] The effect of this provision was to substitute administrative control vested in a central agency for statutory control. As applied by the Budget Bureau it meant that no new position (not even ones listed in the *Personnel Detail*) could be established or filled without its approval. In 1956, position control was tightened by an amendment to the budget law prohibiting the creation of a position "in addition to or in excess of those specifically provided for in the budget or its supporting documents"[29] without the approval of the Board of Public Works (consisting of the governor, comptroller, and treasurer). In practice, position control was returned to virtually its pre-performance-budgeting situation.

A second form of control regulated the transfer of funds between objects of expense. Initially, the Budget Bureau merely required the agencies to file monthly statements of expenditures by work programs and objects and to report changes in spending plans. No prior approval of transfers between objects was necessary as long as the total expenditure for a work program did not exceed appropriations. However, in 1961 the Budget Bureau imposed the requirement that "transfers of funds between objects within a program shall only become effective upon approval and authorization by the Budget Bureau."[30] Henceforth, items of expense were accorded their pre–performance budgeting status, except that approval by the governor was not needed for transfers within programs.

A third form of control was based on statutory requirements that all purchase vouchers be cleared by the Purchasing Bureau (which to-

28. See Chapter 845 of the Acts of 1963, Section 2.

29. Chapter 318 of the Acts of 1963, Section 16A. Published in *Fiscal Digest of the State of Maryland for the Fiscal Year 1964*, p. 135.

30. Maryland Department of Budget and Procurement, *Instructions for Reporting Monthly Expenditures and Revised Object Estimates to the Budget Bureau* (no date). In a letter to the author, the chief of the Budget Bureau indicated that this control was put into effect in 1961.

gether with the Budget Bureau constituted the Department of Budget and Procurement). Generally, approval was forthcoming if the item was included in the agency's detailed estimates; otherwise, the purchase order was closely reviewed by the central agency. The purchasing controls tended to bind agencies to their original budget specifications.

The chief of the Budget Bureau has acknowledged that when performance budgeting was introduced, the bureau "was afraid that it would lose controls, but in fact no controls have been surrendered." Why the persistence of control? A legislative aide charged that "the Budget Bureau, in form, accepted the performance budget but never really abandoned its object thinking. When you get people who are clearly imbued with the philosophy of one system and install another system, then these people will operate as if the old system were in operation." An examiner argued, "you cannot divorce your transition from line-item to performance budgeting from top personnel and its orientation."

The developments in Maryland did not merely reflect the attitudes of its top officials; they were also in accord with the general character of budget reform during the 1950–65 period. As in the states as a whole, reform in Maryland was confined to the four techniques described above. Once these marginal performance features were installed, the process of reform came to a halt. Maryland's fifteenth performance budget (for the 1968 fiscal year) was basically similar to its first. In its initial performance budget the Budget Bureau promised to concentrate on "improvements in agency programming [and] the development of yardsticks to measure agency workload, performance, and effectiveness."[31] But aside from periodic revisions in the narratives and a slight increase in work and cost statistics, no changes were made.

A further perspective on the kind of hybrid budget implemented in Maryland may be gained by comparing the recommendations and expectations of the 1951 reorganization commission with what was actually accomplished under performance budgeting. The commission recommended that "a system of administrative controls should be established to supplant the controls now afforded through the 'line-

31. *The Maryland State Budget for the Fiscal Year Ending June 30, 1954*, p. 73.

item' budget."[32] This recommendation was not implemented; even after a decade of performance budgeting, the director of Budget and Procurement insisted "it still is necessary to exercise object of expenditure control over agency expenditures."

In its report, the commission charged that the requirement that every minor expenditure be itemized rigidly in the budget means that loose estimates or rough guesses are treated as if they were measurements of exact needs for long periods ahead. Although visible changes were made in the form of the budget and appropriations, the methods of budget preparation were not significantly altered, nor did the budget office relax its demand for precision in the budget estimates. The commission envisioned a performance budget in which "personal services would be shown in a single amount and not listed by occupational classifications as at present."[33] The *Personnel Detail* aborted this expectation.

The commission expressed its "firm conviction that standards can be developed for evaluating performance in departments and agencies of government."[34] But the only systematic use of performance standards in the entire Maryland budget was in the schedules for the Department of Employment Security, using standards developed by the U.S. Bureau of Employment Security. This solitary instance of factorial budgeting illustrates the gap between the potential and the actual application of performance budgeting.

Finally, the commission questioned the value of monthly operating reports, which "show whether funds are being spent too rapidly to last throughout the fiscal year," but fail to show "whether the expenditure of funds has gotten for the state the services it ought to be paying for." The commission anticipated that "when the budget has been set up in terms of programs," it will be possible to ascertain what each agency has accomplished "in acceptable quality and quantity in . . . performing its prescribed functions."[35] This expectation was not realized. The monthly reports still concentrated on the rate of expenditure and were completely silent about work and performance.

No significant efforts to change the budget system in Maryland were made until the late 1960s, when Governor Agnew's Task Force on

32. *The Maryland Budget System,* p. 14.
33. *Ibid.,* p. 20.
34. *Ibid.,* p. 23.
35. *Ibid.,* p. 41.

Modern Management proposed the installation of a Management Information and Program Evaluation System (MIPES).[36]

New York State's Performance Budgeting Experiment

The development of hybrid budgeting in New York followed an unusual course. Only after a "pure" performance budget was tested in several tuberculosis hospitals, did New York adopt a hybrid version.

For more than twenty-five years, beginning with the initial attempts to establish a coordinated budget system in New York State, the governor and legislature battled for control of the budget machinery. A constitutional amendment in 1927 (establishing an executive budget system), court decisions in 1929 and 1939 (curbing the legislature's control over the form of appropriation), and the growth of party discipline and administrative centralization finally and indisputably settled the issue in favor of executive supremacy.[37] "In budget preparation and execution," Frederick Mosher wrote in 1952, "all roads lead to the Governor's administrative right arm, the director of the budget."[38] With its 150-man staff, the Budget Division was reputed to be the most powerful state budget office in the nation, and it used its power to operate a network of centralized controls grounded in itemized appropriations. In other states, the legislature imposed the itemization of expenses, but in New York "detailed itemization seems to prevent the intent of the Legislature from being expressed at all; it operates as an aid to executive dominance."[39] In New York, pressure for detailed control came from the Budget Division, which determined the form of classification. Agencies had to itemize their estimates in great detail; these estimates were incorporated into voluminous budget documents and appropriations acts. In certain instances (for example, in the case

36. John G. Lauber, "PPBS in State Government—Maryland's Approach," *State Government*, Vol. 42 (Winter 1969), pp. 31–37.

37. This supremacy recently was challenged in a suit brought by three state assemblymen. The suit charged that the 1970 budget was in violation of the New York State Constitution because substantial portions of the budget were submitted in lump-sum rather than line-item form. The challenge was upheld, and the 1970 budget was ruled in violation of the New York State Constitution. But this decision was reversed on technical grounds by the New York Court of Appeals. See the *New York Times*, Sept. 25, 1969.

38. "The Executive Budget: Empire State Style," *Public Administration Review*, Vol. 12 (1952), p. 77.

39. *Ibid.*, p. 82.

of new agencies or agencies with unstable workloads) appropriations were made in lump sums, but no money could be spent until the budget director "lined out" the appropriation.

After the appropriations were voted by the legislature (often in exactly the amount and detail recommended by the governor), agencies were expected to adhere to the original itemization of expenditures. Prior consent of the budget director was required for transfers among "maintenance" and "operation" items (no transfer was permitted between personal services and other items) or among subdivisions within a department. Under state law, no new positions were to be authorized without the budget director's approval. The director also had final review over position reclassifications, and he was empowered to bar the filling of vacant positions. He had authority to line out unappropriated and federal funds.

The first inroads into New York's renowned control traditions derived from the recommendation of the Bird Commission (the Temporary Commission on the Fiscal Affairs of State Government). In cooperation with several state agencies (including the administrative management unit in the Budget Division), the commission designed and installed a performance budgeting system in the Homer Folks tuberculosis hospital. In its final report issued in February 1955, the commission recommended "as a next step that test installations be made in as many other areas of the State as are necessary to determine the usefulness of the system."[40] Subsequently performance budgeting was installed in five of the seven state tuberculosis hospitals. However, the system was not extended to any other state agency or institution. Throughout its duration, performance budgeting was regarded as an "experiment," not as a regular or legitimate feature of state budgeting. In 1960, following five years of languid experimentation, the Budget Division terminated performance budgeting in the state hospitals.

Though objects were retained in a minor capacity, the tuberculosis hospitals budgeted for their activities with detailed work and cost measurements.[41] Planned and actual performance rates were compared

40. State of New York, Temporary Commission on the Fiscal Affairs of State Government, *A Program for Continued Progress in Fiscal Management* (Albany, February 1955), p. 27.

41. The experiment has been reported in several articles. See Marion L. Henry and Willis Proctor, "New York State's Performance Budget Experiment," *Public Administration Review*, Vol. 20 (1960), pp. 69–74; Daniel Klepak, *Performance*

in quarterly reports that spotlighted variances from the original plans. To give the performance budget system a full and fair test, the ordinary object controls were suspended. In lieu of items of expense, the budget document presented workload and unit cost data for each cost center. For information purposes, the performance accounts were reconciled with the line items in a separate schedule. Appropriations were voted in lump sum to each cost center, and provisions in the state law requiring the budget director to line out the sums were waived. Under pressure from the Health Department, the Budget Division agreed to relinquish its position controls over cost centers with variable workloads.

Virtually everyone directly associated with the experiment considered it a *technical* success. Writing in the *Public Administration Review*, two Health Department officials reported that the experiment produced timelier and more accurate estimates, simplified the task of budget preparation, increased managerial flexibility, provided useful cost data, and made possible the evaluation of performance. Even the budget examiner who recommended that it be discontinued lauded the performance reports as well as the flexibility afforded by the new method. Despite this technical success, the Budget Division rebuffed efforts of the Health Department to extend the experiment to additional institutions. Its demise in 1960 attracted none of the fanfare that had attended its inception five years earlier.

No single factor accounted for the abandonment of performance budgeting. In an unpublished report, Frank Sherwood suggested "that the decision was made not so much in terms of dissatisfaction with the limited experiment itself as in terms of an unwillingness to see it spread further."[42] He correctly perceived that "the decision not to expand the program . . . makes it quite clear that those in positions of power did not see that their interests would be furthered through performance budgeting." Obviously performance budgeting was deemed salient by those who advocated it. But these were technical and management people, not budget and policy officials. Few people in the

---

Budgeting for Hospitals and Health Departments (Municipal Finance Officers Association, 1956); George James, Daniel Klepak, and Herman Hilleboe, "Fiscal Research in Public Health," *American Journal of Public Health*, Vol. 45 (1955), pp. 906–14.

42. "Performance Budgeting in New York State," Report to the Governor's Committee on Fiscal Organization of New York State (Nov. 15, 1960; processed), p. 20.

top echelons of state government regarded it as a matter of high priority.

The agency with the greatest stake in the experiment was the Budget Division, not the Health Department. From the start, performance budgeting was identified with the administrative management staff; the separate examinations units had little to do with it, though they had command over the basic budget preparation and execution processes. "The examiners were not really brought into the performance budgeting experiment, and they never really understood it." As a result, they never developed the attachments and commitments that those associated with the project had. Throughout the experiment, the examiners were outsiders, and they acquired the doubts and anxieties of outsiders. The experiment suffered from rivalry between the management and the examinations staffs. "Every examiner," a leader of the team that installed performance budgeting said, "resents Research and Management. They are Johnnys-come-lately who want to change everything. If control over this experiment had been under Examinations, it would have made it." A memorandum by Hugo Gentilcore (the examiner who had responsibility for monitoring the experiment) recommended the termination of performance budgeting, and this was approved by the budget director because "the examiners are in the best position to decide whether performance budgeting has sufficient advantages."

Performance budgeting meant abandoning control traditions, in which the examiners had strong interests and over which they served as guardians. Gentilcore certainly spoke for the majority of examiners when he posited (in the memorandum) "the fact" that line-item budgeting

has resulted in explicit, accurate budgets with a minimum of deficiencies and supplementals. It has enabled the State to carry out a multitude of simple and very complex programs. In the main, I am convinced that these programs have been carried out well and economically.[43]

As long as budget officials continued to believe that "there's no quicker way to know about agency thinking than to look at what's happening with line items," they would not view with favor the radical reforms promised by performance budgeters.

Although most of those involved in the experiment considered it a

43. Unpublished memorandum from Hugo J. Gentilcore to John J. Corrigan, Dec. 19, 1958.

technical success, a number of complaints were voiced. These centered around the reliability and detail of performance data. Gentilcore questioned the usefulness of data comparing the cost performance of different institutions. In the interviews legislators indicated their displeasure with the detailed performance statistics: "Performance budgeting as they tried to sell it to us is supplemental. You sure as hell can't cut a budget with it"; "it was not giving the legislature the information it needed and wanted. Legislators came in complaining, 'What does all this mean'? The legislature is not interested in the detailed unit cost information."

Performance budgeting was castigated as too radical and too complicated. Some of Gentilcore's most critical comments pertained to "over-refinement in details."

... we have gone to the extreme in the refinement of activity classification and relating cost concepts to budgeting. Our major concern in these institutions should be the total cost involved in caring for the individual patient. ... Overrefinement can obscure the prime purpose of an agency's program with the result that budgeting becomes a mere exercise in accounting.

But the budgeters also felt that it makes little difference whether one method or another is used. "My general feeling," Gentilcore concluded in his memorandum, "is that during the period of this experiment we have merely gone through an exercise in accounting." He could not find "a single example that this changing emphasis and increased cost information had been used as a management tool." Many old-line budgeters expressed faith in common-sense—in contrast to scientific—budgeting. "Budgeting is 90 percent common sense and don't let anybody tell you anything else." This latent fear of the technical skills required for performance budgeting prompted Gentilcore's statement that "under any system of budgeting, in the last analysis, the end results are determined by the competency, integrity, and interest of the administrator directly responsible for the program."

The decision to terminate the experiment was coupled with an accelerated transition to a hybrid system that combined activity classifications and object controls. To the Budget Division, program budgeting (as the new hybrid approach was designated to distinguish it from performance budgeting) meant "moving more slowly, taking small steps instead of big ones. . . . It is a compromise which everyone can live with." Program budgeting was viewed as a reform that avoided the pitfalls of performance budgeting. It did not eliminate objects of expense or threaten the control-minded traditions of the budget examiner; it was easy to understand and implement and was compatible with budget conventions. As it was installed in New York, program budgeting was in line with Gentilcore's recommendation that

It should be possible and perhaps desirable to combine the best features of several systems. It seems to me that as a starting point, the present methods of budget preparation should be reviewed and, where feasible, revised to reflect the programs and services that New York State renders and relate them to the total cost of each. At the same time, we should present and budget in the object-of-expense manner.

The first transitional steps toward hybrid budgeting were taken in the mid-1950s, and they centered on the form of budget presentation. Beginning with the 1955 budget document, there was a steady expansion of narrative and work content, but there were no significant changes in the form of appropriation or in the centralized control over objects. In his 1955 budget message, the governor commented that the inclusion of narratives and workload statistics "conflict(s) in no way with the preservation of our time-tested type of budgetary presentation." He also suggested that "a combination of the best features of program budgeting" and "our traditional type of budget may prove to be one of the truly new and effective tools in contemporary public fiscal management."[44]

The governor's budget message for 1957 devoted three pages to a discussion of improvements in budget presentation and to the performance budgeting experiment still under way. The next stage in the movement toward hybridization was spurred by an inventory of state programs launched in April 1959. This inventory identified more than two thousand activities and thereby facilitated the incorporation of program data into the budget document.

With the abandonment of the performance budget experiment, development of a hybridized version was pushed. In 1962 much of the detailed listing of positions was deleted, and the expenditures of three departments were presented on an activity basis. By 1964 the functional budget form was extended to each agency, and the budget document furnished a brief description of the major activities of each department along with explanations of program changes and, where available, workload statistics. Yet the form of appropriation was not affected by these changes, for the Budget Division took the position

44. State of New York, *The Executive Budget, 1954–55,* p. 24.

that the state constitution requires the itemization of appropriations.[45] The next modifications to be made in New York State budgeting were under the aegis of PPB, and they took a different tack than the one taken by the performance budget experiment.

Ohio: The Abandonment of Performance Budgeting

Not every state that tried to apply performance budgeting ended with a hybrid system. Ohio was one state to adopt and subsequently discard its performance budgeting innovations. Until 1957 Ohio had a straight object-of-expense approach. In both the budget and the appropriations, expenditures were grouped into forty-two object accounts. In that year the governor recommended, and the legislature authorized, the formation of a budget study group. At the outset this group (consisting entirely of administrators) decided to adopt performance budgeting; consequently, most of its efforts were devoted to designing a system for the 1961–63 biennium.

Meanwhile the familiar shift from legislative to administrative control over objects was accomplished. In 1959 a proposal to abolish the forty-two object classes and to appropriate in lump sums was modified by the legislature to allow appropriations in only six object categories. In that year also the Department of Finance established a system of position controls requiring agencies to obtain central approval of new positions and of changes in their tables of organization. The department also centralized data processing and accounting under its purview. Thus the environment into which performance budgeting was introduced was characterized by the growing power of the Finance Department and its budget division. Accordingly the new performance budget was perceived by many department officials as another step in centralizing financial control.

The first performance budget—for the 1961–63 period—was a gargantuan fifteen hundred–page document; the presentation for the Department of Mental Hygiene and Corrections covered almost three hun-

45. See Mosher, *Program Budgeting*, p. 82, where he concludes that "it would seem legally possible to convert the entire budget to a performance or program basis." In 1971 the New York State Court of Appeals dismissed on technical grounds a suit by state employees, who contended that the lump-sum budget violates the state constitution (*New York Times*, May 15, 1971). However, the litigation dealt with a lump-sum budget and not with whether a program or performance budget would meet the constitutional standards.

dred pages. In his budget message, the governor expressed the hope that the program format "will serve as a beginning on which to build future presentations in a manner which allows the total effort of the state to be measured as to its purpose and as to effectiveness."[46] In designing the new budget, the overriding strategy "was to leave no one with the excuse that he had not enough information. So we gave them everything." The "give them everything" tactic was evident throughout the budget document. For each department, there was a one-page description of major activities, an organization chart, a breakdown of expenditures by activities and major objects, and a tabulation of the number of positions per activity. Following this summary, the budget detail for each activity included a lengthy narrative description, information about organizational structure, and an itemization of personal services, positions, and minor objects. Institutional budgets were especially detailed; for example, the budget for the Marion Correctional Institution was divided into twenty-five separate activities, each of which carried a full load of work and object information. Work and cost statistics were sprinkled throughout the budget, but in no regular pattern. The budget's unwieldiness was complicated by the separation of the governor's spending proposals into Alternative I and Alternative II categories, the first category pegged at continuation levels, the latter carrying a higher level of support for new undertakings. This dual presentation was designed to force the legislature to choose between a tax increase or opposition to program improvements. The number of major objects in the appropriations was reduced to three, but the addition of activity accounts resulted in an overall increase in the number of appropriation units.

The new approach—admittedly "an unfinished product"—generated complaints over the centralization of financial control and the effort required to produce the massive budget document. Performance budgeting was seen by some departments as an acceleration of the process of administrative centralization begun in 1957. The departments had not been consulted in the development of performance budgeting. They knew little of its purposes, but they were affected by the extension of position controls down to the activity level and by the centralization of the accounting system. A department business officer complained bitterly, "All they see in the Department of Finance is con-

46. State of Ohio, *Executive Budget for the Biennium, 1961–63*, p. i.

trol. They don't care enough about management." A budget examiner reported "considerable feeling that the performance budget means more control." A high budget official acknowledged that Finance "has tightened up its controls over expenditures in the budget execution stage." When it admixed objects and activities, the Finance Department multiplied the number of control points and reporting requirements, thereby increasing the inflexibility and central surveillance that performance budgeting was intended to alleviate. Comments from institution officials (who were hardest hit by the proliferation of budget accounts) reveal the frustration and resentment stirred by the way performance budgeting was applied in Ohio. "For some budgeteers, flexibility means flexibility for the budget office, not for the departments." "The budget division does not understand how these changes have affected the business offices. More types of information have been added. The controls have remained. The change has been made for the benefit of the Department of Finance, not for the institutions." "It has caused confusion from one end of the department to the other. In this department there is a theoretical possibility of fourteen thousand accounts to maintain. Are we running hospitals or an accounting office?"

Understandably the budget document attracted a good deal of criticism from those who had to use it as well as from those who had to provide information for it. "Most legislators," one of their aides commented, "were confused by it. It provided more information but it was more difficult to understand." A committee chairman exploded: "Who laid out the format of this budget? Who cut it into so many pieces so that we don't know what's being done?" Department staffers resented the enormous burden of putting the documents together. "Some departments feel that they did more than ever before." "Preparing our budget this year cost us twenty times as much in terms of personnel than in the past."

"I'm going to do my utmost to wreck this whole thing," an irate department official vowed in 1961. He attained his objective without having to lift a finger. Midway in the preparation of the 1963–65 budget, there was a change in administration. The Republican gubernatorial candidate, James Rhodes, defeated the Democratic incumbent, Michael DiSalle, in a contest that revolved around the fiscal condition of the state. One of the first moves of the new administration was to discard most of the performance budget material prepared for the forthcoming bienniel budget. Under Governor Rhodes, the budget and appropriations retained the tripartite classification of objects, but no other vestiges of performance budgeting remained. Into the 120 pages of the 1965–67 budget were crammed summaries of departmental and institutional expenditures by major object and fund. Gone were the narratives, activity accounts, and workload information.

The abandonment of performance budgeting did not mark a return to centralized line-item control. The Finance Department did not revert to the itemization of minor objects; rather it continued with the threefold breakdown established under performance budgeting. "The basic philosophy of this administration," the Finance Director said, "is placing more responsibility at the department level." This view was seconded by a former supporter of performance budgeting, who acknowledged that "the Department of Finance has done an exceptional job in decentralizing autonomy and responsibility to the agencies." Hence, relations between the agencies and Finance were improved, even though the departments probably received smaller appropriations from Rhodes than they would have obtained under DiSalle. Departments welcomed the elimination of most of the paperwork mandated by the performance budget apparatus. For the 1965–67 biennium, each agency was furnished a computer printout of its expenditures for the preceding and current biennia and was requested to supply corresponding estimates for the next two years. Only a handful of forms were used, the amount of detail was kept to a minimum, and no program or performance information was solicited.

Abandoning performance budgeting also meant freeing departments from the constraints imposed by the combination of object and activity units in the appropriations. A few statistics tell the story here. The 1959 appropriations act contained approximately 180 units; there were 310 units in the 1961 act and only 120 units in the 1965 appropriations. The Department of Mental Hygiene and Corrections suffered most from the installation of performance budgeting and benefited most from its abandonment. In 1961 its appropriations were fragmented in 66 appropriation units and 207 appropriation items; in 1965 it was down to 3 units and 22 items.[47] Because of the relaxation of control

---

47. "Appropriation items" are defined as appropriations "made for personal service, maintenance equipment, special purpose, subsidy or rotary"; "appropriation unit" means a "part of a department, office or institution to which an item of appropriation was made." Roughly speaking, items correspond to objects of expense and units to organization subdivisions.

and the reduction in budgetary labors, the rejection of performance budgeting attracted widespread support among state officials.

Concluding Comment

Performance budgeting failed to achieve its aspirations and potential. It did not undo decades of budget tradition. What it did accomplish were changes in the forms and procedures of budgeting. Yet it was not to be the last word in budget innovation, and the disappointing career of this proposed reform did not deter a new generation of reformers from striving to convert the tradition-bound budget apparatus to new purposes.

4

The Status of PPB in the States

A few years ago planning-programming-budgeting was little more than a concept and a set of initials. Today it appears, in more than half of the states, to be in some stage of consideration or implementation and to be associated with specific applications and procedures. In March 1969 the Council of State Governments surveyed the states to measure the progress of PPB. Twenty-four of the responding states replied affirmatively to the question "Are you now developing an integrated planning and budgeting (or PPB) system?" Sixteen states indicated that they plan to undertake PPB development in the future, and only two states reported that they have no plans for installing PPB.[1] As for diffusion, the spread of PPB seems to be comparable to that of the executive budget and probably swifter than the dissemination of performance budgeting.

Yet these encouraging statistics hide the true status of PPB in the states. Except for one or two states, PPB has not penetrated the decision-making arenas of state governments. Its actual progress is far less advanced than the yes-no questionnaire responses imply. Furthermore, the short-term prospects of PPB—over the next three to five years —are not favorable unless the course of innovation is altered and the pace of implementation significantly accelerated.

In this chapter, PPB is subjected to a closer scrutiny than is afforded by the survey replies. What does the preponderance of "yes" responses mean? Do they indicate that there has been action or only interest,

1. See Council of State Governments, *State Progress in Planning and Budgeting Systems* (Lexington, Kentucky, 1969), pp. 8–17.

commitment or only fashion? Necessarily a survey of PPB in the states must be couched in fairly general terms. Hence the next chapter examines PPB innovation in five states that are among the most—if not *the* most—advanced in the nation in budget reform.

Problems of Assessment

Before considering the status of PPB, it is appropriate to specify the limitations that stand in the way of a complete and accurate assessment. First, it is possible to offer only an interim appraisal, since PPB has yet to be fully implemented in a single state. Although PPB in the federal government dates back to August 1965, many states entered the field only recently, and few have moved beyond planning for PPB to the implementation stage. It appears that the lead time between promise and delivery will be several years or more, certainly longer than the period experienced thus far. A few states have planned for PPB three or four years ahead, but they have little to show for it now. Other states have stepped in only to test the water and are unsure of their future intentions. Very few budget directors expect to achieve their PPB goals within a year or two. In fact, when they were asked at the 1969 convention of the National Association of State Budget Officers (NASBO), "How long do you estimate it would take to fully install PPB in your state?" only one budget director projected a complete installation within one to two years, while ten thought it would take three to five years, and a dozen estimated that more than five years would be required.[2] Accordingly, it is difficult to tell whether the first stirrings will blossom into an innovative restructuring of state decisional processes or fade away without leaving a durable imprint on state administration. Nor is it possible to foresee precisely whether the initial difficulties will be overcome once state officials gain an understanding of the PPB system, or whether they will lead to the abandonment or the scaling down of PPB intentions.

2. The questionnaire, in which this was one of many items, was distributed directly to the budget directors in attendance at the convention, and returns were received from twenty-four of them. The purpose of this form of distribution was to avoid the common occurrence where questionnaires signed in the name of the director actually are prepared by lower ranking employees. Since most of this questionnaire dealt with attitudes, the views of subordinates would not have adequately reflected those of the budget directors.

A second problem arises from the sheer difficulty of monitoring actions in fifty states. The task is complicated enormously by the different approaches emerging in the states. Each state has its own conception of what PPB means and how it should be implemented; each uses the language and the techniques somewhat differently; each is proceeding with its particular sequence and ranking of priorities; each strives to differentiate its version from those of its peers and neighbors; each is confident that it will avoid the pitfalls and errors that have stymied other states. One state stresses a multiyear planning feature; another concentrates on overhauling its information systems; a third gives priority to the preparation of policy analyses. Will these differences narrow or widen as the states gain self-confidence, or become discouraged? Will states starting along the same road reach the same destination? The PPB concept has become sufficiently elastic and diffuse to cover diverse efforts to bolster the planning or analytic processes of the states. Although most of the differences in state approaches can be fitted into a set of generalizations, one cannot be certain that small distinctions will not grow into major ones.

The problem of tracking PPB development is complicated further by diverse sponsorship. Where the budget office takes the lead, a central budget perspective will give a reasonably accurate picture of what is being done. However, in some states little is being done by budgeters, but the planners are trying to incorporate aspects of PPB into their operation. In still other states the main impetus has come from a special task force or from the governor's policy staff. In a few states the initiative has been taken by professionals in certain agencies rather than by central staffers, and in some instances specialized PPB-type activities are concentrated in particular programs where federal money is the spur. There are even a few states where the legislature has been the active force in prodding the executive to consider PPB. One must look for PPB wherever it is, but this is not an easy task. Anything less than a field inspection in each state could not yield a comprehensive or completely accurate account.

The third problem arises from the fact that PPB is a two-sided phenomenon. There is the public side, easy to identify because it is embodied in official pronouncements, new forms and procedures, and new staff units. But there is also a private side, manifested in the kinds of decisions made by public officials. This aspect is not necessarily revealed in the budget document or in the forms, but is seen in executive sessions, when program plans are formulated, the budget is marked up, and expenditure decisions are made. Though these sessions are closed to public scrutiny, they are the real testing ground of planning and analysis. Unlike performance budgeting, PPB gives little attention to the form of budget presentation. It is possible to achieve all the goals of PPB and yet keep the traditional budget format intact. Is an effort made to relate programs to objectives, to compare the costs and effectiveness of program alternatives, to consider the future implications of current policies? If the answer is yes, the state is "doing PPB" regardless of the form in which its budget is cast; if no, PPB is not operative even if the forms appear to attest otherwise. But how does one evaluate the returns from thinking analytically? Rarely are there clearcut "before and after" or "with and without" comparisons to dramatize the results. As William Gorham has said, "It is difficult—and will remain difficult—to point to specific decisions and say, 'that one was different because of PPB.' "[3]

Any evaluation of what has happened thus far can be made to show either a favorable record or a dismal outlook. One can read promising portents into the early moves, or one can interpret them bleakly. Nevertheless, a tentative statement is useful. First steps are clues to later ones; early problems often foreshadow more difficult ones to come. Let us try to determine whether the seemingly slow pace is the product of a "deliberate speed" strategy or of troubles that might persist even if the start-up obstacles were surmounted.

Elements of PPB

Since its beginning, PPB has been identified with a set of distinctive procedures and documents. The technical antecedents of most state PPB systems were the bulletins issued by the U.S. Bureau of the Budget for the guidance of federal agencies.[4] Many of the techniques are not new; multiyear forecasting, for example, was applied in a few

3. See testimony of William Gorham before the Subcommittee on Economy in Government of the Joint Economic Committee, *The Planning-Programming-Budgeting System: Progress and Potentials* (September 1967), p. 9.

4. U.S. Bureau of the Budget, Bulletin 66-3 (Oct. 12, 1965); Bulletin 68-2 (July 18, 1967); and Bulletin 68-9 (April 12, 1968).

governments and agencies before PPB. What is new is the effort to integrate a number of separable elements into a PPB system.

Structure of the Budgetary Process

PPB envisions a particular relationship between planning and budgeting, one that is at odds with the conventional budget process. In practice planning is to precede budgeting. This planning emphasis would mean a radical departure in the operating procedures of governments that have followed a bottom-up sequence in budgeting; that is, lower levels formulate their requests without substantive financial or program guidance from above. The logic of PPB is that planning must come at the start, or it will not come at all; after the estimates have been submitted and when budgeters are hurrying to meet administrative deadlines, it will be too late to consider purpose, future implications, and program alternatives.

To accommodate the planning function, two adjustments probably would have to be made in the budget calendar. First, the budget process would have to begin earlier—in a pre-preparation stage, during which policy previews would be conducted. In this period, systematic analyses of selected programs and issues would be made. Not all programs and budget categories would have to be covered, only those that seem to offer the most favorable opportunities for analysis and action. The previews could be formal hearings, attended by the governor and his aides, or informal discussions between central and departmental staffs. The exact format of the previews is not important, but it is essential that they deal with major budget issues, not with detailed estimates. Before the previews, departmental and central staffs would identify prospective issues and prepare brief papers outlining possible courses of action. After the policy sessions, some of the projected issues would be set aside, while others would be analyzed thoroughly in preparation for the next round of budget, program, and legislative decisions.

The second change needed in the budget calendar is a reduction in the amount of time allocated to budget estimation—centrally and in the departments. If budget estimation continues to consume half or more of each fiscal year, there will be neither opportunity nor inclination for policy analysis. This probably calls for the use of automated data processing techniques that eliminate much of the manual work in budget estimation.

Program Budget

In most developed budget systems, expenditures are classified according to organizational units, appropriation categories, items of expense, and (where performance budgeting is being used) activity units. It is hard to make or use analyses with these traditional informational and decisional categories. From the standpoint of planning and analysis, they have three limitations: they do not show total program costs, they retard trading off among program alternatives, and they do not provide a channel from program analysis to budget decisions.

The program structure proposes to remedy these deficiencies by organizing budget information according to the objectives of government. To what extent the program structure would add to or displace the existing budget classifications need not be considered here, but it is certain that governments will always need various kinds of information to serve the control and management functions of budgeting. The program structure would be superior to all the other classifications, at least for the planning and analytic aspects of budgeting.

In some writings, there is a tendency to identify the program structure as the dominant component in PPB. This has led to a good deal of distortion and misunderstanding. On the one hand are those—represented primarily in the *Program Budgeting* anthology published by the RAND Corporation—who imply that once a government has arrayed its budget accounts by programs, it has achieved the main benefits of PPB. On the other hand, there are those who, like Aaron Wildavsky, say that the program structure is either harmful or useless.[5] A balanced view is that the program budget is only one of the elements of PPB; it is definitely not the whole story. In the Defense Department, program packages helped to reorient the budget process and to bolster the position of the secretary of defense vis-à-vis the military services. But in state governments, other aspects of PPB probably will be more useful. In any case, the utility of a program structure cannot be divorced from the quality of the analysis and decisions it engenders.

5. Aaron Wildavsky, "Rescuing Policy Analysis from PBB," *Public Administration Review*, Vol. 29 (March/April 1969), pp. 189–202.

Two criteria govern the construction of program categories: substitution and complementarity. According to the rule of substitution, all elements that serve a common objective and can be substituted for one another should be grouped in the same category. This makes it possible to trade off within categories: highways versus public transit; welfare payments versus income guarantees; Polaris versus Minuteman, and so on across the full range of public activities and expenditures. The complementarity rule requires that all items that contribute jointly to the same objective should be placed together so that the full cost of each program is displayed. Scholarships for medical students and grants to medical schools serve to improve health care; flood control and hydroelectric installations contribute to a region's economic growth; police and judicial activities promote law enforcement. Even under these rules, different classification schemes are conceivable because (a) there are multiple ways of defining public objectives, and (b) many activities serve several objectives. Consequently the design of program categories must be based on additional factors, such as the preferences of policy officials.

Organization boundaries are not the paramount factor in the design of program structures, but they are likely to be given more weight if the task is entrusted to the departments rather than to some central unit. Nevertheless, existing organizational lines cannot be ignored altogether because excessive divergences between the departmental and program structures might adversely affect the accounting and budget routines.[6]

Multiyear Plans and Projections

The routines of the budget process necessarily revolve around a one- or two-year cycle. Whatever amount of planning is introduced into budgeting, the budget process must be controlled and managed according to the fiscal year calendar. But programs do not begin and end

---

6. This problem plagued the first years of federal PPB. To avoid excessive fragmentation of organization and appropriation units, U.S. Bureau of the Budget Bulletin 68-9 cautioned: "There are many instances where the program structure, if it is to facilitate decision-making, must cut across organization lines, appropriations, and other classifications. Pursuit of absolute uniformity and consistency in development of a program structure will, however, be counterproductive in some instances in terms of the major objective of PPB: the improvement of the basis for decision-making."

when the fiscal year does. The systems costs of each program are the aggregate of many years' expenditures, as are its benefits.

Furthermore, within the bounds of a single year, it is virtually impossible to make a genuine evaluation of alternatives. When a budgeter's horizon is limited to the next year, he can do little more than make incremental adjustments in the existing distribution of funds. Most of his potential options already have been foreclosed by built-in cost increases and by political and bureaucratic constraints against change. Only when he escapes from the immediate budget predicament and views expenditures in terms of aggregate spending increases over a number of years can the budgeter give serious thought to significant program changes. Also, within a single year, objectives inevitably get crowded out of the picture. One looks backward to what was spent or to present problems and pressures, not forward to program opportunities and end results five or ten years hence. Program analysis therefore requires the identification of costs and benefits for a span of years, ideally for as many years as it will take to complete the program, or in the case of continuing programs, for enough years to indicate the prospective trend of costs and benefits.

A multiyear plan has two sides: an input statement of costs by programs (and program elements) for each year of the plan and a parallel report of estimated output of each program. To construct a full-blown multiyear plan therefore requires the prior identification of appropriate output indicators for each program. The output measures pertain to the purposes, not the work, of government agencies. Preferably there should be a limited number of key indicators for each program unit; otherwise, it will be hard to relate costs to accomplishments. Of course, some program outcomes cannot and should not be stated in quantitative terms. In those instances, it is much better to describe the outputs verbally than to use inappropriate measures or make no statement concerning output.

Many kinds of multiyear statements can be developed within a PPB system. (1) The statements can be plans for the future or only projections of likely trends. While the plan is not rooted to current commitments and activities, projections of the future costs and results of existing programs ordinarily are made under a fixed assumption, such as a rate of program growth consistent with recent experience. (2) The statements may be estimates of what departments would *like to* spend and accomplish, or they may be constrained by what central officials consider a reasonable planning target. The constraints may be dollar or percentage limits on expenditures, and they can be varied for different departments and programs. (3) The statements may present alternative plans for the future, or they may project a single state of affairs. For example, the multiyear plan for an education program might estimate costs and benefits based on 100, 150, and 200 percent of current spending. This kind of plan has an analytical function in that it facilitates the comparison of alternative programs.

Program Analyses and Program Statements

As a system for analysis, PPB's main purpose is to provide for the effective use of analysis in making budgetary decisions. The program categories and the multiyear documents furnish a needed informational base for analysis, but they cannot ensure that an analysis is made or used. PPB requires procedures for determining what analysis should be undertaken, for tying the analysis to the budget process, and for keeping track of the analytic and decisional status of each program.

PPB offers procedures for making and for using analysis. In connection with the policy previews discussed above, a formal procedure might be used for deciding what issues shall be examined. It would be folly to try to analyze everything every year; analysis must be selective, and the selections must be made with considerable care and with a keen awareness of policy and program matters. In addition to the program analyses, some governments use program memoranda as concise and authoritative reports of the status of each program. The memorandum informs officials of the judgments and studies behind each program, so that they can be aware of the policies and objectives that are represented in the budget requests.

Crosswalk Relations

An operative planning-programming-budgeting system needs a diversified and specialized information base. The requirements of control and management cannot be satisfied within a planning-only framework. PPB tries to cope with this multipurpose budget problem by means of a "crosswalk" arrangement, whereby program categories are translated into the other informational structures, and vice versa. In this way, a budgeter can quickly obtain data on the distribution of a health program's budget among various organizational units and appropriations categories and on the item-of-expense detail.

In a technical sense, crosswalking is not difficult. Most successful private firms do it routinely, but few governments have had experience with it. Part of the problem is the lack of an adequate accounting structure for crosswalking. This can be remedied by developing comprehensive cost and activity codes and by automating the accounting system. Beyond the technical problems, however, there are more intractable difficulties in operating a budget system that has heterogeneous functions. These difficulties are examined in Chapter 7.

Alternative Approaches to the Implementation of PPB

When a state decides to introduce PPB, it is faced with alternative strategies. It can concentrate on immediate payoffs by gearing the analytic staffs to pending program issues, or it can concentrate on establishing a system for analysis. Some states have pursued the former course, but most of those that have advanced beyond the talking stage have preferred a strategy of long-term survival. In part, this tactic has been due to a reluctance to move too quickly before the system has been accommodated to the existing decisional processes; in part, it has been forced by the dearth of analytic resources in the states.

Analytic versus Systematic Approaches

The states that are following a "systematic" rather than an "analytic" strategy are those that give priority to developing and installing an overall structure for planning and budgeting. This systematic structure contains the informational base of planning and analysis, the documentation and calendar for linking the plans to the budget, the extension of PPB procedures to all sectors of the state government, and the means of relating multiyear projections to current budget choices. Pennsylvania has opted for a systematic approach, with the installation of PPB phased over several years to provide for the training of participating officials, the design of a program structure, multiyear reports, the determination of state goals, the development of output and impact measures, and the evaluation of results. When a systematic course is followed, the state will have few returns in the early years. The expectation is, however, that once the system is operational, it will produce analytic budgets on a continuing basis, with the requisite staff and data available for operating the system.

The analytic strategy favors a short-term payoff in the hope that as budgeters and other policy officials gain confidence in PPB they will be willing to invest in the installation of a system. Under the analytic approach, a select number of program issues are removed from the ordinary budget stream and given special analytic treatment. The analysis is ad hoc, without the benefit of an overall informational or decisional structure, and it is injected into the budget cycle "out of turn," rather than through prescribed procedures. While the pioneering PPB states tended to favor a systematic route, some of the later ones were unwilling to bear the considerable costs and difficulties of imposing an elaborate system on the existing budgeting and planning structures. Therefore, they have preferred to aim for short-term payoffs from analysis.

Piecemeal versus Comprehensive

Along with their systems strategies, the early PPBers tried to apply PPB across the board to all state agencies. This was the case in the five states participating in the State-Local Finances Project. These states felt that it would be unproductive to treat PPB as a "pilot" effort that had to prove its feasibility and worth in limited areas before it could be judged ready for widespread application. Many feared that PPB would inevitably fail if it were stigmatized as an experiment, and though they knew that a comprehensive effort entails many uncertainties, they were willing to take the risks rather than see their project fail for lack of initial confidence and investment.

But as the difficulties of the comprehensive approach have become recognized, the recent tendency has been to apply PPB to a few agencies or programs. Rhode Island has concentrated on welfare and social programs; New Jersey, on health, transportation, and education; Hawaii, initially on education, though now across the board. The states that are approaching it piecemeal do not see their efforts as trials but rather as the deployment of limited resources in a few areas. They see the choice as being between spreading available resources (staff, money, and analytic talent) thinly across all state programs or concentrating them on "targets of opportunity," where a small investment can stimulate the extension of PPB to other areas.

Informational Resources

One of the popular strategies for installing PPB incrementally is to begin with the development of informational resources for planning and analysis. Ordinarily this takes one of two forms: either the construction and installation of a government-wide program structure, along with suitable adjustments in the accounting and budget codes, or the development of a new, computerized information system for the state, with the financial accounts being a main segment of the system. During the past several years, Wisconsin's PPB effort has focused on the development of a program structure and ancillary informational resources. The State of Washington has given considerable attention to designing a computer-based Budget Reporting System. In both states, information has been the priority concern, while multiyear planning and program analysis have been deferred until the information systems become capable of supplying analytic data for budget making.

Multiyear Perspectives

A few states use PPB for projecting or evaluating the future implications (costs and effectiveness) of current budget decisions. California is one state that has moved in this direction, and Pennsylvania published a five-year budget projection together with its regular 1970 and 1971 budget documents. In the first years of its PPB efforts, New York State emphasized long-range projections, but this aspect has been curtailed in later versions. While the multiyear projections do not have much analytic content, they serve to stretch the budget beyond its narrow time constraints.

Attempts to Institutionalize PPB

The attempt to institutionalize PPB has proceeded in a number of ways. One of the first steps has been an expression of interest and support from the governor, especially in those states where the impetus for PPB has emanated from the governor's policy staff. Often this backing has been nominal rather than active—a pronouncement issued in the governor's name, a few remarks at a PPB conference or at a meeting of department heads, a memorandum from the governor reporting his interest in the new system. None of these moves commits the governor to act according to the dictates of PPB; in fact, in no state has the governor so acted in regard to his key program and budget decisions (though in a few states major statements of gubernatorial policy have been issued as PPB documents). Nevertheless, the governor's name has helped in launching PPB, attracting publicity, and getting potentially recalcitrant or uninterested agencies to go along with the new system.

Second, many PPB states have established new analytic staffs, either within the budget agency or in close relationship to it. In some PPB states, staffs (or liaison positions) have been set up in the departments as well. These staffs have given PPB an institutional base from which to campaign for the support of budgeters and other policy officials. PPB need not depend on the regular budget staff in order to survive and gain a foothold in state decision making. The staffs also provide spokesmen for PPB who have vested interests in the survival and success of the system, people who are not bound to the old ways of budgeting and have some analytic skills.

Third, in most states, PPB comes with its distinctive package of techniques and procedures: program structures, multiyear plans and projections, program memoranda, and the like. These techniques have enabled practitioners to relate PPB to the routines of budgeting and to identify it with concrete actions and requirements. As a result, PPB is seen not as an amorphous attempt to apply analytic thinking but as a set of specific procedures leading to budget decisions.

Fourth, many states are striving to develop informational bases for PPB. In some, this effort is concentrated on the design of program structures for classifying expenditures into functional or analytic form; in others, a substantial investment is being made in comprehensive informational systems. The development of new informational structures furthers the institutionalization of PPB in two ways: it provides visible evidence of the new system, and it lays the groundwork for applying analysis to government programs.

Finally, various training approaches have been used to orient state officials to the operations of PPB and to the rudiments of economic and systems analysis. Thousands of high and middle level officials have attended PPB courses varying in duration from a single day to a month or longer. These courses have brought the message and techniques of PPB to officials who otherwise would know little or nothing about it. While it cannot be said that the training efforts have overcome the formidable obstacles to PPB, or even that they have been effective in communicating its concepts and practices, at least there has been an educational effort to supplement the large amount of publicity that has accompanied the announced introduction of PPB.

Each aspect of institutionalization imposes some costs and constraints. Statements by a governor in support of PPB can backfire if they are not followed by specific actions that indicate a genuine interest in PPB. It does not take a bureaucrat long to distinguish between publicity and reality and to discover that a superficial promise of change has not penetrated the organization. If a governor preaches PPB but practices the old budgeting, he will create a credibility gap that PPB cannot overcome. Of course, the fact is that a governor (or budget director) cannot use PPB until it is capable of producing for him, but it is questionable whether PPB will be productive if it is not reinforced by gubernatorial action.

The analytic staffs have given PPB a home base but denied it direct entry into the heartland of budgeting—the examinations units in budget agencies. Separate does not mean equal as long as budgeters command the decisional apparatus and the analysts are on the outside engaged in their specialized irrelevancies. From the standpoint of PPB institutionalization, staff separation seems to be desirable because it protects the embryonic analytic enterprise against bureaucratic subversion and inertia. But separation also serves to protect budget traditions against attempted change because it isolates the PPBers from budgeting and channels the inevitable (and not so inevitable) criticism of PPB away from the budget office to the analytic staffs. The analysts get blamed for the problems of PPB, including those provoked by the noncooperation of the budgeters. Moreover, the separate analytic staffs are cast in the role of supervising the implementation of PPB rather than conducting policy analysis. Central monitors rarely are popular, especially when they have the job of prodding agencies to change their ways and of calling into question some of the favored budget traditions of the past.

Another form of separation, the association of PPB with its own techniques, also has exacted a heavy cost. For many, PPB has meant designing a program structure, drafting a program memorandum, and filling the columns of a financial plan. Techniques that were intended to serve analysis have become its masters, with the result that the early PPB documents have contained a great deal of routine description and justification but little analysis. Perhaps the triumph of technique is inevitable; it is a regular occurrence in bureaucratic life. Yet the way in which PPB has been institutionalized has heightened the emphasis on technique, first by giving prominence to the documents themselves and second by keeping these documents apart from the main—and still decisive—budget procedures.

In sum, the attempt to institutionalize PPB has been engineered in a way that greatly compromises its chances for success. Except in a few states, the effort has been premised on a separation between PPB and budgeting. While this division has given PPB a measure of protection, it inevitably has meant that the budget process is barely affected by the new institutions. It is one thing to incorporate PPB into the central decisional structure or to modify the budget process substantially in order to accommodate the new methods, but quite another thing to set up a separate and peripheral apparatus. The course taken in most states minimizes the risks of innovation, but only at the cost of also minimizing the possibility of change. In its quarantined institutions, PPB can do its thing, provided it remains cut off from decision and action.

Significantly, one of the main components of PPB separatism has begun to disappear. In 1969 New York, California, and Hawaii abolished the separate PPB staffs that once were deemed de rigueur among PPB promoters. Each state had its own motives, but each concluded that the costs of separation far exceeded the gains.

Training for PPB

The conspicuous first step in many PPB states has been to set up training sessions for state officials. In this area enough PPB action has occurred to provide a firm basis for evaluation. Each of the states in the State-Local Finances Project ("the 5-5-5 project") has made some attempt at training, as have almost all the states reporting some PPB activity. While the length of the programs and the numbers participating vary widely, most training efforts have been one- or two-day orientations for a small number of managerial and policy officials.[7]

7. See Council of State Governments, *State Progress in Planning and Budgeting Systems*, pp. 18–23; also State-Local Finances Project, *Implementing PPB in State, City, and County* (Washington, D.C., 1969), pp. 109–26.

Training for PPB has been taxed with many difficult responsibilities, most of which are beyond the reach of even the most effective programs. Within a few days or a week—the usual length of training courses—participants must be stripped of their old budget views and perceptions and clothed with new analytic orientations and outlooks. Administrators who have operated successfully in a justificatory budget environment must be re-equipped with basic and advanced analytic skills and techniques. The training program must break down the barriers between planners and budgeters, and it must build up cooperative work relationships between program operators and program analysts. Training must help the new budgeters resolve the tensions between advocacy and analysis, and it must show them how loose justifications can be turned into concrete statements of purpose and effectiveness.

The training program must take the lead in promoting and developing PPB; it must convert PPB from idea to practice, yet it has a meager fund of experience to work with. The trainers have few precedents to follow, and the governments for which they are training have made little headway in applying PPB to the core program and budget decisions. Often the training program is loaded with incompatible missions: to sell and to instruct, to produce converts and to produce analysts, to accommodate PPB to the established budget framework, and yet to modify the traditional incremental routines of budgeting. Recalcitrants are thrown together with enthusiasts, each side drawing from the same "hard sell" to nourish its doubt or buoy its confidence. Doers of analysis and users of analysis are run through the same course as if they had identical roles and perceptions. Advanced students and beginners are given the same instruction as if they were starting with the same capabilities and would end up with identical jobs. And all this and more must be done in a week or less.

Given these difficult tasks and constraints, it is no wonder that most of the training efforts undertaken in the 5-5-5 jurisdictions and in other governments have not yielded startling payoffs. Training has been expected to compensate for the difficulties and limitations of PPB, to succeed where PPB itself has not succeeded. As a result, much of the training has not been *for* PPB but *as a substitute for* PPB. In some governments, hundreds and thousands have been put through the training mill, but only a few have done any planning or analytic work. In a number of governments, training has been the only action taken to implement PPB. For many trainees, the last day of the course is the last time they hear about PPB. They quickly sense that what was portrayed in the classroom will not be delivered in the field. In part, this is because it is easier to set a training program into motion than to stir a bureaucracy into action. Those who are turned on by the training course soon will be turned off by the lack of visible results. When that happens (as it has in more than one place), selling inevitably becomes overselling, and public officials become disenchanted by the gap between publicity and performance.

In the typical training program, participants are taught the elements of PPB (program structures, program memoranda, program and financial plans, etc.) and are given some basic ideas about analysis (identification of objective and evaluation of alternatives, output measurement, discounting, and the like). The entire effort is pervaded with the impression that PPB is a proven product, that all its parts have been tested, and that the job of the trainee is to conform faithfully to the specifications of the PPB model. The limited focus of PPB means that trainees learn the elements of the system without gaining any appreciation of its purpose. They are shown program categories, for example, but they are not able to associate this form of accounts with the purposes of planning and analysis. As a result, the techniques of PPB are seen as its end-products. The tacit message of so many courses has been that doing PPB means getting a program structure, filling in a program statement, and filling out some multiyear form. The mechanistic character of the course is then replicated in the mechanistic application of PPB.

One of the anomalies of PPB training is that few courses are aimed at budgeters. Often agencies and programs are well represented, but few budgeters enroll in the course. There are several explanations for this. First, budgeters are (or seem to be) busier than most other administrators, and they find it hard to take the time for training. Second, many of the courses are run by new analytic units (located within or outside the budget apparatus) that have not yet established effective working relationships with the budgeters. Third, budgeters may not relish the criticism of their roles implied by PPB and may prefer to withdraw from contact with their critics rather than have their work challenged in the training forum. Whatever the reasons, the absence of the budgeters means that training fails to reach those who have an important responsibility for shaping the course of government budgeting and who have a major voice in the application of PPB.

Of course, the training strategy itself cannot be held accountable for the disappointing pace of PPB. Yet training has been one of the few PPB activities in which states have been willing to make fairly substantial investments. The failure to develop effective training has added to the substantial impediments to innovation. By supporting training programs, state officials have satisfied themselves that they have taken the necessary first step. That step often has been the last, and, even when it has been followed by others, it has contributed only marginally to the advancement of PPB.

What Has Been Accomplished?

The most important fact to note about PPB is that it is approaching operational status in only a few states. Most states have gone no further than the preliminaries—training courses and program structures—and have not taken adequate steps to build PPB into the decisional structure. Only a few have made the critical investment in commitment, resources, and boldness to give PPB a fair chance against the prevailing budget traditions. Even in these states, PPB has yet to produce many concrete results, though the future prospects are significantly brighter than they are in the majority of states that have engaged in marginal maneuvers that seem destined to disappointment. In spite of the fact that most state budget officials profess an interest in PPB, there are few success stories to emulate, few examples of what works, and no solid evidence of the benefits to be derived from PPB. The traditions established in earlier years continue to dominate the budget process, while PPB stands on the outside, a fashionable but peripheral feature of state administration.

The strategy of state budget innovators seems to rest on a mixture of resignation and hope. Through their actions, they are saying "PPB will take many years to install fully, since the current obstacles are greater than the resources we can marshal against them. About all we can do at present is the preparatory work, not the installation itself. Somehow time will rescue us from the difficulties that now encumber state budgeting. What is not now possible will become feasible in the future." Of course, this approach is self-justifying but self-defeating. The problems will continue to be intractable three or five years hence unless steps are taken to remedy them. Precisely because the difficulties are so great, a minimal effort cannot succeed.

The Limited Application of PPB

During PPB's first years, several kinds of accomplishment have been reported. (1) Some states have tried to institutionalize PPB, that is, either to establish a separate PPB framework or to make PPB a prominent part of the budget process. (2) Certain aspects of PPB, such as program structures and multiyear projections, have been incorporated into the budget processes of some states. (3) In a few states, some decisions have been made as a product (or byproduct) of PPB activity. However, the character of these accomplishments suggests that innovation has been very limited and that the mode of budget choice has not been significantly changed.

As was explained above, the institutional framework erected for PPB virtually assures that it will remain apart from the regular decisional processes. Moreover, while the adoption of selected PPB features may upgrade the budget process, PPB may leave its legacy of forms and procedures—just as performance budgeting did—without making a durable impact on the use of budget power. Finally, one should not place undue importance on the use of analysis in a very few budget decisions. PPB does not represent the first use of analysis in budgeting, though it may be more economic and systemic than earlier methods. What is new is the effort to make planning and analysis regular and critical elements of public choice. When state officials offer a particular analysis as evidence of PPB's accomplishments, they often are really testifying to the limited use of PPB. Rarely, if ever, is the indicated analysis representative of the prevailing mode of budget choice; indeed, it is pointed out because it is unique. There is a "museum piece" quality to these analyses; they are exuberantly displayed for outsiders, but a "hands off" practice bars their use in actual decisions.

The argument often is made that PPB has not been in operation long enough to mature, that it takes time to break down the barriers to change and to build bureaucratic and political support. Perhaps this is so, but several factors suggest that the future course of PPB will not be markedly different from what has happened thus far. (1) Although most budget directors expect the full implementation of PPB to take three to five years or longer, few have definite plans for the phased development of the new system. They expect implementation to take many years because they are stymied by current difficulties, not because they have plotted the steps that must be taken to install an operational PPB system. (2) In many states the pace of PPB development has slowed considerably. Although it may be premature to conclude that PPB has passed its peak, definite signs of a standstill are visible in many states. Perhaps they are merely pausing to take stock and reassess their expectations, perhaps they are beginning to recognize the paucity of accomplishment under PPB. (3) The faults in PPB design and the inadequacy of investment in PPB mean that past difficulties are likely to continue in the future. If a state devises a PPB system that is purposely outside the stream of budget choice, or if it maintains its PPB effort at a bare subsistence level, what prospects are there for a brighter future? Hope and good intentions are just not enough to do the job.

There is nothing inevitable about this dismal prognosis for PPB. What has been said above about the states as a whole does not fit the condition in a few states, notably Hawaii and Pennsylvania, and possibly California and Wisconsin as well. In these states, the commitment is much more commensurate with the problem. Moreover, they are trying to build PPB into the budget process and not to establish it at a protected but remote place in the state's administrative structure. As will be seen in Chapter 5, the states that have made the greatest commitment to PPB differ significantly from one another in the approach taken. But what is common to their efforts are the scale of investment and intent to create a budget system that is oriented to a planning role.

However, more than half of the states that place themselves in the PPB column have done nothing more than sponsor some training courses, hire a few people, or design an unused program structure. In this category are many small and medium-sized states that have been prompted to act by federal assistance. But their actions have progressed only as far as their federal assistance has carried them. It is of some significance that in three of the states with the boldest plans, the federal involvement has been marginal or totally absent.

A Resurgence of Performance Budgeting?

When PPB arrived, one could not point to a single state that had reliable cost and work data for major segments of its budget or had successfully used performance controls in place of the traditional input controls. In some ways PPB has enabled state budgeters to accomplish some of the unfinished business of performance budgeting. Thus the informational systems established through PPB tend to be functional rather than analytic; they group expenditures according to standard functional categories (health, education, public safety) rather than according to objectives (economic well-being, community development, protection of the environment).[8] Another indication of the influence of performance budgeting on PPB is the enormous investment being made in Management Information Systems (MIS), Statewide Information Systems (SWIS), Financial Information Systems (FIS), and similar management accounting systems. Generally these systems provide informational support for the internal operations of state agencies but do not deal with the objectives of the state. Moreover, these systems tend to be geared to organizational structures rather than to programs.

Some states are trying to design performance controls either to replace or to supplement the existing financial controls. One of the principal components of Hawaii's PPB system is an annual *variance* report presented by the governor to the legislature, which shows deviations from actual performance. Performance auditing is receiving growing attention in several states that are trying to reorient the post-audit from fiduciary control to the evaluation of performance.[9]

The resurgence of performance budgeting through PPB has developed because the latter makes many more demands on the information resources and decisional capabilities of government. Agencies that lacked reliable data on what they were doing were called upon to evaluate the effectiveness of their programs. They were expected to leap from input controls to command over outcomes, from a focus on

8. For example, New York State's program structure contains these central categories: governmental affairs, education, health, transportation and traffic safety, social development, housing and community development, business and industry, natural resources, recreation and cultural enrichment, and personal safety. Wisconsin uses a smaller number of units for its broadest categories: commerce, education, environmental resources, human relations and resources, and general executive functions.

9. In one of the first recognitions of this development, Article IV, Section 53 of the 1963 Michigan Constitution provides that the auditor general shall conduct performance post-audits of all state agencies and institutions. These types of audit still are quite rare. The legislative auditor of the State of Hawaii has conducted a *General Audit of the Department of Personnel Services* (Honolulu, February 1969), which is heavily oriented to performance.

one fiscal year to a multiyear view, from concern over what is being spent to awareness of what is being accomplished—all without basic information on the work and activities of government. While it might be unwarranted to define performance budgeting as a prerequisite for PPB, there can be no doubt that governments cannot easily move from a pre-performance budgeting situation to PPB.[10]

Attitudes and Intentions

In the absence of firm indicators of PPB success, it has become common to point to the mood of budget makers rather than to the decisions themselves as evidence of PPB's achievement. Thus the final report of the State-Local Finances Project refers to the progress made by one of the participating governments:

It is not possible to point to one reallocation of budget made by that government, or even to one analytical study completed on the use of resources. But a spirit of inquiry was aroused, analytical studies are underway, and highly competent analytical support has been sought for the work.[11]

Though a person's views are not always a faithful guide to what he will do, attitudes often are clues to action. Because the PPB activities of state governments have been limited, the attitudes of state officials must be examined for a fuller understanding of current intentions about budget innovation. The attitudes of innovators are a matter of public record. As spokesmen and sponsors they have vigorously promoted and publicized PPB. The attitudes of state budget leaders, however, are not clearly revealed in their actions, and therefore interview data has been relied on to obtain their views. (See Table 3.)

The questionnaire circulated among budget directors at the 1969 NASBO meeting measures three dimensions of attitudes toward PPB: (1) the extent to which budget directors believe that PPB will help

10. Interestingly, the architect of PPB in the Defense Department (Charles Hitch) was succeeded as comptroller by a prominent management accountant (Robert Anthony), and in the mid-1960s PPB in Defense was modified by Project PRIME, an attempt to install a system of expense accounting for activities of the department. The purpose of Project PRIME was "to achieve a correspondence of operating costs among program, budget, accounting system, and reporting system. Such consistency would eliminate the necessity for the unrewarding "torque conversion [crosswalk]...." Steven Lazarus, "Planning-Programming-Budgeting Systems and Project PRIME," *Defense Industry Bulletin* (January 1967), p. S-18.

11. State-Local Finances Project, *Implementing PPB*, p. 13.

Table 3. Attitudes toward PPB

Statement	Agree[a]	Disagree[a]	No opinion[b]
With PPB, we will be able to do a better job deciding what to spend.	15	3	6
PPB gives us a good opportunity to find out what agencies are doing with their funds.	9	7	7
It's about time that somebody did a cost-effectiveness study of PPB.	15	1	8
Ten years from now, they'll be asking, why all the fuss about PPB?	7	7	9
PPB is a lot of fancy words but not much results.	11	12	1
When agencies get hold of PPB, they'll use it for getting more big programs.	4	15	4
There's nothing new in PPB; we've been doing it all along.	3	20	1

Source: Answers to questionnaire distributed at 1969 annual meetings of the National Association of State Budget Officers.

a. The questionnaire actually offered five possible responses: (1) agree strongly, (2) agree, (3) no opinion, (4) disagree, (5) disagree strongly. For this tabulation, the "agree strongly" and "agree" responses have been combined into a single category, as have the "disagree" and "disagree strongly" responses.

b. In view of the positioning of the choices on the questionnaire, the "No opinion" response may convey a position of neutrality or uncertainty on the statement.

them to do a better job or are cynical about the claims made in behalf of PPB; (2) their ratings of different facets of PPB in terms of priority and ease of accomplishment; and (3) the views of budget directors concerning the best way to install PPB.[12]

Is PPB Worth It?

Two-thirds of the budget directors agreed with the statement, "With PPB, we will be able to do a better job deciding what to spend." This solid agreement may indicate that the budgeters have examined the implications and potential of PPB and have come to the conclusion that it will improve budget making. Or it might indicate that the directors *want* to believe that PPB will enable them to do a better job, that is,

12. To the extent that attendance at the NASBO meeting was not representative of the state budget profession as a whole, the questionnaire responses may be biased. There is reason to believe that the budget directors who do not generally participate in NASBO (representing one-third of the states) are less interested in, and less informed of, current budget developments than are those who do attend.

that they are favorably disposed toward PPB because they perceive a need for budget improvement even though they don't know enough about the new approach to make a definite judgment. Although most believe that PPB will help them do a better job, the directors are fairly evenly divided on the statement, "PPB gives us a good opportunity to find out what the agencies are doing with their funds." It thus seems that a large number of the budget directors are not certain that PPB will equip them to make more informed judgments on agency spending requests, or they believe that it will not help them.

The interpretation that directors *want* to believe (rather than are certain) that PPB will enable them to do a better job is supported by their agreement, by a ratio of two to one, with the statement, "It's about time that somebody did a cost effectiveness study of PPB." Many directors want more information about PPB; they want an objective study that will clear away the conflicting claims and tell them how to proceed. Again, they want to believe that PPB will work, but they also want definite confirmation of their hopes. Another possible indication of the "want to believe" attitude is provided by the responses to "Ten years from now, they'll be asking, why all the fuss about PPB?" Equal numbers agreed and disagreed with this statement, but the largest number of responses were in the "No opinion" category, the group that is withholding judgment until it learns more about PPB. The budget directors also are split in their reaction to the expression of cynicism, "PPB is a lot of fancy words but not much results." Yet on this statement, only one director sought refuge in the "No opinion" response, while the overwhelming majority took their stand on either side of this issue. Finally, most directors perceive that PPB is something new; it is not a different term for old practices. They, therefore, reject the statement, "There's nothing new in PPB; we've been doing it all along." The very newness of PPB contributes to the uncertainty about its potential and implications. Budget directors are familiar with the claims made in its behalf but are unsure of what it can or will do for them.

At this time, the budget officials appear to be divided into three groups, with the size of each group definitely sensitive to changes in the professional status of PPB. In the first group are those who are reasonably confident that PPB is a worthwhile investment, that it will improve budgeting, and that it is workable. This group probably consists of budget directors who have promoted PPB in their states and who have self- and professional images to sustain, but who will be willing to cut their losses if PPB fails to produce for them or entails unwanted costs. A second group consists of a hard core of skeptics who believe that PPB has been oversold and will not be able to deliver on its promises. These people tend to agree with another of the statements in the questionnaire—"Budgeting is mostly experience and common sense"—and they are convinced that a cost-effectiveness study would show that PPB is not worth its cost. A final group is composed of people who recognize the need for budget improvement, like the "paper" version of PPB, and hope that it will produce according to expectations. But they are unwilling to move vigorously in their own states until more results are available. These directors probably will move into the doubting category if PPB's performance fails to match its publicity in the next several years.

At the present time, the doubters are a small minority, perhaps no more than three to five directors among those represented in the interviews. The group favorably disposed toward PPB is a somewhat larger minority, five to ten from PPB-active states. The "want to believe" group is the largest and consists of directors from states that have indicated an intention to try PPB but have not invested many resources in the effort thus far. The present doubters probably cannot be moved from their positions, and their ranks certainly will swell as PPB loses some of its glamour. Moreover, some of those who are at present favorably disposed as well as some who want to believe may become doubters. It will not take much to plant cynicism in the minds of budgeters; it will be much more difficult to maintain the current level of favorable views and to convert those who want to believe into true believers.

Desirability and Feasibility

Apart from perceptions about PPB, budgeters have views about its particular features. An attempt was made to obtain ratings of the priority and feasibility of the fifteen PPB elements and activities listed in Table 4. For each of these items, the budget directors were asked (1) whether its accomplishment should be "top priority," "desirable," "deferred," or "not desirable," and (2) whether its accomplishment would be "easy," "not so easy," "difficult," or "very difficult." The replies can be interpreted as ratings of the value of specific PPB elements.

Table 4. Desirability and Feasibility of PPB Components[a]

Desirability (ranked from most to least desirable)	*Feasibility* (ranked from most to least feasible)
Training and recruiting staff	Support from the governor
Support from the governor	Rewarding agencies that use PPB
Program identification	Relaxing control over line items
Developing output measures	Program identification
Establishing goals and priorities	Setting up a PPB staff
Analyzing program alternatives	Establishing goals and priorities
Developing supporting information	Using PPB in budget decisions
Selling system to legislature	Getting planners and budgeters to work together
Getting planners and budgeters to work together	Developing supporting information
Using PPB in budget decisions	Making multiyear plans
Establishing criteria for evaluation	Training and recruiting staff
Making multiyear plans	Selling system to legislature
Setting up a PPB staff	Analyzing program alternatives
Relaxing control over line items	Developing output measures
Rewarding agencies that use PPB	Establishing criteria for evaluation

Source: Answers to questionnaire distributed at 1969 annual meetings of the National Association of State Budget Officers.

a. The scores were computed on a scale of 1 to 4. Desirability ratings were scored: 4—top priority, 3—desirable, 2—can be deferred, 1—not desirable. Feasibility was scored: 4—easy, 3—not so easy, 2—difficult, 1—very difficult. Thus the higher the score the more desirable or feasible the particular PPB element.

Budget directors give high priority both to the development of an institutional base for PPB and to some of the core elements of planning and analysis. At the top of the desirability list, they place training and recruiting and obtaining the support of the governor. Immediately below these are four of the main components of PPB—program identification, output measures, goal determination, and analysis of program alternatives. However, not all institutional or analytic features receive high desirability ratings. Thus, selling the system to the legislature, getting planners and budgeters to work together, and setting up a PPB staff are lower down on the list, as are multiyear planning and evaluation criteria. That budgeters prefer to analyze rather than to evaluate is not surprising, but the relatively low rank given multiyear planning is at variance with what was expected. For although no state has made any significant commitment to evaluation, many of the PPB states have emphasized the multiyear feature.

Lowest priority is accorded to two items that have a considerable bearing on the success of PPB. Budget directors do not consider it important to relax controls over line items or to reward agencies that use PPB. Yet it is precisely the feeling that PPB means an additional layer of control and that there is nothing to be gained (in budget outcomes) from using PPB that discourages many agency officials from an enthusiastic acceptance of PPB. Either budget officials do not have much understanding of agency perspectives, or they are unwilling to take the major steps necessary to make PPB popular.

One item in the middle range of the list is particularly interesting because it dramatizes the distance between image and reality. Budget directors do not regard using PPB in budget decisions as among the most important actions. They still value many of the features of PPB, but they stop short of using it. One possible interpretation is that PPB per se is perceived as something different from its elements. If this is so, budget officials can be expected to promote desired features, such as program identification and goal determination, even if they do not formally adopt PPB.

The feasibility rankings are in a significantly different order than the desirability ratings. High on the feasibility list are three low-priority items—rewarding agencies, relaxing the controls, and setting up a staff. At the bottom of the feasibility list are several of the priority features of PPB—criteria for evaluation, output measures, and program analysis. Evidently the things that are easy to do, the directors do not want to do; the actions that are hard to accomplish are the ones they regard as important. The gap between what is desired and what is feasible seems to augur a difficult future for PPB. Yet the gap is not uniform for all components of PPB. The feasibility score is lower than the desirability score for all items except relaxing controls and rewarding agencies.[13] The desirability deficit is comparatively small for some of the institutional aspects of PPB (support from the governor and setting up a staff) and largest for the several core analytic components (output measures, evaluation, and program analysis).

Apparently budget directors feel that they will have no difficulty gaining gubernatorial support for their PPB activities, for that item

13. Strictly speaking, the desirability and feasibility scores are not comparable because they measure different responses. Both are 4-point scales. The desirability scale was computed by assigning a 4, 3, 2, or 1 score respectively to the following responses: "top priority," "desirable," "can be deferred," "not desirable." In like fashion, the feasibility scores were determined by giving "easy to accomplish"—4; "not so easy"—3; "difficult"—2; "very difficult"—1. In each scale, the higher the number, the more feasible or desired the item is rated.

ranks number one on the feasibility list. Yet they believe that it will be difficult to sell PPB to the legislature and to train and recruit staff. Inasmuch as training and recruiting were lumped together, it is not possible to determine whether the low feasibility score applies to both or only to training or recruiting. But in view of the considerable training activity in the states, it is questionable whether the budgeters regard it as infeasible. (Perhaps their replies refer to the feasibility of *effective* training rather than to the training activity itself.)

The Best Way to Install PPB

Earlier in this chapter, several approaches to the installation of PPB were discussed. To ascertain the views of budget directors on some of these and on other approaches, a series of forced-choice alternatives was presented. The responses give a fairly clearcut picture of current attitudes, since on most issues one alternative was favored by a wide margin. (See Table 5.)

Over all, budget directors favor a "deliberate speed" policy that does not upset budget traditions and that involves a wide spectrum of participants. The composite "best way to install PPB" is: in a few agencies at a time rather than across the board; with the regular budget staff rather than with a special PPB staff; by revising the existing budget procedures rather than by establishing special new procedures; by working with the agencies rather than by concentrating the work in the central budget office; by concentrating on the legislature rather than by circumventing it; by giving planners an advisory rather than a leading role; by relying on people who know state budgeting; by establishing state goals rather than by developing supporting data; by focusing on program alternatives rather than on cost projections.

Clearly, budget officials feel that PPB should not be isolated from the regular budget process, not in terms of the staffs or skills involved nor in terms of the procedures used. They do not want PPB to be an ex parte exercise, walled off from agency or legislative involvement, nor do they want to proceed more rapidly than the results or resources warrant. As with traditional budgeting, they prefer to concentrate on the current year (by analyzing program alternatives) rather than on future years, and they would give precedence to the job of determining staff objectives over the construction of the state's information systems.

Table 5. Attitudes of Budget Officials Concerning the Installation of PPB

Pairs of contrasting attitudes ("*The best way to install PPB is . . .*")	*Number of officials sharing same attitude*
Across the board	3
In a few agencies at a time	20
With a special PPB staff	5
Through the regular budget staff	18
Revising the budget document	15
Setting up special procedures	8
Working with the agencies	20
Doing the job in the budget bureau	2
Concentrating on the legislature	21
Bypassing the legislature	2
Giving planners a leading role	4
Giving planners an advisory role	17
With economists and analysts	3
With people who know state budgeting	18
Establishing state goals	17
Developing supporting data	6
Analyzing program alternatives	20
Projecting future costs	3

Source: Answers to questionnaire distributed at 1969 annual meetings of the National Association of State Budget Officers.

What is remarkable about these views is that they diverge on almost every count from the way PPB initially was launched in the federal government and in the states. Initially the states proceeded across the board and established special PPB staffs and an array of special PPB procedures. Although they professed otherwise, the first states did most of the installation centrally, with only marginal inputs from the agencies, and they gave scant (or no) attention to legislative participation. To the extent that they progressed, it was in the direction of supporting information (through the program categories) and cost projections rather than in the direction of program analyses or broad goal determinations.

Judging from their expressed views, most states now seek a cautious application of planning and analysis, as opposed to their ambitious intentions of a few years ago. The states now are aware of the need to secure the cooperation of agency officials and of the difficulties involved, as well as of the risks of giving full responsibility for PPB to imported economists and analysts isolated in a PPB enclave. Yet it is not certain that the states will apply their lessons from experience. For while it is easier to move piecemeal and it is desirable to solicit the involvement of the various participants, it will not be easy to incorporate PPB into the established budget process. It seems far easier to minimize the disturbance to the ongoing process by setting the new PPB institutions apart from the arenas of budget making.

Attitudes sometimes express images rather than reality, and in some of the attitudes toward PPB installation, there seems to be a divorce between image and reality. For example, by a vote of twenty-one to two, the budget directors favor concentrating on, rather than bypassing, the legislature. In fact, however, the state legislature typically is not consulted when changes are being considered or implemented, or is brought into the picture after the changes have been developed. Ordinarily the legislature gets its first direct involvement in PPB when it is given a dual budget—the usual budget document and a PPB prototype. There are some notable exceptions, for example, Wisconsin during its early program budgeting development, in which the legislature was drawn in as a partner to the proposed innovations. In Hawaii the state legislature took the initiative in developing PPB, and in some states individual members of the legislature have involved themselves in budget innovation. Budget officials also may be responding to an image rather than indicating their intent when they say they favor the analysis of program alternatives, since very little has been accomplished in this area.

Concluding Comments

The introduction of PPB has brought a damaging gap between publicity and performance. Agencies go through the motions of preparing PPB documents—in addition to their regular budget work. The regular submissions get all the attention, while the analyses and plans are disregarded. In the final days of budget decision, months of promotional and analytic work can go down the drain as budgeters forsake the long view in favor of the short run, and the analytic in favor of the justificatory material. (Analyses raise questions, justifications give answers, and these are what decision makers want in the final stages.) Thus, PPB seems out of place in the final moments of budget making.

The future of PPB will be dismal if it exhausts itself in formal routines. The governor wants programs, not program structures, and he will lose all interest in PPB if it is only an accounting exercise. All the participants have a subsidiary interest in the forms and a major stake in the outcomes; PPB can endure as form, but the routines will not mean that budget decisions are made within analytic or planning frameworks.

Part of the problem of PPB implementation is the failure to recognize that what might have been appropriate at the start may not be appropriate several years later. Without concrete steps to create a permanent structure for PPB, it might have withered for lack of support, even if some useful analyses had been produced under it. In the long run, therefore, the survival of PPB can be enhanced by institutionalization, provided that the institution created for PPB is within the ambit of budget making. However, this has not often been the case, and as a result the separate PPB machinery has been remote from the budget process.

In some ways, PPB's main accomplishment thus far has been to raise the level of expectation far above what it was a few years ago. The prevailing standard of "good enough" has been redefined, as budget participants have been exposed to PPB's criticism of the established order and its criteria for public choice.

The stakes in PPB are high not only for the planners and analysts but also for the perennial budget participants. Planning is more salient than management, since it goes directly to the outcomes of the budget process, the purposes and valuation of public expenditures and activities, and the "who gets what" of budgeting. One can ignore the cost per pound of laundry if he wishes, but he had better get involved in the work of defining his agency's or the government's programs. Each of the stakeholders in the budget process has something to gain or lose from the way future costs are projected, effectiveness measured, and alternatives framed and presented. Participants can withdraw from program planning only at the risk of losing their say in these matters. Consequently, even if PPB fails to make the grade, state officials can be expected to retain their interest in planning and analysis. In the long run, there may be planning, programming, and budgeting without PPB; that is, each of the main components may be adopted but without the systems umbrella and identification currently provided by the PPB label.

5

PPB in Five States

In Chapter 4 it was argued that PPB in most states has not advanced beyond "first steps" and that as states acquire more experience with PPB, they do not necessarily get better results. While this general conclusion is derived from a survey of the states as a whole, there is still considerable variety among them in application and approach. The five states examined in this chapter represent most, if not all, of the states that have made enough progress with PPB to warrant at least an interim appraisal.

In three of these states—California, New York, and Wisconsin—the contemporary wave of budget improvements predates the decision made in 1965 to implement PPB in the federal government. These three states participated in the State-Local Finances Project ("the 5-5-5 project") designed to demonstrate the feasibility of PPB for state, county, and local governments. The two remaining states—Hawaii and Pennsylvania—were influenced substantially by the federal model, though their PPB plans—if not their progress—were bolder than what was attempted in the federal government.

New York State: From Long-Range Planning to Program Analysis

New York was the first state to adopt PPB and the first to discard it.[1] PPB was initiated in 1964 (though it is uncertain when these

1. Although the program analysis and review (PAR) system, which replaced PPB in New York in 1970, resembles the approach to PPB taken in other states,

initials were first used), and it was replaced in 1970 by PAR (Program Analysis and Review). Many of the factors that contributed to the rise and fall of its performance budgeting experiment (discussed in Chapter 3) also accounted for New York State's early acceptance and quick abandonment of PPB a decade later. In fact, there have been few major changes in New York State budgeting since the 1950s, though the form and content of the budget have been modified and the environment in which the budget process functions has been changed significantly. Except during the Harriman administration (1955–59), the same person served as budget director from 1950 to 1970. Moreover, there have been remarkably few changes in the top leadership of the examinations sections of the Budget Division during the past twenty years. There also has been a continuing belief in the efficacy of central fiscal controls, though effective use of these controls has been weakened by the steep growth in state spending and programs. The trend toward more program data in the budget and appropriations, which developed during the performance budgeting era, has continued, but this has more to do with legislative (line-item) versus administrative (lump-sum) control than with the functions and orientation of the budget process.[2]

Role of the Secretary to the Governor

Yet despite these continuities and trends, the position of the budget process within the state's policymaking structure has undergone an unheralded but important upheaval. While the Budget Division has continued to conduct primarily a control operation, the office of the Secretary to the Governor has taken the lead in developing the large new programs that characterized Nelson Rockefeller's first three terms as governor. With his one hundred-man staff (many of whom serve as "program associates" assigned to particular functions), the secretary's office has become the center of policymaking and pro-

---

PPB was discarded in the sense that the initials were officially and deliberately dropped in an effort to make a break with the past. But because it does in fact have some key features of PPB, PAR is treated in this chapter as the third stage through which PPB has gone in New York State.

2. "Almost invariably those who favor program budgeting have lump sums in mind." John van Laak, quoted in a report of the State of New York Joint Legislative Committee on State-Local Fiscal Relations, *Foundations of the Fiscal System* (March 31, 1966), p. 49.

gram formulation in New York State.[3] Rivalry between the Budget Division and the secretary's staff rarely flares in the open, but it does affect the linkage between program and financial decision making. For their part, the program associates often are skeptical of Budget's responsiveness to the governor's wide-ranging program interests. "They would give you ten reasons why it couldn't work, but not one way to make it work." The budget examiners, on the other hand, sometimes are critical of the spending attitude of the program staff. "They don't care how much it will cost or how it will be financed as long as it's a big, new program." With both his budget and his program staffs, Governor Rockefeller has been able to maintain financial control and program development without one function impeding the other. However, the effect has been to separate what PPB strives to bring together —program and financial decisions. Moreover, in order to finance its many ambitious programs, the state has resorted to various devices (primarily public corporations and lease-back arrangements) that have had the effect of loosening budgetary control over both the selection and the financing of state programs.

Role of the State Planning Agency

Besides the expanding role of the governor's secretary, the role of the Budget Division has been affected by the activities of the state planning agency. In New York, as in many other states, comprehensive planning was revived in the early 1960s. Under the auspices of the Office for Regional Development (ORD), which was transformed into the Office of Planning Coordination (OPC) in the mid-1960s, the planners brought their urban land use and physical facilities orientation to state government. In a 1964 report dealing with the future role of planning, ORD advocated comprehensive state and regional planning, one aspect of which would be the preparation of long-range resource plans.[4] The Budget Division saw this expanded concept of

3. The role of this office and its relationship with the Budget Division has varied during Governor Rockefeller's administration. During periods of program expansion, the office has been more powerful than at times when the governor's policies were tuned to fiscal conservatism. Also the two men who occupied the office between 1959 and 1971 were quite different. William Ronan was a close confidant and adviser of the governor, while his successor, Alton Marshall, previously had been deputy director of the budget.

4. State of New York, Office for Regional Development, *Change/Challenge/Response* (1964).

planning as a threat to its established leadership in capital programming and financial management. In the "power struggle" that ensued, each side staked its claim to long-range resource planning: the planners argued that this type of planning was not being covered through the budget process; the budgeters insisted that it would be unwise to sever resource planning from the annual budget cycle. Out of this jurisdictional squabble emerged Planning-Programming-Budgeting in New York State, for Governor Rockefeller resolved the dispute by giving the Budget Division and ORD joint responsibility for developing and operating what was to become the state's PPB effort.

The pressured commitment to PPB had significant consequences for its subsequent course and ultimate fate. PPB "fell between the stools," as one observer put it. Both the Budget Division and ORD established separate PPB staffs, but neither organization treated PPB as a truly salient part of its work. At the start, the handful of PPB personnel in Budget had a close relationship with the director; within a few years, they were housed in a special unit that was formally responsible to, but actually remote from, the budget director. This new staff was walled off from the examinations unit as well as from a potential ally (which became an adversary)—the management section. This separation was due as much to the eagerness of the PBBers to be free from the constraints of the old-timers as to the desire of the old-timers to operate without PPB interference. "By and large, the examiners were enemies of PPB. They were not really consulted. The PPBers had come to government out of nowhere or out of physical planning." Thriving on their separateness, the PPBers did "not recognize that there are other decisional processes outside PPB."

Under the pressured circumstances of its adoption, little forethought was given to the purposes or operation of the new system, to how it would relate to the existing decisional processes, to which procedures should be used and why, to the respective roles of central staffs and departments, or to the availability of personnel and information. One of the staff members assigned to evaluate the PPB experience claims, "No analysis preceded the introduction of PPB, no timetable, no explanation of why we need the forms and the information. We could not find a single document laying out in advance what PPB was supposed to do, how, and why."

Still another consequence was that PPB in New York, perhaps more than in any other state, started primarily as a statewide planning system with budgeting as a subordinate component. After all, the rivalry between the Budget Division and ORD was over long-range resource planning, and the terms of settlement provided for joint sponsorship of a new planning process. Hence, when PPB was launched, it was virtually taken for granted that planning should be its main feature. Moreover, the budgeters were in it as much to protect their jurisdiction as to improve the budget process, and this objective was achieved through joint participation. As a matter of fact, the Budget Division willingly placed a planner from ORD second-in-command over its own PPB operations.

While the first years of PPB were marked by its planning origins, there have been three discrete stages of budget-related innovation during the brief career of PPB (and its successor, PAR).

1965–67: PPB as planning with a little budgeting

1968–70: PPB as budgeting with some program reporting

1970: PAR as old budgeting with some analysis

The characteristics of each of these stages, as well as the factors that led to the several transitions, are sufficiently distinct to warrant a discussion of each stage.

PPB: Planning with a Little Budgeting

As originally conceived, PPB was a planning process, with budgeting as just one of its many components, *not* a budget process to which a planning element had been added. Thus, long-range planning was the dominant focus of the first set of guidelines issued in 1965 and 1966. These guidelines directed state agencies to "project relevant indicators as far into the future as possible. Twenty-year projections are desirable."[5] The full PPB cycle was to have seven stages; five pertained to the preparation of long-range projections and were to take most of the period from January to September; the two final stages were to coincide with the preparation of the budget. Departments were instructed to "present their budget requests in the context of the long-range goals of their programs."[6]

Agency program projections were to be prepared in accordance with standard planning methodology, beginning with the determination of

5. State of New York, Office for Regional Development and Division of the Budget, *Guidelines for Integrated Planning, Programming, Budgeting* (1966), p. 2.
6. *Ibid.*, p. 3.

goals and objectives. For each of its programs, a department was to provide twenty-year estimates of basic "influencing factors" and ten-year projections of relevant private, intergovernmental, and interdepartmental factors. In typical planning style, these projections were to be funneled into medium-range (five-year) program plans and targets, and the program plans were to be translated into five-year projections of resource requirements, including personnel, capital facilities, and fiscal needs.

In bringing long-range planning to state government, the planners also brought their distinctive values and perspectives. The PPB system was to be integrated, uniform, and comprehensive and to serve the purposes of central planners rather than those of program administrators. PPB, according to the 1967 edition of the guidelines, "treats the entire operational structure of State government as an integrated system which is directed toward the fulfillment of a great variety of governmental goals established to meet State needs."[7] Integration meant that there was to be a direct and specific linkage between the long-range plans and the annual budget and between program goals and agency expenditures. Both the 1965 and the 1966 guidelines insisted that projections should be prepared under a uniform format "designed to apply to all departments." Use of this format would "facilitate the review, evaluation and interdepartmental coordination of the program projections by the Governor's executive staff agencies."[8] Unlike the earlier performance budget, which was to be pretested in a single activity, PPB was to be applied in all major state agencies. Once PPB was cast in a planning framework, the decision to apply it comprehensively was virtually inevitable; after all, comprehensiveness traditionally has been deemed one of the marks of good planning. Even the examiners agreed to go along with an across-the-board implementation, albeit for their own reasons. They preferred an "all for one, one for all" approach that would distribute credit or blame among all agencies rather than a selective strategy that would isolate an agency or program for special treatment. Finally, PPB was conceived from the vantage point of central planning; in effect, department administrators were to serve as the suppliers of information to be used by planners in developing and coordinating state policy.

7. State of New York, Office of Planning Coordination and Division of the Budget, *Guidelines for Integrated Planning, Programming, Budgeting* (1967), p. 5.
8. Office for Regional Development and Division of the Budget, *Guidelines* (1966), p. 7.

The new system lacked many of the conspicuous features that were associated with PPB elsewhere. There was little emphasis on the delineation of program structures, on formal policy analysis, or on the measurement of program effectiveness. The focus was on the future, not on current policy choices, and the language was drawn from planning—goals, targets, needs, requirements—rather than from budgeting or economic analysis.

PPB got off to a favorable start in New York. The governor gave it verbal support, liaison staffs were established in many departments, and a new flow of documents was implemented. Yet the new planning approach did not operate effectively, and within a few years it was jettisoned in favor of a PPB system more closely tied to the budget process. The main problem with this approach was that it made impossible demands on the data and decisional resources of the participating agencies. As one of the architects of the initial PPB effort acknowledged, "It looked good on paper, but when we tried to work it out, the data base wasn't there, the staffing wasn't there." It is generally agreed that the documents submitted by the agencies were superficial and useless, "top-of-the-head guesses about the future." Agencies would have to wait months before receiving official reaction from OPC and Budget, and then they would be castigated for failing to achieve the expectations of the planners. It did not take long for the agencies to perceive that the annual budget cycle continued to operate independently of the PPB apparatus, and they came to view the new documents as burdensome paperwork, unrelated to their programs or to state policymaking. These views were shared by many examiners in the Budget Division, who had little voice in the design of PPB but nonetheless had to cope with the additional paperwork. As they became better acquainted with the conception and operation of PPB, the budgeters grew more skeptical of the value of planning.

By 1967 PPB had gained a national reputation, but one tied closely to the budget process and almost totally divorced from planning. New York budget men examined federal practices and decided that they were more suited to the realities of budgeting than was the existing PPB process. True to its image as a leader in budget innovation, the Budget Division expanded its PPB operation, enrolled as one of the five states in the State-Local Finances Project, and began to redirect the PPB system to its own perspective.

The entry of the budgeters was facilitated by the waning interests of the planners. The planners did not relish the day-to-day involvement in the routines of financial management, nor did they have the capability for responding to departmental submissions. With the establishment of the Office of Program Coordination, the main focus of planning shifted to the preparation of a long-term, statewide development plan.

PPB: Budgeting with Some Program Reporting

The first hint of the shift to a budgetary orientation was provided in the 1967 guidelines, which included this caveat:

... PPBS is designed with full recognition of the continuing need for expenditure controls, management control, and management improvement to assure that specific activities are carried out effectively and efficiently. A carefully conceived balance among all these administrative functions is vital to the optimal management of State government.[9]

These guidelines also made the five-year program plan "the core of the planning-programming-budgeting submission," and stressed the importance of making the various documents relevant to policy decisions.[10] In their program plans, departments were to identify goals and constraints, rank objectives according to priority, and estimate future workload and performance levels.

But the main changes came in the 1968 guidelines, which dropped "integrated" from the title and listed the Budget Division before OPC on the title page. The guidelines said that modifications were being made in the PPB system "to make it more useful for executive decision making."[11] Four major types of changes were identified. (1) The comprehensive planning component was significantly downgraded, and the long-range planning requirements (twenty- and ten-year projections) were dropped altogether. (2) In line with conventional PPB methodology, agencies were instructed to refine their program structures and to make these the basic categories for program analysis, effectiveness studies, and the presentation of budget requests. Fully one-fourth (fifteen pages) of these guidelines was devoted to instructions for preparing the program structures. This emphasis was in accord with the conviction of PPBers in the Budget Division that "a compre-

9. Office of Planning Coordination and Division of the Budget, *Guidelines* (1967), p. 6.
10. *Ibid.*, p. 29.
11. State of New York, Division of the Budget and Office of Planning Coordination, *Guidelines for Planning, Programming, Budgeting* (1968), p. 7.

hensive set of output-oriented categories classified according to objectives" constitutes "the necessary base" for PPB.[12] (3) The five-year program plans were expanded into a program reporting system to provide data on authorized programs and proposed program changes, program size indicators and effectiveness measures, and projections of personnel, capital facilities, and fiscal requirements. New program proposals were to be presented separately, alternatives to the proposed program were to be identified, and the criteria used in choosing the proposed alternative were to be discussed. Finally, increased attention was given to program analysis, and each agency was asked to undertake at least one program effectiveness study during the next year.

In its published reports, the Budget Division conveyed the impression that PPB was making significant progress. Thus in its final report for the State-Local Finances Project it said: ". . . Decision makers now place more emphasis on program objectives than they did prior to PPBS." "Agency heads are taking an increasing interest in the PPB system." "Budget examiners have become heavily involved in PPBS over the past four years."[13] Signs of progress were found in the revision of the budget and appropriation formats and in the development of a reporting system for the annual budget process.

Beneath this facade of progress, however, was the plain fact that PPB never made it in New York. The overhaul of the PPB system could not rescue it from the disrepute and disuse into which it had fallen. From the standpoint of the departments, the new guidelines merely substituted one mass of irrelevant and burdensome reports for another. Second-generation PPB was little more than a reporting system, as distant from program and financial decision making as its predecessor had been. At most, it was a compilation of data and documents, with the agencies uncertain as to why the information was wanted and the Budget Division uncertain as to what to do with it.[14]

In fact, the Budget Division never gave PPB enough support to enable it to influence the course of budgeting in New York State.

12. State-Local Finances Project, *PPB Pilot Project Reports*, "The State of New York" (Washington, D.C., 1969), p. 25.
13. *Ibid.*, p. 27.
14. The assessment of the Joint Legislative Committee on State-Local Fiscal Relations, made during the early years of PPB, is relevant: "The revisions which have emerged from this line of development have, in fact, had very little effect on the basic character of budgeting in New York State. Any effect would be superficial, procedural, formal." P. 57.

"PPB had top-level rhetorical support, but not top-level decisional support." Only minor changes were made in traditional budget procedures, and after five years of PPB, the rules of budget preparation and expenditure control were not much different than they had been before.

Budgeting with Some Program Analysis

In 1969 operation of the PPB system came to a virtual halt. There was widespread noncompliance among the agencies, and the submissions were inferior to those of the previous year. Where agency heads once showed some interest and involvement, clerks were now preparing the forms. The State-Local Finances Project had ended, and key personnel were departing or looking for positions elsewhere. Agencies did not want to continue with another round of PPB submissions, and the examiners and management specialists in the Budget Division were receiving a stream of complaints from disgruntled administrators. Matters reached a boil in the Interdepartmental Management Improvement Council (IMIC), where a motion was passed to set up a task force to study the PPB system and recommend possible changes. In the summer of 1969 the program analysis and coordination unit, which was responsible for directing the PPB effort in the Budget Division, was abolished. Shortly thereafter, a Program Analysis and Review Committee (PARC) was established to evaluate the PPB system and decide what to do with it. PARC worked closely with the IMIC task force and visited the agencies to ascertain their views concerning the value of PPB.

The appraisal of PPB revealed a nearly unanimous opinion that the new system "had bombed." Even those who favored budget improvement had cooled to PPB. "It tended to discredit all reform efforts. We lost five years because of it." Persons who had been skeptical about PPB from the start took the opportunity to vent their anger. "PPB is a vast mindless, useless, garbage collection system," an unusually vehement critic said.

In their evaluation of PPB, both PARC and IMIC had three options: to continue the existing system, perhaps with some modifications; to abandon all efforts to improve the budget process; or to replace PPB with some other budget improvement effort. To continue with PPB or some variant closely identified with it was quickly ruled out. "It would have been disastrous to go again with the old submissions or even with revised ones. Age had not improved them; in fact, there was negative deceleration [sic] and we were regressing rather than progressing." But despite the adverse experiences of the previous five years, PARC decided to recommend still another drive for budget improvement. Though PPB had failed to change budget traditions, it had succeeded in making budgeters aware of the shortcomings of the budget process. Accordingly PARC decided to turn from an evaluation of PPB to identifying those aspects of the budget process that need improvement. In meetings with the chiefs of the various units in the Budget Division, PARC identified five deficiencies. The budget process (1) did not deal effectively with interdepartmental issues, (2) failed to handle multiyear implications of current choices, (3) did not facilitate the consideration of alternative proposals, (4) did not identify critical problems before they became crises, (5) did not make effective use of the tools of analysis.

In 1970 PPB was replaced by PAR—Program Analysis and Review, which is intended to correct some of the perceived defects of the budget process and at the same time avoid the problems that beset PPB. PAR diverges from its predecessor in several ways. First, it is selective where PPB was comprehensive. As the introductory statement for the PAR guidelines says,

The revised system recognizes the difficulty in applying any single budgeting or planning system to all problems in every agency. Selectivity, therefore, is a keystone of the new approach, with increased cooperation between staff and operating agencies to arrive at mutual decisions on problems requiring special attention.[15]

Second, PAR is agency-oriented in contrast to PPB in both versions, which were oriented to the perspectives and reporting needs of central staffs. Third, PAR tries to draw the governor's office into certain parts of the new process, unlike PPB, which generally ignored the fact that much policymaking is concentrated in the governor's office rather than in Budget or Planning. Fourth, PAR does not try to reform the basic budget process but instead tries to inject some analysis into program and financial decisions. Issue analysis, as the new acronym suggests, is the heart of the new system.

The operative components of PAR are fewer and simpler than those

15. State of New York, Division of the Budget and Office of Planning Coordination, *Guidelines for Program Analysis and Review* (June 1970).

of PPB. First, each department is to file an *agency appraisal report*, in effect a brief "state of the agency" report prepared by the head of each agency. He should "discuss the success of his agency in meeting its major program objectives, problems that need to be overcome, and expected future directions."[16] Second, agency heads are to submit *program papers* that justify requests for new programs and for program changes. A program paper should explain why the particular program was proposed and what alternatives were considered and rejected. It should estimate the probable effect of the proposal on existing programs and indicate program size and costs for the first two years and for the "target year," the farthest year in the future for which planning has been done. Third, PAR establishes a formal issue analysis process "to identify and resolve questions where independent action by an agency is impossible or undesirable, or where an individual agency simply does not have adequate resources to carry out the analysis."[17] As part of the process, the governor is to have final approval of the issues to be examined. Finally, most of the formal trappings of PPB have fallen by the wayside. Agencies no longer are required to submit program structures or annual statements of objectives, nor are they required to file multiyear projections or effectiveness measurements.

PAR is intended to operate in low key compared to PPB, but it is by no means certain that it will fare better than its predecessor. Nevertheless, its objectives are much more modest, and if it should fail, its failure would be less conspicuous. Because it is an accommodation to the fixed traditions of the budget process, PAR's fate may depend on future attempts to reform that process. During the late 1960s, there were growing rumblings of dissatisfaction in the legislature concerning the budget process, and it is possible that in the 1970s the state legislature will play a more vigorous role in pressing for an overhaul of the executive budget process that has prevailed in New York for almost half a century.[18]

Wisconsin: From Program Budgeting to PPB

The development of PPB in Wisconsin has been almost the reverse of New York's. In Wisconsin, change has come gradually and in rela-

16. *Ibid.*, p. 1.
17. *Ibid.*, p. 4.
18. See State of New York, *Report of The Joint Legislative Committee on Fiscal Analysis and Review* (March 31, 1970).

tively small doses; the first steps were taken in 1959, and, according to the present schedule, complete PPB will not be achieved until the mid-1970s or later. The pace has been cautious and controlled, with the rate of change governed primarily by the availability of support and resources. Throughout the long period of budgetary improvement, support has been forthcoming from the state's budget leaders, and the entire effort has been designed and directed by the central budget staff. Wisconsin's main objective has been to improve the programming features of the budget process, not to recast that process into a planning and analytic framework. Wisconsin began where New York appears to have left off—with fairly limited changes in budget procedures and information—and is striving to end where New York began—with an integrated planning and budgeting system for all state activities. Yet it is not certain that Wisconsin's evolutionary strategy will yield more accomplishments than will be attained through New York's zigzagging experiences.

From a Line-Item to a Program Budget

The first steps toward budget improvement in Wisconsin were taken at the end of the performance budgeting period and were very much influenced by the conceptions that were then popular. The prime task was to convert from a line-item to a program budget, with a "program budget" conceived (as it was during the performance budgeting era) as involving classification of expenditures according to the activities and services provided by government agencies. Considerable emphasis was placed on improving the budget document and the other fiscal records and accounts of the state. Only after PPB arrived on the scene in the mid-1960s was Wisconsin's conception of budget improvement expanded to encompass the analytic and planning processes commonly associated with PPB. But the program budget origins still are dominant; in terms of concrete changes, Wisconsin can show little more than the program classifications, a substantially revised budget document, and a partly computerized information system. Still in their early stages or on the drawing boards are multiyear planning, program analysis, and measurements of program effectiveness.

A necessary first step in the evolution of budgeting was the creation of a central budget staff with the willingness and capability to spearhead the drive for budget improvement. The Department of Administration was established in 1959, and within it were placed budgeting, accounting, personnel, purchasing, and other administrative functions. With the exception of state planning, which was lodged in the Department of Natural Resources (also created in 1959), the Department of Administration had jurisdiction over all the central staff and management activities in Wisconsin. Its budget unit (the Bureau of Management) inherited a host of line-item controls, while its accounting unit (the Bureau of Finance) pre-audited vouchers and other items to determine their correctness, legality, and propriety. Under state law the budget was presented, and appropriations were voted, in line-item form. In sum, the Department of Administration started as a control agency; its conversion to a management orientation opened the door to subsequent changes in the budget process. This conversion was facilitated by a large increase in the staff of the department. Most of its new staff were schooled in public administration and were favorable toward performance budgeting. During its first decade, the department more than tripled the size of its staff and expanded its scope of operations to include data services, management improvement, and (in 1967) planning. Most importantly, the department "came to be relied upon by the Governor as almost his sole source of program analysis and advice."[19]

In converting from control to management and from line-item to program budgeting, the department's Bureau of Management (where most of the new men were placed) marshaled substantial legislative and executive support before introducing any changes. Because of this, the conversion to program budgeting took much more time than might have been required had the department acted unilaterally, but the changes were much more thorough than might have been possible through unilateral action. (Not only the budget but also the appropriations and accounting code were converted.)

The evolution toward program budgeting was marked by several developments. First, a number of agencies financed by special funds were allowed to try program budgeting. Second, the Bureau of Management provided staff for task forces of business leaders who were invited by the governor to examine the administrative practices of the state and to propose improvements. One of the major recommendations of these task forces was that program budgeting should be applied to

19. Roger Schrantz, "Planning-Budgeting Relationships: Wisconsin Case Study," in National Association of State Budget Officers, *Newsletter*, Vol. 10 (July 22, 1968), p. 5.

all state agencies. The next stage in this consensus building process was a similar call for program budgeting by a legislative group, the Interim Committee on Efficiency and Economy in Government. Pursuant to these recommendations, the Department of Administration was directed by the governor and the legislature's Joint Finance Committee to proceed with the development of program budgeting. Still, the department worked carefully. In 1964 it developed prototype program budgets for seven state agencies and recast the 1963–65 budget (which had been voted in 1963) into program form. In this way, the governor and the legislature had a concrete and convenient comparison of the existing and proposed formats. There was widespread agreement that the new format contained a great deal of useful information not previously available, but some legislators were concerned that abandonment of line-item budgeting would mean the loss of detailed expenditure information, as well as of the controls associated with that type of budgeting. It was necessary for the Department of Administration to provide assurance "that all of the detail data currently available would continue to be available under program budgeting,"[20] and in the legislation that removed the requirement for line-item appropriations, the legislature directed the department to maintain allotment controls to assure that "the intentions of the joint committee on finance, legislature and governor, as expressed by them in the budget determinations" are properly fulfilled.[21]

The Department of Administration lavished considerable time and care on the preparation of the new classifications. It decided to make the programs the common informational base of the budget, appropriations, and accounting code, not merely an additional layer of accounts. The department had to decide what is meant by "program," and it developed a "what for whom" rationale. A program is "a broad category of similar services for an identifiable group or segment of the population for a specific purpose."[22] Thus, the programs were not classified to facilitate analysis or trade-offs among activities serving the same purpose, but were functional groupings of related activities.

20. *Report of the Subcommittee on Program Budget of the Joint Finance Committee* (April 20, 1964), reproduced in Paul L. Brown, "Wisconsin's Conversion to Program Budgeting" (Dec. 1, 1966; processed), p. 18.

21. Chapter 553, Laws of 1963, Section 2.

22. Paul L. Brown, "An Operational Model for a Planning-Programming-Budgeting System" (January 1968; processed), p. 15.

In explaining this approach, the director of the Bureau of Budget and Management expressed his belief that there is "more of a payoff in concentrating initial attention at a lower level of activity than the goals and objectives of government."[23] Finally, the Department of Administration decided to devise the program categories centrally rather than give the agencies responsibility for the task. "We decided that since we had developed the rationale, or set of principles for defining the agency programs, the proper application of this rationale could assure us that we could get consistent definitions of programs even though there would be 76 different agencies involved in defining programs."[24]

The first program budget was presented in 1965, for the biennium beginning on July 1 of that year. During the next several years, the Department of Administration devoted considerable effort to refining the program budgets, and this task was often at the top of the list of budget improvements to be undertaken in the near future. Refinement meant improving the program classifications and the accuracy of the expenditure and work information, increasing the program content of the budget document, revamping the accounting code, and further computerizing the budget process. The department also modified the line-item controls, which it had traditionally exercised. Relaxation of these controls was facilitated by the increased discretion in the management of funds afforded by the program appropriations, the rise to leadership positions of the management-oriented officials in the Department of Administration, and the department's increasingly active role as the program and policy adviser to the governor.

Measured against the general trend of performance budgeting in the states, the program budget implemented in Wisconsin was a creditable accomplishment. The program accounts were solidly grounded on what the agencies were doing and spending, the budget document contained more useful program information than did the documents of other states, and the program budget was successfully integrated with the appropriations and the accounting system. In a retrospective appraisal of its program budget, the Department of Administration pointed to this integration as one of the factors that saved it from problems confronting other states. For unlike the PPB conception of program budgeting, which provides for a crosswalk among the several different informational structures, Wisconsin had a homogeneous informational

23. *Ibid.*, p. 3.
24. *Ibid.*, p. 21.

scheme. In view of "the problems encountered in other states and in the federal government . . . a close identification between programs and appropriations is a very wise first step. . . . By converting to a program budget orientation and appropriating on this basis we eliminated a lot of work and problems."[25]

While its conception of program budgeting was concordant with performance budgeting, Wisconsin did not make much progress toward the development of workload and other performance measurements. It regarded these measurements as the next step beyond program budgeting:

. . . We plan to introduce new techniques of performance measurement which will help administrators, the Governor and the legislature to evaluate programs better and to make more meaningful budget policy decisions. These performance measurement techniques, in our view, are not an integral part of program budgeting, but they do evolve logically out of it and enhance the entire budgeting system.[26]

These intentions had not been realized at the time PPB was announced by President Johnson.

The Influence of PPB

The year in which program budgeting was implemented in Wisconsin was also the year in which PPB was introduced in the federal government. The quick spread of PPB to the states and the renewed interest in budget innovation attracted attention to the changes then under way in Wisconsin. State budget officials were able to point to the successful implementation of program budgeting as evidence that Wisconsin was in the forefront of PPB development. This claim drew to Wisconsin from other states officials who wanted to find out what PPB is and how to do it. Many of these visitors left convinced that either Wisconsin wasn't doing PPB or PPB wasn't much different from what they had been doing all along. As they became exposed to PPB writings and spokesmen, Wisconsin budget leaders were forced to reevaluate budget improvement in their own state and to move beyond program budgeting, which no longer was to be the end goal but only the first step in the development of PPB. Wisconsin joined the State-Local Finances Project as one of the five participating states. Increas-

25. *Ibid.*, p. 5.
26. John W. Reynolds and Walter G. Hollander, "Program Budgeting in Wisconsin," *State Government*, Vol. 37 (Autumn 1964), p. 211.

ingly, state publications referred to PPB rather than to program budgeting, though sometimes "planning, budgeting, management process" or "planning budgeting system" was the favored term. Under this broadened conception, Wisconsin officials have added (or are developing) several new features, in particular: (1) the discussion of policy positions taken by the governor, (2) multiyear program planning, and (3) the measurement of program performance and effectiveness.

1. *Policy analysis.* State budget officials have taken the position that program analysis should not be cut off from the main channels of state decision making. Accordingly, they have not tried to develop formal analytic procedures apart from the regular budget process, but have tried to make analysis a feature of the biennial budget preparation cycle. This strategy flows from their view of innovation as budget improvement rather than as the establishment of a new process for planning and analysis. The position of the Department of Administration as the policy adviser to the governor has enabled it to apply analysis to areas where the governor makes major program decisions. A *Program Policy Reports* manual instructs the agencies on the identification and analysis of important issues confronting the governor, and much of the work of the Department of Administration is devoted to the resolution of policy issues rather than to routine budget decisions. Summaries of the program analyses are published in a volume that accompanies the governor's budget message. The *Governor's Policy Positions* for the 1969–71 biennium discusses fifty-three issues, many of which involve only small sums of money or minor policy changes, although a few (such as the examination of public assistance policy) deal with costly and possibly controversial matters.[27] The form of presentation is uniform, with approximately three pages allotted to each issue. Each issue is discussed in four parts: the issue is presented in question form, the problem is discussed briefly, several alternatives are explained, and the course of action proposed by the governor is justified.

The policy position report enables the governor to draw public attention to his program objectives and to spell out (in a form suitable for public presentation) the reasons for his decisions. It also enables legislators to pick out the interesting items in the budget without having to read the voluminous documents in detail. Finally, the close

27. State of Wisconsin, *Governor's Policy Positions* (January 1969).

linkage of analysis to the governor's program policies lends a sense of relevance and realism to the analytic efforts.

2. *Multiyear planning.* The budget improvement perspective of state officials meant that comparatively little attention was given during the early program budgeting period to multiyear planning. Moreover, planning was under the jurisdiction of the Department of Natural Resources, and it was concerned primarily with the development of the state's resources, not with programs and budget policies. However, with the rise of the Department of Administration to a position of policy leadership, relations between the planners and budgeters became strained, and "the planning agency came to be isolated from the political policy formulation process and from significant contact with the Governor."[28] In 1967 the planning function was shifted to the Department of Administration, and the Bureau of Planning was established as one of the main policy units in the department.

The influence of planning is now making its appearance in the budget process. The instructions for the 1971–73 budget alert agencies to the fact that in 1970 Wisconsin was electing its first four-year governor. "Consequently, it is desirable that all departments project the impact of anticipated developments, program objectives and policies and workload data through 1975 wherever possible, since that is the time period in which the governor will be most interested."[29] One section of the program narrative submitted by agencies as part of their budget preparation contains four-year projections of anticipated developments. In addition the Bureau of Planning has developed guidelines for an integrated planning-budgeting system that strongly resembles the initial PPB effort in New York State but operates with a six-year time frame rather than with the ten- and twenty-year planning horizons used in New York. Wisconsin regards multiyear program plans as the core element of the planning process and as the bridge between long-range plans and the biennial budget. The total planning framework is to contain eight sections, beginning with a projection and analysis of basic factors and objectives, moving to concrete multiyear program plans, and concluding with specific estimates of the manpower, facilities, and funds required to implement the proposed pro-

28. Schrantz, "Planning-Budgeting Relationships," p. 6.
29. *Manual on Program Budget Preparation for the 1971–73 Biennium,* Letter of Transmittal (Feb. 6, 1970).

grams.[30] The *Program Planning Guidelines* provide detailed listings of the types of data to be included in the various reports but do not standardize the form in which the data are to be presented. However, the guidelines distinguish between basic information (descriptive material to be supplied by all agencies), supplemental data (analytic material to be supplied by agencies with advanced planning capabilities), and background information (identification of data needed for future planning exercises).

Although they have approximately the same scope as New York's original PPB guidelines and conceive the same link between long-range planning and the budget process, the Wisconsin guidelines place considerably more emphasis on the analysis of alternative courses of action. Thus one section of the plans is the analysis of issues and problems, and another is the analysis of alternative program policy directions. Moreover, the pivotal multiyear program plans are to identify both program priorities and alternative programs and strategies.

The Bureau of Planning is aware that many agencies will not be able to complete all the plans within the tight timetable it has set. Accordingly it has authorized agencies to determine their own "planning effort priorities," that is, to decide which aspects of the total planning guidelines should be attempted during the first planning cycle. Nevertheless, it is possible that the ambitious goals set for planning will lead to demoralization if the agencies cannot satisfy the requirements and their plans are not used in policy formulation. Despite its professed commitment to an integration of planning and budgeting and despite the close organizational relationship between its planners and budgeters, Wisconsin has not adjusted its latest budget instructions to the planning guidelines. As was indicated above, the 1971–73 instructions ask for consideration of the four-year implications of the budget proposals, not the six years specified in the guidelines. Furthermore, there is not a single reference in the instructions to the new planning efforts, nor is there any indication that the program plans are to be used in connection with the preparation of the 1971–73 budget.

3. *Performance measurements and reports.* Wisconsin budget leaders long have regarded performance measurements as one of the next steps

---

30. The eight "topics" (as they are called in the guidelines) are: projected needs and influencing factors, public-private roles, analysis of issues and problems, alternative program policy directions, multiyear program plans, and (in three parts) estimated resource requirements.

beyond program budgeting. Their view has been that "development of unit costs and yardsticks to measure the performance of state agency operations is feasible only if these operations are divided into meaningful [program] units."[31] Now that the program budget is operational, budget officials have moved to develop performance measurements for determining budget allocations and for evaluating agency accomplishments. Several distinct types of performance measures have been defined in various state publications: extensiveness measures pertain to the amount of work being performed and the quantity of services provided; efficiency measures deal with the resources expended to produce public services, and generally are expressed as a ratio of output to input; effectiveness measures relate program results to program accomplishments; benefit measures pertain to the social or economic value of a public program.[32]

The 1971–73 budget instructions emphasize the importance of effectiveness measures and urge agencies to define their objectives in measurable terms in order to provide a basis for annual reports to the governor and the legislature on the performance and accomplishments of state agencies. When fully operational, the performance reports are to be the final stage of a recurring biennial planning-budgeting cycle.

Budget officials in Wisconsin repeatedly have stressed that it will take many years to install a complete PPB system. As early as 1967 one official expressed his "hope to complete development of the component parts of a PPB system and achieve implementation of a comprehensive process by the middle 1970s."[33] Whether or not it reaches full implementation, Wisconsin already has two major accomplishments: a program budget that is genuinely and closely related to the accounting and appropriations processes, and possibly the most informative budget documents of any state. In each succeeding biennium the scope and amount of program information in the budget has been expanded, and the increasing emphasis on planning, analysis, and evaluation—as reflected in the 1971–73 budget instructions—promises

31. Reynolds and Hollander, "Program Budgeting in Wisconsin," p. 215.

32. See *Manual on Program Budget Preparation for the 1971–73 Biennium*, pp. 14–16.

33. Warren D. Exo, "Statement," in *The Planning-Programming-Budgeting System: Progress and Potentials*, Hearings before the Subcommittee on Economy in Government of the Joint Economic Committee, 90 Cong. 1 sess. (1967), p. 106.

a further broadening of Wisconsin's PPB efforts. Yet the goals that Wisconsin has set for the future are much more difficult than those it has already achieved. The state has established the informational groundwork for planning, analysis, and evaluation; it remains to be seen whether the information will be put to these purposes.

California: Applying Federal PPB to State Government

California's Programming and Budgeting System (PABS) conforms in most essentials to the PPB approach introduced in the federal government. Many of the strategies and methods have been similar, and differences generally have been terminological rather than procedural or conceptual. However, the California system seems to have been more successful and to have better prospects for survival, perhaps because of the commitment of state officials to budget change, modifications made in the PABS format, and the comparative ease of implementing a PPB-type system in a state government.

Even before PPB there was some dissatisfaction with the budget process in the state, and a few steps were taken to improve it. A 1963 report of the Assembly Interim Committee on Ways and Means called for "a substantial change in the content and format of the budget document" and urged that long-range program planning be made a vital part of the annual budget process.[34] In the same year, the governor's budget message suggested the need for revisions in the budget format to improve legislative review of state expenditures. Pursuant to this, sample program budgets were prepared for three agencies in 1964 and for twenty-one agencies in 1965. On May 16, 1966, Governor Brown ordered the establishment of a Programming and Budgeting System; "planning" was dropped from the title because "there was a natural tendency for us to have wanted a title different from that of the Federal Government."[35] Otherwise, there were few notable differences between the federal and the California approaches; indeed, the PABS guidelines suggested that "*anyone* seriously interested in

34. State of California, Assembly Interim Committee on Ways and Means, *Report on Long-Range Program and Budget Planning* (January 1963), p. 30.

35. State of California, *Programming and Budgeting System* (Oct. 1, 1968), p. 13.

PABS should study the Federal PPBS program."[36] During the next several months, a flow of instructional memoranda came from the Department of Finance, and in October 1966 a four-man PABS staff was formed in the department. The task of this unit was to issue guidelines and instructions, monitor the efforts of the various agencies, and review their PABS submissions. When the State-Local Finances Project was established in 1967, California joined, but the project had little influence over the course of budget reform in this state.

PABS incorporated most of the elements originally designed into the federal PPB system, namely, a program structure, program memoranda, and multiyear financial plans. The first task assigned to agencies was to classify their activities into program categories and prepare "program statements" that explain the objectives of each program and the activities taken to accomplish them. Although each department was to prepare its own program statements (with guidance from the central PABS staff), it was hoped "that a coordinated, statewide program structure will evolve eventually . . ."[37] a hope that was shared but never realized by the federal PPB leaders. California's definition of programs was analytic rather than functional, but the agencies had considerable leeway in determining the classification scheme to be used.[38]

Program memoranda were to be the analytic components of the PABS system. Each memorandum was to contain the agency's program recommendations, along with information on objectives and effectiveness and an analysis of program alternatives. Multiyear program statements represented the planning component of PABS. These five-year projections of the costs and output of each program were to be updated periodically in response to actions taken by the agencies, the governor, and the legislature. The several planning and analytic documents were to be the informational base for the annual budget. Line-

36. *Ibid.*, p. 10. Earlier versions of the PABS guidelines republished the PPB bulletins issued by the U.S. Bureau of the Budget.

37. State of California, Department of Finance, Management Memo No. 66-16 (June 3, 1966).

38. The definition of "program," or, more accurately, one of the several definitions used from time to time, was: "A program is a group of interdependent government activities that are in closer relationship with each other than with those outside the program. . . . It should be end-product or intermediate-product oriented. Meaningful programs should be concerned with specific objectives of the department. Each program should bring together all costs associated with its execution." *Ibid.*, Attachment "A."

item detail was to be eliminated from the budget once the program format was fully developed, though it still was to be collected. Each department's budget was to be arrayed programmatically, with a "crossover" technique used for allocating program costs among organization units. A standard format—based on the sample program budgets—was developed.[39]

The initial PABS efforts met with some success, but they had little impact on California budgeting. Shortly after·it was introduced, Governor Reagan replaced Governor Brown, yet PABS managed to survive this relatively radical transition, and it continued to have official support from the governor's office and the top leadership of the Department of Finance. The agencies' responses ranged from enthusiastic to lukewarm, but they did produce the requisite program structures, memoranda, and plans. An ambitious training program was begun, and several thousand state administrators received classroom instruction. Within one year after it was launched, PABS was a going concern.

The PABS Problems

But all these were superficial accomplishments. In fact, the materials produced under the auspices of PABS were not used in budget making, and their quality generally was unsatisfactory. Part of the problem was that, despite the training efforts, few administrators had an adequate understanding of PABS or of what was expected. On many points the guidelines were unclear, and key terms were poorly defined. For example, it was unclear whether program memoranda were to be prepared annually for each program or for only those programs that had been analyzed. The term "program" was ambiguously defined, and few concrete illustrations of PABS applications were furnished. In-

---

39. The recommended format contained program information under seven headings: (1) *Need* ("why is the program, element or component needed?"); (2) *Objective* ("what is to be accomplished? How do the program objectives relate to the need for the service?"); (3) *Output* ("what product is delivered? How may the effectiveness of the program be measured?"); (4) *Authority* ("by what or how is the program authorized?"); (5) *General Description* ("how will the department organization be used to accomplish the objectives?"); (6) *Work Plan* ("what performance standards and workload measures are used to indicate levels of performance?"); (7) *Input* ("what will the program cost?"). State of California, *State Administrative Manual* (Draft #4), Section 6830.2. Appended to *Programming and Budgeting System.*

stead, there were frequent references to federal publications and practices, but these were of dubious value to administrators who lacked first-hand knowledge of the federal PPB system. Because the instructions were issued initially in piecemeal form, it was difficult for administrators to gain an understanding of the whole system or of the relations among its various parts. Most important, agencies were unsure of the connection between the new documents and the line-item budgets, which they still were required to prepare.

The lack of agency understanding was damaging because PABS—like federal PPB but unlike Wisconsin's program budget—vested implementation in the hands of the departments. Inevitably, technique came to be regarded as the end-product, and many departments came to regard PABS as going through the motions of preparing program memoranda, multiyear statements, and other documents—not as a means of relating activities to objectives and budgets to programs.

The understanding gap was fueled by the de facto divorcement of the PABS system from the ongoing budget process. PABS was built, promoted, and perceived as budgeting's "fifth wheel," separated from the established budget process both procedurally and organizationally. Whatever it was, PABS was different and apart from budgeting. Agencies had to prepare two budgets each year in order to satisfy the ambivalences of the Department of Finance and the persistent demands of legislators for line-item information. Despite the sample program budgets and the attempts to forge a transition from line-item to program formats, the legislature has been unwilling to yield its claim to traditional budget detail. Thus, after it was given only the program budget in 1970, the legislature demanded and received multilith copies of the line-item budgets that the agencies had prepared previously.

The separation between PABS and budgeting also was manifest in the organization and operations of the Department of Finance. The nucleic PABS staffs was cut off from direct involvement in budget making, while many examiners clung to their line-item routines and openly disparaged the PABS endeavor. The top leadership of Finance gave strong verbal backing to PABS, but when the chips were down and the final budget decisions were being made, the line items got the lion's share of attention. The focus of the early PABS effort was on the implementation of systematic techniques, not on the use of planning and analysis in budgeting. The rationale was that the long-term durability and success of the new system would depend on its effective installation throughout state administration. Whatever the ultimate merits of this strategy, the immediate results were meager.

In this regard, PABS suffered from the same disability that has plagued and virtually aborted federal PPB as well as similar approaches which leave the established budget practice intact and try to inject change through a new planning and analytic system that is tied to the budget process. This tactic explains why California, unlike Wisconsin, did not overhaul its accounting and appropriations codes or change the procedures and organizational structure of the budget process.[40] PABS and its spokesmen were outside the mainstream of budgeting, whatever the publicity garnered in its behalf.

By all accounts, the materials produced under PABS were not very useful. The output measurements generally have "emphasized workload data rather than measures relating to objectives achieved," and the multiyear statements "have generally been arithmetic extensions of currently authorized programs."[41] One of the reasons why the legislature refused to rely on the program budgets was its lack of confidence in the allocation of costs among programs and in the criteria used for measuring outputs. The inadequacy of the PABS documents placed the Department of Finance in a dilemma. On the one hand, it continued to preach the virtues and benefits of PABS; on the other, it was unwilling to release the documents to the legislature. In effect, Finance was caught in the predicament of being unable to use the materials because they were not good enough, but also unable to spur agencies to improve documents that were of doubtful relevance in budget making.

Prospects for the Future

Despite its limited applicability PABS has managed to survive. One explanation for its endurance is the considerable investment that has been made in training, which has muted potential opposition to PABS

40. In justification of this approach, the PABS guidelines argued, "expensive changes in data systems, including accounting systems, should not be made until we are assured that the program structure reflects, at least to some significant degree, the framework around which management decisions are made." *Programming and Budgeting System,* p. 10.

41. See Edwin W. Beach, "California's Programming and Budgeting System," in U.S. Congress, Joint Economic Committee, *Innovations in Planning, Programming, and Budgeting in State and Local Governments,* 91 Cong. 1 sess. (1969), p. 31.

and even converted some administrators to the cause. A second explanation lies in the consistent verbal backing that has come from the top. Early in his administration, Governor Reagan gave PABS a boost by directing all agencies to prepare multiyear projections of expenditures.[42] Although this had been a feature of PABS from the start, the governor took an interest in the projections and has used them to justify his pleas for austerity in state government. The leadership of Finance has been committed to PABS, even though few concrete actions to build it into the budget process were taken until 1969. Support also has been forthcoming from another quarter—the Cabinet and agency secretaries. Under a reorganization plan implemented in 1968, most of the departments responsible to the governor have been grouped into four agencies, each of which is headed by a secretary. The four secretaries, together with other gubernatorial aides, form the Cabinet, which is charged with direction of overall state policies. The Cabinet and the agency secretaries have viewed PABS as a means of increasing their control over the many departments that have been brought under their jurisdiction. Several secretaries have used PABS techniques enthusiastically, if not always successfully.

Beginning in 1968 the Department of Finance moved on several fronts to modify the budget process and to make PABS more relevant for state policymaking. Finance delegated a significant number of routine controls to the agencies and terminated the time-consuming central editing of line-item submissions. Among the transactions that no longer require final central review are most contract approvals, fund transfers within budget allocations, and many personnel actions. These changes have been made with the concurrence—indeed prodding—of the legislature and the legislative analyst.[43] As a result of the changes, it has been possible to reduce the size of the central budget staff, while redirecting examiners to program and analytic tasks. Finance lost approximately thirty-five positions in the 1971 budget, some 15 percent of its work force. The separate PABS unit has been abolished, and its functions have been assigned to four newly constituted program budget staffs. This reorganization has brought to positions of influence budgeters who are committed to the planning and analytic aims of PABS.

42. State of California, Governor's Office, Memorandum 68-5 (March 11, 1968).
43. State of California, Legislative Analysts, *Analysis of the Budget Bill for the Fiscal Year July 1, 1969 to June 30, 1970*, p. 525.

The calendar of the budget cycle was adjusted in 1969 to facilitate central policy review and program analysis prior to preparation of the next budget. The policy and program hearings that previously had been scheduled for the fall were held in April and May, before the detailed work on the forthcoming budget had begun. In preparation for these sessions, agencies submitted issue papers that identified the major program and policy questions confronting them. These papers were to be the first step in the analytic process and were to provide the agenda for the hearings. Following the hearings, program memoranda were prepared for the issues that, in the judgment of the Cabinet, warranted intensive analysis. It is difficult to assess the impact of these hearings because shortly after they were concluded the governor anounced a radical and unexpected change in the procedures for submitting agency budget requests.[44] The program and policy hearings were continued in 1970, but at the agency level rather than centrally. It was hoped that this modification would make the hearings more useful for agency secretaries and enable them to provide effective leadership for the departments within their jurisdiction.

The Department of Finance also has moved to establish a budget data system that would computerize much of the routine work of the budget process, give both Finance and the legislature immediate access to current budget information, and provide a continuous updating of multiyear budget projections and the regular financial records. Future expansions of the budget data system are envisioned to accommodate much of the information produced through PABS.

The net effect of these changes has been to close the gap between PABS and the budget process. Yet PABS is still a long way from becoming a full and productive partner in the state's program decision process. The legislature has refused to give up its line-item detail, and

44. Under the procedure announced on July 28, 1969, after the policy hearings had concluded and when many agencies were already involved in preparation of their 1971 budget requests, each agency was given a basic allocation, within which it could request whatever programs it wanted. Program requests in excess of the allocations were to be presented separately. The basic and supplemental requests were to be program lists without supporting detail. Only after the requests had been reviewed by the governor were agencies to "prepare detailed program budgets, as well as line item expenditure budgets." Thus, the new emphasis was "on making decisions first, and then upon preparing detailed budgets for approved programs." See State of California, Department of Finance Memorandum (July 28, 1969).

the program and output information presented in the budget are generally deemed inadequate. In order for California to achieve the objectives of PABS, the state might have to discard or recast some of the techniques and procedures associated with it.

Pennsylvania: A Systems Approach to PPB

The genesis of PPB in Pennsylvania can be traced to two factors that converged in 1967: the growing interest among state officials in the newly established federal PPB and the election of a new governor who brought men from outside government into the top leadership positions of the Office of Administration (which serves as the main policy and management arm of the governor) and the Budget Bureau. Following their first round of experiences with the state's budget process, these officials were sufficiently dissatisfied with it to want to make substantial changes. They had heard of PPB but knew little about it. Accordingly the Office of Administration contracted with a private consulting organization to study the feasibility of PPB. The study made a strong recommendation for PPB, and the legislature voted a $450,000 appropriation to implement the new system, a commitment of resources probably far above that made in any other state.

PPB was officially inaugurated in March 1968, when the Office of Administration contracted with the Institute of Public Administration at Pennsylvania State University to design and direct the implementation of the new system. In its role as consultant, the institute had overall responsibility for the PPB project, but most of the tasks, including the collection of data, design of categories and measurement, and preparation of documents were to be done by Office of Administration and departmental staffs. One of the first decisions of the project leaders was to aim for implementation of PPB during the term of the incumbent governor. Since the Pennsylvania Constitution limited the governor to one term, this meant that full implementation would have to be completed by January 1971, when the next governor was to take office.[45] Thus approximately thirty-four months were available for completing the changeover. The project leaders decided to use approxi-

---

45. This provision of the constitution has been amended, effective with the governor who enters office in January 1971. The new governor will be able to succeed himself for one additional term.

mately two-thirds of the time for design and implementation and the final year (calendar 1970) for refining and debugging the system.

Despite this tight schedule, the Office of Administration and the institute decided to develop a full-blown PPB system that would have major planning, analytic, and evaluation components and that would closely link the program planning and budgetary processes. "It was recognized from the outset that if the decision making processes of the Commonwealth were to be revised . . . fundamental changes in the decision process had to take place."[46] The PPBers were convinced that only a systematic and radical overhaul of the way in which the state makes policy and financial decisions would have any prospect of success. In the words of the director of the PPB project:

A piecemeal approach to the installation of a "system" is a contradiction in terms. Unless those necessarily related elements of the system are installed simultaneously, the system itself cannot be assembled. That means that some type of systems management approach to the installation, such as PERT [Program Evaluation and Review Technique], must be employed to schedule and monitor progress.[47]

To achieve its systems goals, the project operated according to a timetable under which all important actions to be taken during the thirty-four months were time-linked to one another. A PERT-type flow chart was constructed showing the several streams of events that were to occur during the lifetime of the project, the relationships among the various events, and target dates for completion of each of the actions. Very little slack was provided in the timetable. "Since events are interdependent . . . any delay in the occurrence of one event can significantly delay others. Particularly important is the need for phasing the planning and programming cycle with the budget cycle. A sizeable delay in the former could endanger the prospects for inclusion of planning-programming in the budget process."[48] To a considerable extent, the actions and milestones specified in the timetable have been achieved according to schedule.

The first set of actions covered the establishment of organizational responsibilities and capabilities for PPB. The Office of Administration was realigned into five bureaus—for budgeting, systems analysis, man-

46. Robert J. Mowitz, "The Present Status of the Planning-Programming-Budgeting System in Pennsylvania" (July 1, 1969; processed), p. 1.

47. *Ibid.*, p. 4.

48. Robert J. Mowitz, "Event Schedule Planning, Programming and Budgeting System" (no date; processed).

agement information systems, personnel, and financial administration. Each bureau had designated PPB-related functions, with the Bureau of the Budget (which had been reorganized into three divisions for planning and program, budget analysis, and program auditing) serving as the key bridge between the program planning and the budgeting processes. In addition, a PPB coordinator was assigned to the Office of Administration to provide linkage among the bureaus, the operating agencies, and the outside consultant. PPB coordinators also were appointed in each of the major agencies, and special task forces were set up to furnish start-up guidance for the effort.

A related set of actions was concerned with the recruitment and training of state officials. Additional slots were given to the Office of Administration and to some of the agencies. The training effort had the objective of giving every program manager in state government some exposure to the basic principles and techniques of PPB. While the actual numbers trained fell far short of this goal, more than fifteen hundred administrators attended brief orientation sessions, and several hundred completed courses in analytic methods.

The Program Structure

The core of the PPB system is a multiyear program planning process, which is integrated directly into the annual budget process. The main components of this system are commonwealth (statewide) and agency program structures, commonwealth and agency program plans, gubernatorial policy guidelines, and a procedure for revising authorized programs. Following initial implementation and refinement, there is to be a continuing annual cycle for revising and updating these documents in response to annual budget decisions or other policy actions. Nominally, the initial phase in the establishment of Pennsylvania's PPB system is the same as in other states—the development of a scheme for classifying activities into a program format. But there are several notable differences between the conception of program structure adopted in Pennsylvania and that used in the other states that were studied. Pennsylvania's program structure is conceived as much more than a classification scheme; indeed, classification appears to be subordinate to the identification of the goals and objectives of government programs and the measurement of the outputs and impacts of state activities. At each level of the program structure, there are program statements, ranging from broad statements about goals at the common-wealth-wide level to specific output targets for program elements at the lowest level in the program structure.

Pennsylvania officials had to decide whether to develop the program structure centrally (as in Wisconsin) or to allow each department to define its own structure (as in California). The solution adopted was to combine both approaches, with central determination of the com-monwealth program structure (CPS) and departmental determination of the agency program structure (APS). Centrally the Office of Administration devised the commonwealth program structure, based on general government-wide goals and consisting of eight broad programs that transcend organizational lines.[49] For example, the activities of the Department of Agriculture were distributed among three of the pro-grams. The next step involved departmental classification of their activities into the eight commonwealth programs and into a three-level agency program structure (program categories, subcategories, and ele-ments). Like the commonwealth programs, the agency structure is based upon missions and objectives crossing organizational lines. Each program category contains statements of the goals of the various activities comprising that category. At the subcategory level, impact indicators are in quantifiable form to provide measures of the im-pact of the program upon society or the environment. Finally, each of the elements is associated with specific outputs produced as a result of the activity. Thus there is a distinction between impact measures pertaining to the effect of state programs and output measures relating to the amount of service performed. Only outputs are measured at the lowest level of aggregation, while impacts are measured at the program subcategory level. This distinction has been applied consistently to all the PPB documents and reports.

The program structure is a permanent record of the objectives, activ-ities, and intended outputs and impacts of state programs. When changes are made in programs, corresponding modifications are made in the program structure. The program structure also serves as the framework for agency program plans and for the annual budget. Moreover, the programs and their components have been coded to pro-

49. The eight commonwealth programs are: general administration and support, protection of persons and property, health—physical and mental well-being, intellec-tual development and education, social development, economic development, trans-portation and communications, and recreation and cultural enrichment.

vide a basis for program accounting and the computerization of the PPB system.

The Program Plans

The next set of PPB documents are the agency program plans and the commonwealth program plan. The latter is an aggregation of the agency program plans, and it "reports total plans and programs for each category and subcategory irrespective of agency source."[50] Agency plans consist of three statements (program, financial, and manpower requirements), with standardized but simple forms for each. Each statement provides five-year projections based on existing decisions and commitments. Whenever there is a program change, the agency plans are revised. It is anticipated that updating will occur at least three times a year.

The program statement contains four parts, with information comparable to that presented in the program structure. (1) For each subcategory, there is a listing of four or fewer impact indicators, ranked according to priority. The indicators can be stated in unit as well as percentage terms. (2) A backup statement explains why the particular indicators were selected and how the impact projections for the next five years were derived. (3) At the element level, there is a listing of four or fewer output measures, together with explanations of their use and derivation. (4) A final statement projects "needs" and "demands" over the next five years.

The program structure and program plans furnish an authoritative file on what the state is doing, what it expects to accomplish, and the costs of attaining its objectives. These documents are linked to the budget cycle through a program revision process, which takes place before the agencies begin work on the next year's budget (though, of course, program revisions can be considered throughout the year). During 1968 this facet of PPB was not yet operational; instead, the governor relied on a Commonwealth Priorities Commission, consisting of civic and professional leaders, to recommend program changes for the 1969–70 budget.[51] However, for the 1971 and 1972 budgets, the

50. The Pennsylvania State University, Institute of Public Administration, PPB Project Staff, "Instructions for Preparing the Commonwealth Program Plan and Agency Program Plans" (no date; processed), p. 2.

51. Commonwealth Priorities Commission, *Report to Governor Raymond P. Shafer* (December 1968).

intended procedures have been used. The process starts with the issuance of program policy guidelines by the governor's office. These guidelines include economic, demographic, and other trend data, a gubernatorial statement of program priorities and concerns, and identification of issues requiring further analysis. The seventy-six-page guidelines issued for fiscal 1971–72 directed attention to more than thirty issues. Presentation of the issues was along program structure lines.

In response to the guidelines or on its own initiative, an agency may submit a program revision request. Here is where systems analysis—in the form of special studies—formally enters the PPB cycle, since each request should have "extensive documentation of the need for a program revision including analytic studies demonstrating the benefits to be derived as well as the cost involved."[52] The forms used in the program revision procedures are virtually identical to those used for agency program plans. The main differences are that the program revision forms provide for lengthy narrative explanations and that the key statistical indicators (impacts, outputs, needs, and demands) are measured in terms of both the approved program and the proposed revision. In this way it is possible to estimate the effects of a program change and to provide a basis for determining whether a program revision has accomplished its objectives. The data in these forms are projected five years ahead so that they can be time-related to the other PPB documents.

Pursuant to an agency's request for a program change, the governor's office issues a program revision action (PRA), which announces his decision. If the PRA authorizes a revision, corresponding adjustments are made in the agency program plan, and the next budget submissions reflect the change. Beginning with the preparation of the 1971–72 budget, the program plan is the core document in agency budget requests. Thus there is no divorcement between the materials used for program planning and those used for budget making. It also is intended that the budget document will be structured according to the planning and programming data produced through PPB.

Implementation of Program Budgeting

Execution of the program budget is tied to an integrated accounting system and to the automation of all PPB documents and data. Every

52. Commonwealth of Pennsylvania, "Program Policy Guidelines, Fiscal 1971–72" (no date; processed), p. 2.

item of PPB data is coded and processed in machine-readable form. Computerized data codes cover program statements, multiyear projects, analytic data, the various statistical measures, and data on actual performance.[53] In order to solve the "dilemma of supplying financial data for several divergent needs," the Office of Administration intends "to use the cost-center concept of breaking costs into discrete units which can be assembled into any format that is desired."[54] The automated PPB data system will be capable of providing program audits and performance reports on a regular schedule. Periodic reports will compare actual with targeted impacts and outputs, and special reports will show which agencies and programs have failed to meet impact and output tolerance levels. Output reports (for each program element) probably will be issued quarterly, but the impact reports (for subcategories) will come out semiannually because it often takes some time before programs show significant impacts.

Steps have been taken to integrate PPB with the existing budget process. Thus the position of PPB coordinator has been abolished, the accounting codes are being integrated, and the same documents, types of data, and time frames are being used for all parts of the PPB system. However, state officials acknowledge that "it is too early to tell the results of PPB," but they "can already see that the concept is valid." Thus far the reliability of the program statistics has not been tested, and PPB still stands somewhat outside the decisional stream. The main accomplishment has been the institutionalization of a new structure for program and budgetary choices. This is in line with the Pennsylvania PPB leaders' conviction that "structure has to come first because analysis is viable only if you are capable of plugging it into the decisional stream." Now that the structure has been developed, it still is uncertain whether the new governor will give PPB as much support as it had from Governor Shafer. Legislative reaction also is an uncertain factor, for until mid-1970 the legislature was shown few concrete applications of PPB, and its appropriations process was barely affected by the new system.

Much of the implementation of PPB occurred under rather unusual circumstances—a prolonged budgetary dispute between the governor and the legislature and a net reduction in state revenues. In 1969 the

53. Planning Research Corporation, "PPBS Automation" (Draft, May 21, 1970).
54. Commonwealth of Pennsylvania, Governor's Office of Administration, PPBS Project Office, "Application of Pennsylvania's Planning-Programming-Budgeting to Pre-School Education" (July 1969; processed).

governor submitted a budget calling for substantial tax increases, as well as $160 million in program increases, as recommended by his priorities commission. For almost fifteen months, the governor and the legislature were deadlocked on certain tax and spending proposals, and, as a result, submission of the 1970–71 budget was delayed until April 20, 1970, three months after the usual date. More important, the revenue program worked out by the legislature in 1969 relied on non-recurring tax windfalls, and therefore the funds available for 1970–71 were substantially lower than the amount spent in the preceding year.

This impending scarcity meant that the 1970–71 budget was to be unusually austere, with few program expansions and some significant cuts.[55] PPBers interpret this situation "as a godsend"—first, because it meant that their meager analytic resources would not be overwhelmed by a flood of program revision requests, and second, because they could promote PPB as a means of responding to the emergent fiscal crisis in state government. The 1969–70 budget document contained some PPB information, including five-year projections that the governor said were "the most innovative, long-range financial plan ever presented to a legislative body in the United States."[56] But the 1970–71 budget shows how PPB might operate and look once it is incorporated into the budget process. Some six weeks after the regular budget went to the legislature the governor submitted an entirely new PPB document, covering in program form much of the material presented in the regular budget. Not all programs or agencies are included in the PPB budget; "the amount of program detail available for inclusion in this document was not uniform from agency to agency."[57] The document is structured according to programs, with organizational identities virtually omitted from the budget. The program format is closely patterned after the basic PPB documents—the agency program plans and the program revision requests. For each subcategory, there are five-year projections of impacts and outputs and some narrative explanation. No line data are presented, except as part of the narrative. Whenever a change is proposed in a program, a program revision

55. Despite mandatory cost increases in many programs, the governor's 1970–71 budget called for $70 million less spending than in the previous year.

56. Commonwealth of Pennsylvania, *Executive Budget, July 1, 1968 to June 30, 1970*, Vol. 1, *Summary*, "Executive Budget Message," Jan. 28, 1969, p. 1.

57. Letter of Governor Raymond P. Shafer to Members of the General Assembly (June 8, 1970).

appendix compares the current and revised program in terms of impacts and outputs for the full five-year span. Thus the reader has easy access to statistical indicators of the estimated effects of all program changes. Because of the fiscal conditions in 1970, only a handful of program revisions were proposed, all in the "protection of persons and property category."

For the most part, what has been described above is the drawing-board version of PPB in Pennsylvania. Certainly in design and on paper, Pennsylvania's PPB system is a more comprehensive and bolder departure than has been tried elsewhere in the United States. But it is one thing to design and install, and quite another to use, a new system. A key test of the utility and survivability of the new system will be the extent to which Governor Shapp (who took office in January 1971) retains and uses the PPB framework constructed by his predecessor. Therefore, a complete assessment must be deferred, pending at least one or two years of budgeting with PPB in full operation.

Hawaii: Legislature versus Executive

The development of PPB in Hawaii has followed a very unusual course, for Hawaii is the only state in which sustained and forceful promotion of PPB has come from the legislature. Indeed Hawaii is the only state to have fully incorporated PPB into its budget law and legislated the form in which PPB is to be developed. Many of the techniques and practices introduced in Hawaii can be found in the PPB efforts of other states, though Hawaii ranks next to Pennsylvania in the fullness and scope of its PPB system. Inasmuch as the main significance of PPB in Hawaii relates to the respective roles of the legislature and the executive, this section gives only incidental attention to the forms of PPB and instead focuses primarily on the activities of the legislative and executive branches.

Legislative Initiative

PPB in Hawaii began as part of a search for new methods of legislative control over spending for public education. In Hawaii, public elementary and secondary education is entirely a state function, administered by the Department of Education (DOE), which is a state agency. Education long has been the leading function of the state, with DOE and the University of Hawaii consuming about 40 percent of all state funds. In 1966 the Hawaii legislature decided to appropriate funds for DOE in a single lump sum, thereby freeing the department from line-item controls and enabling it to operate with considerably more flexibility than state agencies usually have. In the following year the legislature removed the ceiling on the number of personnel the department could hire, and subject only to its overall appropriation limit, DOE could spend for whatever activities and objects of expense it considered appropriate.

In abandoning their customary line-item controls, legislative leaders hoped that DOE would use its new fiscal autonomy to develop and implement an overall state education plan and to improve the efficiency and effectiveness of its programs. They also hoped that DOE would develop new means for holding itself accountable to the legislature for its actions and expenditures.

The first results under lump-sum appropriations were very disappointing to legislative leaders. DOE had used simple formulas in allocating its lump sums, the budget contained no new data on performance and effectiveness, and the legislature continued to be poorly informed on the objectives and programs of DOE. A major portion of the report of the conference committee on the appropriations bill dealt with DOE's actions under the lump-sum method. The committee found that DOE's reports

reveal little overall progress in the development of educational programs within the framework of the legislative directives, and they fail to supply that kind of information which the Legislature needs to evaluate the effectiveness and efficiency with which the Department is operating. Neither the reports nor the allocation method provide information as to where the Department is headed, what results the Department is striving for, what programs are being pursued in an effort to attain those results, how much resources are being used in each program, and how much more resources will be required in future years.[58]

The committee took the position that the inadequacies of the lump-sum method were due in part to the legislature's failure to give DOE specific instructions. Accordingly it decided that the grant of fiscal autonomy "must be accompanied by means whereby the Department shall properly account to the Legislature."[59] The committee directed

58. State of Hawaii Legislature, Conference Committee Report No. 22 (April 29, 1967), p. 14.
59. *Ibid.*, p. 17.

DOE to adopt a planning-programming-budgeting system, and a joint Senate-House Interim Education Committee was established to oversee DOE compliance with the PPB directives.

Subsequently several legislators became ardent supporters of PPB, and together with members of the legislative auditor's office they vigorously promoted this innovation.

The 1967 conference committee took the position that in order for its intent to be fulfilled, it would be necessary to stipulate in detail the kind of system it envisioned and to maintain close supervision over the DOE's work. Thus, in addition to prescribing PPB for the Department of Education, the committee also specified the kinds of statements of objectives, program analyses, and financial statements to be included in the new system.[60]

Between 1967 and 1970 many meetings were held between legislative representatives and officials of the Department of Education. Often the relationship was stormy as the legislators pressed their point of view and DOE officials tried to win approval of a slower, more cautious approach. The special interim committee set up to supervise the introduction of PPB in DOE took an active role, even to the point of specifying in detail how the department should proceed. Thus the committee directed DOE to develop a "vertical" program structure that would align the objectives and activities of the department according to major curricular areas, such as language arts, social studies, and science. DOE had preferred a "horizontal" approach, in which attention would be directed to discrete grade levels, but it was overruled by the interim committee. Moreover, the special committee annually issued detailed instructions to the department and checked on the progress made to date. It generally found many deficiencies in the DOE effort, including a failure to modify the accounting and information system in accord with PPB, inadequacy of the program

60. "The Department of Education shall continue to develop the planning, programming, and budgeting system. . . . The system is to include, among other things, the following: (a) Statements of objectives for all areas of educational endeavor. The objectives are to be stated in such a way that they: (1) describe the specific results which the Department seeks to achieve; (2) prescribe attainment on a long-term basis—that is, the end results being sought are those which will require five or six years for full attainment; (3) where appropriate, set forth different levels of expectations for the different grades, mental capacities, districts, schools, etc.; and (4) specify the measurement for success or failure." *Ibid.*, p. 18.

analyses, and failure of DOE leadership to give PPB full support.[61] Each year also the interim committee reaffirmed its confidence in PPB and pressed DOE to accelerate its implementation schedule.

In responding to the forceful legislative initiatives, the Department of Education was in an uncomfortable predicament. While it welcomed the flexibility afforded by lump-sum appropriations, the department did not relish the close surveillance exercised by the legislature or the manner in which PPB had been thrust upon it. Many education officials felt that they, rather than the legislature, should have final say on the implementation of PPB and that they should be allowed to introduce PPB in a way that would not disrupt the traditions and operations of the public education system. These officials feared that the PPB approach mandated by the legislature would cause the centralization of curriculum decisions, which could best be handled locally, and would force the use of spurious and potentially harmful measurements of educational achievements.

Moreover, DOE was being pulled simultaneously in a number of different directions, which strained its ability to embrace the legislature's version of PPB. As is indicated below, the governor's office launched its own PPB efforts in 1967 with the result that DOE had to satisfy two diverse sets of PPB instructions in addition to the continuing requirements of the budget process. Finally, DOE was engaged in preparing a master plan for education, but this task was only weakly linked to the PPB effort. Confronted with these various cross-pressures, DOE inevitably engaged in what the legislature interpreted as foot-dragging, and it gave less than wholehearted support to the PPB effort, though it did not openly oppose the legislature's directives and it did produce a series of documents along the lines mandated by the interim committee. Occasionally, DOE gave vent to its resentments and frustrations, though the criticism tended to be softened by the need to maintain satisfactory relationships with the legislature. Generally DOE tried to draw a distinction between PPB as a concept and PPB as the technique for managing the department and making major education decisions. The education master plan issued in 1969 professed that "PPBS, conceptually, is a tremendous improvement over the existing budget system. . . . From a long-range standpoint, PPBS is surely the direction we must move toward if we are to do more

61. See State of Hawaii Legislature, Special Committee Report No. 2 (Feb. 24, 1969).

than survive in a rapidly approaching computerized world."[62] Nevertheless, the planners found serious fault with the way PPB had been operated within DOE. ". . . We experienced difficulties that have tried our capacities and our patience. At times we felt as though we were trying from a management standpoint, to vault into the 21st century without passing through the 20th." Among the problems encountered in the application of PPB were a lack "of reliable data about input-output relationships"; "the multiplicity and complexity of objectives and the difficulty of quantifying human behavior"; and how to define "the proper mix of values and . . . factor it into the array of alternatives and the decision-making process."[63] In private documents circulated within DOE, the criticisms were much more vehement and impassioned,[64] but in the master plan, the education leaders tamely pleaded "the need to tread lightly and to conduct frequent, candid evaluations as we move ahead."[65]

Executive Action

While the first legislative forays were confined to the education program, they undoubtedly prodded the governor's office to institute its own effort. Executive action was formally inaugurated in November 1967 with the issuance of *A Recommended Program for Improving Management Methods* in the state government and of a memorandum that detailed certain new procedures for planning and budgeting.[66] The new procedures included the identification of statewide objectives, the grouping of all activities into a program structure, and the preparation of department program plans and multiyear output and financial

62. State of Hawaii, Department of Education, *Master Plan for Public Education in Hawaii* (September 1969), p. 97.

63. *Ibid.*, pp. 97–98.

64. Two draft reports (the authors of which were not identified) were circulated within DOE in 1969, and some excerpts found their way, in modified form, into the master plan. The two reports are "Analysis of PPB Effort in the DOE" (Jan. 14, 1969), and "Department of Education and Planning, Programming, Budgeting System" (no date).

65. *Master Plan*, p. 98.

66. See "A Recommended Program for Improving Management Methods in the State Government." No date or author is given, but references in other reports indicate that it was made in October 1967, in the form of a memorandum from Myron Thompson to Governor John A. Burns; also, a memorandum on "Procedures for Planning and Budgeting," from Myron Thompson to all department heads (Nov. 2, 1967).

plans. A small central analysis group (CAG) in the governor's office was given overall responsibility for implementing the system. During 1968 (and to a lesser extent in 1969) there was considerable official PPB activity in the executive branch. Additional guidelines, including revised instructions for preparing the annual budget requests, were issued, an outside consultant was retained to analyze selected programs, and CAG tried to relate PPB to the planning, budgeting, and accounting processes of the state government.[67]

Whatever the quality of the documents generated through PPB, it appears that the new system had very little impact on either budget or program decisions. From the start, CAG was isolated from the central decisional organs of the state. Although it was formally lodged in the governor's office, CAG's influence was meager, and its small staff was headed by two planners who had little experience with the operating side of state government. CAG designed complex forms but never succeeded in developing effective working relationships with the central staff agencies or with the operating departments. Moreover, the central administrative functions of the state were divided among three separate departments: the Department of Planning and Economic Development had jurisdiction over statewide planning and preparation of the capital budget; Budget and Finance was responsible for the operating budget and for certain management functions; and the Department of Accounting and General Services controlled the state's accounting and information systems. In addition, the state was going through a costly and difficult process of developing a statewide information system. Finally, the governor and his staff never backed PPB wholeheartedly.

Although spokesmen for the governor sometimes indicated substantial dissatisfaction with the budget process, they generally viewed PPB as "a program to accelerate and consolidate existing efforts"[68] rather than as a radical break with established practices. This attitude was expressed in the 1970 budget message, in which the governor cautioned "that the full employment of sophisticated techniques will require time, talent and training."[69]

67. Most of the major documents relating to the first year of executive-sponsored PPB were reprinted in State of Hawaii, Office of the Governor, *A Program to Introduce Improved Management Methods in Hawaii State Government: A Planning-Budgeting System*, Vol. 2 (March 1969).

68. See "A Recommended Program for Improving Management Methods," p. 1.

69. State of Hawaii, *The Executive Budget for the Fiscal Year 1970–1971*, Part I, *The Operating Budget*, "Budget Message of the Governor," p. iv.

The deficiencies of the executive PPB system were candidly discussed in a report prepared as part of an application for federal funds. Two major problems were identified:

(a) The quality of the program plans and their relationship to the budget. . . . The initial program plans were often an inadequate basis for making program decisions. In addition to the quality of the plan, a major problem revolved around the relationship between the plan and the budget. Plans were often prepared simultaneously with the budget, sometimes by different personnel and often with little coordination. This resulted, in part, from the desire not to disturb the usual budgeting procedures during the first year of the program. The problem was, however, intensified by the failure of coordination between individuals having planning and budgeting functions within the same department. The two operations of planning and budgeting were often undertaken at the same time by different individuals so that one had no effect on the other. In other cases, the plan which was prepared first was laid aside and ignored when the budget was developed. There were a great many variations but all lead to the fundamental problem that unless program plans are explicitly made the basis of the Administration's program decisions then they will continue to be regarded as an "exercise," having little impact on budget decisions, and their quality will not be improved.

(b) Timing of the review and inadequate coordination between agencies reviewing plans and agencies reviewing budgets. The review of program plans was undertaken too late in the fiscal year. Budget preparation was already underway in many departments. . . . But an additional problem was generated by the fact that the review of program plans was made entirely by the Central Analysis Group, which does not review detailed budgets. This group can only effectively review program plans for the adequacy or inadequacy of their technical content. Program decisions based on these plans must be the responsibility of the Central Budget Agencies which must participate in this review.[70]

Legislative-Executive Relations: Antagonism and Convergence

As long as the legislature confined its efforts to education, its PPB interests could proceed largely independently of the executive's, and as long as the governor's budget reforms stopped short of impinging on the appropriations process, there was no need for the legislature to get involved. Of course DOE would feel the strain of competing and divergent approaches, but otherwise PPB could spread, even in the absence of joint legislative-executive activity.

70. State of Hawaii, "Design for Planning-Budgeting Program of the State Government, March 1969 to March 1970," Pt. III, "Description of Program" (no date or author given; processed), pp. 4–6.

However, the legislative auditor and certain legislative leaders never perceived their role or PPB as being limited to education. Once they adopted PPB as the desired innovation, they deemed it appropriate to convert the entire planning and budgeting process to the cause. This view found early expression in the report of the 1967 conference committee on the appropriation bill. "We are confident that the procedure and format for accountability, when finally developed, will be a major advancement in budgeting, and hopefully the procedure and format may be extended at a later date to other departments of the state."[71] At the start of the 1968 legislative session, the legislative auditor sponsored a four-day seminar on PPB for all the members of the state legislature. Most of the legislators attended regularly, and strong support for PPB was voiced by members of the interim committee and by the analysts assigned to the PPB project in the Department of Education.[72] In June 1968 the legislative auditor issued a report that was severely critical of the state's capital improvements planning process. The report recommended "that the State adopt that system commonly referred to as the *Planning-Programming-Budgeting System*,"[73] as a means of integrating the capital and operating budgets. Finally, the legislative auditor recommended that the Department of Budget and Finance require that agencies analyze rather than justify their budget requests.

In response to the strong legislative push for PPB, the governor took the position that changes should be made slowly and carefully. "In my view, the present process, which is the product of many decades of evolution, is susceptible to only minor adjustments and refinements." Accordingly, the governor preferred an approach that

is introducing incremental improvements into the existing planning and budgeting process rather than making revolutionary changes. It is selective in the sense that it recognizes and is building upon the past efforts . . . to improve program planning and planning for capital facilities.[74]

As long as it had only an advisory role, the legislature could do little to prod the executive to quicker and more dramatic changes. But the

71. Conference Committee Report, No. 22, p. 21.

72. See State of Hawaii, Office of the Legislative Auditor, *Transcript of Seminar in Planning-Programming-Budgeting* (Jan. 30–Feb. 2, 1968), pp. 223–36.

73. State of Hawaii, Office of the Legislative Auditor, *State Capital Improvements Planning Process* (June 1968), p. 40.

74. Letter of Governor John A. Burns to the Joint House-Senate Interim Committee to Study the Capital Improvement Program (July 9, 1968).

1968 Hawaii Constitutional Convention made two significant changes in the state's budget process that opened the door to an active legislative role in the reform of the budget process. First, the state constitution was amended to remove the requirement of separate capital and operating budgets. In its place, the constitution provided that "the budget shall be submitted in a form prescribed by law."[75] Second, Hawaii became the only state in recent times to shift from an annual to a biennial budget. These two changes thrust upon the legislature an opportunity to enact its conception of the budget process. Since one of the main reasons for the shift to biennial budgets was to enhance planning and analysis, it is not surprising that the legislature used its power to mandate the PPB system.

The 1969 legislature established a Joint Interim Committee on Budget Format and Review to recommend an appropriate budget format, and the governor was asked to submit the 1970 budget both in the traditional format and in the new form. However, the only response from the executive branch was in the form of suggestions from the central analysis group. But the legislature was informed that these suggestions "represented the views only of that group." Consequently, "the task of developing a new budget format devolved solely to a legislative effort," in which the deputy legislative auditor played the leading role.[76]

Early in 1970 the interim committee presented a bill for a new budget format based on the concepts and techniques of PPB. Several months later the bill was adopted by the legislature, and on July 6, 1970, it was signed by the governor. Section 4 of the act declares in part: "The system shall be governed by the following general principles: (a) Planning, programming, budgeting, evaluation, appraisal, and reporting shall be by programs grouped by objectives, regardless of their placements in the State or agency organizational structure."[77] Other sections of the act define the character and use of the program structure, call for thorough planning and analysis of state programs, and prescribe the documents and forms for submission of the budget. The new act prescribes three main documents: a six-year program and

75. Article VI, Section 4, Constitution of the State of Hawaii, as amended in 1968.
76. State of Hawaii, Legislature, *Report of the Joint Interim Committee on Budget Format and Review* (January 1970), p. 2.
77. Act 185, State Legislature of Hawaii, 1970.

financial plan, a biennial program budget, and an annual variance report. Each of these documents is to be structured according to programs, and the budget law spells out the kinds of data to be provided in each, including precise measures of program size and effectiveness and combined capital and operating estimates. The annual variance report is to compare anticipated and actual program costs, size, and effectiveness.[78]

As specified in law, the Hawaii legislature requires more than executive agencies are able to produce at this time. In the view of the deputy legislative auditor, the statute "presents the ideal. How it might be implemented presents a question of strategy. Over the next three years, I expect much give and take between the legislature and the executive."[79] Because it was not a party to the deliberations that led to the new budget law, the Department of Budget and Finance had little influence over the legislation. But the law cannot work without the active cooperation of Budget and Finance. The present director of Budget and Finance previously served as a legislator and in fact was a member of the special committee that supervised the implementation of PPB in the Department of Education. In that capacity, he was the lone dissenter from the recommendation that DOE adopt a "vertical" program structure. While he believes that the budget process needs improvement and that PPB has many worthwhile features, the director laments that "PPB has been overbought."

Nevertheless, the director, as well as other executive officials, have moved quite rapidly to meet the new budgetary requirements. During the summer of 1970, extensive training sessions were held for top and middle-level management. The Statewide Information System (SWIS) project has been transferred to the Department of Budget and Finance, and the department also has set up a Program Evaluation office to coordinate all its PPB activities. An effort has been launched to revamp the program structure in accord with legislative intent, and new budget formats and program analyses are promised for a number of state programs. It is the official policy of the governor—as communicated to the legislature—"to implement on a comprehensive basis the new Programming and Budgeting System for the 1973–75 biennium."[80]

78. *Ibid.*, Section 14.
79. Letter of Mr. Yukio Naito to the author (March 9, 1970).
80. Letter from Mr. Hiram Kamaka, director of Budget and Finance, to the Joint Interim Committee on Legislative Review and Organization (Nov. 15, 1970).

Yet for all the recent innovation, there persists a wide gap between the strivings of the legislature and the capabilities of executive budget makers. It remains to be seen to what extent an accommodation will be forged through a scaling down of legislative aspiration or through a build-up in executive competence.

Conclusion

There are many roads to PPB, but they do not all lead to the same results. The five states examined in this chapter were selected because they differ from the states as a whole as well as among themselves. In none of the states is PPB a complete failure; in none has it been a clearcut success. The lessons to be derived from the five states' experiences are few and simple. PPB can be little more than a technical exercise if it lacks key support and resources. Or PPB can come close to overhauling the state's decisional structure if such support and resources are forthcoming. PPB can begin as an attempt to improve the informational bases of budgeting or as an effort to project planning to the forefront of state policymaking. PPB can begin modestly and grow to a systematic and comprehensive attempt to change state program making, or it can begin ambitiously and shrink into a narrow and piecemeal tampering with the decisional process.

Perhaps the most important parts of these stories remain to be experienced and written. A generation hence, PPB or some later variant of it might be a standard part of program and budget making in many states. But as the 1970s began, PPB was still struggling to become a relevant part of the decisional structure in the states. The outcome is uncertain, and it will not be the same in every state.

6

Budgetary Men:
Roles and Relationships

Budget players have multiple, overlapping, and reciprocal roles. Each participates in the cyclic budget-building and budget-cutting processes; each has a hand in the formulation of budget policy and in the spending of public moneys; each is motivated both by strategic and by "public-interest" inclinations; each shares in the control, management, and planning functions. But each participant has his distinctive "role mix" that distinguishes him from the others.

In an ideal world, budget making would be done by Budgetary Men, counterparts of the classical Economic Man and Simon's Administrative Man.[1] Budget Man could be administrator or legislator, governor or budget worker; all would be linked together by a rationalized division of labor. Budgetary Man, whatever his station or role, would act rationally and efficiently, regardless of his personal or organizational stakes in budget outcomes. In a budget process ruled by such men, there would be an unswerving commitment to efficiency, explicit and prior delineation of goals and purposes, objective evalua-

1. See Herbert A. Simon, *Administrative Behavior* (The Macmillan Company, 1957), pp. 38–39: "A fundamental principle of administration ... is that among several alternatives involving the same expenditure the one should always be selected which leads to the greatest accomplishment of administrative objectives; and among several alternatives that lead to the same accomplishment the one should be selected which involves the least expenditure. Since this 'principle of efficiency' is characteristic of any activity that attempts rationally to maximize the attainment of certain ends with the use of scarce means, it is as characteristic of economic theory as it is of administrative theory. The 'administrative man' takes his place alongside the classical 'economic man.' "

tion of the cost-effectiveness of spending policies, and no bias in the interchange of data and analyses. If these norms were operative and the requisite data and skills were available, a radical transformation would occur in budgetary behavior and action. In every instance, Budgetary Man would adopt the alternative that optimizes the use of public resources.

As an ideal type, Budgetary Man serves to indicate the discrepancy between the roles and behavior called for by budget reform and those that exist in actual budget practice. The budget world is populated by partisans, advocates, and bargainers. For each participant, there is a tension between the ideal (or preferred) role and the actual one. Legislative oversight competes with legislative policymaking; the former invites interest in spending details, the latter would rivet attention on programs and objectives. The administrator's role as a claimant for scarce funds is in conflict with his role as the producer of public benefits. While the claimant role impels the administrator to be concerned with the size of his staff, his equipment budget, the status of his accounts, and similar "internal" matters, the benefit-producer role demands attention to end-products. De facto, the central budget office serves as a budget-cutter, reducing agency estimates to manageable levels. Ideally, it would serve a budget planning role—formulating and evaluating programs in terms of public policy objectives.

The purpose of this chapter is to identify the effects of the roles and relationships of the budget participants on the innovations that have been proposed in recent years. It first discusses the potential for dissatisfaction latent in the budget process, and then explains why this potential is not realized. The roles of each set of budget participants are then considered.

The Potential for Dissatisfaction

To win consideration of a reform it is necessary "to get established the conviction on the part of those responsible for the conduct of affairs that present conditions are unsatisfactory."[2] As March and Simon explain, organization leaders do not "search for or consider alternatives to the present course of action unless that present course

2. William F. Willoughby, *The Movement for Budgetary Reform in the States* (D. Appleton and Company, 1918), p. 208.

is in some sense 'unsatisfactory'."[3] Under satisficing criteria, the status quo enjoys a preferred position; organization men will accept a "good enough" situation rather than strive for an optimal solution. The warm welcome initially accorded performance budgeting and PPB suggests that there is considerable dissatisfaction with the budget process. Though they ordinarily lack a means for expressing their discontent, people in all walks of budgeting have reason to feel that the prevailing practices are inadequate. Consider the possibility for discontent in the roles of each of the major budget makers: operating officials, central budgeters, the governor, and the legislature.

Program officials usually are invited to request more funds than they will receive. They are allowed to inflate their expectations and to invest costly effort in preparing futile claims. When their requests are trimmed, usually at *in camera* proceedings conducted by the central budget agency, these officials are apt to feel that they were unjustly treated, that much of their extra effort was wasted, and that they failed to communicate the importance of their programs to central authorities. They resent the complicated and seemingly foolish rituals that must be followed in preparing their budgets and the detailed paperwork associated with budget execution. They tend to be annoyed by the layers of central control that rob them of wanted discretion and the constant intervention of central authorities in their fiscal and operating affairs. Program officials tend to regard annual (or biennial) budget preparation as a bothersome diversion from their work, and they see the role of central budgeters as an unwarranted violation of their program prerogatives.

Central budgeters also may feel aggrieved by the limitations of the budget process. Every year or two, the estimates come in, expanded far beyond what they regard as reasonable or what can be funded. The budgeters have to labor around the clock to separate the substance from the chaff and to reduce the budget to acceptable levels. They must struggle to penetrate the confusing and irrelevant statistical and verbal justifications prepared by the departments, and they have considerable difficulty in ascertaining the validity of the estimates and the efficiency of the expenditures. Despite their efforts, the budget grows larger all the time, and they know that when this year's budget is done there will be only a brief respite before the next cycle begins.

3. James G. March and Herbert A. Simon, *Organizations* (John Wiley & Sons, 1958), p. 173.

Large chunks of the budget escape effective scrutiny, either because they are uncontrollable expenditures or because policy officials lack the will to control them. The budgeter has enormous power over small items, but he has a weak voice in the major issues that determine the growth of spending.

The governor often comes away from budget sessions less than satisfied. He took office either intent on slashing spending or with a desire to launch new programs. But whether he wants to retrench or to expand, the governor's budget expectations are likely to be thwarted. The retrencher quickly learns of all the mandatory items that cannot be cut, of all the reasons why the budget must be increased, and of all the political and bureaucratic pressures for spending more. If he forcefully intervenes in budget matters, the governor may succeed in slowing down the rate of increase, and he may even be able to use some bookkeeping devices to show a reduction, but he knows that the budget process did not give him an effective means for implementing his policies. A governor with expansionist views may want to provide a prominent place in his budget for new programs, but find that the prior claims of departments consume almost all available funds. By the time the budget reaches his desk, the expansionist governor is forced into a budget-cutting role, and the programs that must be cut are often his own, not the ones that are entrenched because of bygone budget decisions. The budget reflects his limited ability to determine the course of government, though of course, he dresses it up to show some program accomplishments.

Finally, the legislature has reason to feel disadvantaged by the distribution of influence over the budget. As the budget has increased in size and developed into a tool of executive leadership, the legislature has suffered a decline in its budget power. It can no longer play an effective role as "watchdog of the treasury," and its oversight of administrative actions is confined to a few areas on a hit-or-miss basis. The legislature lacks adequate staff and time to review the executive's budget recommendations, and so it is forced to "rubber stamp" the budget rather than exercise its independent judgment. Neither line-item nor lump-sum appropriations give the legislature satisfactory budget control: the former enable it to control purchases but deny it a voice in policy; the latter give departments a virtual carte blanche to spend as they wish.

Yet the existence of discontent does not guarantee the success of a reform. The conditions portrayed above do not mean either that PPB will be regarded as an appropriate improvement or that it will be embraced by the various parties to the budget process. For the most part, the *potential* for dissatisfaction has been discussed rather than the *perception* or *expression* of discontent. Certainly some budgeters, legislators, and executives have these feelings, but undoubtedly there are many for whom the process is working well. The important question is whether latent dissatisfactions are brought to the surface by PPB. Does the appearance of PPB make the status quo less attractive? Does it impel once-satisfied participants to reexamine the process and to establish higher standards for what is good enough? After all, an evaluation of *what is* hinges on one's awareness of *what might be*, so that PPB might impel a devaluation of traditional budgeting. But it is also possible that participants will revert to a satisficing acceptance of the status quo after the initial PPB excitement wanes.

The potential for dissatisfaction is not equal among all the participants, nor is PPB likely to be perceived by all the participants in the same way. For example, legislators probably rank among the most disadvantaged by the contemporary distribution of budget roles, yet PPB seems to offer them less than it does the administrative participants. Moreover, one person's dissatisfaction can be offset by another's contentment. It often takes more than the dissatisfaction of one participant to implement a major change.

Often feelings of dissatisfaction derive from the outcomes of the budget process rather than from the way budgeting is conducted. An agency participant may blame the process if he is dissatisfied with his agency's share of the budget. Or a budgeter may translate his concern over the rise in public spending into an adverse appraisal of the budget system. But in neither instance is there any assurance that the disaffected party will subscribe to a particular course of reform because of his discontent over the outcomes.

Much discontent is a permanent part of the budget process, rooted in its bargaining/incremental mode, which requires the participants to play adversary roles and each to get less than he wants. But each party to the budget gains something from the traditional arrangements. The countervailing satisfactions may outweigh the latent discontents and thereby frustrate efforts to change the process. Accordingly, in the following sections the implications of the roles of the various budget participants for PPB are examined. The actors are considered in the

sequence in which they usually become involved in the budget cycle
—spending agencies, central budget office, governor, and legislature.

The Spenders

Budget making in the agencies, according to reform standards,
"should provide the occasion for evaluating agency policy—an investigation of the program areas which should be expanded or contracted,
and the investigation of new programs which are required."[4] At this
stage the budget machinery should be used first for asking questions
about the ends to be sought and the activities to be undertaken in
pursuit of those ends. In the course of budget preparation, "all factors
affecting departmental operations and costs should be subject to a
most searching and critical analysis." Budget people "should challenge
the entire basis of operations, suitability of policies, efficiency of
methods. . . . Nothing should be taken for granted just because it has
been done in such and such a way in the past."[5] Only after the overriding policy questions have been settled and the proposed agenda of
future activities has been drafted should a reckoning be made of the
inputs required for accomplishing the goals and programs. However,
the inputs should serve as "building blocks" for estimating the costs
of proposed activities and not as ends in themselves. Moreover, the
estimates should be supported, to the extent possible, by objective fore-
casts of the volume of work to be performed and the projected cost
per unit of work. In sum, the budget estimates transmitted to central
authorities would consist of a statement on goals and purposes, a concrete plan of programs and activities, estimates of the quantity of
work to be performed and of unit costs, and *provisional* estimates of
objects of expense. The agency, of course, would be an advocate for its
special interests, but its advocacy would be grounded in explicit policy
and objective cost statements, which, together with the submissions of
other agencies, are to be appraised by central officials.

Organizationally, the budget process should reflect this planning
and programming emphasis. Goals and purposes should be determined

4. Jesse Burkhead, *Government Budgeting* (John Wiley & Sons, 1956), p. 246.
5. From "It's Always Budget Time," reprinted in Albert Lepawsky (ed.),
Administration: The Art and Science of Organization and Management (Alfred
A. Knopf, 1949), p. 471.

at the highest levels within the agency, but these should be strictly in accordance with the policy guidelines and instructions issued by the chief executive. At each lower level, successively narrower and more detailed plans should be prepared until, at the lowest levels, all the detailed work and cost components have been put into place. Then the process would be reversed as the subordinate levels transmit upwards detailed input and output estimates for consolidation and review. Finally, the agency's complete estimate would be forwarded to the central budget office for evaluation and revision in accordance with the governor's policies. This procedure would ensure central determination of policies as plans and decisions are transmitted from the higher to the lower levels and objective information moves from subordinate to superior echelons.

After appropriations have been voted, the agencies would again move into the foreground and assume direct responsibility for implementing the authorized plan of expenditure. Execution of the budget would be decentralized. Central clearance would not be required for changes in the distribution of expenditures among objects, provided that the program totals are not exceeded. The central budget office would monitor adherence to authorized plans by means of periodic (usually monthly or quarterly) performance reports. Their newly won flexibility, plus the availability of performance indicators, would prod the agencies to execute the commitments embodied in the budget and appropriations faithfully and efficiently.

But compared with this idealized conception of agency roles, actual practice falls far short of the mark. To be sure, the preparation of estimates, to a considerable and growing extent, is directed by budget specialists, who rely on work projections, cost formulas, and performance records in determining how much money to request. But rarely is the making of a budget an explicit exercise in planning the future course of an agency. Policy considerations, though they are ever present, are decidedly secondary to the main foci: deciding *how much money* and *what things* to request.

Budgeting in the agencies ordinarily begins in response to (or in anticipation of) a "call for estimates" issued by the central budget bureau. The call, it should be noted, is not for plans or objectives, but for estimates: agencies are asked to submit projections of their money requirements for the next year or the next two years. Monetary considerations are given a primacy at the start, and they retain center stage throughout the budget cycle. Sometimes the call for estimates contains vague warnings about the need for efficiency or about holding expenditures to minimum levels. Occasionally it sets ceilings on the amounts of money the agencies may request. These instructions are intended to inhibit the ambitions and demands of the agencies, but because they are couched in strictly monetary terms, the agencies still lack meaningful policy guidelines when they begin the task of budget preparation. Nor are policy considerations foremost in the internal budget procedures of most agencies. The usual pattern is to distribute forms to the lowest budget-making units within the department and to withhold policy directives until the bits and pieces have been assembled.

The call for estimates interrupts the work patterns of operating agencies. The task of seeking funds for the next year or two may be perceived as a distraction or as a threat to ongoing programs. Budgeting comes to be regarded as "a burdensome routine which must be got through as the price of existence."[6] Agencies handle this burden in diverse ways, but it is unusual for top officials to handle it themselves. Budget preparation is assigned to professionally staffed budget offices that operate as, or within, "business offices," a designation that suggests the paramountcy of financial routines over budgetary planning. Regardless of the classifications used, the preparation of estimates seldom is interpreted, as reformers would have it, as an opportunity for taking a new look at programs and goals. Activities are taken for granted just because they have been carried on in the past. Last year's level of spending is accepted as a base for next year's, and its legitimacy is not challenged by central authorities. Consequently the business of budget estimation is reduced, for the most part, to computations of the costs of desired supplies, personnel, equipment, and other objects. It doesn't make much difference whether the items of expense are encased within organizational or program units.

In the performance budgeting and PPB literature, objects of expense are considered necessary for internal management. But besides their informational and control functions, objects have great value for administrators. Much of the budget game revolves around such pressing wants as additional staff, more office space, and new equipment. As things of value, these immediate requirements may take on greater

6. Burkhead, *Government Budgeting*, p. 246.

meaning and relevance than do program matters. These, after all, are the daily bread of administrative life, and these are key aspirations that administrators seek to satisfy through the budget process. Of course, this focus on objects may open the door to programmatic concerns; additional staff may enable an agency to adopt new activities. But it is precisely the "back door" approach to programming that has been the bane of reformers.

There is more than a touch of Christmas wishing in the making of budget estimates. Like the child compiling a list of his wants, each agency compiles a list of the things it would like to have, knowing all along that it is not likely to get everything. But unlike the child, the agencies are up against a tough Santa, who often asks difficult questions and gives them only what he thinks they deserve or what he can afford. Thus, while the child tries to flatter his Santa, the agencies must try to outwit theirs. They provide as little "hard" evidence as possible and wrap their estimates in tinseled justifications.

This political circumstance helps to explain why the agencies like object-of-expense budgeting (despite their frequent disclaimers). Budgeting by objects gives the agencies many opportunities to manipulate the facts to their advantage and considerable leeway in estimating the projected benefits of proposed activities. Agencies are able to express their subjective interpretations of anticipated benefits without being encumbered by analytic measurements. Nor are they required to weigh, in a systematic and uniform manner, the cost-effectiveness of their proposals. Object budgeting makes the "best case" for the agencies; an agency needs only to promise benefits in order to demonstrate the worthwhileness of its requests.

Agencies are forever playing the "numbers game" to their advantage. They invent staffing formulas, minimum standards of performance, grading systems, and similar seemingly scientific measurements in order to obtain more money for recreation, libraries, education, or some other "neglected" concern. They revel in demonstrating that they are understaffed or underfinanced by comparison with their peers. They develop measurements to show how much more money is needed in order to meet minimum standards. And, of course, the standards are raised once the coveted level is reached. These numbers games are palpably subjective devices, but nevertheless effective because they have the outward appearance of scientific objectivity. The manipulation of subjective standards by the agencies does not mean that they would accept standards formulated by others. The appearance of scientific reliability often is more useful for the agencies than is genuine objectivity.

Performance budgeting and PPB strive to place data beyond the subjective influences of the agencies. Each agency's interpretation of the facts becomes vulnerable to at least two challenges: first, the benefits (or effectiveness) are measured by standards of results external to the agency; second, the projected benefits are weighed against their costs. It is no longer so easy for an agency to point to subjectively estimated benefits as prima facie justification for its requests.

For the agencies, then, the opportunity cost of budget reform includes an impairment of their ability to "sell" their budgets. Much of the early resistance to cost accounting and scientific management, as well as the recent skepticism about performance and effectiveness measurements, stems from agency preferences for free-wheeling subjectivity. Agencies are doers of government work and producers of public benefits, but in the context of budgeting they are primarily spenders of public funds. The spending role influences not only how the agencies behave, but also how they relate to the other budget players, for in the division of labor it is the job of central authorities to control the spenders, much as it is the job of the spenders to mobilize the resources they want.

The Cutters

Budget reform implies and requires much more than adjustments at the agency level. Every role is part of a multilateral network of relationships; none is autonomous. Change in the agencies presupposes change elsewhere, perhaps everywhere. Most directly, it requires changes in the relationship between the agencies and the central budget office, and hence in the budget office's role as well.

Over the past two decades, state budgeters have made sincere, if not bold, efforts to change their roles. For the most part, they have not resisted performance budgeting or PPB, and they have tried to keep up with the latest developments. Even recalcitrant budgeters have been pulled by the tide of events and by the rival activities of planners to pursue a more active policy role. Few budgeters today have the same definition of good budgeting that they or their predecessors had twenty years ago, before performance budgeting was introduced.

In the PPB interviews for this study, state budget officers were asked: "Which of these functions do you consider the *most* important for your office: (a) control over expenditures; (b) assisting agencies to do their work efficiently; (c) serving as a policy staff for the Governor?" Twenty-four replies were received, most of which came from PPB-active states. None of the budget directors placed his operation in the control category; seven regard their offices as management assistance operations; and seventeen prefer to be regarded as policy staffs. The responses to this question clearly show that budgeters view themselves as policymakers and want to eschew a financial control role.

A similar image is projected in "Principles for State Executive Budget Officers," presented to the 1968 meeting of the National Association of State Budget Officers (NASBO) by its Committee on State Budget Research. Although it is necessarily general and eclectic in tone, this statement ranks program planning and evaluation as the number one budget role. This role encompasses

assistance to the agencies in the development of long-term operating budgets; guidance in developing long-range goals and objectives and analyzing alternative ways to achieve these; assistance in determining programs to accomplish goals; estimating program financial requirements; and evaluating alternate programs within a monetary ceiling.[7]

These are images and aspirations, but they are not easily convertible into action. The budget office cannot escape the consequences of fiscal scarcity, budget uncontrollability, central-agency mistrust, and other control-orienting factors. Nor can it easily abandon the traditional division of budgetary labors, which has cast the agencies as spenders and the central budget office as cutters. It has been pointed out above that in the preparation of estimates the budget office usually does not transmit policy instructions to the agencies. By the time the budget office gets into the act, it is faced with the overriding task of bringing estimates into line with available resources. All other functions must defer to the exigencies of budget cutting. Given the tradition against

7. In addition, the functions of the budget office should include management improvement, financial planning, and budget execution. See "Principles for State Executive Budget Offices," *Proceedings,* Twenty-fourth Annual Meeting, the National Association of State Budget Officers, Aug. 11–15, 1968 (The Council of State Governments, 1968), p. 74.

cutting existing programs, the budget-cutting function impels the budget office to take a negativistic role. As explained by Paul H. Appleby,

... There is no point in denying, the budget function is preponderantly negative. It is on the whole rather strongly against program and expenditure expansion. This approach is desirable, because the programmatic agencies and most of the potent pressure groups are so expansive that there will be little danger that the undeniable values they represent will be overlooked or smothered by budgeteers.[8]

Appleby offered this forthright defense of budget office negativism during his service as New York State Budget Director. His audience was the staff of the Budget Division, and the occasion was the beginning of budget preparation. Appleby did not consider the possibility of containing agency pressures before they have been allowed expression in the estimates, and consequently he could not conceive of an alternative to the budget-cutting role.

A budget-cutting role does not preclude program development and policy planning activities by the budget office, but it does rule out a dominant planning orientation, except during rare interludes when there is considerable fiscal slack and the governor is committed to substantial program development. In ordinary times, abandonment of the budget-cutting responsibility would upset the adversary relationships that enable the agencies to claim and the budgeters to ration. If the budgeters joined in on the side of the "yes-men," the state quickly would be confronted by a serious supply-demand imbalance. As much as budgeters want to be program developers and policy leaders, they are held back by the unceasing exigencies of budget balancing. The budgeter is stuck with the role that the web of budget relationships assigns him.

As a result, there is a growing disparity between budget aspirations and budget actions. More and more, the budgeter talks the language of programming and planning, but he is hesitant to fully embrace a policy role. The budgeter no longer has firm peer guideposts as to what constitutes good budgeting and what is the proper role of his office. Increasingly one senses ambivalence and confusion, and even a touch of despair, as budgeters seek to comprehend the enormous program

8. Paul Appleby, "The Role of the Budget Division," *Public Administration Review*, Vol. 17 (1957), p. 156.

explosions of these times. The budgeter is caught in a crossfire of conflicting demands. He knows that the old role is not good enough, but
is unsure what alternative is feasible.

There are many ways to cut the budget. One way is to look at program proposals and decide which shall be recommended and which
shall not. This is the approach of program budgeting; the program decisions are explicit and open to direct challenge by program supporters. Another method is to cut the program indirectly by reducing
the inputs that are invested in it. This is the approach of traditional
budgeting; the program decisions are covert—understood by the insiders, but not easily open to direct or vigorous challenge.

Covert programming facilitates budget cutting by making it possible
to conceal the impact of reductions on programs. The agencies are
inhibited from expressing their wants in terms of benefits and accomplishments and are forced instead to peg their requests on such suspect items as staff additions, travel costs, and new equipment. These
items can be eliminated without any *visible* reduction in programs.
Overt programming, however, compels the budget office (as well as
the legislature and the governor) to deal head-on with the programmatic implications of budget cuts. The program classifications readily
show the effect of budget cuts on agency plans and activities. Central
officials are aware of the potential proliferation of expenditure pressures that might result from program budgeting. During interviews
for this study, budget officials repeatedly mentioned the difficulties
involved in cutting programs and the consequent advantages of object-
of-expense budgeting:

You don't have guys defending postage or telephone costs. But if you had
program control, you would be proliferating the pressures on government.

. . .

Cutting on a program basis would cause a lot of hard feelings in the agencies.

. . .

It's one thing to vote to cut five million dollars; it's another thing to vote to
cut two thousand hospital beds.

. . .

Were we to draw out a particular program, we would give pressure groups
the opportunity to single it out for attention.

. . .

If we were to budget by programs, we'd be multiplying the number of
bureaucratic interests in the budget. In addition to the organization interests,
there would be the program interests.

The budget office's behavior depends on relationships with other actors in the budget system. As an agent of the governor, the budget office takes many of its cues from the way the governor interprets his role and from the mission he delegates to it. If the governor is unwilling or unable to re-evaluate existing programs, it is improbable that the budget office will be able to break away from its limited budget-cutting assignment.

The Gatekeeper

The executive budget places the governor at the apex of state budgeting. Formally, it empowers the governor to review departmental estimates, to propose a plan of expenditure, and to control expenditures by executive agencies. Throughout its long history, budget reform has been conceived primarily from the perspective of, and as an aid to, the chief executive. Performance budgeting and PPB, like the earlier executive budget movement, have been regarded as instruments of executive leadership, as means of making the budget an effective statement of gubernatorial policy.

In the view of reformers, the traditional budget classification is deficient on several counts. First, it enables the agencies to partly conceal their programs and performance from central scrutiny, and it thus becomes more difficult for the executive to translate his policy objectives into the budget. Second, the arrangement of data along organizational lines reinforces the separatist tendencies of the agencies and impedes interdepartmental comparisons. Third, it emphasizes objects that are important for agency management, rather than objectives that are relevant for central policymaking. Fourth, the organization-object classification tends to accept the previous year's level and distribution as the base for next year's and thus makes it difficult for the chief executive to implement new or changing policies.

The program budget, by contrast, abets executive leadership and administrative integration by bringing the policy implications of interdepartmental expenditure alternatives to the explicit attention of the chief executive. The program budget pits one department against another and last year's level of spending against all requests for next year in the competition for executive approval. Moreover, because they are the product of a comprehensive evaluation of alternatives, the

spending estimates in the program budget are more likely to be co-
herently and consistently related to the executive's policies than are
recommendations based on give and take among competing units of
government. The program budget thus should be a potent centralizing
force, for no longer would the budget be a bargain struck by dispersed
groups, with the marginal participation of the chief executive in the
final stages of negotiation.

Not much published research is available on the governor's budget
role, though there have been a number of studies of his formal budgetary powers.[9] The case literature on state budgeting, however, provides some insights into the governor's special place in the budget
system.[10] In one study of budgeting in Illinois, the author concluded
that, although the governor was "the most powerful actor in the system," this power was of a limited sort.

In neither year [1961 or 1963] was the Governor actively involved in the
process of putting together any given agency budget from the inside out,
nor was he even involved in hearings designed to review requests. Instead,
he entered the process much later, after preliminary decisions were
already made, and was asked for nothing more than approval or disapproval.
In both years the Governor's problem was to eliminate a sufficient amount
from agency requests to bring them into line with anticipated revenues. And
in both years he did this, not by close examination of the total cost of every
program run by each and every agency, but by cutting what he could from
the *increases* requested by the various agencies, leaving the bulk of the
budget unexamined and untouched.[11]

The governor's involvement in budgeting is reserved for special
matters that cannot be handled by others within the established decisional framework. In the division of budgetary labors, the governor
does not use the budget machinery to evaluate all the expenditure proposals made by the agencies. Instead, while a few are evaluated by
him, most are handled by others in accordance with established rules.

The governor has a very specialized role; he is the chief gatekeeper
of state budgeting.[12] In this role, he directs the pace of spending in-

9. See Joseph A. Schlesinger, "The Politics of the Executive," in Herbert Jacob
and Kenneth N. Vines (eds.), *Politics in the American States* (Little, Brown & Co.,
1965), pp. 207–34.
10. Thomas Flinn, *Governor Freeman and the Minnesota Budget* (Inter-Univer-
sity Case Program, University of Alabama Press, 1961).
11. Thomas J. Anton, *The Politics of Public Expenditure in Illinois* (University
of Illinois Press, 1966), p. 146.
12. Gatekeeping is a central function in David Easton's *A Systems Analysis of*

crease and program expansion by deciding which of the programs proposed by the agencies or by his own office shall be included in the budget. As gatekeeper, the governor rarely looks back at programs that have already passed through the gate; his attention is focused on those programs that have not previously gained approval. That is, he rarely reviews existing programs. Moreover, even a gatekeeper who wants to close the door to program expansions (such as Governor Rhodes of Ohio) ultimately is forced to approve many new programs.

As the gatekeeper of state budgeting, the governor is constrained by the agencies and his budget office. The agencies control the pressure gauge of state spending. By increasing their pressure, the agencies can compel the governor to open the gate wide to new programs. As a result, even a powerful governor has an unsure grip on the gate. To exercise greater control over the pace of expenditure increases, the governor would have to step in earlier, before the initial agency decisions were made. The governor also is dependent on his budget office for determining whether an agency request falls in the "continuation" or the "new" category. In other words, the budget office determines which matters shall be brought to the attention of the gatekeeper.

The gatekeeping function helps to explain the growing popularity of classifications that distinguish between continuation and expansion levels. This method facilitates the governor's review of the expansion items while enabling the budget office to handle the continuation requests routinely. Program budgeting, by contrast, demands equal treatment of new and old programs; all compete on an equal footing for scarce funds. For a gatekeeping governor, therefore, program budgeting is not the most useful method because it fails to inform him adequately about proposed expansions.

However, not all gatekeepers are alike, and hence, program classifications are of more use to some kinds of governors. The gatekeeper we have described is neither an active expansionist nor an austere retrencher. He balances the programmatic pressures emanating from the agencies against available revenues and opens the gate to moderate ex-

---

Political Life (John Wiley & Sons, 1965). In Easton's framework, "gatekeepers are not only those who initiate a demand by first voicing it . . . [but also] those whose actions, once a demand is moving through the channels of the system, at some point have the opportunity to determine its destiny." (P. 88.) Clearly, the governor is not the only gatekeeper in state government, but in regard to state budgeting, he is its chief gatekeeper.

pansions. But an expansionist governor might consider program budgeting as a mechanism for spotlighting the new programs in his budget, while a conservative governor might view program budgeting as a mechanism for intensifying the pressures on his office. Performance budgeting is not related to the governor's role as gatekeeper, nor does it strengthen his policy leadership. The judgment of New York State officials that the decision to terminate performance budgeting was not important enough to warrant the governor's attention probably was an accurate appraisal of the situation. Although many governors recommended performance budgeting, few were interested in taking on its management duties. Performance budgeting would have made the governor the state's budget director and would have gotten him involved in detailed budget matters.

The situation is substantially different in the case of PPB because that system directs central budgetary attention to matters that are awaiting the governor's decision. In recent years, the governor's office has assumed a more vigorous policy role in many states. Increasingly it is staffed by a corps of program and policy advisers who keep him abreast of program developments and formulate his legislative and political program. PPB would appear to be a useful tool of executive authority because it redirects budgeting from internal administration to program planning. Whether or not PPB succeeds, gubernatorial policy analysis can be expected to emerge in a growing number of states, as it already has in a number of larger ones. This development may portend a major reorientation in the governor's budget role.

The Uprooted

In the seesaw of budgetary relationships, the course of reform has been marked by a series of gubernatorial "ups" and legislative "downs." Every budget reform, from the executive budget to the present, has been promoted as an aid to the legislature. The argument always has been the same: a more responsible executive will enable the legislature to play its appropriate policy role. But there is an anomalous discrepancy between the intentions of reformers and the implications of their reforms. Because they have assumed a harmony in executive-legislative relations, reformers have failed to perceive the potential decline in the status of the legislature resulting from the loss of its traditional role as a check on the executive. Whether performance budgeting and PPB presage further declines in legislative power, or whether they will, as some reformers promise, open the door to a revitalization of legislative authority will be considered below. First, consider the role of the legislature as it is usually conceived by reformers.

Generally, budget reformers envision a shift in legislative functions from control over administration to formulation of public policy. Control by the legislature over administration would be stymied by depriving it of object data; control over policy would be facilitated by supplying it with program data. The alleged violation of the policy-administration dichotomy—the legislature's trespass into administrative matters and its corresponding neglect of policy functions—has been the target of much reformist ire. Congress and state legislatures alike have felt the brunt of condemnation, expressed so forcefully by Leonard D. White two decades ago. Legislative control over administration, he said,

is basically control over details, not over essentials. It is negative and repressive rather than positive and constructive. It reflects fear rather than confidence. It is sometimes irresponsible. It is based on no rational plan, but is an accumulation of particulars whose consequences are seldom seen in perspective.[13]

The 1967 report on *Modernizing State Government*, issued by the Committee on Economic Development, expressed the belief "that each state legislature has responsibility for making policy decisions on matters of major concern to people of the state. This cannot be done if the focus is on administrative trivia or matters of local concern."[14] This theme has been echoed in many studies of state legislatures and in recommendations pertaining to the fiscal operations of state governments. Brushing aside the dismal record of performance budgeting in Illinois, the state's Commission on the Organization of the General Assembly "continue[s] to believe that the concept of a program or functional budget is not only sound, but offers the best long-term method of improving the quality of legislative participation in the appropriations process."[15]

13. Quoted in William Keefe and Morris Ogul, *The American Legislative Process: Congress and the States* (Prentice-Hall, Inc., 1964), p. 427.

14. P. 35.

15. Illinois Commission on the Organization of the General Assembly, *Improving the State Legislature* (University of Illinois Press, 1967), p. 114. For a survey of legislative reform in the states, see Citizens Conference on State Legislatures, *Compilation of Recommendations Pertaining to Legislative Improvement in the Fifty States* (Kansas City, Missouri, April 1967).

In these and many other statements there is a normative conception of the legislative function and a judgment that the norm is being infringed by most legislatures. This conception of the legislature has been defined by William Keefe and Morris Ogul in *The American Legislative Process: Congress and the States,* as follows:

Legislative bodies should set only broad policy and not interfere with the details of administration. Legislative bodies can represent the interests of society, but neither their structure, organization, personnel, nor practices seems conducive to effective control over details. . . . Legislative bodies should set structure, personnel, and fiscal policies only in the broadest sense. Their objectives should be to promote centralization of control through the top echelons of the executive branch.[16]

But there is another model of legislative-executive relations that predicates responsibility as the basic norm.

A primary task of legislative bodies is to further bureaucratic responsibility. The legislative body must be concerned with all policy—both broad and detailed. . . . Lines of responsibility ultimately run to the people; since the people are best represented by legislative assemblies, the chief excutive cannot be as effective as the legislature in controlling the bureaucracy in the public interest. Indeed, legislative bodies must watch the chief executive himself to insure that responsible government is achieved.[17]

The two divergent approaches lock horns on such down-to-earth matters as the amount of detail that should be written into appropriations acts, piecemeal versus comprehensive evaluations of expenditures, and concern of the legislature with objects of expense versus its concern with programs. The efficiency model dominates reform thinking, while the responsibility model dominates legislative practice. Whereas the efficiency model postulates a dichotomy between policy and administration, the responsibility model asserts the inseparability of politics and administration. Robert Ash Wallace states this position effectively in challenging proposals to divest Congress of administrative details. Congress, he maintains, "interferes with administrative particulars for only one reason: details affect policy." Moreover, "if Congress is to control spending . . . [it] must concern itself with details which affect substantive policies."[18] Richard Fenno has come to similar

16. Pp. 424–25.
17. *Ibid.,* p. 425.
18. *Congressional Control of Federal Spending* (Wayne State University Press, 1960), p. 14. Wallace adds: "the idea that Congress should avoid administrative detail is wishful thinking. Congress has the constitutional power to affect details, and experience has shown that it will exercise it. This being the case . . . [Congress]

conclusions on the basis of his careful study of congressional use of the appropriations power.

The truth of the matter, from the [appropriations] committee's standpoint, is that the only way they can effectively find out what is going on in the executive branch is through detailed and specific inquiry. . . . Furthermore, the only way the committee can effectively influence the executive branch is through detailed and specific intervention (or threat thereof) in the processes of administration. . . .

PPBS or no PPBS, the Appropriations Committee is going to want to proceed by inquiring into and acting upon the specifics and details of executive programs, just as it has in the past.[19]

Legislative oversight of administration, Arthur MacMahon observed more than two decades ago, is a peculiarly modern function of legislatures. This contemporary function is a product of the growth of the administrative state and the concentration of administrative power in the chief executive. Nowadays, according to Theodore J. Lowi, "the major problem and major focus of Congress is no longer simply that of prescribing the behavior of citizens but more often that of *affecting the behavior of administrators*."[20] Legislative control over details, once a guard against administrative transgression, now is a device for influencing the course of administration-made policies. In this sense, then, Fenno and Wallace are correct; control over details has become a mechanism for control over policy. Externally, legislative surveillance over objects has remained the same, but in fact it has acquired new purposes.

This transformed executive-legislative relationship also accounts for the reluctance of legislatures to take on program-development and evaluation functions. The rise of the integrated administrative state, the growing complexity of administrative matters, and increasing specialization have impaired the capacity of legislatures to decide and evaluate. The contention that legislatures would be able to make program evaluations if they were provided the right kinds of information

---

should have access to more information and analytical data in order to ascertain better the consequences of their actions. This would result in a greater degree of congressional control over spending policy." P. 17.

19. Richard F. Fenno, "The Impact of PPBS on the Congressional Appropriations Process," in Robert L. Chartrand, Kenneth Janda, and Michael Hugo (eds.), *Information Support, Program Budgeting and the Congress* (Spartan Books, 1969), p. 184.

20. *Legislative Politics U.S.A.* (2nd ed., Little, Brown & Company, 1965), p. xvi.

might be appealing to a legislature seeking to recover a substantial role in budgeting. Paradoxically, however, the shift from objects to programs might erode the tenuous hold on spending that legislatures have retained. Stripped of their control over objects of expense, legislatures might be unwilling or unable to function as budget makers. That this is a real possibility is revealed in Eghtedari's and Sherwood's study of performance budgeting in Los Angeles. One of the unanticipated consequences of performance budgeting was that "the legislative adoption phase of the traditional budget cycle has been fairly well obliterated in Los Angeles."[21] If the legislators shy away from programs, it is because they don't feel competent and confident, either politically or administratively, about program matters. If they show a relish for object details, it is because objects are things that legislators can comprehend.

All this does not mean that legislators actively oppose budget reform, but it does suggest that they are not often likely to lead the parade for it. Several different sets of circumstances can lead to legislative acceptance or promotion of budget reforms. First, a legislature may acquiesce in the installation of PPB even if its own interests might be adversely affected by the move. The legislature may defer to executive judgment on technical matters, such as the form of expenditure accounts; the issue may be considered unimportant by legislative leaders, or they may lack adequate information concerning it; or the legislature may be so enfeebled as to be incapable of resisting the executive's budget innovations.

Second, the legislature may be dissatisfied with its budget role and hence willing to try a reform that promises more effective control over spending. In Maryland, constitutional restraints on the legislature's

21. "The [performance] budget is a well-researched document. It cannot be attacked in its details; and, if anything, the councilman is glutted with information supporting all proposals. Thus the old lines of inquiry are pretty well closed to the legislator. . . .

"As a consequence, the only avenue of debate left is broad policy, just as performance budgeting theorists intended. But the unanticipated consequence is that legislators seem to have found an alternative: *not* to participate in the debate at all. . . . The effect, then, of the performance budget has been to kill off some of the old legislative irrationalities and most particularly 'across-the-board' economy slashes. It has not, however, forced the legislator to pick up a new mantle as budget policy statesman." Ali Eghterdari and Frank Sherwood, "Performance Budgeting in Los Angeles," *Public Administration Review*, Vol. 20 (1960), p. 66.

power to alter the governor's budget was one of the factors enhancing the attractiveness of performance budgeting for legislators. In California, Wisconsin, Pennsylvania, and other states, the legislature has supported budget reform and contributed to its advancement. And in Hawaii, the legislature has played an extraordinary role in the application of PPB to the Department of Education and the design of a new budget system for the state based on PPB principles and procedures.

Dissatisfaction with its budgetary role may derive from a legislature's awareness of contemporary budget reforms or from a sense of impotence about the state's spending policy. If a legislature is convinced that it effectively controls the purse strings, it will not search for budgetary innovations, nor will it be attentive to those that have issued from executive offices. If a legislature perceives that it has lost, and wants to recover, effective budget control, it might find PPB a useful instrument.

Fragmentation and Interdependence of Budget Roles

Budgeting is characterized by two opposing tendencies that inhibit its innovative capability. It is at once a highly fragmented and a highly interdependent process. Fragmentation comes from the dispersion of political power, the tradition of building budget requests from the bottom up, and the heterogeneous roles and interests of budget officers, operating officials, elected executives, and legislators. Interdependence is an inherent characteristic of all budgeting, deriving from the scarcity of resources and the necessity to secure the cooperation of many parties in the making of expenditure policy. Budgeting can be interpreted as an effort to impose some coordination in the face of the centrifugal pressures of agencies and interests.

Both fragmentation and interdependence hamper innovation. Fragmentation means that no single official can unilaterally impose his administrative preferences on the other actors. Not even the governor can dictate the form and use of the budget process when agencies and legislators have different views. Yet, interdependence means that the preferences of all major participants must be taken into account. Thus budget reform is pulled by conflicting forces: interdependence requires that all parties consent to a budget change; fragmentation makes it hard to get that consent. Performance budgeting and PPB add to the difficulty by expanding the scope and variety of interests that must be harmonized. To implement performance budgeting, the comptroller, the auditor, and data processors must be consulted, in addition to the usual complement of budget participants. Even organization structure, the second Hoover Commission recommended, should be brought into alignment with the performance classifications. To accomplish this would require coordination of budget reform with administrative reorganization. This widened scope makes it essential to attract the support of diverse parties, but often it invites opposition instead.

PPB further expands the circle of involved parties to include planners, policy and program officials, and analysts. To solicit the cooperation of the various (old and new) participants, it has been necessary to spend considerable effort on building lines of communication, probing for areas of common interest, and orienting others to the new system. It has been necessary to work out new relationships between budgeters and planners and to close the gap between the old liners and the new analysts. The large amount of resources expended on these activities have detracted from PPB's planning and analytic work.

The fragmentation-interdependence problem is partly mitigated by the fortuitous circumstance that budget reform tends to be of unequal importance to the various participants. Ordinarily the budget office gives higher priority to the budget format and procedures than does the governor or the legislature. If the budget office endorses a reform, it may be able to take advantage of the indifference of others. (Of course, the success of PPB requires that budget makers at all levels of government not be indifferent to the use of planning and analysis.) Moreover, it is possible to minimize the impact and scope of reform by means of the hybridization and institutionalization strategies described in earlier chapters. Performance budgeting could be implemented ex parte in many instances because it added to rather than withdrew from the stockpile of data and controls available to the governor and the legislature. PPB's institutionalization strategy segregates the new elements from the old and thereby allows budgeters and others to retain their accustomed practices.

Other ways to improve the innovation capability of the budget process are to negotiate compromises satisfactory to the major participants, to mount a consensus-building campaign, and to restrict the innovation to areas within the purview of the implementing officials.

Many state program structures are compromises between what the central analysts wanted and what department officials preferred. Accordingly they tend to sidestep interdepartmental and interfunctional categories. In Wisconsin, careful negotiations between the governor and the legislature overcame partisan cleavages and culminated in the decision to introduce program budgeting. The myriad PPB training programs have been designed as much to sell the system as to train practitioners and analysts. A classic case of the implementation of reform by limiting its scope occurred in the Department of Defense. Without altering its appropriation accounts or changing the basic structure of the armed forces, Secretary McNamara used a set of program categories for comparing the cost-effectiveness of alternative defense expenditures. By limiting the reform to matters within the jurisdiction of his office, McNamara was able to install PPB unilaterally.[22] Many states have followed this strategy in establishing their own PPB systems. They have not tampered with organization structure, appropriation accounts, or the accounting code. Other ways to limit the impact of reform are to restrict its application to agencies or programs where the response appears to be favorable or to proceed on a trial basis in a handful of selected areas where the prospects of success are favorable.

Finally, the fragmentation-interdependence problem is reduced when the budget process has a good deal of slack (the "disparity between the resources available to the organization and the payments required to maintain" it).[23] When resources are plentiful, the need for interdependent budget choice is diminished.[24] Applied to PPB, this sug-

22. Robert J. Massey maintains that "it took so long to arrive at this reasonably straightforward means of achieving the goals of the program budget" because of two erroneous assumptions: (1) "that the program budget could become a reality only when agencies were reorganized so that they could function along major-purpose lines"; and (2) "that little significant progress toward a *program budget* could be achieved without willing congressional participation." The Defense Department overcame these obstacles when it decided to use the program budget for decision making in the department, but to submit the annual budget to Congress in the traditional format. "Program Packages and the Program Budget in the Department of Defense," *Public Administration Review*, Vol. 23 (1963), pp. 30–34, at p. 33.

23. Richard M. Cyert and James G. March, *A Behavioral Theory of the Firm* (Prentice-Hall, Inc., 1963), p. 36.

24. "When resources are relatively unlimited, organizations need not resolve the relative merits of subgroup claims. Thus, these claims and the rationalizations for them tend not to be challenged; substantial differentiation of goals occurs within the organization." March and Simon, *Organizations*, p. 126.

gests that when uncommitted funds are available, program analysis can be concentrated on new programs while continuing activities are allowed to escape analytic scrutiny. De facto, much of the early PPB effort has been applied in this manner.

Information Specialization and Budget Roles

PPB introduces a specialized and selective distribution of information. Specialization is determined by both the role and the level of each participant and agency. Both criteria are covered in Arthur Smithies's dictum that "an executive at any level should be instructed to confine his attention to policy issues that the specialized nature of his activity entitles him to consider."[25] Ideally the distribution of information would be dictated by an objective prescription of functions, not by the subjective preferences of the participants. Information would be made available "to each according to his needs" in contrast to the usual "to each according to his wants" formula. Data would be packaged in one way for policymaking and in another way for agency management. There would be a reasonably clearcut demarcation of control, management, and planning data—earmarked to controllers, managers, and planners in the budget system. The information produced for legislators, agency heads, operating officials, and budget staff would vary in scope and focus. As the information moved up or down the government hierarchy, its functional composition would be changed. At the top, data would be heavily weighted to planning; at the bottom, to control.

Although PPB means an increase in the total supply of information, it deprives certain participants of some data they have been accustomed to receiving. As a rule, object of expense data is reserved for internal administration at the department level and below. This sort of specialization replaces the relatively undifferentiated system under which the various participants receive roughly similar kinds and quanta of information. Although there always has been some informal differentiation—central authorities generally have used less detailed data than has been available to operating officials—PPB would mark out clearcut and formal differentials in the information supplied each par-

25. Arthur Smithies, *The Budgetary Process in the United States* (McGraw-Hill Book Company, 1955), p. 35.

ticipant. In the view of reformers, a main stumbling block to correct budgetary behavior has been the malapportionment of roles resulting from the indiscriminate distribution and use of information.

In the psychology of PPB, it is assumed that the link between informational resources and behavior is direct and significant. If the form of information is changed, the door will be opened to changes in the actions and perceptions of the participants. It is assumed that if the participants are given the right kinds of data and deprived of the wrong kinds, they will conform to their assigned roles, and the whole budget system will achieve a concerted mix of planning, management, and control operations. The roles of the participants will differ from one another, but they will be linked by a rationalized division of labor built upon a corresponding division of information. But the power to determine the distribution and use of information depends on (1) the willingness of participants to work within a specialized and objective information system and (2) the power to prescribe roles. If the participants are able to veto or circumvent changes in the form and use of information, PPB will not be able to accomplish its objectives. And if the change in informational resources fails to trigger expected changes in behavior, the conversion to PPB will be a meaningless gesture.

These are real possibilities; data are not neutral elements of budgetary mechanics but instruments of power in budgeting and appropriations. To protect their established positions, participants may resist the foreclosure of traditional information resources or reject the offering of new types of data. Or they may insist that program data supplement, rather than replace, the traditional input and organization data. This, of course, is the familiar route of hybridization, the end product of which is the breakdown of the effort to bring budget roles into alignment with prescribed norms. If they have both object and analytic data, the participants can continue their roles and avoid the new ones even as they work with the new forms. Rather than take on unwanted roles, budget people may try to develop alternative types of information. Still another option is to abandon the old role, but also spurn the proffered one; that is, to withdraw from effective participation in budgeting.

The variety of possible responses to the imposition of a selective, planning-oriented informational system suggests that the interaction between information and roles is bilateral. Information influences roles, but the reverse also is true. Indeed, data are more tractable than are roles; participants are likely to seek and use the kinds of data that suit their preferred roles rather than to adjust to assigned informational resources. Accordingly the distribution and use of information will be determined largely by strategic factors rather than by an objective division of labor.

When the power to prescribe roles is dispersed, it is difficult to establish a fixed and specialized information structure. The actual distribution probably is based on reciprocal arrangements among the participants rather than on a specific formula that carves out distinct domains for each. In a fragmented political environment, budgetary roles tend to overlap and to be ambiguously and informally defined, with a resulting tendency to use similar data throughout the budget process. Furthermore, the fragmented budget situation allows each player to call his own tune and to have considerable autonomy in responding to the tunes of others. There is no Pied Piper orchestrating the actions of the diverse participants. The outcome often is an undifferentiated, unifunctional budget system.

To relate these observations to the purposes of PPB: (1) The form of information has a limited impact on roles. Changes in the classification and measurement of expenditures do not automatically produce equivalent changes in budgetary policy. The introduction of program information may have little bearing on the conduct and actions of those who have vital stakes in budget decisions. (2) The shift from control to planning and analytic data may be incompatible with established and preferred roles. The withdrawal of object data may thwart central oversight of purchases and personnel, while the tender of program data may force some actors into an unwelcome policy position. Consequently participants may prefer to retain the object of expense controls rather than to adjust their behavior. (3) The tendency to homogenize information resources has impeded the full development of PPB. What is likely to emerge from the effort to innovate is a hybridized version geared to the common (rather than the differential) needs of the participants. And (4) each budget player has multiple and ambivalent roles. There is a bit of the planner and a bit of the controller in each. It is one thing to split the roles, but quite another to split the persons who play them. No budget participant will want to be denied information that others have.

Changing Budgetary Roles

Every budget player derives some benefits from the traditional rules and roles, perhaps enough to make him content with the established ways or apprehensive of the costs of change. If any of the major participants had felt truly disadvantaged by the traditional division of budget roles and powers, the process probably would have been changed to accommodate his interests. Budget reformers must convince the participants that they will be better off by virtue of a change of roles, that the shift to performance budgeting or PPB will not cost more in budget power than is gained in budget information.

In the PPB framework, technique is the translation of planning and analytic concepts into operational form. But the techniques are supposed to be only the instruments of PPB, not its end product. Without them, Planning-Programming-Budgeting would be a hollow gesture, a futile plea for improved budget analysis. But technique alone cannot change the way budget makers behave and decide; it cannot produce analysis or compel budgeters to ground their decisions on a thorough appraisal of public objectives. The acid test of every technique must be the programs and decisions it stimulates, not the documents that are turned out. As the most visible part of the PPB process, the techniques inevitably acquire some independence from their objectives; yet it is essential that their installation be accompanied by "invisible" changes in the use of the budget process, in the roles and skills of budgetary men, and in the dispositions of decision makers toward analysis. These always are the most difficult changes to accomplish.

7

Is Budget Innovation Possible?

In budgeting, no reform is won easily. The cards are stacked in favor of repeating next year what was done this year and in earlier years. Small changes are achieved through large efforts; each wave of reform leaves its modest legacy and prepares the way for future improvements. Compared to pre-World War II practices, budgeting today stands on a much better informational base. There now are procedures for costing out work and activities, projecting future spendings, and presenting program comparisons. Yet the basic structure of budgeting —the roles and relationships of the participants—has not changed much, nor is it certain that the quality and character of budget choice is much better than it once was. Although judgment on PPB must be delayed until more evidence is in, it does not appear at this time that dramatic changes in program evaluation and analysis are imminent. Budget choices still are made without much reckoning of the results of past decisions; major programs and legislation are adopted with little prior consideration of their costs and impacts; budgets are made with scant analysis of program or spending alternatives; the future is shunted aside as decisions narrow down to the current and the following year.

Is budget innovation possible? Beyond procedural changes, what can be accomplished in changing budget policy? The experts know how to change the format of the budget or the classification of expenditures. They even know how to apply analytic techniques to budget problems. But do they know how to change the way people decide? Can they change the rules of evidence for budget choice?

Regardless of its substantive merits, any attempt to change the budget process faces a difficult future. When it comes to reform, budgeting is not a risk-taking process. It has a low tolerance for (visibly) bad decisions, bureaucratic disorder, and loss of morale—problems that often accompany changes in administrative procedures. As budgeting has become more vital to the control of public expenditures and the administration of state governments, its opportunities for adventurous reform have diminished. There have been only two serious challenges to tradition during the half century of modern budgeting. Reorganization of a state budget agency is rare and usually triggered by other changes in state administration rather than by a desire to reorient the budget process.

Despite the difficulties of altering the budget process, and despite the disappointments with performance budgeting and PPB, budget innovation *is* possible. In this concluding chapter, it is argued that faults in PPB design have accounted for many of the obstacles to budget innovation. Before considering these problems and the ways in which they may be remedied, an answer must be offered to those who have contended that rationalized budgeting would destroy some valued characteristics of the American political process.

Reason and Politics in Budgeting

A budget process must be in harmony with its political environment. Regardless of the organization functions it serves, budgeting must be compatible with the processes and rules of political choice. Wildavsky is right: "No significant change can be made in the budgetary process without affecting the political process."[1] But does this mean that political factors make budget reform impossible?

First it should be noted that the clash between budget functions offers a *sufficient* explanation of the difficulties that have beset performance budgeting and PPB. A half century of tradition building has produced an entrenched "budgetocracy," set in its ways and habituated to its routines. There is the habit of looking at the lines and not at the results, the habit of cutting a budget and of justifying a budget, the habit of control and management. Moreover, although budgeting has

1. Aaron Wildavsky, *The Politics of the Budgetary Process* (Little, Brown & Company, 1964), p. 132.

major political implications, support of, or opposition to, a proposed reform is not often based on a calculation of expected political wins and losses; for example, more money for my agency, or injury to the programs I want. Except for the commonplace, "It's all politics," there appears to be very little political interest in, or opposition to, budget reform.

Unless one is prepared to argue that every aspect of budgeting (and of administration for that matter) is political, it is not plausible to regard budgeting as a perfect replica of politics or as beholden to politics for its character and practice.[2] Not everything that happens in budgeting must be accompanied by political upheaval. There is considerable slack in the linkage of budgeting to politics. The American polity can accommodate a variety of budgetary forms. Budget traditions have a life of their own and often are sustained as much by internal organizational dynamics as by exogenous political influences. Moreover, in assessing the politics of budget reform, and especially of PPB, it is essential to keep in mind that there are many PPBs, many ways of applying the rudiments of planning and analysis to public choice. (Even the Gospel has four versions.) There is no need for forcibly transplanting *the* PPB onto alien political soil. A government can design its PPB to suit its political conditions. In the states, a variety of different PPB experiences are emerging, with each state shaping PPB to its particular circumstances.

"Politics" sometimes is used as an excuse for whatever happens to be. Whatever is, exists because it conforms to political tests; whatever isn't, cannot be because it violates political reality. This argument really has very little to do with politics; it's a way of favoring the status quo over the potential. The charge of political implications was made against executive budgeting fifty years ago;[3] yet that method of budgeting is the standard operating procedure in most state governments today, though it was a much more radical political innovation than either performance budgeting or PPB claims to be. It is easy

2. Wildavsky begins his study with the reasonable statement "that the purposes of budgets are as varied as the purposes of men. . . . Nothing is gained, therefore, by insisting that a budget is only one of these things when it may be all of them or many other kinds of things as well." *Ibid.*, p. 4. But toward the end of his study, Wildavsky writes: "Perhaps the 'study of budgeting' is just another expression for the 'study of politics'. . . ." *Ibid.*, p. 126.

3. See Edward A. Fitzpatrick, *Budget Making in a Democracy* (The Macmillan Company, 1918).

to conjure up an imaginary PPB that uproots political traditions and rides roughshod over political values. But the first years of PPB offer no justification for fearing that there is a political revolution in the making.

Bureaucratic Influences in Budgeting

Budget form is more a product of bureaucratic than of political influences. For example, line-item budgeting is a common mode in most governments, regardless of their political forms. Whether developed or developing, presidential or parliamentary, democratic or authoritarian, local or national, governments generally adhere to the itemization of supplies and purchases, and they use the budget process to control spending by departments and agencies.[4] Rarely do governments use their budget machinery directly for planning and policy purposes; where planning is a major function, it often is entrusted to a separate agency that has many of the same problems that U.S. planning agencies have in relating to their budget counterparts. What is common to most governments is their bureaucratic machinery for resource allocation. The lack of market tests, the striving for organization growth and status, and the scarcity of public resources have induced governments of divergent political colors to use the budget power to control their agencies. As bureaucracies mature and establish internal controls, they often graduate from exclusive use for control purposes to some form of performance budgeting in which attention is given to management functions. While there is no law that budget systems must pass sequentially through the several stages of budgeting, it is quite difficult to leap from control to planning, or from line-item to analytic data.

The important facts of budgeting have been accurately and attractively portrayed by Aaron Wildavsky in *The Politics of the Budgetary Process*. This year's budget tends to be used as a basis for next year's. An array of nonanalytic tactics is used to reduce the complexities of budget making and strengthen the opportunities for agencies to increase their funds and for central budgeters to cut the requests. These

4. Several United Nations publications deal with the problems involved in changing the form of the budget to serve management and planning functions. These include *A Manual for Economic and Functional Classification of Government Transactions* (1958), *A Manual for Programme and Performance Budgeting* (1965), and reports on Budgetary Classification and Management workshops held in Africa, South America, and Central America and Panama.

tactics have become the rules and strategies of bargaining that govern the incremental outcomes of budgeting. The bargaining mode limits the conflicts and antagonisms engendered by the annual budget competition. Although Wildavsky underestimates the program content of the federal budget, he correctly observes that there is little explicit consideration of objectives and policies and almost no search for alternatives.

Budget innovators do not directly address the issue of how a proposed change might affect political values and interests. Most of the ideas and inspiration for innovation are grounded in rationalist conceptions of efficiency. "Budget making," the mayor of New York City was advised in 1911, "is a science and should be dealt with scientifically."[5] This rationalist theme has been a basis of reform efforts to the present time. The following compilation of rationalist norms, based on Arthur Smithies's *The Budgetary Process in the United States*, is selected from a list prepared by Charles E. Lindblom.[6]

1. Government policies should be as clearly and explicitly defined as possible.

2. Alternative policies should be explicitly regarded as alternative means toward the achievement of objectives.

3. Revenue and expenditure decisions should be deliberately coordinated.

4. For each expenditure, some systematic and deliberate appraisal of benefits and costs should be made.

5. Policymaking, including budgetary policymaking, should achieve a unified policy.

6. All taxation and expenditure decisions should be somehow embraced in the budgetary process.

7. The legislature should undertake a comprehensive unified, rather than segmented, review of the budget.

This model does not view the efficacy of the budget process from the standpoint of political rationality; that is, in terms of how well it satisfies the interests of the participants. But political rationality has been given careful and imaginative treatment in the writings of

5. Quoted in Arnold W. Lahee, "The New York City Budget," *Municipal Research*, Vol. 88 (1917), p. 19.
6. Charles E. Lindblom, "Decision-Making in Taxation and Expenditure," in National Bureau of Economic Research, *Public Finances: Needs, Sources, and Utilization* (Princeton University Press, 1961), pp. 297–98.

Charles E. Lindblom[7] and Aaron Wildavsky. The gist of their theory is: (1) that the fragmented and seemingly uncoordinated budget process does a better job of allocating public resources than might a system in which central planners make a comprehensive and consistent evaluation of budget alternatives where actions taken are explicitly related to a discrete set of objectives, and (2) that a fragmented budget process is less likely than a system directed by "synoptic" decision makers to neglect important political interests.

The Incremental Method

Thus the key to their theory is a twofold division of labor among partisan decision makers. (A partisan is "one who makes decisions calculated to serve his own goals, not goals presumably shared by all other decision makers with whom he is interdependent.")[8] Partisans include agencies, legislators, budgeters, and other participants. Each partisan's function is to make the best case for the interests he represents, not to be concerned with the totality of interests or with the total public interest.[9] An analytic division of labor among partisans reduces the complexity of budget choice and aids the participants in calculating a rational budget outcome; a political division of labor ensures that no represented interest will be neglected in the budget outcome.

This incrementalist strategy diverges from the standard model of rationality, which requires the budget maker "to choose among alternatives after careful and complete study of all possible courses of action and all their possible consequences and after an evaluation of those consequences in the light of one's values."[10] But this prescription to be comprehensive fails to reckon with man's limited and inadequate information, the costliness of analysis, or the lack of a clear ordering of values and objectives. If it were followed in practice, the rationalist

7. See *Ibid.;* also Lindblom, *The Intelligence of Democracy* (The Free Press, 1965), and with David Braybrooke, *A Strategy of Decision* (The Free Press, 1963).

8. Lindblom, *The Intelligence of Democracy*, p. 29.

9. As a matter of fact, Wildavsky argues that "a partial view of the public interest" will achieve a satisfaction of values preferable to what would be obtained through a "total view of the public interest." See Wildavsky, *The Politics of the Budgetary Process*, pp. 165–67.

10. Lindblom and Braybrooke, *A Strategy of Decision*, p. 40.

ideal would induce paralysis and inaction, not the global rationality it promises.

In contrast to the rationalist insistence on comprehensiveness, incremental analysis is adapted to man's cognitive limits. Under incremental analysis, the task of deciding is simplified in a number of ways. Rather than being concerned with everything, the decision maker deals with (1) only that limited set of policy alternatives that are politically relevant, these typically being policies only incrementally different from existing policies; (2) analysis of only those aspects of policies with respect to which the alternatives differ; (3) a view of the policy choice as one in a succession of choices; (4) the *marginal* values of various social objectives and constraints; (5) an intermixture of evaluation and empirical analysis rather than an empirical analysis of the consequences of policies for objectives independently determined; and (6) only a small number out of all the important relevant values.[11]

The advantage of the incremental method is that it "enormously reduces the range of investigations that the decision maker must undertake, and enormously reduces the strains on his cognitive capacity that attend the attempt to comprehensively evaluate social states."[12]

In budgeting, the incremental approach calls for the acceptance of the previous year's level as a base. Rather than concern themselves with deciding anew a complete set of expenditure policies, budget makers limit their analysis to the increments above the base and to the marginal differences between various expenditure alternatives. There is no hierarchy of values as a guiding beacon, nor is there a comprehensive inventory of all the implications of expenditure policies. Rather, values and decisions are "muddled through" on the basis of incomplete information, a hazy system of values, and neglect of all but the most immediate implications. Further, the problem of deciding is compartmentalized and handled in sequence. No attempt is made to compare each alternative with every other alternative. The problem is divided among separate decision makers (subcommittee members or budget examiners, for example), each of whom specializes in his portion of the problem. Even at the higher coordinating levels (such as the whole legislature, the budget director, or the chief executive) the sub-problems are handled sequentially rather than simultaneously. As Wildavsky concludes, "budgeting turns out to be an incremental process, proceeding from a historical base . . . in which decisions are fragmented, made in sequence by specialized bodies, and coordinated through

11. Lindblom, "Decision-Making in Taxation and Expenditure," p. 306.
12. Lindblom, *The Intelligence of Democracy,* p. 144.

repeated attacks on problems and through multiple feedback mechanisms."[13]

Incrementalism and Mutual Adjustment

Incremental analysis fits hand-in-glove with, indeed is contingent upon, partisan mutual adjustment. Mutual adjustment compensates for the major deficiencies of incremental analysis—the neglect of important consequences and values and the lack of central coordination. Mutual adjustment among partisans is a condition in which decision makers "coordinate with each other without anyone's coordinating them, without a dominant common purpose, and without rules that fully prescribe their relations to each other."[14]

If policymaking were centralized as in the rationalist model, incremental analysis inevitably would lead to the neglect of certain important interests and consequences. But if decision making were dispersed among a multiplicity of partisans, each acting as the watchman for his particular interest, what is neglected by one decision maker would be covered by another. Incrementalism, therefore, "points directly to the need for a multiplicity of decision makers and, more than that, to a multiplicity marked by great variety of attitudes and interests, so that no line of adverse consequence fails to come to the attention of some decision maker."[15]

In budgeting, the various participants behave in this fashion. There is a multiplicity of interests, each with its own spokesman, each staking out the strongest claim for its goals, each making the best case possible for its demands, each using an array of strategies to get what it wants, and each looking primarily at its own interest rather than at the interest of the public as a whole. All these characteristics, and particularly the last, have been maligned by reformers. But partisanship protects important interests against neglect. In his defense of the "partial-view-of-the-public-interest," Wildavsky writes that "the danger of omitting important values is much greater when participants neglect the values in their immediate care in favor of what seems to them a broader view."[16]

Does not the partisan approach introduce complications of its own

13. *The Politics of the Budgetary Process*, p. 62.
14. Lindblom, *The Intelligence of Democracy*, p. 3.
15. *Ibid.*, p. 151; also see pp. 153–57.
16. Wildavsky, *The Politics of the Budgetary Process*, p. 166.

into decision making? How are the conflicting views of partisans co-ordinated in the absence of a central coordinator? If the prime determinant of success is the strategic skill of partisans, how does the weighing of interests satisfy conditions of democracy? And what happens to the public interest if it is neglected by all? Lindblom and his followers contend that the partisan method does produce agreements that give appropriate scope to widely shared collective values.[17] Like the classical economists, Lindblom and Wildavsky rely on some "unseen hand" to orchestrate the roles, interests, cues, strategies, and calculations into a coherent and fair set of expenditure decisions—a "budget."[18]

The positivist aspects of the Lindblom-Wildavsky theory have received substantial empirical confirmation in some recent budget research. Using a variety of statistical techniques, several writers have demonstrated that budget decisions are "incremental, fragmental, non-programmatic, and sequential."[19] As to the norms implied or derived from the theory, there is considerable controversy, with some writers questioning the normative implications of a theory that fails to examine budgetary outcomes and others retaining confidence in the capability of the budgetary process to make the right choices.[20] Regardless of its normative implications, the incrementalism–partisanship school appears to challenge the rationalist model of budget reform on three grounds: "muddling through" versus planned action; advocacy versus analysis; systematic versus piecemeal decision making.

PPB and the Incremental Method

Because of the inflated promises and expectations associated with it, PPB has been vulnerable to caricature and distortion. The strategy

17. See *The Intelligence of Democracy*, Chaps. 14–18.

18. Thus, "the process we have developed for dealing with interpersonal comparisons in government is not economic but political. Conflicts are resolved (under agreed-upon rules) by translating different preferences through the political system into units called votes or into types of authority like a veto power." Wildavsky, *The Politics of the Budgetary Process*, p. 130.

19. *Ibid.*, p. 136; also see John P. Crecine, *Governmental Problem Solving: A Computer Simulation of Municipal Budgeting* (Rand McNally & Company, 1969), and Ira Sharkansky, *Spending in the American States* (Rand McNally & Company, 1968).

20. See Allen Schick, "Systems Politics and Systems Budgeting," *Public Administration Review*, Vol. 29 (March/April 1969), pp. 137–51.

of caricature goes something like this: (1) Select the most extreme statements from the PPB literature and take them at face value; (2) insist that PPB must be portrayed radically, or it would not be worth the effort and attention; (3) polarize PPB versus traditional budgeting, especially the incremental method versus the zero-base dogmatism of PPB; (4) contrast the political success of traditional budgeting versus the political naïveté of PPB; (5) argue that PPB is both harmful and unattainable.[21]

Certainly PPB can be portrayed as requiring that all ends be specified in advance, that these be ordered hierarchically according to some overall valuation, that agreement on objectives be obtained as a prerequisite for choice, that the budget be built from a zero base, that all factors be evaluated before decisions are made, and that each program compete for funds with all others. If these were indeed its prerequisites, there would be no feasible way to apply PPB. The burdens thrust upon the budgeters' analytic and political competences would far exceed their capability for rational choice and social cohesion. PPB would be strangled by its own dogmatism long before it was capable of being used. Officials still would be wrestling with the uncertainties and controversies of last year's budget (or, more likely, the budget of some previous decade) when decision time came for this year's. It is a rank absurdity to expect budget men to make all value judgments and program calculations de novo every year, or to insist on perfect knowledge or perfect agreement as a precondition for choice.

At least for its main implementers, PPB is a modest and pragmatic effort to extend the bounds of collective rationality. Whatever its conceptual roots, PPB tries to stretch the use of planning and analysis at the margins. Its purpose is to improve the bargaining process, not to eliminate it.[22] PPB is premised on the conviction that public problems today are too complex to be left solely to guesswork, uninformed debate, or the hurried judgments of bargainers. It aims to create rational partisans—advocates who are informed of the potential consequences

21. See Aaron Wildavsky, "The Political Economy of Efficiency: Cost-Benefit Analysis, Systems Analysis, and Program Budgeting," *Public Administration Review*, Vol. 26 (December 1966), pp. 292–310.

22. See William Capron, "The Impact of Analysis on Bargaining in Government," presented at the 1966 Annual Meeting of the American Political Science Association and published in Alan A. Altshuler (ed.), *The Politics of the Federal Bureaucracy* (Dodd, Mead, 1968), pp. 196–211; and Charles L. Schultze, *The Politics and Economics of Public Spending* (Brookings Institution, 1968).

of their positions and of the possible alternatives. In *The Politics and Economics of Public Spending*, Charles L. Schultze puts the case for analysis effectively: "While it is often strategically and tactically important for participants in the bargaining process to conceal their objectives from their adversaries, it hardly behooves them to conceal them from themselves."[23] Aaron Wildavsky, probably the most effective critic of PPB, has come around to the view that policy analysis is desirable, though he maintains that PPB is not the proper vehicle for getting it.[24]

Perhaps the main distinction between PPB and traditional budgeting is in the treatment of objectives and outputs. PPB calls for budget calculations to be made with some awareness of objectives and effects. "Muddling through" cannot be the optimal means of incremental choice. "Precisely because means and ends are so intertwined, as Lindblom suggests, sophisticated analysis of objectives is a critical component of the decision process."[25] But the objectives need not be regarded as fixed and immutable statements of intent that cannot be changed in the course of planning. After all, a person is least informed about his objectives when he starts to plan; as he learns more about constraints and opportunities, his initial idea of what is possible and desirable may undergo radical change.[26]

On all other counts, however, the difference between the incremental and the analytic methods is considerably narrower than is usually realized. PPB does not force an all-or-nothing choice. The alternatives are always at the margins, and the increments can be either large or small. PPB does not require that every program be compared with all others, nor does it mean that everything must be decided all at once. PPB does not require zero base decisions. Only a portion of the budget can be analyzed during a single cycle, with most of the programs continuing according to standard incremental procedures.

23. Schultze, *The Politics and Economics of Public Spending*, p. 66.

24. See Aaron Wildavsky, "Rescuing Policy Analysis from PPB," *Public Administration Review*, Vol. 29 (March/April 1969), pp. 189–202.

25. Schultze, *The Politics and Economics of Public Spending*, p. 71.

26. Charles Hitch writes: "We must learn to look at objectives as critically and as professionally as we look at our models and our other inputs. We may, of course, begin with tentative obejectives, but we must expect to modify or replace them as we learn about the systems we are studying—and related systems. The feedback on objectives may in some cases be the most important result of our study." *On the Choice of Objectives in Systems Studies* (The RAND Corporation, 1960), p. 19.

There are many ways of assessing the political implications of a PPB-type reform. One way is to impute to PPB an omnipotence and omniscience it does not possess. In this form, PPB is chimerical; it stands no chance of implementation, and it poses no threat to existing political processes because it is totally imaginary. Another way is to regard PPB as tinkering with budget form. This version is plausible, but it is mostly irrelevant to politics. The political process can easily swallow changes in budget form without any adjustments of its own. A preferable approach is to look on the core of PPB—the analysis of objectives, programs, and outcomes—as a means of effecting substantial changes in the processes and quality of public choice. In this form, PPB is both political and realistic. The very shift in focus from process to outcome is likely to modify the decisions made, the processes used, the winners and losers. In Lowi's frame of reference, budgeting will become more "redistributive" in its character and performance.[27]

The Problem of Crosswalking

During the first decades of this century, when budgeting was unidimensional and dedicated to control activities, it was possible to operate with a homogeneous informational structure and to cycle the budget calender to the requirements of control. The development of performance budgeting brought a host of problems, for budgeting acquired a management function besides that of control. And the addition of planning complicates matters further, for all three functions now have to be served. The disparities between planning and control are wider and less tractable than those between management and control. Both of the older functions deal primarily with the internal operations of government agencies; planning takes the budget process outside government, since it is concerned with the impact of public programs on individual and social values. Moreover, performance budgeting followed, and in a sense was a product of, the de facto spread of management into budgeting; PPB appeared on the scene before planning had made a substantial penetration of budgeting.

Briefly stated, the problem stems from the coexistence of budgeting's several functions: how to provide for control without driving out plan-

27. Theodore J. Lowi, "American Business, Public Policy, Case-Studies and Political Theory," in *World Politics*, Vol. 16 (1964), pp. 677–715.

ning and how to accommodate planning without neglecting the vital control functions.

The process for integrating the planning, control, and management functions is *crosswalking*. In a technical sense, crosswalking refers to the data processing routine for switching from one informational form to another, for example, from organization to program classifications.[28] Viewed from this perspective, crosswalking is merely the small price that must be paid for PPB's inability to restructure all the budget accounts along program lines. In the interim, crosswalking will be a "nuts and bolts" routine that has no significant bearing on the budgetary process. It can be handled by computer technicians and need not concern budget or policy staff.

However, in contrast to the foregoing view, crosswalking is defined here as the process of reconciling the many informational and institutional diversities that spring from the multiple purposes of budgeting. The reconciliation of the budget and appropriations is just one aspect of crosswalking, and the need for crosswalking will persist even if the accounts are recast into program form. In this sense, crosswalking is neither routine nor automatic; it cannot be turned over to technicians and then forgotten. In a full-blown PPB system, the crosswalking problem appears in the relationships between planning and budgeting, the supply and use of budgetary information, the schedule of budget work, and the connection between organizational and budget structures. The multipurpose budget problem will persist as long as budgeting is assigned heterogeneous responsibilities. Since it is unlikely that budgeting will revert to its simple, unifunctional past, this problem is likely to be a permanent fixture of modern budgeting.

The Crosswalk System

In structure, PPB is a crosswalk system. Its distinctive characteristic is that plans and analyses are commissioned, produced, and reported expressly for purposes of budget making. The procedure for selecting planning studies and for reporting their findings are governed by the requirements and priorities of budgeting. The calendar for planning is

28. Thus, the PPB glossary prepared by the U.S. General Accounting Office defines crosswalk as "the expression of the relationship between the program structure and the appropriation budget structure." *Planning-Programming-Budgeting and Systems Analysis Glossary* (January 1968), p. 14.

phased to the ongoing budget cycle; budgetary deadlines, not the shape of the problem, determine the timetable for planning. In a cross-walk system, the job of central authorities is to manage the crosswalk apparatus and to monitor agency activity, not to do the planning work itself. For this purpose, a small staff (the size of California's four-man PABS group or New York State's eight-man program analysis and co-ordination unit) is sufficient. The conventional budget documents are not modified significantly; rather, new reporting documents (such as program memoranda and program and financial plans) feed the plans into the budget stream. It should be stressed that these new documents are not plans or analyses but are rather the means of conveying plans to budget makers. The crosswalk arrangement requires a precise and routine reconciliation of the financial and organizational accounts with the program structure. The planning enterprise is only a small com-ponent of the total system, for the main effort is spent on the delivery of plans to budget clients.

In the federal government, the Bureau of the Budget opted for crosswalking because it was the easiest, least disruptive course of action. The entrenched budget machine was left alone, and no major planning organization rivaling the bureau was established. All that was necessary was to couple a small-scale planning capability to the budget cycle. This was accomplished via the program categories, pro-gram memoranda, and program and financial plans—the constituent routines of PPB. Planning and analysis would bloom slowly in the safe and relevant context of budgeting. There would not have to be major upheavals to accommodate the newcomer. The press releases would announce a major innovation, but insiders would know that the core had remained intact and that changes at the periphery would not chal-lenge the established way. Nothing old would have to be traded away to get the new, not a single beat would be missed in the cycle of budget events. The figures in the big document would continue to have their old meaning and reliability. State officials did not have to make these strategic calculations when they decided for PPB, but they were lured to the crosswalk alternative by the same factors that made it attractive to federal officials.

The pivotal position of budgeting was strengthened by the leading role of economists and analysts in the formulation of PPB. They almost instinctively view the budget as the key instrument for rationing public resources and disciplining the wants of public agencies. Understandably they preferred a system that terminates in a budgetary outcome and uses the power of the budget to obtain the best possible expenditure mix.[29]

In terms of minimizing budget risks, as well as the difficulties in budget implementation, the crosswalk alternative was the clear and necessary choice. But this is an insular view, perhaps inevitable from the confining perspective of the budget process. Viewed from the outside, in terms of the quality of public choice, the crosswalk relation of planning and budgeting has a number of major defects. These defects are rooted in the character and traditions of the budget process. Thus the problem of budget innovation turns out to be the problem of the budget process itself. By making planning and analysis so heavily dependent on budgeting, the innovators have denied PPB the possibility of accomplishing what was initially expected of it. Accordingly, the budget process must be examined to learn why the buoyant prospects set in motion by the PPB movement have not been realized.

The Routine of Budgeting

Budgeting has become one of the great triumphs of bureaucratic order. Decisions involving billions of dollars are made quietly and routinely according to prescribed procedures. The books are opened and closed for each fiscal year, the accounts maintained and forms filled, the purchases made and the payments disbursed—all with fidelity to the deadlines and the rules. Routine goes hand in hand with incrementalism: incrementalism makes routine necessary; routine makes incrementalism possible.

Routine is the nemesis of innovation, for every bureaucratic change spells a disruption in regularity, even if its intent is to impose a superior set of routines. Most budget operations are staffed—in terms

29. The prototypic application of PPB occurred in the Defense Department, where the secretary has enormous budgetary discretion and leverage over weapons policies, particularly over the big strategic weapons systems. Each year, old weapons are scrapped and new ones requisitioned. The annual budget, in tandem with allied decisional processes, gives the secretary a powerful role in weapons policy. He lacks comparable power over other sectors of Defense spending. Similarly, most welfare and human resources policies are fixed in basic legislation and administrative rules. In these circumstances, the budget serves as a second order translation of established policy into fiscal terms. Yet in the hurly burly of PPB's debut, there was not much inclination to look at the Defense experience to appraise its relevance for different public programs.

of size and orientation—to handle the routine work of preparing and executing the budget. Anyone who has worked in a state budget office can attest to the constant rush of deadlines, the endless flow of paperwork, and the difficulty of completing long-range work. The task of implementing new procedures places added work burdens on the budget office, and this problem was aggravated in the case of performance budgeting and PPB because both reforms meant a net increase in the amount of data that has to be collected and processed. Even when the initiative for reform emanates from some outside source, much of the implementation is the responsibility of the budget office or is accomplished in close liaison with it. Unless the budget office is staunchly committed to the reform, it may be unwilling to allocate staff to the innovation, and even when staff is assigned, it may be pulled back to its routines by an approaching deadline or a bureaucratic crisis.

A routinized decisional process tends to establish its own internal success indicators. Closed from public view and notice, the routines of budgeting are presided over by "armchair" budgeters, who maintain the flow of paper between the central office and the agencies. If the deadlines are met and the budget is presented on time, the budgeter is tempted to accept the view that the process is working properly and is not in need of overhaul. Given the insularity of the budget process, there are not likely to be many effective challenges to this self-perception. From the budgeter's point of view, failure means the breakdown of relations with departments or within the office, the inability to meet budget deadlines, errors in budgetary arithmetic, and the like. These perceptions are only indirectly related to the uses to which the budget process is put, the quality of budget choice, or the results of public service.

A routinized outlook, therefore, induces insulation from the winds of change that blow outside. Budget makers come to esteem and rely on that which can be routinized; the things that can be routinized generally pertain to internal operations rather than to public outcomes. March and Simon speak of "Gresham's Law of Planning: Daily routine drives out planning"[30] as a common organization phenomenon. An examiner confronts a large stack of papers when he begins his chores in the morning and an equally large pile when he departs in the evening.

30. James G. March and Herbert A. Simon, *Organizations* (John Wiley & Sons, 1958), p. 185.

During the intervening hours, there probably has been little opportunity or inclination for field work, planning and analysis, or evaluation of programs. The forms and routines force one's mind to the worksheets and ledgers, and away from the schoolroom, hospital, or ghetto.

Finally, the net effect of routinization is that budget reforms themselves become routine. The only way for the new orientations to gain entry into the processes of budget choice is to become incorporated into the calendar of procedures and forms. Early in its career, performance budgeting was transformed into activity classifications, workload statistics, and budget justifications. PPB has undergone the same kind of transformation, from a conception of rational choice into a mechanism for projecting future costs and gathering limited kinds of output data. Once planning and analysis were tied to the budget process, they were fated to become part of its routine.

The crosswalk system forces planning into a time frame that is suited for control and management. The conventional cycle of budget routines, with its lengthy and detailed preparation of estimates, demands a strict sequence of steps, uniformly time-phased throughout the government with a constant awareness of when the fiscal year begins and when a particular action (among many) leading to that date must be commenced or completed. The control and management of spending similarly operate within discrete time frames—days, weeks, pay periods, months, quarters, and so on—during which actions must be promptly checked and reported. Estimates must be prepared in time for central review; the governor must make his recommendations in time for legislative consideration; the legislature must act before expenses can be obligated. There are salaries to pay, vouchers to process, checks to disburse, accounts to maintain. The treasurer must be sure that he has enough funds on hand to pay the bills, and the comptroller must be sure that spending is not outpacing appropriations. On some matters, the control and management schedule allows a little slippage—a state can make do if the legislature votes funds some time after the fiscal year begins—but the budget clock cannot tick erratically, with some events occurring weeks after they were expected.

The Timing Dilemma

Genuine planning is destroyed by fixed routines and omnipresent deadlines. Planning must be opportunistic and episodic, taking its cues and clues from wherever they come: expiring legislation, a new department head, changes in federal grant policy, shifts in public opinion, policy signals from the governor, a crisis, breakthroughs in technology. Most of these are nonroutine events, and few can be programmed in advance. Although short-term planning can be—and has been—compressed into the budget calendar, fundamental policy planning leading to major program changes must have some independence from budget routines. Without time-distance from budgeting, planning itself becomes routine.

Unlike control and management, which necessarily operate within a fiscal year calendar, planning must have a variable time frame, depending on the scope, complexity, and timeliness of the issue. Planning cannot be coterminous with the fiscal year, nor can it have uniform beginnings and endings. Normally, planning must have a multiyear frame; otherwise, there will not be much opportunity to consider alternatives to the present course of action.

Within the crosswalk system, no reliable way has been found to synchronize the budget and planning timetables. The budget clock works with minutes and days, especially during the "home stretch" when final budget decisions are made; budget-linked planning, therefore, has been compressed into a schedule that compels routine rather than thought. Of course, consultants and governments can construct fanciful schemes and charts, with the vectors aimed in the right direction and the boxes properly positioned, with feed-in from plans to budgets and feedback from performance to plans, with a circular or linear flow of processes or stages, all sequenced in a logical fashion. But in practice it just doesn't work that way, not in a single government that tries to bring planning and analysis into the central policy-making arenas.

PPB has muddled through the time problem by letting budgeters and budgeting retain their paramountcy at the expense of policy planning. Budgeting deals with the immediate and is favored by the bureaucratic impulse to respond to the nearest deadline and to defer faraway problems. When the budget becomes tighter, the budgeters become stronger, for they have direct command over current spending. (It need hardly be mentioned that budgets have been tight in most states in recent years.) Planners and analysts have had to work within the budget calendar, with the predictable result that little planning and analysis have been done. In many cases the planners have been converted into budgeters; that is, they have been diverted from analytic work to pending budget business. Where they have not been tied to the budget process, the planners and analysts often have been isolated from the decisional centers. In short, the alternatives confronting the new planning staffs have been to stay on the outside or to join the budget game.

The timing dilemma is due to a faulty conception of the analytic input into policy. It is a mistake to assume that planning can be influential only if it "gets to the church on time," when the budget is waiting at the door. Because of this misconception, it is always the upcoming round of budget actions that determines the course of PPB. If more patience had been shown in the attempt to apply planning and analysis, PPB probably would have much more to show after two or three years than it has been able to produce in the "pressure cooker" environment of budgeting. But the understandable desire to produce immediate results in order to demonstrate the usefulness of planning does not afford much opportunity for farsightedness in installing the new system.

The Planning Gap

In summary, the crosswalk system offers no remedy to the anti-planning orientation of traditional budgeting. Control and management routines remain dominant and probably preemptive. Because it is dependent on a tight integration of budgeting and planning, the crosswalk system is hamstrung by the inevitable tensions and disparities of the two processes. And because budgeting is the entrenched process, it will continue to dominate whatever alliance is formed. The result will be the withering of planning and analysis. Some slack is necessary if planning is to stand on its own feet and make a creditable input into the policy process. This is applicable especially to the contemporary situation, when planning is still struggling to establish roots and linkages.

A crosswalk system in which budgeting is dominant may push planning to the fringes of public policymaking. In order to avoid being dominated by budgeting, the planners move away from the relevant policy arenas. They gain some autonomy but lose the influential role anticipated for planning.

Maintenance of the crosswalk system consumes most of the resources and support available for planning and analysis. The crosswalk machinery necessarily is cumbersome because of the need to link plans to the budget. Program categories are counterparts of the regular budget and appropriation categories, and multiyear financial statements and program reports are the equivalents of the fiscal year budget statements and justifications. It takes a great deal of work to prepare these documents, yet they are a means of delivering plans to budgets, not of increasing the supply of analysis. Unfortunately there has been very little planning and analysis to deliver because very little has been done. State governments have invested more in keeping the system going than in producing plans and analyses.

Alternatives to PPB: Systems for Planning and Analysis

In one of his recent appraisals of budget reform, Aaron Wildavsky has made a strong case *for* policy analysis, but *against* PPB. He rests his argument on the conviction that the costs of maintaining a system will drive out rather than abet analysis.[31] However, some formal system for analysis is necessary because the established budget process is anti-analytic.[32] If budgeting were hospitable to analysis, the maintenance of a formal system would be counter-productive. But given the control environment in which budgeting operates, it is doubtful that the analysis done will be used unless there is some permanent mechanism for commissioning, doing, and using the analysis.

That a system for analysis is necessary does not mean that the PPB-type crosswalk is the one to be preferred. The decisive factor in favor of the crosswalk system is its linkage to budgeting, which is perhaps the most powerful action-forcing process of government. However, this advantage seems to be offset by the liabilities of budgeting's heritage and encumbrances, particularly its control and management ties. Accordingly, it would be desirable to proceed independently to bolster the processes for legislation and program development. Regardless of the fate of PBB, resources invested in improving program planning will yield a high and continuing return.

Planning, like control and management, is an organizational function. It becomes a prime budget function only when the resources and leverage of the budget process are used for policy purposes. PPB tries

31. "Rescuing Policy Analysis from PPB."
32. Allen Schick, "Systems for Analysis: PPB and Its Alternatives," in U.S. Congress, Joint Economic Committee, *The Analysis and Evaluation of Public Expenditures: The PPB System* (Government Printing Office, 1969), pp. 817–34.

to do precisely this, to move planning from the periphery to the center of budget operations. But there are alternative ways of satisfying government's need for planning. Another way would be to attach planning to other decisional arenas, such as legislation and program development. Within the budget sphere, alternatives to PPB are possible. One alternative would be to convert budgeting into a planning process by stripping it of all its management and control chores. Another would be to retain the budget process in its traditional form but to set up a parallel planning process that is only loosely connected with the budget.

Proposals for separating planning and analysis from the routines of budgeting predate PPB. During the performance budgeting era, Arthur Smithies proposed dividing the budget process into program policy and performance review components.

Under present procedures, the appropriations process serves the dual purpose of reviewing the past and of programming for the future, and, because of this duality, it is satisfactory in neither respect. . . . The solution proposed here is that a review of actual performance should focus attention on economy and efficiency, while a program budget should be related to policy objectives.[33]

Frederick Mosher carried the argument a step further and suggested that "it may well be that the single budget process has been overloaded with different kinds of problems, not basically consistent with each other." According to Mosher, "the two purposes of budgeting, the making of program decisions and the provision of an effective system of administration, must be linked; but they should not have to ride the same track at the same time." To remedy this dilemma, Mosher proposed

two different budget systems: one designed for the development, appraisal, and authorization of future policies and programs at top levels; the other, to facilitate internal programming, management and control. These we shall refer to respectively as the program budget and the administrative budget.[34]

Altogether, three alternatives to PPB can be identified. One alternative is a policy planning system. Its principal target is the policymaking arena, legislative and administrative. A second alternative is an *analytic budget* system; the budget process is overhauled and made

33. Arthur Smithies, *The Budgetary Process in the United States* (McGraw-Hill Book Company, 1955), pp. 171–72.

34. Frederick C. Mosher, *Program Budgeting: Theory and Practices* (Public Administration Service, 1954), pp. 236–37.

analytic by bringing in new skills and perspectives, changing central budget roles, and developing informational resources and a calendar suited to planning and analysis. A final alternative can be called a *two track* system because under it, planning is largely independent of budgeting and is allowed to develop at its own pace and according to its own opportunities.

Policy Planning Systems

Budgeting is not the only policymaking arena of U.S. government. At least two other public decisional processes exist alongside, and often dominate, the budget process. These less formalized processes for legislation and program development often are the avenues for major policy departures from the status quo, while the budget process handles continuing programs and incremental adjustments. Indirectly, of course, legislation and programming feed into the budget, as least to the extent that the budget becomes a costing out of decisions already made elsewhere. The legislative and programming processes generally lack a steady flow of information, ideas, and attention. The purpose of a policy planning system would be to remedy these defects by establishing a permanent policy staff, possibly in the governor's office, to prepare the legislative program, review departmental program proposals, develop objectives and priorities for gubernatorial action, and coordinate the policy planning operations of state agencies. There would be a comprehensive policy system for the collection and use of analytic data, the preparation of plans and analyses, and the making of policy decisions. Much of the prescribed procedure would resemble the PPB apparatus, but there would be no formal tie-in to budgeting. The budget process would be drawn in only after programs had been formulated, when it became necessary to get firm cost estimates for next year's budget.

This divorcement of planning from budgeting would offer several advantages. It would remedy the usual neglect of legislative and administrative decision making. Often major decisions in these arenas are made with scant forethought or analysis. At the same time it would free planning from the formidable and perhaps inherent constraints of the budget process. While the popular image of the budget process is one of great power over expenditures and programs, the true picture often is that of a feeble response to decisions already made. Thus, rather than being the instrument for making policy choices, frequently the budget is used merely to cost out the decisions for the next fiscal year. Consequently, when planning is dependent on the budget, there may be little opportunity to apply planning. The opportunities will have been foreclosed by previous decisions regarding programs and legislation.

In a separate policy planning system, planning would not be loaded with the traditions and habits of the budget process. It would not have to compete directly and on unfavorable terms with the entrenched control and management functions. Nor would it be necessary to reshape budgeting radically in order to make way for planning. Budgeting could continue its old ways while planning developed separately.

Analytic Budgeting

Under PPB's crosswalk arrangement, budgeting remains largely unchanged, with modifications introduced through the new planning process attached to it. Analytic budgeting would mean revamping the budget process so that it would become a planning instrument. There would be no separation of planning from budgeting and hence no need for a formal (crosswalk) or informal (two-track) connection. But in order to achieve analytic budgeting, radical changes would have to be made in many facets of the budget process. The central budget agency would spin off its control and management and take on a program development and policy leadership role. The budget staff's skills and perspectives would be brought into accord with this new orientation. The budget process would be purged of a good deal of its detail, as well as of the conventional budget forms and procedures that relate to policy outcomes rather than to the internal affairs of government agencies. The bottom-up budget tradition would be reversed as top levels transmitted policy guidance to subordinates prior to the preparation of budget estimates. The bulk of analysis would be done by mainline units in the central budget agency and by department staffs. A special planning unit might have responsibility for matters that did not fit into the analytic routines of budgeting.

In a fully developed analytic budget system, there would be routine and explicit trading off among alternatives in the course of budget making. Top decisional channels would be reserved for matters warranting analytic action. Issues would be presented in an informational structure that enabled policymakers to consider prospective outcomes. The budget calendar would be cycled to suit the needs of planning and analysis rather than those of control and management. Thus the budget horizon would be lengthened to an appropriate multiyear span, and decisions regularly would be made in the light of multiyear rather than next-year impacts. Adjustments in the appropriations process also would have to be made to conform to this lengthened time frame. Instead of trying to review every item in the budget annually (or biennially), central executives and legislators would cycle the budget process to examine selected segments of the budget each year, with the remaining portions funded under continuing appropriations until their scheduled time for review. Of course, allowances would have to be made for program changes that could not be deferred (or that policy officials did not want to defer) until the program's turn was reached in the multiyear cycle. In addition, methods would have to be provided for coping with unanticipated situations: a fiscal crisis, a change in political leadership, new federal grant programs, a steep rise in welfare costs. Probably there would be a need to authorize the governor (or perhaps a joint executive-legislative committee, such as Ohio's Controlling Board) to adjust a program's budget within a range, and according to rules set by the state legislature.

Though it is a very radical alternative, analytic budgeting has two impressive advantages compared to the crosswalk arrangement: (1) It does not accept the budget process with all its encumbrances and limitations as a given but tries to do something to alleviate them, and (2) more than any alternative, it brings planning and analysis directly into the centers of public policymaking. All the other systems impose some distance between planning and budgeting. But the price for obtaining these benefits may be too high for practical executives and legislators. They may prefer a crosswalk arrangement that leaves the existing budget system intact (allowing change to seep in gradually) rather than an upheaval in traditional practices.

Two-Track Systems

The two-track alternative takes a middle ground between the alternatives discussed thus far. Unlike the planning system, it establishes a relation with the budget process; unlike analytic budgeting, it does not uproot half a century of budget practice. Yet it also differs from the crosswalk setup; its relation to budgeting is less formal, and the planning component is not just a satellite of the much larger and better entrenched budget control and management process.

In a two-track system, planning is allowed "to do its thing" according to its own timetable and procedures. The objective continues to be plans and analyses that influence budget choice, but their impact depends on their quality and strength as well as on organizational and political circumstances, not on some standard formula tying them to the budget. Accordingly, the use of analysis will be spasmodic, rising or falling as support at the top is granted or withheld. The budget process is not revamped substantially; routines and procedures continue as they were. But the activation of a large planning and analytic staff (not the small units provided under PPB) lends status and potency to policy analysis and enables it to compete with the budget process when important program decisions are being made. The mission of the central staff is to plan and analyze, not merely to maintain the PPB system.

The two-track arrangement recognizes that planning and budgeting have different data requirements and that planners and budgeters have different perspectives and operate under different constraints. Planning is not bent to the routines of budgeting, but it can develop its own pace and place in policy formulation. It is not unduly constricted by the necessities and habits of budgeting.

A two-track system can work only when it is supported by policy officials at the top and staffed with a critical mass of planning and analytic resources. Top support is necessary for providing convergence of the parallel budgeting and planning operations and for injecting a sense of relevance and opportunity into the planning work. If sustained interest is lacking, planning will drift away from the operative policy channels and become irrelevant or futile. But a planning center that has both resources and support can challenge the authority and status of the budget agency. For this reason, a two-track system rarely is adopted, though certain of its features have been incorporated in some state PPB systems.

The Possibility of Budgetary Improvement

Regardless of the approach it takes, a state will enhance both its budget practices and the prospects for innovation by reexamining the uses to which it puts its budget process. By addressing the uses of the process, the state can arrange its budget reforms in an effective sequence. It faces squarely the issue of control, and it perceives that one of the very first orders of business must be the reconstruction of the control machinery so that the critical requirements of control will be served while the budget process is being revamped to accommodate planning. The state that invests a good deal of its PPB energy in the design of new control patterns will have a high payoff in the opportunities for planning that are opened up.

If a state perceives its reform problem as one of changing the use of its budget process, it also will gain an enlarged view of what must be done in order to carry out that transformation. It will recognize that much more must be changed than the information categories or the flow of documents. Roles and relationships appropriate for control will have to be modified for planning. This means placing the planning component ahead of budget preparation, adjusting the budget calendar to suit the timetables of policy formulation, reversing the flow of budgetary instructions from bottom-up to top-down, and possibly creating some joint enterprise in which the budgeters participate with the spenders in program development. If the process is reconstructed on a planning basis, the changes in information categories will be among the least dramatic, though possibly the most visible, of the accomplishments.

A related change is to examine the types of evidence required for budget choice. The current criteria are well known: How much was spent last year? What is the cost of the mandatories? What items can be pared?, and so on. If these continue to be the dominant rules, all changes made in the accounts or the structures will have been in vain. PPB means applying analytic criteria in making budget choices: What alternatives are available, and how do they compare in cost and effectiveness? What will the program cost in the years ahead? What results does it promise to produce? If these kinds of questions are raised in the course of budget making, analysis and planning will be effectively drawn into the process instead of remaining apart, as is generally the case at the present time. The questions don't have to be asked in all sectors of the budget; analysis can be applied more rigorously to selected targets of opportunity rather than across the board. But the habit of looking at the budget analytically should be pervasive, even if the specialized analysis is not.

PPB analyses cannot survive unless the states do much more than they are doing currently in the way of program evaluation, that is, in appraising ongoing programs. Any analytic enterprise can be discredited if it is predicated on no more than speculations about the future and makes no attempt to apply actual experience to budget decisions. From an analytic standpoint, it seems to be much easier to evaluate the results of previous decisions than to conjecture about what might be. But there are pitifully few incentives in bureaucracy for sustained program evaluation, and this deficiency ultimately may lead to the discrediting of analysis.

Program evaluation does not have to proceed as a zero-base exercise. Even under a successfully operating PPB, established programs will enjoy some preference over proposed new ones. The purpose of program evaluation is not to build up the budget from the beginning, but to supply the evidence on which analytic choices can be based. The rules can be applied opportunistically, and the availability of evaluative evidence will promote an expansion of the spheres of opportunity, but not everything can or has to be evaluated every year. It long has been a costly fiction in budgeting that all components are equally deserving of support. We ought not to replace it with another fiction that all components are equally in need of scrutiny. It is useless to evaluate the program and budget of the state university as if it had no past, no items that are less capable of change than others, no areas in which evaluation promises a higher payoff. We can expect the university to continue in operation next year and to continue doing most of the things it has done. Program evaluation will provide data on the performance and effectiveness of the university, and we may use some of the data in deciding next year's budget, or we may decide to let things ride along or to look at certain segments more closely.

The business of budget improvement will not be concluded with the current cycle of innovation. PPB will leave in its wake many unfulfilled expectations, much as performance budgeting departed the scene only partly realized. A future round of reform will look at the unrealized potential of PPB, cast it into somewhat different and more contemporary form, and provide new standards for analysis and planning. PPB itself might fail or fade away, but its concepts will have an increasing influence over budget practice. If PPB is an idea whose time has not quite come, it also is an idea that cannot be repressed by momentary setbacks.

Index

Activity classification: in executive budget, 20; in hybrid budget, 56–57, 59–60; in performance budget, 8, 44–46, 48, 68
Agnew, Spiro T., 74
Alternative expenditures: in PPB process, 8–9, 92, 136; and welfare economics, 33–34
Altshuler, Alan A., 201n
Analytic budgeting: alternative to PPB, 214–15
Anthony, Robert, 107n
Anton, Thomas J., 178n
Appleby, Paul H., 175
Arkansas, 12

Banfield, Edward C., 42n
Beach, Edwin W., 142n
Beard, Charles A., 3–4
Bell, David, 39
Bird Commission (Temporary Commission on the Fiscal Affairs of State Government), 76
Bosworth, Karl A., 64n
Braybrooke, David, 42n, 197n
Briggs, John E., 60n
Brown, Edmund G. (Pat), 138, 140
Brown, Paul L., 131
Buck, Arthur Eugene, 14n, 17n, 21, 28n
Budget and Accounting Act of 1921, 6
Budget officials: ideal, 164–65; reform attitudes, 66–69, 165–69, 192–93
Budgeting: agency role in, 169–73, 177–80; analytic, 214–15; budgeters, 23, 66–69, 164–69; bureaucratic influence in, 195–97; central office role, 23, 173–

77; control element (see Control element); economists' role, 32–36; fragmentation-interdependence problem, 185–88, 197; governor's role (see Governor); incremental analysis method, 197–99; Keynesian effect, 28, 32; legislative role (see Legislature); line-item (see Line-item budgeting); management element (see Management element); mutual adjustment coordinate, 199–200; New Deal impact on, 26–30; planning element (see Planning); and political process, 193–95; reform attitudes, 66–69, 165–69, 192–93; routinization in, 206–08; systems analysis in, 6, 36–37; time element, 90–91, 208–10; uses, 3–8; welfare economics effect, 33–34. See also Executive budgeting; Legislative budgeting; Performance budgeting; Planning-programming-budgeting system (PPB)
Burkhead, Jesse, 44n, 61, 62n, 169n, 171n
Burns, John A., 157n, 160n

California, 12, 42, 58, 97, 100, 105, 117, 185; PABS in, 138–45
Capron, William M., 201n
Chartrand, Robert L., 183n
Cleveland, Frederick A., 14n, 15–17, 19, 21
Colorado, 43n
Commission on Economy and Efficiency (1912), 13, 20
Computers. See Data technology

Connecticut, 11, 52, 62, 64, 69
Control element: budgeters' attitude, 66–68; in crosswalking, 203–04, 208; defined, 4; in executive budget, 16–20, 24–25; in Maryland budget reform, 70–73; in performance budget, 48–52; in PPB, 7; in traditional budget, 4–6; in Wisconsin budget reform, 129–31. *See also* Line-item budgeting
Corrigan, John J., 78*n*
Cost measurements: in hybrid budget, 56–57, 60–61; in performance budget, 46–47
Council of State Governments, 31*n*, 86
Crecine, John P., 200*n*
Crosswalk system: in California PABS, 140; defined, 203–04; need for, 206–08; planning gap in, 210–11; structure of, 204–06; time problem in, 208–10
Cyert, Richard M., 187*n*

Data technology: in PPB process, 36–37, 41–42, 90–91, 150–51
Dawes, Charles G., 21
DiSalle, Michael, 83–84
Downs, Anthony, 23
Dye, Thomas R., 12*n*

Easton, David, 178*n*–79*n*
Economics, 6; Keynesian, 28, 32; in PPB process, 32–36, 42; welfare, 33–34
Eghtedari, Ali, 184
Executive budgeting: concepts, 15–17; control element in, 16–20; governor's role, 177–80; interest in, 63–65; legislator's role, 18; management element in, 16–17; planning element in, 15–16
Exo, Warren D., 137*n*

"Factorial budgeting," 47–48
Fenno, Richard F., 182–83
Fitzpatrick, Edward A., 194*n*
Financial Information Systems (FIS), 106
Flinn, Thomas, 178*n*
Functional classification. *See* Activity classification

Gentilcore, Hugo, 78–80
Goodnow, Frank J., 15, 20
Gorham, William, 89
Governor: California PABS role, 138, 140, 143; and control tradition, 24–25; executive budget role, 17–19, 65, 177; "gatekeeper" role, 167, 177–80; Hawaii budget reform role, 156–60, 162;

Pennsylvania budget reform role, 150–53; performance budgeting role, 64–65, 180; PPB role, 97–99, 177, 180; Wisconsin budget reform role, 134–35
Graves, Mark, 24
Gross, Bertram, 6*n*
Gulick, Luther H., 18, 28*n*

Harriman, Averell, 118
Hawaii, 12, 54, 59, 96, 100, 105–06, 117, 185; PPB in, 153–63
Henry, Marion L., 76*n*
Hilleboe, Herman, 77*n*
Hitch, Charles J., 37, 107*n*, 202*n*
Hollander, Walter G., 133*n*, 137*n*
Hoover, Herbert C., 30*n*
Hoover Commission, 2, 6, 8, 29–31, 52, 54, 62
Hoover Commission (*second*), 8, 45, 186
Hugo, Michael, 183*n*
Hybrid budgeting: extent of, 55–58; and information specialization, 190; innovations in, 59–60; New York model, 80–81; objects of expense in, 58–59; and performance budgeting, 52–62; strategy of, 60–62

Illinois, 181
Incremental analysis: budget method, 197–99; and PPB, 200–03
Information specialization: in hybrid budget, 190; in PPB, 188–90
Institute of Public Administration (Pennsylvania), 145–46
Interdepartmental Management Improvement Council (IMIC), 126
International City Managers' Association, 31, 55
Itemization. *See* Line-item budgeting

Jacob, Herbert, 12*n*, 178*n*
James, George, 77*n*
Janda, Kenneth, 183*n*
Johnson, Lyndon B., 1, 13, 133

Kamaka, Hiram, 162*n*
Keefe, William, 181*n*, 182
Key, V. O., 33
Killian, Kathryn W., 9*n*, 45*n*
Kilpatrick, Wylie, 26
Klepak, Daniel, 76*n*–77*n*
Kraemer, Kenneth L., 40*n*

Lahee, Arnold W., 196*n*
Lauber, John G., 75*n*
Lazarus, Steven, 107*n*

Legislative budgeting: characteristics, 14–15

Legislature: budget role decline, 167–68, 180–85; California PABS role, 141–42, 144; executive budget reform role, 18; Hawaii budget reform role, 153–63; Maryland performance budget role, 70–72; Pennsylvania PPB role, 151

Lepawsky, Albert, 169*n*

Lewis, Verne B., 34

Lindblom, Charles E., 42, 196–97, 198*n*–99*n*, 200, 202

Line-item budgeting: advantages in, 22–23; agency preference for, 171–72; in California PABS, 139–41, 143–44; in control budget era, 6–7, 22–23; in executive budget, 20; in hybrid budget, 52–54, 58–59; in Maryland budget reform, 70–72; in performance budget, 10, 50, 75–76; in Wisconsin budget reform, 129–32

"Little Hoover Commissions," 13, 52, 63

Lowi, Theodore J., 183, 203

MacMahon, Arthur, 183

Management element: defined, 4–7; Bureau of the Budget role, 28–29; in crosswalking, 204–05, 208; in executive budget, 16–17; in New Deal era, 29–30; in PPB, 7–8; in Wisconsin budget reform, 130–33. *See also* Performance budgeting

Management Information and Program Evaluation System (MIPES), 75

Management Information Systems (MIS), 106

March, James G., 68*n*, 166*n*, 187*n*, 207

Marginal utility, doctrine of: and welfare economics, 33

Marshall, Alton, 119*n*

Martin, James W., 12*n*

Marx, Fritz Morstein, 28*n*

Maryland, 11, 52, 58, 62, 64, 69; performance budgeting in, 70–75

Maryland Commission on Administrative Organization, 70

Massachusetts, 11, 18, 69

Massey, Robert J., 187*n*

McKean, Roland B., 34

McNamara, Robert S., 37, 187

Michigan, 12, 106*n*

Mitchell, George W., 55*n*

Moak, Lennox L., 9*n*, 45*n*

Mosher, Frederick C., 30*n*, 37*n*, 48, 75, 81*n*, 212

Mowitz, Robert J., 146*n*

Multiyear projections: in California PABS, 139, 141, 143; defined, 93; PPB characteristic, 9, 38–39, 97; single-year v., 93, variants of, 93–94; in Wisconsin budget reform, 135–38

Municipal Finance Officers Association, 31*n*

Mushkin, Selma J., 43*n*

Naito, Yukio, 162*n*

Narrative statements, 29; in hybrid budget, 56–57, 59, 61; in performance budget, 68

National Association of State Budget Officers (NASBO), 54, 63, 87, 107, 108*n*, 174

National Governors' Conference: and PPB, 41

New Deal era: and budget process, 6–7, 26–30

New Jersey, 11, 58, 69, 96

New Mexico, 43*n*

New York, 11, 42, 58, 64, 69, 81*n*, 100, 106*n*, 135–36; budget machinery in, 118–21; performance budgeting experiment in, 75–81, 180; PPB experiment in, 117–28

New York Bureau of Municipal Research, 13

Novick, David, 36–37

Object of expense budgeting. *See* Line-item budgeting

Office of Planning Coordination (OPC), 119, 123–24

Office for Regional Development (ORD), 119–21

Ogul, Morris, 181*n*, 182

Ohio, 11, 26, 69, 179; performance budgeting experiment, 81–85

Oregon, 12

Pearson, Norman, 28*n*

Pennsylvania, 11, 54, 64, 69, 95, 97, 105, 117, 185; PPB experiment in, 145–53

Performance budgeting: activity classifications of, 8, 44–46, 48, 68; attitudes toward, 66–69, 77–79, 82–83, 173; case studies of, 70–85; control methods in, 48–52; emergence of, 2, 8, 30–31; fragmentation and interdependence problem, 185–86; governor's role, 64–65, 180; hybridization of, 52–62; interest in, 62–69; line-itemization in,

10, 50, 75–76; management element in, 4–7; measurements in, 47–48; New York experiment in, 75–81; Ohio experiment in, 81–85; and PPB, 8–10, 106–07; reports in, 48; techniques of, 44–48

Planning: "701" state grants, 40–41; in analytic budgeting, 214–15; conventional v. PPB, 37–40; in crosswalking, 204–06, 208, 210–11; defined, 5; executive budget concept, 15–16; in PPB, 7, 37–41, 90, 121–24; in policy planning systems, 213–14; rapprochement with budgeting, 37–41; time-distance need in, 208–10; in two-track system, 216. *See also* Planning-programming-budgeting system (PPB)

Planning-programming-budgeting system (PPB): alternatives to, 211–16; alternative expenditure evaluations, 8–9, 92, 136; analytic nature, 9, 94, 134–35, 202–03; analytic v. systematic approaches to, 95–96; attitudes toward, 107–15, 173; and California budget reform, 138–45; control element in, 7; crosswalk arrangement, 94–95, 203–06; data technology and, 36–37, 41–42, 90–91, 150–51; economists' role in, 32–36; elements of, 9, 89–95; emergence of, 31–32; evaluations of, 87–89, 104–05, 115–16, 126–27, 191; fragmentation-interdependence problem, 185–88; governor's role in, 97–99, 177, 180; and Hawaii budget reform, 153–63; incremental method and, 200–03; information specialization in, 188–90; installation methods, 95–100, 113–15; institutionalization of, 97–100; management element in, 7–8; multiyear element, 9, 38–39, 92–94; and New York budget reform, 117–28; and Pennsylvania budget reform, 143–53; performance budgeting as prerequisite, 8–10, 106–07; planning element, 7, 37–41, 90, 121–24; and political process, 193–95, 203; PABS in California, 138–45; PAR and, 127–28; program plans in, 139–40, 149–50; program structure in, 91–92, 97, 106, 124–26, 147–49; routinization and, 207–08; staff separation problem, 99, 120; systems analysis in, 36–37; time-distance element, 90–91, 208–10; training courses in, 98–103, 140, 142–43, 147, 160, 162; and Wisconsin budget reform, 128–38

Policy planning system: alternative to PPB, 212–14

POSDCORB process, 28–29, 31, 37

Powell, Fred Wilbur, 14n, 17

President's Committee on Administrative Management (1937), 28

Proctor, Willis, 76n

Program Analysis and Review (PAR), 118, 126–27; comparison with PPB, 127–28

Program Analysis and Review Committee (PARC), 126

Program budgeting: contrast to performance budgeting, 2, 8, 79–80; executive role in, 177; in Wisconsin, 129–33

Program Evaluation and Review Technique (PERT), 146

Program plans: in PPB, 139–40, 149–50

Program structure: in PPB, 91–92, 97, 106, 124–26, 147–49

Programming and Budgeting System (PABS), 138–45

Public administration: in budgeting, 6, 42

Public Administration Service, 31n

RAND Corporation, 36–37, 91

Reagan, Ronald, 140

Reynolds, John W., 133n, 137n

Rhode Island, 11, 58, 69, 96

Rhodes, James, 83–84, 179

Ridley, Clarence E., 30n, 60n

Rockefeller, Nelson A., 118, 120

Ronan, William, 119n

Sayre, Wallace S., 21n

Schick, Allen, 4n, 200n, 211n, 218n

Schlesinger, Joseph A., 178n

Schrantz, Roger, 130n, 135n

Schultze, Charles L., 42n, 201n, 202

Seckler-Hudson, Catheryn, 53n

Shafer, Raymond P., 151, 152n

Shapp, Milton J., 153

Sharkansky, Ira, 200n

Sherwood, Frank P., 47n, 77, 184

Simon, Herbert A., 30n, 60n, 68n, 164–65, 166n, 187n, 207

Smith, Harold D., 29

Smithies, Arthur, 33, 34n, 188, 196, 212

Stans, Maurice, 39

State-Local Finances Project ("the 5-5-5 project"), 43, 96, 100–01, 107, 117, 123, 125, 133, 139

Statewide Information Systems (SWIS), 106, 162

Sundelson, J. Wilner, 25n

Systems analysis, 6, 36–37

Taft, William Howard, 13, 20
Tennessee, 43n
Tennessee Valley Authority, 30
Thompson, Myron, 157n
Training courses: in California PABS
program, 140, 142–43; evaluation of,
98–103; in Hawaii PPB program, 160,
162; in Pennsylvania PPB program,
147. *See also* State-Local Finances
Project
Tax Foundation, 54
Two-track system: alternative to PPB,
215–16

U.S. Bureau of the Budget: crosswalking,
205; Dawes on role of, 21; establish-
ment of, 6; management responsibil-
ities, 28–29; state PPB role, 43, 89
U.S. Bureau of Reclamation, 30
U.S. Census Bureau, 30
U.S. Civil Service Commission, 43
U.S. Department of Agriculture, 30
U.S. Department of Defense: systems
analysis use by, 36–37; PPB in, 206n
U.S. Department of Housing and Urban
Development, 40–41; "701" state
grants, 43
U.S. Forest Service, 30
U.S. Treasury Department, 28
Upson, Lent D., 25–26
Urwick, L., 28n

van Laak, John, 118n
Vines, Kenneth N., 12n, 178n

Walker, Harvey, 26
Walker, Jack L., 12
Walker, Robert, 37
Wallace, Robert Ash, 182–83
Washington (state), 12, 97
White, Leonard D., 15n, 181
Wildavsky, Aaron B., 42, 91, 193, 194n,
195–201, 202, 211
Willoughby, William Franklin, 14n, 15,
17n, 165n
Wisconsin, 12, 42, 43n, 59, 97, 105, 117,
185, 187; PPB development in, 128–
38
Work-cost units: attitudes toward, 68; in
control budget, 26; in hybrid budget,
56–57, 60–61; in performance budget,
8–10, 71

BOOKS BY
ALEXANDER McCALL SMITH

IN THE NO. 1 LADIES' DETECTIVE AGENCY SERIES

The No. 1 Ladies' Detective Agency
Tears of the Giraffe
Morality for Beautiful Girls
The Kalahari Typing School for Men
The Full Cupboard of Life
In the Company of Cheerful Ladies
Blue Shoes and Happiness
The Good Husband of Zebra Drive
The Miracle at Speedy Motors
Tea Time for the Traditionally Built
The Double Comfort Safari Club
The Saturday Big Tent Wedding Party

IN THE ISABEL DALHOUSIE SERIES

The Sunday Philosophy Club
Friends, Lovers, Chocolate
The Right Attitude to Rain
The Careful Use of Compliments
The Comforts of a Muddy Saturday
The Lost Art of Gratitude
The Charming Quirks of Others

IN THE PORTUGUESE IRREGULAR VERBS SERIES

Portuguese Irregular Verbs
The Finer Points of Sausage Dogs
At the Villa of Reduced Circumstances

IN THE 44 SCOTLAND STREET SERIES

44 Scotland Street
Espresso Tales
Love over Scotland
The World According to Bertie
The Unbearable Lightness of Scones

The Girl Who Married a Lion and Other Tales from Africa
La's Orchestra Saves the World
Corduroy Mansions

THE SATURDAY BIG TENT WEDDING PARTY

THE SATURDAY BIG TENT

WEDDING PARTY

Alexander McCall Smith

Alfred A. Knopf Canada

PUBLISHED BY ALFRED A. KNOPF CANADA

Copyright © 2011 Alexander McCall Smith

Knopf Canada and colophon are trademarks.

www.randomhouse.ca

Library and Archives Canada Cataloguing in Publication

McCall Smith, Alexander, 1948–
The Saturday big tent wedding party / Alexander McCall Smith.

(No. 1 Ladies' Detective Agency series)
Issued also in an electronic format.

ISBN 978-0-307-39826-0

I. Title. II. Series: McCall Smith, Alexander, 1948– . No. 1 Ladies'
Detective Agency series.

PR6063.C326S37 2011   823'.914   C2010-904223-9

First Edition

Printed and bound in the United States of America

2 4 6 8 9 7 5 3 1

This book is for Professor Max Essex
of the Harvard AIDS Initiative,
in admiration of the work that he has done.

THE SATURDAY BIG TENT WEDDING PARTY

CHAPTER ONE

THE MEMORY OF LOST THINGS

MMA RAMOTSWE had by no means forgotten her late white van. It was true that she did not brood upon it, as some people dwell on things of the past, but it still came to mind from time to time, often at unexpected moments. Memories of that which we have lost are curious things—weeks, months, even years may pass without any recollection of them and then, quite suddenly, something will remind us of a lost friend, or of a favourite possession that has been mislaid or destroyed, and then we will think: *Yes, that is what I had and I have no longer.*

Her van had been her companion and friend for many years. Can a vehicle—a collection of mechanical bits and pieces, nuts and bolts and parts the names of which one has not the faintest idea of—can such a thing be a friend? Of course it can: physical objects can have personalities, at least in the eyes of their owners. To others, it may only be a van, but to the owner it may be the friend that has started loyally each morning—except sometimes; that has sat patiently during long hours of waiting outside the houses of suspected adulterers; that has carried one home in the late afternoon, tired after a day's work at the No. 1 Ladies' Detective Agency. And just like a person, a car or a van may have likes and dislikes. A good tar road is balm to man and machine and may produce a humming sound of satisfaction in both car and driver; an unpaved road, concealing behind each bend a deep pothole or tiny mountain range of corrugations, may provoke rattles and groans of protest from even the most tolerant of vehicles. For this reason, the owners of cars may be forgiven for thinking that under the metal there lurks something not all that different from a human soul.

Mma Ramotswe's van had served her well, and she loved it. Its life, though, had been a hard one. Not only had it been obliged to cope with dust, which, as anybody who lives in a dry country will know, can choke a vehicle to death, but its long-suffering suspension had been required to deal with persistent overloading, at least on the driver's side. That, of course, was the side on which Mma Ramotswe sat, and she was, by her own admission and description, a traditionally built person. Such a person can wear down even the toughest suspension, and this is exactly what happened in the case of the tiny white van, which permanently listed to starboard as a result.

Mma Ramotswe's husband, Mr. J.L.B. Matekoni, that excellent man, proprietor of Tlokweng Road Speedy Motors and widely regarded as the best mechanic in all Botswana, had done his best to address the problem, but had tired of having to change the van's shock absorbers from side to side so as to equalise the strain. Yet it went further than that. The engine itself had started to make a sinister sound, which grew in volume until eventually the big-end failed.

"I am just a mechanic, Mma Ramotswe," he had said to his wife. "A mechanic is a man who fixes cars and other vehicles. That is what a mechanic does."

Mma Ramotswe had listened politely, but her heart within her was a stone of fear. She knew that the fate of her van was at stake, and she would prefer not to know that. "I think I understand what a mechanic does, Rra," she said. "And you are a very good mechanic, quite capable of fixing a—"

She did not finish. The normally mild Mr. J.L.B. Matekoni had raised a finger. "A mechanic, Mma," he pronounced, "is different from a miracle-worker. A miracle-worker is a person who . . . works miracles. A mechanic cannot do that. And so when the time comes for a vehicle to die—and they are mortal, Mma, I can assure you— then he cannot wave a wand and make the car new again." He paused, looking at her with the air of a doctor imparting bad news. "And so . . ."

He had done his best for her, of course, and bought her a spanking new van, blue this time, with an array of buttons on the dashboard that she had not yet dared investigate, and with an engine so quiet and unobtrusive that it was sometimes possible to believe that it was not switched on at all and that it was gravity alone, or some other mysterious force, that was propelling the van down the road. She tried to appear grateful, but it was hard. It was true that the point of a vehicle was to get you from one place to another without incident, but that, she thought, was not the only consideration. If efficiency were the only value in this life, then we would be content to eat bland but nutritious food every day—and the same food at that. That would keep us alive, but it would make for very dull mealtimes. And the same was true of transport: there was all the world of difference between travelling along a highway in an air-conditioned bus, behind tinted glass, and making the same journey by a side-road, on a cart pulled by a team of mules, with the morning air fresh against your face and the branches of the acacia trees brushing past so close that you could reach out to touch the delicate green leaves. There was all that difference.

The tiny white van had gone to a scrap dealer, and that, she thought, was the end. But then she encountered a woman who told her that a nephew of hers had acquired the van, and towed it up to his place near the Tuli Block. He loved tinkering, she said, and he might be able to do something with the parts that he could strip from the body of the van. That was all Mma Ramotswe heard, and nothing more. It was a better fate, perhaps, than that of total destruction in the jaws of some metal-crushing predator, but still she hoped that the young man who had bought the van for scrap might exercise his mechanical skills and restore it. And that possibility she kept in her mind, tucked away among the other scraps of hope of the sort that we go through life with, not thinking about them very much but unwilling to let them fade away altogether.

Now, on this crisp Botswana day, at the tail end of a winter that, for all its cold mornings, was still drenched in clear and constant sun, Mma Ramotswe was reminded of her former van by something she saw on the road. She was driving past the Ministry of Water Affairs, her mind on a case that she had been working on for some time and was no nearer resolution than when she had started. She wondered whether she should not begin afresh, abandoning all the information she had obtained, and speaking to everybody again from scratch; possibly, she thought, it might be easier if . . . And then, out of the corner of her eye, she saw what seemed to be her tiny white van. It was not just that she saw a white van—they were common enough in a country where the most popular colour for a vehicle was white—it was the fact that the white vehicle she saw had the *air* of her van, a characteristic gait, so to speak, a way of moving.

Her first instinct was to stop, and this she did, pulling in to the side of the road, her wheels throwing up a cloud of dust and causing the vehicle behind her to swerve angrily. She waved an apology—that was not the sort of driving she condoned in others—before twisting round in her seat to look at the turning down which she had glimpsed the van making its way. She saw nothing, so she decided to reverse a few yards to get a better view. But no, the side-road was empty.

She frowned. Had she imagined it? She had read somewhere that those who mourn will sometimes see those they mourn—or will think they see them. But she was not really mourning her van, even if she regretted its passing; she was not the sort of woman who would allow something like that to get in the way of living. She shook her head, as if to clear it, and then, on impulse, made a sweeping U-turn, heading off on to the side-road down which she had seen the white van disappear.

A woman was sitting on a stone on the edge of the road, a small bundle of possessions on the ground beside her. Mma Ramotswe slowed down, and the woman looked at her enquiringly.

"I'm sorry, Mma," said Mma Ramotswe through her open window. "I haven't stopped to give you a ride to wherever it is you want to go."

"Ah," said the woman. "I hoped you had, Mma, but I don't mind. My son promised to come and collect me, and he will get round to it eventually."

"Sometimes men forget these things," said Mma Ramotswe. "They tell us that they are too busy to do the things we want them to do, but they have plenty of time for their own concerns."

The woman laughed. "Oh, that is right, my sister! I can hear them saying that in those voices that men have!"

Mma Ramotswe joined in the laughter. Then she asked, "Did a white van come down this way, Mma? Not a big one—a small one, same size as this one I'm in but much older—and white."

The woman frowned. "When, Mma? I have only been sitting here for half an hour."

"Oh, not that long ago," said Mma Ramotswe. "About two or three minutes ago. Maybe four."

The woman shook her head. "No, Mma. Nobody has been

down here for at least ten minutes, maybe more. And there have been no white vans—I would have seen one if there had been. I have been watching, you see."

"Are you sure, Mma?"

The woman nodded vigorously. "I am very sure, Mma. I see everything. I was in the police, you see. For three years, a long time ago, I was one of those police ladies. Then I fell off a truck and they said that I could not walk well enough to stay in. They are very foolish sometimes, and that is why the criminals sit there in those bars and tell one another stories of what the police have not done. They laugh at them and drink their beer. That is what is happening today, and God will certainly punish the politicians one day for letting this happen."

Mma Ramotswe smiled. "You are right, Mma. Those criminals need to be taught a lesson. But to go back to the van, are you absolutely sure, Mma?"

"I am one hundred per cent sure," said the woman. "If you made me stand up in the High Court in Lobatse and asked me whether I had seen a van, I would say certainly not and that is the truth."

Mma Ramotswe thanked her. "I hope that your son comes soon, Mma," she said.

"He will. When he has finished dancing with ladies or whatever he is doing, he will come."

MMA RAMOTSWE continued with her journey, completing the tasks she had been on her way to perform. She thought no more of the sighting of the van until she returned to the office a couple of hours later and mentioned the matter to Mma Makutsi.

"I saw something very strange today, Mma," she began as she settled herself at her desk.

"That is no surprise," said Mma Makutsi from the other side of the room. "There are some very strange things happening in Gaborone these days."

Mma Ramotswe would normally have agreed with this—there were very odd things happening—but she did not want Mma Makutsi to get launched on the subject of politics or the behaviour of teenagers, or any of the other subjects on which she harboured strong and sometimes unconventional views. So she went on to describe the sighting of the van and the curiously unsettling conversation she had had with the woman by the side of the road. "She was very sure that there had been no van, Mma, and I believed her. And yet I am just as sure that I saw it. I was not dreaming."

Mma Makutsi listened attentively. "So," she said. "You saw it, but she did not. What does that mean, Mma?"

Mma Ramotswe considered this for a moment. There was something on the issue in Clovis Andersen's book, she seemed to remember; *The Principles of Private Detection* had a great deal to recommend it in all departments, but it was particularly strong on the subject of evidence and the recollection of what people see. *When two or more people see something,* the great authority had written, *you would be astonished at how many different versions of events you will get! This is not because people are lying; it is more because we see things differently. One person sees one thing, and another sees something altogether different. Both believe that they are telling the truth.*

Mma Makutsi did not wait for Mma Ramotswe to answer her question. "It means that one of you saw something that the other did not."

Mma Ramotswe pondered this answer. It did not advance the matter very much, she thought.

"So the fact that one of you saw nothing," Mma Makutsi continued, "does not mean that there was nothing. She saw nothing because she did not notice anything. You saw something that she did not notice *because it was not there,* or it was not there in the way that you thought it was there."

"I'm not sure I follow you, Mma Makutsi . . ."

Mma Makutsi drew herself up behind her desk. "That van, Mma Ramotswe, was a ghost van. It was the spirit of a late van. That's what you must have seen."

Mma Ramotswe was not certain whether her assistant was being serious. Mma Makutsi could make peculiar remarks, but she had never before said anything quite as ridiculous as this. That was what made her feel that perhaps she was joking and that the proper reaction for her was to laugh. But if she laughed and her assistant was in fact being serious, then offence would be taken and this could be followed by a period of huffiness. So she confined her reaction to an innocent question: "Do vans have ghosts, Mma? Do you think that likely?"

"I don't see why not," said Mma Makutsi. "If people have ghosts, then why shouldn't other things have them? What makes us so special that only we can have ghosts? What makes us think that, Mma?"

"Well, I'm not so sure that there are ghosts of people anyway," said Mma Ramotswe. "If we go to heaven when we die, then who are these ghosts that people talk about? No, it doesn't seem likely to me."

Mma Makutsi frowned. "Ah, but who says that everybody goes to heaven?" she asked. "There are people who will not get any-where near heaven. I can think of many . . ."

Mma Ramotswe's curiosity was too much for her. "Such as, Mma?"

Mma Makutsi showed no hesitation in replying. "Violet Sepho-tho," she said quickly. "There will be no place for her in heaven—

that is well known. So she will have to stay down here in Gaborone, walking around and not being seen by anybody because she will be a ghost." She paused, an expression of delight crossing her face. "And, Mma, she will be a ghost in high-heeled shoes! Can you imagine that, Mma? A ghost tottering around on those silly high heels that she wears. It is a very funny thought, Mma. Even those who saw such a ghost would not be frightened but would burst out laughing. Other ghosts would laugh, Mma—they would, although we wouldn't hear them, of course."

"Unless we were ghosts ourselves by that stage," interjected Mma Ramotswe. "Then we would hear them."

This warning made Mma Makutsi fall silent. It had been an appetising picture that she had been painting, and she slightly resented Mma Ramotswe's spoiling it like this. But her resentment did not persist, as it occurred to her that Mma Ramotswe, having possibly just seen a ghost herself—even if only a ghost van—might be in need of a restorative cup of red bush tea.

"I think it is time that I put the kettle on," she said. "All this talk of ghosts . . ."

Mma Ramotswe laughed. "There are no ghosts, Mma. No ghost people, no ghost vans. These things are just stories we make up to frighten ourselves."

Mma Makutsi, now standing beside the kettle, looked out of the window. Yes, she thought, one can say that sort of thing in broad daylight, under this wide and sunlit Botswana sky, but would one say the same thing with equal conviction at night, when one was out in the bush, perhaps, away from the streetlights of town, and surrounded by the sounds of the night—sounds that could not be easily explained away and could be anything, things known or unknown, things friendly or unfriendly, things that it was better not to think about? She shuddered. It was not a good idea to let one's mind dwell on these matters, and she was sure it was best to think about something quite different. And so she said to Mma Ramotswe, "Mma, I am worried about Charlie. I am very worried."

Mma Ramotswe looked up from her desk. "Charlie, Mma Makutsi? But we have always been worried about Charlie, right from the beginning." She smiled at her assistant. "I'm sure that even when he was a very small boy, this high, his mother was shaking her head and saying that she was worried about Charlie. And all those girls, I'm sure that they have been saying the same thing for years. It is what people say about him."

Mma Makutsi smiled too, but only weakly. "Yes, Mma," she said. "But this time it's different. I think now that we have to do something about him."

Mma Ramotswe sighed. Whatever it was, Mma Makutsi was probably right. But she was not sure that it was the responsibility of the No. 1 Ladies' Detective Agency to deal with Charlie's problems—whatever they were. Charlie was an apprentice of Tlokweng Road Speedy Motors, and it would have to be Mr. J.L.B. Matekoni who took action.

She looked across the room at her assistant, who was frowning with concentration as she poured the boiling water into the teapot. "Very well, Mma Makutsi," she said. "Tell me what the trouble is. What has our young friend been up to now?"

CHAPTER TWO

THE CHARLIE PROBLEM

THAT EVENING, Mma Ramotswe pondered what she had been told by Mma Makutsi. She thought about this while she prepared the evening meal, in an empty house, as Mr. J.L.B. Matekoni had taken Puso and Motholeli to choir practice in the school hall. Both children had good voices, although Puso was plagued by embarrassment when he sang, closing his eyes as a result.

"Puso," the choirmaster scolded him, "we do not close our eyes when we sing. We keep them open so that people who are listening know that we are not asleep. If you close your eyes, then maybe next you will start to close your mouth, and that is not good for singing, is it?"

In spite of this public upbraiding, Puso continued to close his eyes. The choirmaster learned to ignore the matter, though: the boy had a naturally good ear for music, and that was something that was worth cultivating in spite of other failings.

Mma Ramotswe went over Mma Makutsi's revelations about Charlie and made sure that she knew how best to relate them to Mr. J.L.B. Matekoni. It was a matter for adults to discuss among themselves, not one for the ears of children, so when the three of them eventually returned she fed the children first; that way, she and Mr. J.L.B. Matekoni would be able to talk freely.

"We shall have our dinner a bit later," she said to her husband. "If you are too hungry to wait, I can give you something. But it might be better not to eat until we can talk privately."

Mr. J.L.B. Matekoni nodded, and sniffed at the cooking smells drifting out from the kitchen. "It smells very good, Mma Ramotswe," he said. "So I shall wait."

"I have made—" she began, but he silenced her with a finger to his lips.

"It will be a surprise." He paused, before whispering, "What do we have to talk about that cannot be spoken of in front of the children? Is it one of your cases?"

She shook her head. "No, it is one of *your* cases, Rra."

He was puzzled. "I have no cases," he said. "You are the detective; I am only—"

She leaned forward. "Charlie," she whispered. "He is your responsibility, is he not?"

He looked grave. Ever since he had taken on Charlie as his apprentice—and that had been an inordinately long time ago—he had worried about the young man. At first his anxiety had been kept in check by the knowledge that apprenticeships do not last forever, but then the realisation slowly dawned on him that some apprenticeships appeared to disprove that rule. Charlie and Fanwell, his fellow apprentice, should have finished their training years earlier. Fanwell, at least, was now only a month or two short of completion, having at last passed the examinations of the Mechanical Apprenticeship Board and needing only a final period of assessment—a formality—before being registered as a fully qualified mechanic. Charlie, however, had failed his examinations time after time, mainly because he never bothered to prepare himself.

"You could pass very easily, you know," Mr. J.L.B. Matekoni

told him after the last unsuccessful attempt. "All it needs is a bit of study. You are not a stupid young man—you have a brain in that head of yours, and yet you will not use it. You are like a farmer who has good rich soil and plants no melons in it. That is what you are like."

"Mmm," said Charlie, licking his lips. "I like melons, Boss!"

"There you are," said Mr. J.L.B. Matekoni, with exasperation in his voice. "You are talking about melons when you should be talking about engines. That is exactly what I mean."

"But you are the one who started talking about melons," said Charlie. "I did not start it, Boss!"

It was extraordinarily frustrating, but it seemed that there was little that could be done. Mr. J.L.B. Matekoni was not only the finest mechanic in Botswana, he was also the kindest. And it was for this reason that he could not bring himself to dismiss the young man and give his place to another who was more willing to learn. Charlie would have to content himself with being an unqualified mechanical assistant—a sort of perpetual apprentice.

There were other reasons to worry, of course. There was Charlie's preoccupation with girls, and his constant talking about them. This distracted Fanwell, who was an altogether more serious young man, and it was also potentially bad for the image of the garage. On more than one occasion, Mr. J.L.B. Matekoni had been embarrassed in the presence of a client when the idle, girl-focused chatter of his apprentices had been quite audible. This had even happened once when a client who was a man of the cloth had been collecting his car and had heard Charlie talking about a girl. The two young men were under a truck and were probably unaware of the presence of the minister, but even so it had been a very awkward moment for their employer.

"Boy, oh boy," Charlie had said, "that one is very fast! She is fast all right!"

Mr. J.L.B. Matekoni had cleared his throat and done his best to spare the minister's blushes. "They are talking about a car," he explained hurriedly. "A very fast car. You know how young men are about speed."

He had raised his voice as he gave this explanation, in the hope that Charlie would realise they were not alone. But this had been to no avail.

"And she drinks too," Charlie continued. "I'm telling you, Fanwell, she likes her drink. Ow!"

"That is fuel consumption," said Mr. J.L.B. Matekoni to the minister. "Some cars these days have a very thirsty engine. It's because modern engines are so powerful. Unlike your car here, Reverend." And with that, he had given the side of the minister's car a loud tap, again in the hope of sending a message to the young men.

It made Mr. J.L.B. Matekoni feel hot at the back of the neck just to think about that moment—the minister had not been fooled—and he did not like to remember it. So when Mma Ramotswe told him that they needed to talk about Charlie, he sighed with a dread that seemed quite to take away any pleasure brought by the anticipation of dinner. A good meal is not nearly so attractive, he mused, if it is accompanied by thoughts of young men like Charlie.

SO, MMA RAMOTSWE," said Mr. J.L.B. Matekoni. "So you have made me a very good stew." He sniffed at the delicious steam rising up from his plate. "But you have also warned me that we have a Charlie problem. Tell me: Is it a big Charlie problem or a little one?"

Mma Ramotswe could not stop herself from smiling.

"Did I say something funny?" asked Mr. J.L.B. Matekoni. "You did say that—"

"Oh yes, Rra. I did say that we have to talk about Charlie. And it is a serious matter. It's just that the answer to your question is that this problem is both big and little."

Mr. J.L.B. Matekoni stared at her. Perhaps his wife had spent too long a time as a private detective and solver of mysteries; maybe too much time in that profession made one inherently enigmatic. He had seen that sort of thing before—cases where people had been so affected by their jobs as to change in their very nature. His cousin who had worked for the immigration authorities had become so suspicious that he began to suspect that just about everybody was in the country illegally. And then there was that butcher who had ended up not eating meat at all and would only eat potatoes and beans—that had been a very surprising development in a country as committed to cattle as was Botswana. Was something similar happening to Mma Ramotswe, he wondered?

"You'll have to explain, Mma Ramotswe," he said. "I am a simple mechanic; I am not a solver of puzzles and things like that."

Mma Ramotswe dipped her fork into her mashed pumpkin. "It is a big problem because it's serious," she said. "It is a small problem because it involves something small. A small person. In fact, it involves . . . a baby."

Mr. J.L.B. Matekoni closed his eyes. It did not matter if Mma Ramotswe said nothing more. He understood.

He opened his eyes again. Mma Ramotswe was looking at him, and she was no longer smiling. "Yes," she said. "You know what I'm going to say, don't you, Rra?"

"Charlie has a baby."

"Yes." And then she added, "Two. Twins. Two boys."

There was a silence.

"You had better tell me, Mma Ramotswe. I am strong. I have heard everything before. There can be no surprises when it comes to that young man."

"Listen to this, then," she said.

She retold the story she had heard from Mma Makutsi. It was related in a quiet, matter-of-fact way, without any of the short gasps of disapproval and tut-tuts with which Mma Makutsi had punctuated her narrative. But it was still enough to distract Mr. J.L.B. Matekoni from his stew, which became colder and colder on the plate.

Mma Makutsi had heard the story from an entirely unimpeachable source—the mother of the young woman who had given birth to Charlie's twins. She was related in a distant way to Phuti Radiphuti, and together with her husband ran a painting and decorating business in the west of the city. The business had prospered and now employed more than fifty painters; its name, Second Coat, could be seen on vans throughout the town, and they had several important contracts with large concerns, including diamond companies.

This couple, Mma Makutsi had gone on to explain, were called Leonard and Mercy Ramkhwane. They were hard-working and were thought to have deserved every bit of their success. They had only one child, Prudence, who was now in her early twenties. She had been at Gaborone Secondary School and had been a very well-known high-school athlete who had taken all the trophies for running. "It was a big pity that she did not run away from Charlie," Mma Makutsi had observed. "Many girls would do far better to run away from men, Mma."

The story continued. Charlie had met Prudence when Leonard brought a car into the garage for attention. On hearing this, Mr. J.L.B. Matekoni groaned. "I know that man," he said, putting a hand to his head. "I do not know him well, but I know him."

Mma Ramotswe lowered her eyes. "Well, he brought his daughter with him to the garage."

Mr. J.L.B. Matekoni groaned again. "So that means she met Charlie under my roof."

"No," said Mma Ramotswe. "The garage roof is not your roof. This is your roof here—in this house. There is a difference, Rra."

He shook his head. "It is my roof. I own it. When it leaks, I am the one who must fix it. That means it is my roof, and I am responsible for what happens under it."

She tried, with gentle persuasion, to convince him that he could not possibly be held responsible for Charlie's meeting Prudence, but his view was not to be changed. So she continued the tale, just as it had been told her by Mma Makutsi.

Charlie had somehow managed to make an arrangement with Prudence—under the very eyes of her father—to meet at a club that young people favoured. Good music, he had said; the latest thing. And what girl could resist such an invitation? Not Prudence, it seemed, and the inevitable happened. At first their relationship was kept secret from her parents; she still lived at home, but, at twenty, was largely independent. But then Charlie became the established boyfriend, and although not what Leonard and Mercy had had in mind for their daughter, he was treated with the courtesy and graciousness a couple like that would always accord to others.

"They are good people, you see," said Mma Ramotswe. "They follow the old Botswana ways. They are polite."

Mr. J.L.B. Matekoni nodded. Charlie did not follow the old Botswana ways. The old Botswana ways would never have approved of using a hammer to move a reluctant nut on an engine manifold. The old Botswana ways respected the *thread* of a bolt; the old Botswana ways understood the consequences of putting diesel in a petrol engine; the old Botswana ways . . . You could go on.

The relationship had been going on for a month or two when Prudence realised that she was pregnant. She told Charlie, and then she told her parents. Charlie left.

"Left her entirely?" asked Mr. J.L.B. Matekoni. "Altogether?"

It was Mma Ramotswe's turn to sigh. "No more calls on that phone of his, the silver one. No more going round to her parents' house. Nothing."

"They call that leaving somebody in the lurch," muttered Mr. J.L.B. Matekoni. "So what happened, Mma Ramotswe?"

"The girl calmed her father down. Apparently the old Botswana ways deserted him for a while, but he did not do anything. And that was that. Twins arrived. So Charlie is now the father of twins."

"He knows that?"

"Oh, he knows that all right. I'm sure she told him."

"And . . ."

Mma Ramotswe spread her hands in resignation. "And nothing. Charlie has done nothing." She sat back in her chair, indicating that this was the end of the story, or at least the end of what she knew of the story.

Mr. J.L.B. Matekoni looked down at his plate. He had touched very little of the stew she had made him—that delicious serving of Botswana beef—and now it was quite cold.

"I shall heat it up again for you," offered Mma Ramotswe.

He shook his head, reaching for his fork. "I do not mind, Mma. Your cooking is always so good that it does not matter whether it is hot or cold. Either way it is all that a man could ever desire. And that is the truth."

She smiled at him. This was how a man should be, she thought. And there was Charlie, working every day with this great man, this embodiment of all that the country stood for, and none of it, not one tiny bit, seemed to rub off on the young man.

She wondered whether to bring up the subject of what they

were to do now, or whether to move on. She decided on the latter. It was sometimes best, she believed, to let things sink in before you took a decision. So they would sleep on this disclosure and talk about it the following day, or even the day after that. Not that there was much to be said, as there was really only one thing to do in these circumstances. And that was to try to get Charlie to face up to his responsibilities.

It was easier said than done—Mma Ramotswe was well aware of that. Charlie would either deny that he was the father, or he would shrug his shoulders in that stubborn way of his and say that the twins were the young woman's affair. "Children are not men's business," he had said once. "It is women who must look after them, not men. These people who say that men must do that work too are talking nonsense, and they are all women anyway. Men have far more important work to do than that. Ha!"

Mma Makutsi had overheard this remark and had been so cross that her glasses misted over; that was always a bad sign, Mma Ramotswe knew. The recollection of this gave her an idea: they could ask Mma Makutsi to deal with the problem of speaking to Charlie. They would give her their full support, she thought, but the leader of the campaign—the general, so to speak—should be Grace Makutsi, recipient of the highest mark in history in the final examinations of the Botswana Secretarial College (ninety-seven per cent) and scourge of all those who would shift their feet, look the other way, or, for that matter, deny the existence of twins.

Yes, she was the one.

CHAPTER THREE

YOU ARE THE LADY TO HELP PEOPLE

SEATED AT THEIR RESPECTIVE DESKS, at a time when the morning air was still fresh and clear and the sky quite empty of clouds, Mma Ramotswe and Mma Makutsi surveyed what the day had in store for them. There were two appointments, one at ten o'clock and one not until well into the afternoon. The second appointment was straightforward enough—a discussion about a statement Mma Ramotswe was to make in a child custody case: simple, perhaps, but emotionally testing nonetheless. "You cannot divide a child's heart in two," she had observed to Mma Makutsi, "and yet that is what some people wish to do. A child has only one heart."

"And the rest of us?" Mma Makutsi had asked. "Do we not have one heart too?"

Mma Ramotswe nodded. "Yes, we have only one heart, but as you grow older, your heart grows bigger. A child loves only one or two things; we love so many things."

"Such as?"

Mma Ramotswe smiled. "Botswana. Rain. Cattle. Friends. Our

children. Our late relatives. The smell of woodsmoke in the morning. Red bush tea . . ."

That was the afternoon appointment; ten o'clock would be different. She knew nothing about the man who had telephoned and arranged to see her, nothing beyond his name and the fact that he lived outside town. He had not wanted to come into the office—a common concern for clients, who appeared to worry they might be seen entering the premises of the No. 1 Ladies' Detective Agency. Mma Ramotswe understood this, even if she sought to reassure them that nobody really paid much attention to those who crossed her doorstep. She wanted to believe that, and almost convinced herself, but she was not sure that it was entirely true. People noticed things in Botswana; they saw who went into which house and they speculated as to what took them there; they noticed who was driving which car and who was in the passenger seat. People saw these things, in much the same way as an expert tracker in the Kalahari will look at the ground and see, written in the sand, the history of all the animal comings and goings.

"I do not wish to come into your office, Mma," the caller had said. "I do not wish to offend you, but when you have a business like mine, you have to be careful. People might see."

"If that is what you wish, Rra, then that is not a problem for me. We can meet somewhere else. There is a café I know at Riverwalk. You know that place?"

There was a mumbling at the other end of the line, as if somebody was being consulted. Then the voice said, "I am a bit out of touch with town, Mma, but I can find out about it. I have friends who know Gaborone well. I can be there."

The caller had given his name, Botsalo Moeti, and had said that he would be coming into town from a place to the south of

Gaborone. "Not a village you will know, Mma, as it is very small. I need not give you its name."

"But that would be helpful, Rra. I might know it."

This was greeted with silence. "I do not think so, Mma. As I said, it is very small."

She had not pressed the issue, and the matter was left there. But after she had rung off and replaced the telephone handset in its cradle, she had looked across the room at Mma Makutsi and said, "That man is scared, Mma. I can tell it in his voice."

Mma Makutsi's eyes had widened behind her large round glasses. "There are many people who are frightened of something or other, Mma," she said. "Even here in Botswana there are people who are frightened."

They had looked at each other without saying anything. Each knew what the other meant; each knew that there were things that people preferred not to acknowledge, not to admit, lest the admission encourage that which needed no encouragement.

It was Mma Ramotswe who broke the silence. "I am not going to be frightened, Mma Makutsi."

Her assistant took off her glasses and polished them energetically with her handkerchief. "And I am not going to be frightened either, Mma. Even if . . ."

"Even if what, Mma?"

Mma Makutsi shook her head; she had said enough, she felt.

AT NINE-FIFTEEN, three-quarters of an hour before Mma Ramotswe was due to meet Mr. Botsalo Moeti, Mma Makutsi made tea. This was an occasion that was an established fixture in the timetable of the No. 1 Ladies' Detective Agency, but less observed in the daily programme of Tlokweng Road Speedy Motors, with whom Mma Ramotswe and Mma Makutsi shared premises. Mr.

J.L.B. Matekoni was happy to punctuate the day with tea, but only downed tools if the work in which he was engaged had reached a natural break. This meant that out of every five tea-breaks, he and his apprentices usually took only three, or sometimes just one or two.

"Everybody else has a regular tea-break, Boss," complained Charlie. "Go into a government office and what do you see? Everybody drinking tea. Same thing in the banks. More tea. Why not us?"

"Because we are not an ordinary business," sighed Mr. J.L.B. Matekoni. "Nor are we a government department. We are like a hospital—a hospital for cars. Hospitals do not suddenly say, 'We have had enough; we are going to stop curing people while we have a cup of tea.' They do not say that, Charlie."

The analogy with a hospital appealed to him, and he developed it in an attempt to get Charlie to understand the need to care about his work. "Yes, we are a hospital for cars, and you and I—what are we? We are surgeons, Charlie; that is what we are. And if you go into a hospital, do you see the surgeons using hammers on their patients? Spanners, not hammers: remember that."

The question was a pointed one. He had tried so often to stop Charlie's tendency to use a hammer on recalcitrant engine parts, but his efforts had met with little success.

"They don't use spanners either," said Charlie, winking at Fanwell.

Mr. J.L.B. Matekoni sighed. He sighed a great deal in his conversations with Charlie. "It is not something to laugh about."

Charlie adopted a serious expression. "I am not laughing, Boss, even if I'm thinking of a surgeon using a spanner on some poor man. Ow! Like this. Ow!"

"He would use an anaesthetic before he got out his spanner," said Fanwell. "We do not give anaesthetics to cars."

That morning the making of tea came at a time when the workshop was quiet, so both apprentices and Mr. J.L.B. Matekoni joined the two ladies in the agency office. Mr. J.L.B. Matekoni came in first, to be greeted politely by Mma Makutsi. Then came Fanwell, wiping his hands on a blue paper towel, and finally Charlie. As Charlie entered, Mma Makutsi glanced over at Mma Ramotswe. Nothing further had been said since their discussion the previous day, and Mma Ramotswe had not yet raised with her assistant the question of her tackling the young man; but nonetheless a meaningful look was exchanged. Mma Ramotswe hoped that Mma Makutsi would not launch into her own attack there and then: she could be impetuous, and might not judge her moment too well. Holding her assistant's eye, she mouthed the word "No."

Returning to her chair, Mma Makutsi took a sip of tea. "Well, Mr. J.L.B. Matekoni," she said brightly, "any well-known cars in trouble?"

Mr. J.L.B. Matekoni nursed his mug in cupped hands. "Nothing," he said. "We fixed Bishop Mwamba's car last week, and that tall government minister's car the week before that. This week it is just ordinary cars—no well-known ones."

"All cars are important, Boss," ventured Fanwell. "You said that yourself."

"Of course they are," said Mr. J.L.B. Matekoni. "We treat all cars the same."

Mma Makutsi was watching Charlie, who was leaning against a filing cabinet. Becoming aware of her scrutiny, the young man gave her a deliberately nonchalant stare.

"What about those vans?" she asked.

Mr. J.L.B. Matekoni frowned. "What vans?"

Mma Makutsi spoke slowly and deliberately. "The painters'

vans. The ones that belong to that nice man—what is his name?—
Leonard something-or-other."

There was a sudden silence, at least in that small office; outside, the cicadas, indifferent to human drama, continued their
screech. Charlie stood quite still, his mug of tea suspended in mid-
air, unsipped.

Mma Makutsi continued regardless. "I thought you were hoping that he would bring all those vans in here. That would be very
good business, wouldn't it?"

Mr. J.L.B. Matekoni looked anxiously in Mma Ramotswe's
direction. "Yes," he muttered, "that would be good. But I'm sure
that he has an arrangement in place for his vans. They do not seem
to be breaking down—somebody must be looking after them."

"I thought he was a very nice man," continued Mma Makutsi.
"But I don't know him, really." She paused. "Phuti does, though. He
knows that whole family. The husband, the wife, the daughter—"

"Mma Makutsi," blurted out Mma Ramotswe, "look at the
time! Here we are drinking tea, and I have to get ready to go to meet
a client. We must get ourselves organised. Come on, everybody,
drink up. Tea-time over. Right now. Over."

SHE WAS EARLY for her appointment and decided to spend a few
minutes window-shopping at one of the clothes shops inside the
rambling Riverwalk complex. She had no intention of buying
anything—money was tight, with several clients being slow to pay
their bills that month—but she felt that it never did any harm just
to look. In fact, Mma Ramotswe found as much pleasure in looking
as in an actual purchase; more perhaps, because looking involved
no guilt, whereas purchasing often did.

This was something that Mr. J.L.B. Matekoni, in common with

most men, simply did not understand. "The whole point about shopping," he had remarked, "is that you go somewhere and you buy something you need. Then you take it home and use it. That is what shopping is about."

Mma Ramotswe had shaken her head. "No, Mr. J.L.B. Matekoni. You are right about many things, Rra, but you are not right about that. That is not what shopping is about."

He had been perplexed. "Then perhaps I'm missing something."

"Yes, you are."

"Tell me, then, Mma Ramotswe, what is shopping for? It seems that I have misunderstood the whole thing."

She smiled. There was much that men simply did not understand, but she had never been much concerned about this lack of understanding. Indeed, in her view it was one of the things that made men so appealing. There were men's things and then there were women's things. The list of which was not written in stone, and it was quite possible for a woman to enter the world of men— and the other way round—but she saw no point in denying that women liked to do certain things and men liked to do other things. Nor did she doubt that these preferences were one of the reasons why women liked men and men liked women. So it was perfectly possible that there were men who liked shopping, and who understood exactly what it was all about, but Mma Ramotswe had yet to meet such a man. Maybe they existed elsewhere—in France, perhaps—but they did not seem to be much in evidence in Botswana.

Of course, she knew that you had to be careful about this sort of thing. Like all women, she had suffered the put-downs of men, and there were still plenty of men who were prepared to say to women, *You cannot do this, you cannot do that, because you are just a woman*. She remembered many years ago, as a girl in the national school at Mochudi, hearing a teacher—a man—say to the class: "These are good jobs for boys, but not for girls; girls can do something else." She had smarted at the injustice. Why could women not do those jobs? You did not have to be strong, with bulging muscles, to be a pilot or an engineer, or a president, for that matter. Such men, she discovered, such men who put women down, were really rather weak themselves, building themselves up by belittling women. A truly strong man would never want that.

A truly strong man . . . Mr. J.L.B. Matekoni was one such, and so, too, had been her father, the late Obed Ramotswe, that great man, that good man, who had never suggested that there were any limits to what she could do with her life. He had been old-fashioned, it was true, but he had always said that women should stand on their own two feet and do what they wanted. And in many respects he had clearly been in advance of his time when he had remarked, as he often did, that the day when women took over important jobs from men would be the day that things got better. But not even Obed Ramotswe, her precious daddy, understood shopping as a woman understands it. He would not have wanted to linger, as Mma Ramotswe now did, before the window of a clothing shop and admire the tempting display within.

She gazed at the window. The proprietors of this shop had understood the situation very well: they sold clothing for both men and women, but in their window the women's clothes were tastefully displayed, adorning coquettishly posed mannequins or draped temptingly on small supports, whereas the men's clothing, distinctly less colourful, was simply placed on a low wooden table with the price tags showing. She saw that the women's clothing had no prices; that was as it should be, because if the price were to be displayed then that would spoil the fun of potential customers outside. They might be put off by realising that they could not afford this dress or that dress, whereas with no prices attached, they could dream of affording them all.

She noticed, too, that the mannequins modelling the dresses— those posturing moulded figures—were all waif-like and thin, as if the slightest wind might come and blow them away like so many leaves. Why were there not any traditionally built mannequins? Why were there not comfortable ladies in the window, ladies with whom those on the other side of the glass—not thin and hungry ladies, but ladies whose breakfast had clearly been generous enough to see them through the day—could identify? That was another thing that women had to be wary of, thought Mma Ramotswe; that was another way of putting women down—telling them that they should stop eating.

Her eye wandered to a small display of women's shoes in one corner of the window. One pair, in particular, caught her attention: cream-coloured, with high heels and two small buttons to fasten the straps. These shoes, she thought, would very much appeal to Mma Makutsi, and would be suitable for her wedding. There was talk of a date now, and she must be thinking about her bridal outfit. These shoes would go well with a white dress, but especially appealing to Mma Makutsi would be the buttons, each of which had a single mock diamond, winking even now in reflected light like little beacons. She would tell her about them; perhaps she would even suggest that they visit the shop together so that she could advise.

She glanced at her watch and dragged herself away from the window display. The café, which was round the corner, overlooking a parking lot, was a favourite of hers as it afforded a good view of one of the entrances to the shopping centre. If you sat there long enough, as Mma Ramotswe occasionally did, you might observe all

Botswana pass by, or at least a large part of it, and you would never fail to see at least one friend to whom you might give a wave.

As she approached the café, she realised that she had said nothing to her client as to how they might recognise one another. What if there were several men sitting at tables by themselves, as sometimes happened? Would she have to go up to each and say, "I am Mma Ramotswe"? This could be embarrassing, as the man would be obliged to give his own name and enquire after her health—if he had any manners at all—and then there would be an awkward silence. And Mma Ramotswe would then say, "And what is troubling you, Rra?" and he would reply, "Well, nothing actually," because he would not be the client but a perfect stranger instead.

She looked about the café. There were several places to sit in the indoor part, and these were all empty. Outside, spilling onto the pavement that ran alongside the parking lot, there were more tables, and these were mostly occupied: a young couple, completely self-absorbed; two middle-aged women with shopping bags at their feet; two teenage girls discussing a photograph one of them was holding—of a boy, no doubt—and highly amused by something—by the boy, of course; and a man sitting by himself. She knew immediately that he was her client and, as he looked up, he knew that she was Mma Ramotswe.

She made her way to his table.

"Mma Ramotswe?"

She reached out and they shook hands.

"Mr. Moeti. *Dumela,* Rra."

There were the usual enquiries of the formal greeting, while she sat down. He had risen to greet her and sat down too, awkwardly, even furtively. Nervousness, she thought. And then, looking for the first time into the eyes of her new client, she saw something else, and that was fear.

It surprised her at first, because this Moeti was a large man, not in girth but in height, and she never expected tall men to show fear. As the waitress came over to take their order, Mma Ramotswe noticed further things about Mr. Moeti: she looked at his shoes and saw that they were well polished, but with a fine layer of dust that had settled since he put them on that morning; she saw the well-pressed khaki trousers, and the two pens in the top pocket of his shirt. So he was a farmer, but he had not been born to it; she was sure of that.

But there was still the fear: that was the predominant impression, and it intrigued and troubled her.

She opened the conversation brightly. "You found this place all right, Rra. I like coming here. You can see everybody." She made a gesture towards the car park. "These big shops are not like the markets we used to have, are they? So we need places like this instead."

He looked out over the car park. Forty-five, she thought. Maybe fifty; old enough to remember how things used to be.

"Yes," he said. "It is a good place."

"And you can talk here," she went on. "The tables are far enough apart to do that. Nobody can hear, except those two girls over there, perhaps, and they would not be interested in what we have to say—their heads are full of boys."

He glanced in the direction of the girls; the photograph was still coming under intense scrutiny. He turned to Mma Ramotswe and smiled weakly. "And their phones," he said.

"Ah," said Mma Ramotswe, "their mobile phones. Yes, that is a big problem, isn't it? So much talking going on. The air above Botswana must be almost full by now with all these words."

He looked down at the ground.

She leaned forward. "I can tell that you are anxious, Rra." She wanted to say that he was frightened, but decided that to refer to anxiety, rather than fear, was more polite—at this stage.

He kept his eyes fixed on the ground. His hands were clasped together on his lap; now she saw them tighten involuntarily. "It is not easy to talk about some things," he muttered.

"Of course it isn't, Rra. I know that. I have many people who come to me who find it very hard. I understand that very well." She paused, watching the effect of her words. "But do you know something, Rra? Talking about it—just saying a few words—is often enough to help. Words can make big things little, you know."

He lifted his gaze. There was still fear in his eyes, she thought; every bit as much fear as there had been at the beginning of their meeting.

"I am a farmer," he said quietly.

"Yes?"

She waited for him to say something more, but he was silent.

"You told me that you lived just south of town," she prompted. "But you did not say where."

"Over there," he said, indicating vaguely. "It's off the Lobatse road. Half an hour."

"Cattle?" she asked.

"Of course." Everyone had cattle, Mma Ramotswe included.

"I was not always a farmer," he continued. "I worked for many years with a mining company. I was in charge of recruitment."

She nodded. "My father was a miner . . . over on that side." She inclined her head in the direction of South Africa.

"That was hard," he said.

"Very. But he came back to Botswana. Then he became late." She realised that she had, in these few words, summed up the life of the man who meant more to her than any other. Yet anybody's life story could be told in such a way, her own as much as anyone else's. She had married a bad man and then been abandoned. She had lost her baby. She had loved her father, and when he died she had opened a detective agency. She had married again, this time to a good man. That was her life in a few sentences.

He started to talk again. "I was left some money by my uncle, and I had also saved hard. So I had enough to stop working for the mining company and buy a small farm. It is not bad land—not the best, but it is good enough for me. We—that is my wife and I—were very happy with it. I bought some cattle and have been living down there."

She nodded encouragingly. It was the commonest dream in Botswana: a small patch of land to call one's own and a herd of cattle. A man who achieved that had achieved everything. Of course it was beyond the reach of most, and sights were lowered accordingly. A share in a small herd of cattle, even half a cow, was as much as many could aspire to. She had been in a room once, a single room lived in by a family struggling to survive financially, and had seen, pinned on the wall, a grubby photograph of a cow. She had known immediately that this was the family's most precious possession—the thing that transformed that mean room into a home.

"So I have had some cattle," Mr. Moeti went on. "Then one died."

"I am sorry, Rra."

"Thank you." He went on: "It did not die of any disease, Mma. Its legs were cut. Like this." He made a sawing motion against his wrist. "It went down on the ground and I found it the next morning. This thing, you see, happened at night."

This thing happened at night. The words made her shiver.

"And then, a week or so ago, it happened again. Another beast down. Same reason." He looked at her. "Now you see, Mma, why I am anxious. That is the thing that is making me anxious."

"Of course. Oh, Rra, this is very bad. Your cattle . . ."

"And it could get worse," he muttered. "If somebody cuts the legs of your cattle, then might they not cut your legs too?"

She was quick to reassure him. "Oh, I don't think so, Rra."

"Don't you, Mma?" There was a note of desperation in his voice. "You may not think that here in the middle of Gaborone, in this place with all its sunlight. But would you say that at night, out at my place, where the only light at night is the light of the moon and stars? And they can't help you, Mma. The moon and stars are no help."

She made a conciliatory gesture. "No, you're right, Rra. I can see why you are frightened." She paused. Why had he come to her, rather than to the authorities? "You have been to the police?"

He shook his head. "What can they do? They will say to me: somebody has killed your cattle, and then they will go away. How can they do anything more than that?"

It was a common view, even if a misguided one. The Botswana Police did act, and the courts did work, even if in other, less fortunate countries one might not be able to say the same thing with great conviction. "They might be able to—if you gave them some idea of who was doing it."

His response came quickly. "I can't. I have no idea."

"You have enemies, Rra? Enemies from the past? Mining enemies?"

He appeared not to have expected this suggestion, and he frowned. "Why would I have enemies from mining? I was just the man who did the recruiting. I had nothing to do with what happened in the mines."

"No, I suppose you didn't. I just think that it's important to consider who may have a reason to do this to you. Is there anybody like that?"

It is hard, she thought; it is hard for us to think of people who dislike us because none of us, in our heart, believes that we deserve the hate of others.

He shook his head. "I have no idea, Mma. And that is why I

have come to you. You are the one to find out these things and save my cattle. I am asking you to do that, Mma Ramotswe, because everybody says that you are the lady to help people."

YOU ARE THE LADY to help people. The words came back to her as she made her way home that evening. It was pleasing to know that people thought that of you, but worrying too. You could not help everybody—nobody could—because the world was too full of need and troubles, a wide ocean of them, and one person could not begin to deal with all that. And yet, even if you were just one person, and even if you could never solve everybody's problems, when somebody came to you and looked frightened, you could not say, *Go away, I cannot do anything for you.* You say, instead, *Yes, I will do what I can.* And then, when you go home from work at the end of the day, you sit on your small verandah watching the day turn to dusk, nursing a cup of red bush tea in your hands, and wonder what on earth you can possibly do to help.

CHAPTER FOUR

RICH PEOPLE HAVE MANY CATTLE

THAT EVENING was one of the nights in the week that Phuti Radiphuti, proprietor of the Double Comfort Furniture Store, came to eat dinner at the modest rented house of his officially betrothed fiancée, Grace Makutsi, associate detective at the No. 1 Ladies' Detective Agency. Their dinner arrangements had changed since the accident in which Phuti had lost his right foot and a small portion of his leg. Rescued from the clutches of his jealous aunt, during the rest of his recuperation he had been looked after by Mma Potokwane, who had found him a spare room in the back of her home at the orphan farm. At first Mma Makutsi had come to see him at the Potokwane house and had meals with him there, but this arrangement was never entirely satisfactory from her point of view.

"It's not that I don't like Mma Potokwane," she had said. "She is a very great lady—one of the greatest ladies in Botswana. But . . ."

"You do not need to say it," said Phuti. "She is also a very bossy lady. A good but bossy lady. I think there are many people like that."

Mma Makutsi smiled. "Yes. Have you noticed how she tells us

to eat up after she has put the food on the table? It is as if she is talking to one of the children. 'Eat up now—leave nothing on your plate.' Have you noticed that?"

Phuti had. "And she even told me the other day that I could have another piece of cake if I was good. I think she forgets that we are adults."

"I think that maybe the time has come for us to have dinner at my house again," said Mma Makutsi. "Do you think that you can drive yet?"

Phuti had shaken his head. He did not yet feel able to do that, he explained, although he hoped that it would not be long. The prosthetic foot he had been provided with by the hospital was taking a bit longer than he had imagined to get used to, and it would be a few weeks, he felt, before he could drive his car again. "But I have somebody from the furniture store who can drive me. He is one of our regular drivers, and we can transfer him from those duties. He is a very safe driver—you will not be worried."

Mma Makutsi had been not so much worried as impressed. Having a driver whom one could casually allocate to new duties was something that seemed to belong to an entirely different world, to a plane of existence of which she had only the slightest inkling. She knew that the Radiphuti family was well-to-do, and she knew that when she and Phuti were married her life would change in certain respects, but she was not yet used to the idea.

"He will drive you all the time?" she asked.

Phuti shrugged. "Yes, if I want that."

If I want that. That, she had thought, was the difference. She had never really been in a position to have what she wanted, and now . . . She imagined what it would be like. If you saw a pair of shoes, you could simply take out your purse and buy them. If you wanted a fridge for your house, or a stove, you could simply go to a shop where they had these things and say, "I will have that one, please. And that one too." She paused. Would she do this? She thought not. Now that she was in a position to indulge such whims, she found that she had no desire to do so, except, perhaps, for the shoes . . . Shoes, of course, were different, and yes, the future looked very positive on the shoe front.

With the driver now available to take Phuti to dinner at his fiancée's house, Phuti had informed Mma Potokwane that he would be eating dinner with Mma Makutsi at her place.

"Is that wise?" Mma Potokwane had asked.

He had looked puzzled, and she had gone on to explain. "You are still recovering from your accident, Rra," she said. "You need very good food."

"But she can make that for me," he protested. "Mma Makutsi is a very good cook."

Mma Potokwane had backed off. "Oh, I am not suggesting she is not a good cook, Rra. It is really just a question of experience. I have many years of experience of cooking for other people. It is not something that anybody can do. Mma Makutsi is a very good secretary, but I do not think that they taught cooking at the Botswana Secretarial College."

He had stood up for his fiancée. "She is an associate detective, Mma," he said firmly. "And she learned to cook at home, not at secretarial college."

Mma Potokwane had recognised defeat. She would never have been bettered in such a discussion by another woman, but Phuti Radiphuti was a man, and Mma Potokwane came from a generation of women that was reticent about arguing with men. "But you will still have breakfast here, Rra?"

"I shall, Mma Potokwane. And thank you for that. Thank you for looking after me so well."

She had smiled broadly. "I have been happy to do that, Rra. And I am so pleased that you are getting better at walking now. Soon you will be one hundred per cent again."

"I hope that I shall not need a stick for much longer."

She hoped that too, she said, although a stick lent a man a certain air of authority. "In my village," she said, "we had a headman who always walked with a stick. He said that it was very useful for beating small boys with if they misbehaved. That is not how headmen conduct themselves these days. Things have changed."

"They have," said Phuti. "It is not good to beat people, I think."

Mma Potokwane had looked thoughtful, wistful perhaps. "Maybe not," she said hesitantly. "Even if they deserve it, maybe not."

DINNER THAT EVENING was a rich oxtail stew made with onions, carrots and mashed potatoes. Phuti arrived at six, and he and Mma Makutsi spent a pleasant half hour sitting at the table waiting for the stew to be ready and discussing the events of the day. Although Mma Makutsi respected the confidentiality of her clients, she did not think that this prevented passing on information to fiancés and spouses, who could be expected to be discreet about what they heard. She knew that Mma Ramotswe discussed her cases with Mr. J.L.B. Matekoni, and she understood why this was necessary. "You have to be able to talk to your husband," Mma Ramotswe had said to her. "If you don't, then everything gets bottled up inside you and pop! it explodes."

Mma Makutsi imagined Mma Ramotswe exploding. It would be like a large bottle of fizzy drink shaken up and then, as she put it so vividly, going pop! "One cannot go pop," she had said. "It is not good for you."

"No," said Mma Ramotswe, "it is not. That is why it's important to be able to talk to somebody."

"Phuti is very careful about these things," said Mma Makutsi. "If I tell him something, he never passes it on to anybody else. He sits there and listens, and then he comes up with some remark that is very helpful. He says, 'What about this?' or, 'What about that?' You know how men are, Mma. They often say 'what about something or other.' "

Now, as she served the oxtail stew, she told Phuti about Mma Ramotswe's meeting with Botsalo Moeti. He listened quietly, and was silent for a moment when she had finished.

"Envy," he said.

She waited for him to explain further.

"Just envy," he said. "That's all."

She had not thought of that. Mma Ramotswe had discussed the case with her on her return to the office, and they had both agreed that Mr. Moeti must have incurred the enmity of somebody who was cruel and spiteful enough to cut the tendons of his cattle; they had not thought of envy. But Mma Makutsi knew all about that; she had grown up in rural Botswana, and knew just how powerful envy could be in the country and in the villages. It was a familiar story.

"Somebody with fewer cattle," she suggested.

Phuti nodded. "Or no cattle at all. Somebody who sees this Moeti doing well and growing fat. Somebody who thinks that it is not fair that he should have what he himself does not have. You know how it is, Grace."

"I do. I have lived in the country. I remember a man having his grain store burned down because he had a much better crop than some other people."

Phuti thought this a very apt example. "And who burned it

down? You don't need to tell me: it was somebody who had a bad crop because they were too lazy to weed the ground or take away the stones. That is the sort of person who is envious."

"So if Mma Ramotswe were to ask Mr. Moeti who is the laziest person in the district, then that will be the person she should look out for?"

Phuti smiled at the suggestion. "That's one way, I suppose."

Mma Makutsi warmed to the theme. "Sometimes the best answer to a difficult problem is the simplest one," she said. "We had a case once when we had to find out who was stealing government food at a college. The answer was the husband of one of the cooks. And how did we find this out? We saw how fat he was getting."

Phuti chuckled. "There you are. It seems that people give themselves away most of the time. They cannot hide things."

"Not from the eyes of a detective," said Mma Makutsi, with an air of satisfaction. "We are trained to spot things, you see."

The conversation moved on to the wedding. A date had at last been set and preparations were being made. The bride price— a tricky issue—had finally been resolved, with a payment of twenty cattle being made by the Radiphuti family to the senior male member of the Makutsi family, Mma Makutsi's father being long dead. The negotiations had been unusually prolonged, that same male person, an uncle with a curious broken nose, having initially made an outrageous demand for ninety-seven cattle, or the cash equivalent, on the grounds that the Radiphuti family was well off and Mma Makutsi had achieved the mark of ninety-seven per cent in the final examinations of the Botswana Secretarial College. This embarrassing demand had eventually been dropped, but only after Mma Makutsi had endured an emotionally draining meeting with her uncle, during which she accused him of threatening her future happiness.

"You cannot ask for that, Uncle," she said.

"Why not? They are rich. Rich people have many cattle. Everybody knows that. And where do they get all that money? From other people—from ordinary people. So there is nothing wrong in getting some of it back."

She had defended the Radiphuti family. "They are rich because they have worked hard. That store of theirs started very small—they have built it up through hard work."

He appeared not to hear. "They can still give some of the money back."

"It is their money, Uncle. They did not steal it. They earned it."

"Rich people think that they can take all the money in the country and put it in their banks in Gaborone. I am just trying to fight back for ordinary people—that is all."

It was no use arguing with him, so she simply issued a threat. "I am not going to stand by and be shamed by this sort of thing. If you are going to ask for that many cattle, then I am going to call this marriage off. I can easily find a poor man to marry."

The prospect of losing the bride price altogether had alarmed him. "All right, I will only ask for twenty-five cattle."

"Twenty."

He had accepted this ungraciously, and the negotiations had resumed. Twenty cattle was still excessive, but it was a figure to which the Radiphuti family could agree.

That done, there was now no impediment to the marriage, and the preparations could begin in earnest. As was customary, there would be two celebrations: one in Gaborone at the home of the Radiphutis, and the other in Bobonong at the home of the Makutsi uncle with the broken nose. Phuti had tactfully offered to pay for both, and his offer had been rapidly accepted by the uncle. "It is right that they should pay for our party too," he said. "With all that money they can easily afford it. I hope that they will give us some new chairs too, for the guests to sit on. We only have four chairs, and there will be two hundred people there. Four chairs will not be enough."

"You must not say anything to Phuti about this," warned Mma Makutsi. "You cannot expect people to give you chairs. I will ask him, though, whether he can lend us some."

"He has many chairs in that big store of his," sniffed the uncle. "He should give us some."

The guest list, as at all weddings, of whatever size, was also proving difficult. On the Radiphuti side there were three hundred and twenty relatives, and that excluded distant cousins who would certainly feel offended if not invited. If this class of distant relatives was included, then the number went up to five hundred and sixteen, with a few places being kept in reserve for relatives of whose existence the family was currently ignorant but who would step forward once the invitations had been issued. Fortunately the Makutsi side was much smaller, with eighty-three relatives appearing on the list agreed by Mma Makutsi and her uncle. To this grand total would have to be added friends and colleagues: Mma Ramotswe and Mr. J.L.B. Matekoni, of course, but also Mr. Polopetsi, who still worked in the garage occasionally, and, more controversially, Charlie and Fanwell. Fanwell's grandmother had asked whether she could come, as it was a long time since she had been to a wedding and she had heard a great deal about Mma Makutsi from her grandson.

"All Botswana then!" Mma Makutsi had sighed. "The whole country. Maybe we should just put an advertisement in the *Botswana Daily News* and say that the whole country can come to the wedding and eat as much beef as it can manage. Maybe that is our patriotic duty now."

"People are happy for you, Mma," Mma Ramotswe had said soothingly. "That is why they wish to come to your wedding."

"They like a large feast too," said Mma Makutsi. "And free beer. That may be another reason why everybody wants to come."

She and Phuti talked about the guest list that night after the oxtail stew had been finished and the plates cleared away. Then Phuti raised the issue of the wedding dress. "You can have whatever you like, Grace," he said. "There is a woman at the store who knows somebody who makes very fine wedding dresses. You can choose whatever you like."

Mma Makutsi looked down at the floor. She did not like to ask Phuti for money, and had been worried about the dress. "You will speak to this person?" she asked. "You will discuss the money?"

He had sensed her embarrassment and had reached over to take her hand. "Of course I will. I will tell her that I will pay the bill."

"And shoes . . ."

"You will certainly need special shoes," said Phuti.

"Mma Ramotswe has spoken about a pair she saw today. She said she thought they would be ideal—if they have them in my size."

"Then you must buy them," said Phuti. "Get them soon. Tomorrow, even. The wedding date is coming soon."

She could not restrain herself, and leaned forward and kissed him on the cheek. He seemed taken aback, and she heard him gasp. She pulled back, unsure of herself. She suddenly felt worried. Phuti had never been physically demonstrative with her. She had put this down to shyness on his part, something to do with his stutter, but now the thought crossed her mind: there were some men for whom the problem ran deeper. What if Phuti were to prove to be such a man?

There were no words in the vocabulary of polite Botswana to express such an intimate matter. Women spoke among themselves of such things, and perhaps men did too. But it was not a subject that a couple like Mma Makutsi and Phuti Radiphuti could easily broach. Perhaps she could ask Mma Potokwane about it. It was too awkward a subject to raise with Mma Ramotswe, but Mma Potokwane was, after all, a qualified matron and had trained as a nurse—even if many years ago—at the Princess Marina Hospital. She would be able to speak to Phuti about such matters, perhaps, and make sure that everything was all right.

Yes, she would ask her.

CHAPTER FIVE

YOU KNOW A GIRL CALLED PRUDENCE?

IT WAS STRANGE, thought Mma Ramotswe, that you could go to sleep thinking one thing, and awake the following morning thinking quite another. And so it was with the question of Charlie.

"I've changed my mind, Mma Makutsi," she said in the office the following day. "We need to tackle Charlie. So let's not put it off. You speak to him today."

Mma Makutsi needed no encouragement. "I am ready, Mma," she said. "I will speak to him, but it will not just be me speaking."

Mma Ramotswe asked her what that meant. It would not just be her speaking, Mma Makutsi reiterated; it would be all the women of Botswana. "I shall be speaking on behalf of all the women of Botswana who have been let down by men," she proclaimed. "On behalf of girls whose boyfriends have pretended that babies have nothing to do with them. On behalf of women whose men go off to bars all the time and leave them at home with the children. On behalf of women whose husbands see other women. On behalf of women whose husbands lie and steal their money and eat all the food and . . ."

As she recited this litany of wrongs, the lenses of Mma

Makutsi's large glasses caught the light, sending flashes like warning semaphore messages across the room. Had a man been present, he would have cowered; as it was, there was only Mma Ramotswe to hear the charge, and she nodded her agreement, even if somewhat awed by her assistant's fervour.

"Don't frighten him too much, Mma," she said. "What you have said is true, but we must remember that Charlie is a young man still and young men—"

"Should not be having twins," shouted Mma Makutsi.

Mma Ramotswe raised an eyebrow. "Yes, Mma, you are right. But he is not all bad. There is something in there that is good—we have all seen it. We need to remind him of his responsibilities. We need to encourage him to take them on his shoulders." She watched her assistant as she spoke; she hoped that the decision to get Mma Makutsi to speak to Charlie was the right one. Her assistant was forceful and could be intimidating, but she was also closer to Charlie in age, and it was possible that he would be more prepared to listen to her than to Mr. J.L.B. Matekoni or to herself.

"I will call him in now," said Mma Makutsi.

Mma Ramotswe asked her whether she wanted her to stay in the room or to find some excuse to go out.

"You stay, Mma. Then you can speak too if he will not listen."

Mma Makutsi rose from her desk, adjusted her skirt, and crossed the room to the door that linked the office with the premises of Tlokweng Road Speedy Motors beyond.

"Charlie!" she called out. "You're wanted in the office."

Charlie came in a few minutes later, wiping his hands. "Better be quick," he said jauntily. "I'm working on a big, big car out there. Major technical problem. Ow! It's no use me trying to explain it to you ladies—you wouldn't understand."

Mma Makutsi glared at him. "Oh yes? So you think that we

don't understand mechanical things. Well, I can tell you, Charlie, there are other things that we *do* understand."

Charlie let out a whistle. "Keep your hair on, Mma. Only a little joke."

"Well this isn't a joke, Charlie," Mma Makutsi snapped back. "You know a girl called Prudence?"

Charlie stiffened. The piece of paper towel on which he was wiping the grease from his hands fluttered slowly to the floor.

Mma Makutsi's voice rose. "Well?"

"Maybe," he said, glancing over his shoulder at Mma Ramotswe. "So what?"

"Maybe?" mocked Mma Makutsi. "Maybe these days you don't have to know people to have babies with them. Maybe you just have to *maybe* know them!"

Charlie was silent. He looked up at the ceiling for a few moments, and then he looked down again. "You shut your face, you warthog! That is none of your business."

"But it is *your* business," crowed Mma Makutsi. "It is your business to look after those twins. It is your business to support them. It is your business to stand by the mother. That is all your business. And Mr. J.L.B. Matekoni agrees." Then she added, "And I am not a warthog."

Charlie looked dismayed. "You've told the boss?"

"He knows," said Mma Makutsi. "He knows. Mma Ramotswe, as you can see, knows. Everyone knows now, Charlie. All Botswana's talking about it. And you can't pretend that it's nothing to do with you. And you know what else?"

"What?" Charlie muttered. His confidence, it seemed, had suddenly deserted him.

"Prudence is going to take you to court," announced Mma Makutsi. "She is going to get an order for you to pay for the twins. And all the other expenses too. That will be for the next sixteen years. And we will all be witnesses in her case. Me, Mma Ramotswe, Mr. J.L.B. Matekoni. Everybody."

"You cannot do that," said Charlie weakly.

"Yes, we can," said Mma Makutsi. "You are caught now, Charlie. There is nothing you can do."

Charlie looked at Mma Ramotswe. His expression was crestfallen, desperate. "Mma Ramotswe . . ."

Mma Ramotswe nodded. "I'm afraid that there is only one thing you can do, Charlie. Mma Makutsi is right. You can go and tell Prudence that you are sorry that you have deserted her, and that you are now ready to accept your responsibilities."

Charlie looked from Mma Ramotswe to Mma Makutsi. The large glasses caught a slanting beam of light from the window and flashed it back in his direction, as the beam of a hunter's lamp may catch its terrified target. Then, quite suddenly, he lurched towards the door and struggled with the handle. His hands, still greasy from work, slipped, but on the third try he got the door open and lunged his way through.

"You cannot run away, Charlie!" Mma Makutsi shouted after him.

"That seems to be what he's doing," said Mma Ramotswe. She looked reproachfully at Mma Makutsi. All that business about Prudence going to court was pure invention; she should have anticipated that her assistant would overdo things.

"I think that I have got him to face up to his responsibilities," said Mma Makutsi, taking off her glasses to polish them.

A moment or two later, Mr. J.L.B. Matekoni came into the office. "Charlie has run away," he said. "He's gone. Right down the road."

"Perhaps he is running off to apologise to Prudence," offered Mma Makutsi, replacing her glasses on her nose.

"I'm not so sure," said Mma Ramotswe.

AFTER CHARLIE'S PRECIPITATE DEPARTURE it was difficult for
Mma Ramotswe to concentrate on her work. Mma Makutsi had
no such difficulty. She sat at her desk with a certain air of triumph,
as judge and prosecutor rolled into one, pleased at the fact that
Charlie had been confronted and dealt with so satisfactorily. The
women of Botswana, her sisters in suffering, had been vindicated
in those few well-chosen words delivered to Charlie, who had, in
the whole business, been standing as a symbol—some might have
said scapegoat—for centuries of accumulated male wrongdoing.
Well, women had now had their say, through her lips; they had
been given their day in court and had seen the defendant roundly
and conclusively vanquished. There was nothing to regret in all
this—it was simply a victory to be celebrated. Mma Ramotswe,
for some odd reason, was silent, sitting at her desk somewhat
morosely. Well, thought Mma Makutsi, her employer had always
been too soft on Charlie—perhaps she was now feeling a bit sorry
for him.

"Are you upset over something, Mma Ramotswe?" asked Mma
Makutsi.

Mma Ramotswe looked up from the account ledger. It was
time to send out bills, a task that she did not relish at the best of
times, let alone now, in the aftermath of this furious row with Charlie. "A little upset," she confessed. "As you may know, Mma, I don't
like conflict. It . . . it disturbs the air."

Mma Makutsi thought about this. "I see," she said. "You heard
him call me a warthog? Did you hear that, Mma?"

Mma Ramotswe sighed. "Yes, I heard that."

"He has called me that before. Do you remember that time? He
called me a warthog."

Mma Ramotswe did remember. It had been a most distressing

occasion, and she had spoken to Charlie sharply about it, telling him that it was unacceptable to call Mma Makutsi anything, let alone a warthog.

"Do I look like a warthog?" blurted out Mma Makutsi. "Do I deserve such an insult, Mma? For a second time?"

Mma Ramotswe sought to reassure her assistant. "Of course not, Mma. Of course you don't look like a warthog."

"Then why did he call me that?" demanded Mma Makutsi.

Mma Ramotswe began an explanation. Young men used ridiculous insults for no real reason. They spoke without thinking. Charlie might call anybody a warthog; it was probably just the first disparaging word that came into his mind; he did not mean it, and she was sure that he would regret it when he realised that it had caused hurt and offence.

Mma Makutsi listened to this explanation carefully. She took off her glasses again, polished them, and replaced them.

"He meant it," she pronounced.

"Charlie needs to grow up," said Mma Ramotswe. "And he will. It's just that it's taking rather a long time—just like his apprenticeship."

They both tried to return to work, but it was impossible. Mma Makutsi, from feeling pleased with the result of her accusation, now seethed at the memory of the insult; Mma Ramotswe, for her part, felt concerned not only about Charlie, but about Mma Makutsi too. It had not been handled well, she thought—and it was her own fault. She should have taken Charlie aside privately and tried to persuade him to do the right thing; it had been an error of judgement to let Mma Makutsi loose on him like that.

Oh well, she thought; things sometimes did not turn out as we had hoped, and the only thing to do was to carry on regardless. If we stopped and brooded all the time over what went wrong, then we would never get anywhere with anything, and one could certainly not run a detective agency, or any business for that matter, in such a way. The day, she decided, would have to be restarted somehow, if it were to get anywhere.

She looked up at Mma Makutsi. "Mma," she said, "I have been thinking."

"And I have been thinking too," interjected Mma Makutsi. "I have been thinking about this warthog business. When that young man comes back, I'm going to ask him why he called me that, and I will carry on asking him until he gives me a proper explanation."

"I haven't been thinking about that," said Mma Ramotswe. "I've been wondering whether we shouldn't shut up shop for a while. Why don't you go out and look at those shoes I mentioned to you? Try them on. Then go and have a cup of coffee—take the money for that from petty cash. I will pay. We can finish off these accounts some other time."

Mma Makutsi smiled. Mma Ramotswe always had a way of defusing a difficult situation; she never failed. "That is a good way of forgetting, Mma. And you are right—I should not sit here thinking about it and making myself all hot and bothered." She paused. "But what about you, Mma?"

Mma Ramotswe explained that she had work to do that would take her out of the office. She needed to go out to Mr. Moeti's place, and there was nothing like a drive into the country to clear one's head and get the small things of life into their proper perspective. Mma Makutsi agreed with all that, but suggested that Mma Ramotswe was overlooking something even better in terms of distraction and balm, and that was shopping for shoes. She pointed this out to Mma Ramotswe, who laughed, and said that each of us needed to find just the right way to take our mind off our problems, and it did not matter what that was—a drive in the country, an expedition to a shoe shop, a quiet cup of tea under a cloudless sky; each of us had something that made it easier to continue in a world that sometimes, just sometimes, was not as we might wish it to be.

TO GET FROM THE OFFICES of the No. 1 Ladies' Detective Agency to the Riverwalk shops—there was not much of a river, it was admitted by all—you could either take a crowded minibus from the side of the Tlokweng Road, and travel no more than a stop or two, or you could drive—if you had a car—or walk. Mma Makutsi could have asked Mma Ramotswe to take her in her van on the way to the Moeti place, and then to drop her off, but she decided instead that it would be better to walk. She was in no hurry to get back to the office, and a walk there and back would add an hour to the pleasant interlude that Mma Ramotswe had so generously arranged.

She set off a few minutes after Mma Ramotswe, locking the office door behind her and leaving a notice pinned to it saying, *Temporarily closed for investigations.* She had been rather proud of this notice, which informed any prospective client that the detectives were somewhere else on unspecified but important-sounding investigative work. But as she pinned the sign into position, it suddenly occurred to her that a quite different impression might be created, namely that the No. 1 Ladies' Detective Agency was itself under investigation, and consequently had been closed down by the authorities. That would never do, so she reopened the office and carefully typed out a new sign. The wording this time was far better, and, she hoped, quite unambiguous: *Temporarily closed while detective personnel are engaged elsewhere.* That was much better . . . or was it? Could it be read as suggesting that the entire staff of the No. 1 Ladies' Detective Agency was, in fact, working for some other concern? That was certainly not the message she wished to convey, so she inserted a third sheet of paper into the typewriter and typed: *Back soon.* There was no room for misunderstanding there, although there might be some people who demanded, "And what does 'soon' mean, may we ask? How soon is that?" Such people, however, would never be satisfied with whatever one said, and would always be picking holes in even the simplest notice. No, you did not need to worry about people like that.

Satisfied with the sign, she set off. As she reached the road that ran past Tlokweng Road Speedy Motors, a struggling minibus, laden to the gunnels with passengers, and tilting dramatically to one side, started to swerve off the tarmac towards her. The driver had scented the prospect of yet another fare and was gesturing from behind the wheel. Mma Makutsi waved him on, and he resumed his journey in a belch of exhaust smoke. As the minibus went past, she saw people staring at her through the windows: a woman with a purple hat pulled down over her ears; a young girl on her mother's lap, hair festooned with tiny ribbons worked carefully into the tight curls; an elderly man, his eyes closed, snatching a few moments of sleep on the journey. *My people,* she thought. *My people.* And she recalled that when she married Phuti Radiphuti she would never again have to travel by minibus, if that was what she wished. She would have a car, and she would be able to go where she wanted, when she wanted, and would not have others squashed in with her, would not have to put up with the discomfort of the elbows of complete strangers digging into one's ribs, nor, even more disconcertingly, their breath hot on the back of one's neck. That would all be a thing of the past—if that was what she wanted. And she was not sure that it was.

She continued her walk. It was not too hot a day, and a breeze had stirred up from the west, from the direction of the Kalahari, the warm heart of the country. There were people who knew what such things meant, who could read the wind, but for Mma Makutsi it was just a breeze that had sprung up to make her walk to the shops that much more comfortable. She looked up. The sky was without cloud, a dome of lightest blue filled with air, great swirls and eddies of it, which you could see—just about—if you stared long enough. She breathed in deeply, and felt the fine dry air fill her with a buoyant optimism. Life was very good: she had behind her a career that was a success by anybody's standards—ninety-seven per cent, associate detective with several significant and challenging cases solved, a new filing system worked out—a comfortable, if rather small, rented house, and now, to top all these achievements, a well-to-do fiancé who loved her and was kind to her in so many little ways. And here she was with three or four hours of time off—and she would not wish to hurry these things—on a mission to purchase shoes for her wedding.

Nice one, Boss!

Pretending not to notice at first, she began to walk a little bit more purposefully.

Yes, said the insistent, rather chirpy voice. *Put your best foot forward!*

She glanced down at her shoes. She had a few more shoes these days, and this was a workaday pair that she had never paid much attention to. But now they were making their presence felt.

It's smart wedding shoes—with diamonds, we hear. So you'll be forgetting about us, we suppose. Well, we won't be forgetting about you, Boss! Know what we mean?

She decided to ignore her shoes. It was absurd, anyway; shoes could not talk, and it was just a trick of the mind, of the same sort that made one think that somebody has said something when they have just been clearing their throat or humming a snatch of tune. The creaking of shoe leather could produce just the same illusion, she thought, and was probably best dealt with by the application of a spot of polish, or a lick of dubbin.

In your dreams, said the shoes.

She was now at the point along the road where a path led off into a stand of gum trees that had been planted forty years ago, when Gaborone was only a small town. The city had grown, of course, but these eucalypts still formed its boundary at this point; beyond them lay a stretch of rough bush—government land—and then the dam that provided the city with its precious water. It was an odd juxtaposition, as the border zones of towns can so often be. On one side lie the works of man—streets and pavements, storm drains, buildings—on the other is nature, and the transition can be so sudden, so sharply delineated. Here the tar and concrete just stopped without warning, and were no more, their place taken by trees, undergrowth, anthills. And the smells were different too: on one side the acrid odour of cars and hot road surfaces and wafting cooking vapours, which on the other side became the scent of dust and grass and dried bark, and cattle somewhere not far away.

A path led off into this stretch of bush, as paths will lead off in Africa, well defined, tramped bare by passing feet, appearing like dusty veins when viewed from above. These paths knew where they were going, and would meander—never a straight line—turn and twist until they reached some human place, a collection of huts perhaps, a rough wooden stockade for cattle or goats, some place of gathering or labour. Or they would peter out, as if the people whose feet had made the path had suddenly remembered something and turned back, or had just forgotten why it was that they were walking that way and had given up, handing the land back to nature.

Mma Makutsi knew where this path led because she had followed it before on one or two occasions and, taking the right fork after five minutes or so, it had brought her out where she thought it would: near the traffic lights at the corner of the Riverwalk shops. She decided to follow it now because it was easier than walking alongside the Tlokweng Road, with its traffic and its stony surface. The path was more peaceful too, because the only sounds were those of birds and, sometimes, the distant and sporadic ringing of cattle bells; some herds, by ancient right, still wandered among these trees. Occasionally, very occasionally, there might be the sound of some other creature in the bush, the startled cracking of twigs as a small antelope was disturbed—a timid duiker, perhaps, or a little bushbuck. There were many of them over by the dam, attracted by the water that would ensure their survival in the surrounding vleis and low boulder-strewn hills or kopjes, creatures clinging to life in the interstices of a bigger, stronger world.

Mma Makutsi walked on. There was no life about, although she could see from the sand on the path that cattle had been this way not long before. She was thinking of the shoes, and making a mental list of the things she had to find out about them. Colour? Would they go with her dress, which was to be ivory. Comfort? She would have to stand for long periods on her wedding day and at the parties; the shoes should not be too tight or she would feel very uncomfortable. Fabric or leather? Her skin, which was troublesome, did not react well to some synthetic materials, so it was important the shoes have leather lining rather than some sort of plastic. Heels? Again there was a comfort issue—

She gave a start, her heart leaping in fright. A sudden noise; a small crashing sound; something in the bush. Instinct took over, and she took a step back and half turned to run; it could be a snake, a cobra or a mamba, which could be very dangerous if she had walked between the snake and its hole. Mambas loved these old anthills, with their cool chambers and the safety of their darkness, and mambas were so quick, so evil, so filled with old hatred for people.

A warthog. It had come through the undergrowth and now it wandered on to the path, saw Mma Makutsi not far away and for a moment itself froze, as she had. Then, turning round sharply, its ridiculous tail erect like an aerial, it trotted off, back into the safety of the sheltering bush.

Mma Makutsi relaxed. "Sorry," she said after the retreating creature. "Sorry. This is your place."

CHAPTER SIX

A SMALL, INCONSEQUENTIAL BOY

THE ROAD TO LOBATSE runs south from Gaborone, heading straight for a pass that opens through low-lying hills on either side. Like all roads in Botswana, for many of those who passed that way regularly each stretch could evoke its memories: here was where we broke down, by that culvert, and waited for help under that tree—the sun was so hot that day; here we turned off once to visit a distant cousin who lived five miles down that track, so bumpy that we were all shaken up and bruised by the time we reached our destination; here lived a man who kept a mangy lion in a large enclosure; here is the turn-off to Mokolodi; here we bought melons from a woman who had flies swarming about her eyes but seemed unconcerned. For Mma Ramotswe, too, there were memories, going right back; of trips by bus when she was a girl, to see her cousin in Lobatse; of a journey with Note, her abusive husband, who broke her heart and then broke it again; of the time she drove this way with her father, just before he died, and he said that he thought he would never see those hills again but no doubt would find some just like them in that place to which he would shortly go, to that other Botswana just beyond that final darkness.

Mr. Botsalo Moeti had eventually told Mma Ramotswe where he lived. His earlier vagueness on this, bordering on reluctance, had puzzled her. Did he not trust her? Was his fear so great? "A road off to the right," he had said. "There is no notice, but if you look for a large thorn tree beside the road just after Otse, then that is the place; there is the chassis of a very old car in the bush. That is my sign."

She saw the tree, and then the remains of the car. These old vehicles were to be seen here and there—in the dry air of Botswana they barely rusted, but became covered in vegetation and dust and merged with the landscape. Often enough they were beautiful old cars or trucks, tractors too, reminders of a time when such things were built with grace and a sense of human proportion, like the implements to be found in an old kitchen, battered and well used, modest and simple. She had suggested once to Mr. J.L.B. Mate-koni that he rescue one of these ancient vehicles some day and tow it back to the garage for restoration. He had laughed, and explained that you could not do something like that; that everything would be solidly fused together now, that the wind would have eroded the cables so that they would turn to dust if touched, that there would be nothing left where once there were dials and tubes and leather seats. The ants would have eaten all those, he said; it would be an exhumation, not a towing. "Cars are just like us, Mma Ramotswe," he went on to say. "When their heart stops—finally stops—then there is nothing left. The life has gone from them. That is true, Mma Ramotswe. That is how it is."

He paused, and then added, "And I do not think they go to heaven, Mma Ramotswe. There is no heaven for cars." He spoke rather wistfully, as such a heaven would be a fine place for a mechanic, surrounded by all the cars that ever were, all those wonderful old cars with their intricate engines and their beautiful, handmade interiors.

He had not meant to be unkind, he had simply wanted to explain the finite life of machinery. Women knew many things, he felt, and there was little, if anything, that he could tell Mma Ramotswe about the world; except when it came to machines. Then, in his view, women seemed less interested; they wanted machines to work, but they did not necessarily want to understand *why* they worked or, more important, why they went wrong. Love was usually quite enough to stop people going wrong, but would not always work with machinery. One of his clients had just demonstrated that. She had brought in her car, which was behaving erratically. "I love it," she said. "I am kind to it. And now it has decided to turn against me. What have I done, Mr. J.L.B. Matekoni, to deserve this?"

"It is not love," he had said. "It is oil."

That is what Mr. J.L.B. Matekoni thought about how women treated cars; but the world was changing, and even as he entertained these thoughts, he began to feel slightly guilty. He was a fair man, who disliked prejudice, but he had yet to be persuaded that women were good with cars. Not that he would ever have dared express such views to Mma Potokwane, for instance, or even Mma Makutsi. These ladies were feminists, he had been told, as he had once informed the apprentices when admonishing them about the things they talked about in the garage, often at the tops of their voices.

"You should watch what you say," he had warned. "What if Mma Potokwane is sitting in the office there and hears these things you say? Or even Mma Makutsi, who has very good hearing? These ladies are feminists, you know."

"What is that?" asked Fanwell. "Do they not like to eat meat?"

"That is vegetarian," said Charlie, scornfully. "Feminists are big, strong ladies. Ow!"

"They are ladies who do not like to hear young men say foolish things about women," said Mr. J.L.B. Matekoni. "They will punish you if you do not watch out."

Charlie had grinned. "If the feminists take over, Fanwell, they will make men sit by the roadside and sell tomatoes. That is their main plan. For you too. That is what is going to happen, big time. Ow!"

Mma Ramotswe steered the blue van off the road. The track—for it was not much more than that—led very quickly to a gate fastened to its post with a twist of wire. She opened this, making sure to close it behind her to keep cattle from straying on to the Lobatse road. That was a major cause of accidents, cattle at night, invisible in the darkness until the last moment when they turned their heads and the driver saw their eyes caught in the headlights, looming large. Everybody knew somebody who had hit a cow, who had lost their vehicle as a result, sometimes their life too.

The track was in good enough condition; a grader, it seemed, had passed along it not all that long ago and had evened out the worst of the ridges and filled the deepest of the holes. This makeshift pact with nature would last until the next rains came, when the dry season's work would be undone with all the quick impatience that nature has for the puny works of man. The first floods of the rainy season were the worst, as the land, parched bone-dry from the winter, would shrug off the sudden deluge, sending it off in red-brown torrents through networks of eroded dongas. Only later would the land drink in the rain and spring to life once more.

On either side of the track, the grey-green bush stretched out, a landscape of struggling shrubs, leaves shrivelled and dusty, filling in the space between the endless forests of thorn trees. The more established acacia provided some cover from the sun, casting pools of shade under which, here and there, cattle clustered, their tails twitching listlessly against the flies. The prevailing note was one of somnolence and stasis, a note taken up and orchestrated by hidden choirs of screeching cicadas: this was a Botswana that had existed since the days when cattle-herding peoples first came to this land; this was a Botswana that was a hundred years from the world of Gaborone, from the world of cars, of white buildings, of commerce and diamonds. But it was the real heart of her country, the heart that she hoped, when her time came to leave this earth, she would see, in her mind's eye at least, before the final darkness set in. And for all that she belonged to Gaborone, and to that other world, Mma Ramotswe belonged here too, and felt beside her quite strongly the presence of her father, the late Obed Ramotswe. As she gazed out through the tangle of acacia, she felt he was there, seated beside her in the van, his familiar old hat resting on his lap, looking out at the cattle and rehearsing in his mind the possible bloodlines of these beasts he knew so well.

Her reverie ended as the van encountered a particularly deep pothole, teetering for a moment before toppling over the rim of the miniature void. Forward momentum prevailed, and the van was soon back on the level, but the creaking and protest from somewhere under the engine made Mma Ramotswe wonder how her white van would have coped with the challenge—not as well, she suspected.

The track changed direction; now came the first signs of human activity: a dip tank, rust-red, with an empty drum lying by its side. The sight brought back a memory—the stench of the dip, that harsh chemical smell, not unlike a mixture of tar and vinegar, which she remembered from her father's cattle post all those years ago. It was an unpleasant smell in itself, but tolerated, perhaps even hankered after, for its association with cattle, and with the life that was led about cattle. Beyond the dip tank there was a rickety enclosure

made of stakes of rough-hewn wood—the trunks of small trees—
driven into the ground and tied together with wire and strips of bark.
Again, this prompted recollections of those long weeks spent out on
the lands and at the distant cattle posts, and of the sound of the cattle lowing in the night when disturbed by some movement in the
bush: some pair of eyes betraying the presence of a hyena or jackal.

Then she saw the house, standing beside a large thorn tree that
had thickened considerably, its upper branches making a dense
crown, like a head of unruly hair among the ranks of the well-
barbered. It was not an imposing house, but it was more than the
single-room structures that served many who lived out in the bush.
The roof, like the roofs of almost all farmhouses, was made of cor-
rugated iron, bolted on and painted red. This covered not only the
main part of the house, but the shady verandah that ran the length
of the front, the space between the whitewashed pillars gauzed in
against flies. Behind the house, in a cluster several hundred yards
away, was a small group of buildings that made up the servants'
quarters. There were always such dwellings—the abode of the
cook, or the man who tended the yard, or the woman who did the
washing and ironing; so normal and unexceptional as to attract
no attention, the places where lives were led in the shadow of the
employer in the larger house. And the cause, Mma Ramotswe
knew from long experience, of deep resentments and, on occasion,
murderous hatreds. Those flowed from exploitation and bad treatment—the things that people would do to one another with utter
predictability and inevitability unless those in authority made it
impossible and laid down conditions of employment. She had seen
shocking things in the course of her work, even here in Botswana, a
good country where things were well run and people had rights;
human nature, of course, would find its way round the best of rules
and regulations.

As she nosed the van into a patch of shade under the large

thorn tree beside the house, the thought came to her that the solution to Mr. Moeti's problem might be simpler than he imagined. It always surprised her that people could be so blind to the obvious; that a person could mistreat a servant and then show surprise when the one they abused hit back. She had seen this time and time again, and she had even thought of writing to Clovis Andersen and proposing a new rule for inclusion in a future edition of *The Principles of Private Detection*. This rule would state, quite simply: *If you are looking for somebody who hates your client, then first of all look under the client's own roof.* And now, getting out of the van and looking over towards the house, she studied the red iron roof under which, perhaps, resentments were burning. The roof looked back at her, impassive and tight-lipped under her suspicion, and she remembered a proposition that was already included in Clovis Andersen's great work which was just as pertinent to this situation as was any suggestion of hers: *Don't think you know all the answers*, Mr. Andersen had written, and had gone on, with admirable economy, to explain why this should be so: *because you don't.*

A figure appeared on the verandah. Smoothing out the creases in her dress, Mma Ramotswe walked towards the house. The figure now revealed itself as a woman, clad in a dull shift dress over which an old blue gingham apron had been donned.

Mma Ramotswe called out the universal greeting of the Tswana world—"*Dumela*, Mma"—and the woman responded appropriately, though in a rather strange, high-pitched voice.

"I have come to see Mr. Moeti. Is he in the house?"

The woman nodded. "He is sleeping."

Mma Ramotswe looked at her watch. "He said I should come."

The woman looked at her blankly. "But he is sleeping, Mma. He cannot talk if he is sleeping."

Mma Ramotswe smiled. "No, nobody can do that. But perhaps he would like you to wake him up."

The woman shook her head. "Men do not like to be woken up, Mma. Sorry."

Mma Ramotswe frowned. There was something strange about this woman, a deliberate obduracy that went beyond the reluctance of a servant to disturb an employer. She wondered: *Is this her? Is this the one?* That might seem impossibly simple, but Mma Ramotswe had often found a culprit on very first enquiry. People gave themselves away, she thought; they so often did. Guilt shone out of their eyes like the beam of a hunter's lamp in the darkness. What, she wondered, would happen if she were to come right out and ask this woman: *Why did you do what you did to the cattle?*

"His cattle," said Mma Ramotswe. She had not planned to say it, but the thought had somehow nudged the word out into the open, as a chance remark will sometimes be made against our better judgement. It was true that words slipped out; they did; they jumped out of our mouths and said, *Look, you've let us loose!*

The woman froze. "His cattle, Mma? What of them?"

Mma Ramotswe watched her eyes carefully. The woman's gaze slid away, off to the unruly thorn tree. Guilt. Unambiguous guilt.

"He has had some trouble with his cattle, Mma. I have come to sort it out. To get to the bottom of it."

The woman's eyes moved. She was looking at Mma Ramotswe again, and the fright that had greeted her initial remark had been replaced by a look of blankness. "I can wake him up if you like, Mma."

"A good idea," said Mma Ramotswe.

SHE WAS READY to detect in Mr. Moeti's expression the fear that she had seen before, but it was not there, at least to begin with. She met him on the verandah, where he shook hands with her and invited her to sit down on a traditional Tswana chair. The supports of the chair were made of panga panga wood; leather thongs, threaded carefully in a criss-cross pattern, formed the seat and back.

"A good chair, Rra," she said. "A village chair."

He smiled at the compliment. "I have always had chairs like that," he said. "They belonged to my father, who was a village head-man, and they came to me when he became late. Now there is only one—the other one was sat in by a very heavy person, one of the fattest men in the country, I think, and it collapsed."

Mma Ramotswe did not stir. The chair beneath her felt solid enough, but it certainly had creaked and even yielded a bit when she had put her weight on it. A chair should be able to support a traditionally built person, and that should apply in particular, she felt, to a traditional chair.

"But you haven't come to see me about chairs, Mma Ramotswe," Mr. Moeti continued, seating himself casually on the low parapet of the verandah.

"I came because of your problem," said Mma Ramotswe. She noticed in the corner of her eye that the woman in the apron was hovering in the doorway. "That private problem you told me about."

Noticing the look, Mr. Moeti flashed a quick dismissive glance in the woman's direction.

"That is the woman who looks after the kitchen," he said. "She has been here forever. Most of these people"—he gestured towards the surrounding bush—"were born on this land. I suppose it's as much theirs as it is mine, except . . . except that it isn't."

She looked at him quizzically. "I'm not sure if I follow you, Rra."

He laughed. "I'm not surprised. I didn't put that very well. What I meant to say is that these people—the people who work for me on the farm—were born here. Their fathers worked for the farmer who owned this place before me. Now they work for me. They're fixtures, really."

Mma Ramotswe nodded. She understood perfectly well; the land came with people, and with the stories of those people. And so when somebody bought the land—as people could do, if they had the money—then they bought not only the land but its people too. For the most part, the new owners would understand that, unless they were foreigners who had no idea of the meaning of land in Africa. But Mr. Moeti, a Motswana, would know exactly what obligations land ownership brought; or she hoped he would. If he did not, then he would soon make enemies, and could easily find that his property came under attack. It was only too easy to start a bush fire, to turn a swathe of golden-grassed cattle range into charred stubble; it was only too easy to take a knife to the Achilles tendon of a cow.

"Are there many such people, Rra? Many here, I mean."

He replied that there were. It was difficult to tell exactly how many people lived on the farm, as not only were babies always being born, but there was also movement away to the towns, or deaths. But if pressed, he would say forty people altogether, in three families. These were all related to one another through complex and convoluted genealogies that only the old people remembered, and even they were now forgetting.

"Do you get on well with them?" asked Mma Ramotswe.

His answer came quickly, and unambiguously. "If you think it's one of them, Mma," he said, "then you couldn't be more wrong. I am their friend, and always have been. There are many children named after me. Go to that place where they live, over there by the dam, and call out 'Botsalo,' and then see how many children come running over. No, it cannot be one of them, Mma Ramotswe."

"I did not say it was, Rra," she said mildly.

"You implied it."

She shrugged. "I have to ask questions. I have to pry—otherwise, how would we find out who has done this terrible thing?"

He said that he understood this.

"And that lady in the kitchen?" Mma Ramotswe went on to ask, looking into the house, her voice lowered. "What about her?"

Mr. Moeti hesitated. "That lady is a very close friend, Mma. She is my wife, but isn't my wife, if you understand me."

She understood, but reflected for a moment on his curious way of throwing opposites together—this was the second time he had done it. "You have a wife, Rra? A legal one?"

He pointed. "She is down in Lobatse. She prefers to be in town. She lives here but she doesn't live here, if you see what I mean."

Now it occurred to Mma Ramotswe that there was another suspect: the wife who was a wife but who also was not. If she knew of the other woman, the resident mistress, then might she not try to get even with her husband? Wronged women did not always take it out on the other woman, Mma Ramotswe knew; often they reserved their venom for the man who had let them down. If there was resentment on the part of the real Mma Moeti—the Mma Moeti who was but was not—then she might well take it out on her errant husband's cattle. After all, a man's cattle were his *representatives* in a sense, and any insult offered to them was an insult to the owner; or so her father, the late Obed Ramotswe, had always maintained, though partly, she thought, with tongue in cheek. She remembered how, when she was a little girl, she saw him raise his battered old hat to some cattle beside the road; she had asked him why, and he had explained that they were cattle of a respected man, of chiefly family, and he was merely according him the respect that such beasts deserved. But then he had smiled, and winked at her, and she realised that the remarks of adults might not always mean what they appeared to mean.

There was a silence as Mma Ramotswe digested Botsalo Moeti's disclosures about his wife. She did not approve of such arrangements, but she did not show her disapproval: he was her client and it was not for her to speak to him about fidelity and those other things that the government advertisements spelled out so carefully. If people like him—well-placed men of experience and status—behaved in a cavalier way towards women, then what hope was there for getting people like Charlie to conduct themselves more responsibly?

Charlie: there was another problem, adding to the list of problems she already had. Moeti, Charlie, the sighting of the white van: these were issues enough to interfere with anybody's sleep.

Moeti's stomach now broke the silence with a loud gurgling sound. "Juices," he explained. "I have too many juices in my stomach."

Mma Ramotswe raised an eyebrow. "Juices are a big problem for some," she said.

There was a note of criticism in her voice—just a touch—but Mr. Moeti did not pick it up, or if he did, gave no indication of having done so.

"I'd like to show you the place where the last attack happened," he said. "Are you ready to come with me, Mma, or would you like some water first?"

She asked for water, and he called out to the woman in the house. "Water for this lady, Mma. A big glass. Very big."

She did not blink. Why did he imagine that she would want a

very big glass? Was it because she was traditionally built? If so, then he had no right to assume that a traditionally built person would drink more than a moderate amount of water. Traditionally built people did not necessarily eat or drink more than those of less substantial construction. It just did not follow.

The woman in the apron brought out a glass on a tray. On the surface of the glass were her greasy fingerprints, each swirl and whorl perfectly outlined, as if etched by an engraver. These prints were about the rim too, which, for some inexplicable reason, the woman had contrived to touch. Although Mma Ramotswe was not unduly fastidious, believing that a reasonable degree of exposure to the germs of others helped maintain healthy resistance, she did not think there was a need to handle a glass quite so thoroughly before offering it to another.

"Look at these wonderful fingerprints," she said, as the woman offered her the tray. "How useful for a detective!"

The woman looked at her blankly.

"Mma Ramotswe is making a joke," said Mr. Moeti to the woman, in a tone of condescension. "It is a joke for Gaborone people, not for rural people like you."

Mma Ramotswe turned to look at him in astonishment. This, she decided, was a man who could well have more enemies than she had imagined.

THEY WALKED FROM THE HOUSE, following a path that took them past the servants' quarters and a shed housing a tractor side by side with an ancient donkey-cart. Mr. Moeti pointed to the cart and told Mma Ramotswe how he believed that the old ways of doing things still had their place. "Donkeys don't go wrong," he said. "Tractors do. And the same goes for everything else. An old radio, for example, has very few buttons. A new one? There are so many buttons that you don't know what to do, even if you're an engineer."

"My husband would agree with you," said Mma Ramotswe. "When people bring in their cars these days, he needs a computer to do everything. He says you even need a computer to work out if you've run out of petrol."

In a small paddock not far from the barn, they saw the donkeys in question, three dispirited creatures standing under the shade of a tree, their heads lowered in that air of utter defeat, of dejection, that marks out their species. A young herd boy, aged no more than seven or eight, was standing beside the donkeys, staring at his employer and Mma Ramotswe as they walked past.

"That child?"

Mr. Moeti glanced in the boy's direction. "Just a herd boy. That was his mother back there in the house."

"Does he know anything?"

Mr. Moeti looked at her in surprise. "No. He's just a boy."

"They have eyes," said Mma Ramotswe quietly—so quietly that he did not hear her and had to ask her to repeat what she had said.

"And?" he asked.

"I have found that children—especially boys—see things and can give you very important information. They notice."

Mr. Moeti shrugged. "You can ask him if you like."

Without waiting, he whistled and gestured for the boy to come over. The child hesitated, and then approached them. He brought flies with him, Mma Ramotswe noticed.

"This lady wants to ask you something," Mr. Moeti said. His tone was gruff, and he stared at the boy as he spoke.

Mma Ramotswe bent down to speak to the boy, reaching for his hand as she addressed him. She asked him his name, and he gave it. He was Mpho.

"So, Mpho, you know about this bad thing with the cattle?"

He moved his head slightly—a nod, but a reluctant one. His eyes, she saw, were fixed on Mr. Moeti.

"Did you see anything?" asked Mma Ramotswe.

He was still watching Mr. Moeti, and Mma Ramotswe glanced up discouragingly at the farmer. "Maybe I should speak to him by himself," she said. "It is sometimes better to speak to children on their own."

"No need," snapped Mr. Moeti. "Mpho, you answer the auntie: You saw nothing, right?"

Mpho shook his head. "I have seen nothing, Mma. I know nothing."

"Are you sure?" she asked.

The boy shivered. He looked up at Mr. Moeti again and then lowered his gaze to the ground. "I am sure, Mma. Can I go now?"

She squeezed his hand. "Of course you can. Goodbye, Mpho, *go siame.*" They continued on their way.

"That's an odd little boy," Mr. Moeti remarked, smiling. "He stands there by the donkeys half the time, doing nothing, or just playing with stones he picks up."

"He's a child," said Mma Ramotswe. "Children should be allowed to spend their time doing things like that."

"He has cattle to watch. That's what he's paid to do."

She did not reply. The child's fear had been so obvious, and she was surprised that Mr. Moeti had not felt obliged to explain it away. Did he imagine she had not noticed it? And the cause of the child's fear was equally apparent: the herd boy was frightened of Mr. Moeti. He had seen something—of course he had—but he knew that he was not supposed to talk about it. She could find out what the child knew, if she really wanted to; if she had the chance to speak to the child by himself, then it would not be difficult to encourage him to speak. All you had to say to a child was that you knew what the secret was, and it would all come tumbling out. No child could keep a secret for long; they claimed to, but it was usually beyond them.

But of course it was not that simple. If she managed to persuade the child to speak, then he would be even more terrified, knowing that Mr. Moeti might find out. And yet, if the boy had witnessed the incident, he would be able to identify the perpetrator. And if he could do that, then why would Mr. Moeti have an interest in concealing the fact? It did not make sense at all, unless, of course, the child had seen something else altogether— some incident that explained the attack. Perhaps Mr. Moeti had done something to somebody else that had then resulted in the attack on his cattle, and perhaps the child had seen whatever it was that the farmer had done. Or—and this was also a possibility, she had to admit—perhaps the herd boy was simply frightened of Mr. Moeti in general and really had seen nothing. What was it that Clovis Andersen said in *The Principles of Private Detection*? It was in the chapter on establishing facts—a very important section in the scheme of the Andersen opus. *Do not forget,* wrote the distinguished authority, *that although a possible explanation may seem likely, there may be an entirely different cause operating in the background. If Mr. Green votes for Mr. Brown, you may think that is because Mr. Green approves of Mr. Brown's politics, but the real reason may be because Mr. Brown is Mr. Green's brother-in-law!*

Mma Ramotswe had been intrigued by this passage, and had read it out loud to Mma Makutsi one morning when business had been slack. Mma Makutsi had listened intently before asking Mma Ramotswe to repeat it. Then she had asked, "Who is this Mr. Green?"

"He is Mr. Brown's brother-in-law," replied Mma Ramotswe. "I do not think they really exist."

"Oh, I know that," said Mma Makutsi. "But I am asking because there may be another reason altogether. What if Mr.

Brown has told Mr. Green that unless he votes for him he will cut off his nose? What then? That is a possible explanation too."

Mma Ramotswe gave this some thought before replying. "A good point, Mma Makutsi. And it shows that Mr. Andersen is correct. There may be even more explanations than those you think you have. That is very true."

It had been a slightly odd conversation—many conversations with Mma Makutsi could take a surprising turn—but it seemed helpful to remember it now. There could be any number of reasons for the boy's fear of Mr. Moeti and none of them might have anything to do with the cattle incident.

Mr. Moeti now stopped and pointed to a patch of grass at the side of the path. "This is where the last bullock was found," he said. "He was a very fine beast. Strong. White patches on his head."

Mma Ramotswe looked about her. They were, she thought, in a place best described as nowhere, surrounded by thin acacia scrub that stretched out to a small outcrop of hills to the south. Through the trees, though, she could just make out a fence that ran die-straight through the bush. She pointed at this.

"The border of my farm," said Mr. Moeti. "My neighbour is on that side—I am on this."

"And who is he?" asked Mma Ramotswe.

Mr. Moeti did not appear to be particularly interested. "He is just a man," he said. "He has a business down in Lobatse. He comes here at weekends."

She nodded. This was not at all unusual. The ambition of any successful businessman in Botswana was to own land, and cattle, of course. Wealth in the bank was one thing; wealth in the shape of cattle was quite another, and for many, much more desirable.

She sighed. "It is very sad, what happened to your cattle. Very sad. People can be so cruel to animals. They do not think of their suffering, do they? Imagine how painful it must be to have your tendons cut and you just lie there and . . ."

She looked at him as she spoke, and saw that his expression remained impassive. That was interesting, she noted. Most people, when reminded of pain, reacted in some way. They winced or gritted their teeth, or simply looked distressed. But Mr. Moeti did none of these.

"Not good," he said.

"No. Not good, Rra."

He gestured to the patch of grass. "Should we look around?"

She saw no point to doing this, but having gone out there she thought that she should at least look; not that there was anything to see, really, other than a small patch of ground on which something cruel had been done. There were numerous such small patches of ground throughout the world, she thought, and Africa, her beloved Africa, had many of them.

She looked up at the sky. That was the real witness to human cruelty, to all our manifold sorrows—the sky.

Her thoughts were interrupted by a grunt from Mr. Moeti. It was a rather odd sound, and she wondered for a moment whether he was in pain; it was that sort of sound, the *oh* that escapes our lips when a sudden awkward movement sends an electric shock of pain from the back. What if Mr. Moeti were to have a heart attack out here? Would she have to leave him lying on the ground—on the very grass on which the bullock had lain in the embrace of its own pain—and run back along the path to the house? And what would happen then? How long would it be before a doctor could be summoned or an ambulance brought out from Gaborone?

"Are you all right, Rra?"

He muttered something inaudible.

"Rra?"

"Come over here, Mma Ramotswe. Come over here."

He was bending over, looking at something on the ground. As she approached, he pointed, the gold band of his wristwatch glinting in the sun as he did so.

"You see that?" he said. "I don't want to touch it before you see it. Look."

She peered down at the ground. There was a small, silver-coloured object, half covered by a dried leaf that had blown across it. She went down on her knees; the ground beneath the meagre covering of vegetation was hard and stony. She reached out and picked up the object. A real detective, she thought, would have used tweezers and immediately dropped the evidence into a convenient plastic bag. But where were the tweezers and plastic bags out here? Or even in the office? She would hardly find tweezers among the rough spanners and wrenches of Tlokweng Road Speedy Motors.

She looked at Mr. Moeti. "A key ring."

He held out his hand. "Let me see it, Mma."

She watched him. "Is it yours, Mr. Moeti?"

He shook his head. "I've never seen this before."

"It is a little thing," she said. "It must be easy to drop something like that."

"Yes," he said. He was staring at her intently. "Mma Ramotswe?"

She took the key ring back from him. "Yes, Rra."

"Was this dropped by the person who did this thing?"

She gestured to the wide expanse of surrounding bush. "This is not a very busy place, Rra."

He looked embarrassed. "Of course. I am not a detective— I am a farmer."

"How did you take the bullock away?"

He pointed towards the farm. "I brought my tractor. I came with my stockman."

"Just the two of you?"

"Yes."

She felt the key ring between her fingers. There was a rough edge to it; it was almost sharp; a small, metal map of Botswana.

"And could this be his?"

He answered quickly: "He has never seen it either."

"Oh? How do you know that?"

He looked away. "I mean that I do not think he has ever seen it. That is what I mean."

CHAPTER SEVEN

A TRUTH ABOUT LIES

MA RAMOTSWE had told Mma Makutsi that they should close the office while they were out, but had said nothing about coming back. Mma Makutsi was conscientious—one did not achieve ninety-seven per cent in the final examinations of the Botswana Secretarial College without demonstrating responsibility and the capacity for hard work—but she felt, nonetheless, that Mma Ramotswe could hardly have meant for her to go back to the office after her shopping trip. Buying shoes was not a simple transaction; one had to take one's time about it, and it was already noon. If the choosing of the shoes took two hours—perhaps three, with time for contemplation—then there would surely be no point in walking back to the office (another half an hour) only to have to close up for the day an hour or two later. No time and motion expert would think that a good idea; such a person, she felt, would be more likely to suggest going home after the purchase of the shoes in order to be fresher and more energetic for work the next day.

Mma Makutsi had attended a lecture by a time and motion expert in her final month at the Botswana Secretarial College. It had been a riveting talk, perhaps the most entertaining of all the lectures they had received at the college, and she remembered almost every detail of what was said. The expert was a rotund man who had immediately engaged the attention of the students—or almost all of them—by telling them how he performed the task of getting dressed each morning. "I am very efficient," he said, smiling as he spoke. "When I get undressed, I hang my shirt on a hanger straightaway. Then, in the morning, if I am wearing the same shirt—and it is not efficient, I believe, to change your shirt every day, unless it is very hot—then in the morning I back up into the shirt like this, while at the same time picking up my trousers with my free hand, like this, and putting first one leg in and then the other. As I put in the first leg I make sure that a shoe is lined up to receive it when it comes out the bottom of the trousers. In this way, I put all my clothes on at the same time. It is a big saving of time. Three minutes and twenty seconds, to be precise. I have plotted it on a graph and taken the average."

The students had all been impressed—or, again, almost all of the students had been impressed. Violet Sephotho, of course, had pretended to be bemused by it all.

"Big nonsense," she said scornfully as they filed out of the lecture room. "No man gets undressed in the way he says they do. Men do not hang their shirts on hangers when they get undressed."

"Yes, they do," said Mma Makutsi. "I do not think that this college invites liars to become visiting lecturers. He said they do, and I believe him."

Violet looked at her pityingly. "What do *you* know about it, Grace Makutsi? What do *you* know about the way men get undressed?"

And then she had smiled knowingly and flounced away, examining her painted fingernails with elaborate interest.

"She is always talking," whispered one of Mma Makutsi's

friends. "Men run away from women like that. They put *on* their clothes when they see her coming. That is the real truth."

Mma Makutsi would have liked to believe that, but felt that the evidence actually pointed the other way. Men had seemed to flock around Violet the moment she left the front gate of the secretarial college. That was a good place for idle men to congregate, for some reason. There was always a small knot of men at the front gate, pretending to have business there, but hoping only to get a glimpse of, and perhaps share a word or two with, girls like Violet. It was sad, thought Mma Makutsi; surely these men had something better to do, but the truth of the matter was that they did not. In the minds of the men who used to attend at the gate, this was by far the best way they could conjure up of spending their time.

As she approached the shop in the Riverwalk shopping centre, Mma Makutsi remembered that time and motion lecture. Efficiency was, in general, a good goal, but she felt, as she saw the mouth-watering selection of shoes displayed in the window, that this was not an occasion on which it should be practised. *Just in from Pariss* panted an enthusiastic sign. *Pariss?* There was an extra *s* there, she concluded; she would have to point it out to them— gently, of course, but one could not let these things go uncorrected. And she doubted, too, whether these shoes came from Paris; Johannesburg, perhaps, or maybe Nairobi. But if they really came from Paris they would surely be even more expensive than they already were.

She looked for the pair of shoes that Mma Ramotswe had identified. There was a pair placed on a pedestal, and she thought they were probably the ones. She peered at them. They were attractive, yes, and she could see how they might be tempting for somebody slightly older, but they were not quite right. Her eye moved to another pair, and then met the gaze of the assistant inside the shop, who was looking back out at her. The assistant waved; they knew each other and got on well.

Mma Makutsi pushed open the glass door of the shop. "*Dumela*, Patricia. You are well?"

The assistant smiled. "I saw you before you saw me, my sister. I could tell that you were coming in here. Shoes for your wedding?"

Mma Makutsi nodded. "Phuti has encouraged me. He says that I can buy whatever shoes I want. There is no budget on these."

Patricia was impressed. She clapped her hands together like a schoolgirl anticipating a treat. "No budget! He is a very good fiancé if he says 'no budget'! You must marry him quickly, Grace, so that he becomes a husband who says 'no budget.' Such husbands are very unusual. In fact, you usually only find them in museums, they are so rare. Husband museums."

They both laughed. But then Patricia leaned forward to touch Mma Makutsi sympathetically on the forearm. "I heard, Mma. I heard that bad news about poor Phuti's accident. So sad!"

Mma Makutsi thanked her. "He has made a very good recovery. You know that he lost a foot?"

Patricia closed her eyes in sympathy. They had a small box of single shoes in the back of the shop—shoes that had been separated from their twin through theft or bad stock control; would one of these fit Phuti, and thus find a home that way? She wondered whether she should ask, but decided that it might not be tactful, particularly so soon after the accident; perhaps later she might say, "Mma, there are some men's single shoes in the back, if they could be of any use . . ." Instead she said now, "Ow! I'd heard that, Mma. That was very bad news."

But bad news should not be allowed to interfere with the business of buying shoes, and the subject was gently changed. Leading Mma Makutsi to the display stands, Patricia gestured to the tempting array of shoes. "Look at this, Mma: Is this not a sight that makes you happy that you're a woman?"

They both laughed again.

"I am always happy I'm a woman," said Mma Makutsi. "Not just when I see nice shoes like this; I think that all the time."

She paused, her eye caught by a pair of black patent-leather shoes with red piping round the sides. They were not wedding shoes, but would be very suitable for wearing to dances—if she was going to go to dances, of course, which was now perhaps rather doubtful after Phuti's injury.

"Being a man is not easy," Mma Makutsi continued. "They are always struggling to prove that they are better than the next man."

"And they have those very rough skins," offered Patricia.

Mma Makutsi had not really reflected on that, but Patricia was right, she thought. Phuti's skin was not all that rough, but there was certainly a place on his neck where it looked as if he had reacted to the razor. Perhaps he should grow a beard. But that would merely exchange roughness for prickliness, and she was not sure which was worse.

"And yet," Mma Makutsi said. "And yet there is much to be said for some men."

"Oh, that is true," said Patricia. "Just as there are some women who are . . ." She left the sentence unfinished.

"Very bad," suggested Mma Makutsi.

There was a silence, finally broken by Patricia. "Such as . . ."

"Violet Sephotho."

"Exactly."

Again there was a silence. Then Patricia said, as if speaking to herself, "Violet Sephotho, the politician."

Mma Makutsi frowned. "Did I hear you correctly, Mma? Did you say, 'Violet Sephotho, the politician'?"

Patricia nodded. "I did. Have you not seen the posters?"

Mma Makutsi had not seen any posters, and now she listened with dismay as Patricia told her about the posters that had appeared in her part of town a day or two previously. These were emblazoned with a large photograph of Violet, under which there was an exhortation to vote for her in a forthcoming by-election. Mma Makutsi said nothing as she absorbed this news. She had heard of the by-election—caused by the death of a popular member of parliament—but she would never have imagined that Violet Sephotho, of all people, would turn out to be a candidate. Violet Sephotho the shameless husband- and fiancé-snatcher; she who at the Botswana Secretarial College had been lazy and uninterested, going so far as to laugh at several members of the teaching staff, and to mock their ways of speaking; she who had achieved barely fifty per cent in the college's final examinations, and yet who had gone on to get glittering job after glittering job (such was the injustice of the world). What possible claim could such a woman have to represent the people of Gaborone?

"I am very shocked," said Mma Makutsi. "It will be a very bad day for Botswana if that woman is elected to parliament. It will be the beginning of the end."

"It will not happen," said Patricia. "God will not allow it."

"God cannot stop everything," said Mma Makutsi. "He is very busy dealing with big things. He cannot watch the results of elections here in Gaborone."

"Then the voters will," said Patricia.

Mma Makutsi pointed out that the voters might not know the full extent of Violet's unsuitability to be their representative. "Not everybody has seen what she is capable of," she said.

"Then we must tell them," said Patricia. "I shall put a notice in the window of the shop saying *Do not vote for Violet Sephotho.*

Many people walk past the shop window every day, and they will see this message."

"Every little bit will help," said Mma Makutsi. "I might make a badge with the same message and wear it every day. And I could ask the Botswana Secretarial College to put it up on the notice board outside the college."

This idea appealed to both of them, and indeed there were others, of varying degrees of practicality. The placing of a notice in the shop window seemed possible, but Mma Makutsi was less sure about the Stop Violet–sponsored half-marathon, or the Violet Sephotho Prevention charity concert in the football stadium. "These are all interesting ideas," she said to Patricia. "But I do not think that we can do them all. For the time being we should just try the notice in your window."

Mma Makutsi now pointed to a pair of shoes near the top of the display. They were white, with a distinct satiny sheen, and had straps crossing at the ankle. She knew immediately that these were the shoes in which she would be married. The knowledge was a relief in a way, as it put an end to doubt, and having the right shoes—as these undoubtedly were—would make everything else, including the dress and handbag, fall into line.

Patricia reached forward and plucked one of the shoes from the display. "I knew it, Mma!" she exclaimed. "I knew that these would be the ones you chose. I didn't want to say anything, because I did not want to interfere, but I knew in my heart, Mma, that these would be the right shoes for you."

She handed the shoe to Mma Makutsi, who took it gingerly, as one might take possession of a great treasure, an item worthy of religious awe.

"Oh, my . . . ," Mma Makutsi muttered, as she examined the shoe. "This is a beautiful shoe."

"A very beautiful shoe," said Patricia. "And do you see that rose,

Mma? We have no other shoes, not one pair, that has a rose on the front. It is very rare."

Mma Makutsi touched the small leather rose; it was supple, soft, and dyed perfectly white, even on the underside of its petals. "So pretty," she whispered.

Patricia lowered her voice. "They will suit you, Mma. You are a very beautiful lady and you deserve these shoes."

Mma Makutsi looked away. She did not think that she was beautiful. She would like to be beautiful—when she was a young girl she had wished for beauty with all her heart, but had become reconciled to the fact that beauty was a gift conferred in the crucible of one's mother's womb and was not on offer at any later stage. But to hear Patricia say it made her wonder, for a moment or two at least, whether it was indeed true; whether beauty had somehow crept up and settled upon her, as age, or the signs of worry, might do.

Patricia consulted a screen to see if the shoe was in stock in the right size. It was, and she retreated into the back of the shop to retrieve the box. Returning a few minutes later, she took the shoes out with a flourish and indicated to Mma Makutsi that she should sit down to try them on.

The ankle straps were fastened with a small silver buckle, which Patricia did up with the facility of one with long experience in such things. "There!" she said, stepping back to survey the effect. "Now stand up, Mma, and see how the shoes feel. They mustn't pinch anywhere, or you will limp down that aisle, and that would never do." For a moment a picture flashed into her mind of Mma Makutsi, her large glasses flashing in the light from the church windows, limping down the aisle with Phuti, still feeling the effects of his injury.

Mma Makutsi stood up. The shoes had reasonably high heels, but they were not meant to be walking boots, after all, and she was accustomed to heels even higher than these. Not, of course, that she wore heels as high as those favoured by Violet Sephotho, who could be toppled, she always felt, brought down with just one judiciously timed push. Violet Sephotho! She did not want to think about that woman at a time like this, but the thought of her as a member of parliament made the back of her neck feel warm with resentment. Members of parliament could become government ministers, and that would be even worse: Violet Sephotho, Minister for Cosmetics and Husband-stealing, perhaps.

"Well, Mma? How do they feel?"

She told Patricia that the shoes were comfortable enough and that she would take them. If they could be put aside, then Phuti Radiphuti would call in later to pay for them, as he had promised.

Patricia looked over her shoulder. She was the assistant manager, not the manager, nor the owner, and her discretion was limited. But everybody knew who Phuti Radiphuti was, and was well aware that he owned the Double Comfort Furniture Store. If credit could not be provided to the fiancée of such a man, then it could be provided to nobody. "I know I'm not meant to do this," she said, "but I think it will be perfectly in order for you to take these shoes now, Mma. Phuti can come in tomorrow, or even the day after that. We trust you."

Mma Makutsi was on the point of saying that it did not matter to her if the shoes remained in the store, but then it occurred to her that it would be useful to break them in before wearing them in earnest. There was walking to be done at a wedding, and standing too, as you talked to relative after relative, friend after friend.

"Thank you, Mma," she said. "I think I'll wear them in."

Patricia looked surprised. "Are you sure, Mma? There is some rough ground round here, even in the parking lot. I've seen people break heels out there. Snap. No heel any more."

Mma Makutsi thanked her for the warning. "I shall be very careful," she said. "I shall watch where I'm putting my feet."

Patricia took Mma Makutsi's old shoes and wrapped them respectfully in tissue paper before putting them in a box. Mma Makutsi watched her friend at work; it was a vocation, this, almost akin to being called to higher secretarial office, or being, as she herself was, an associate detective. Patricia clearly treated shoes with respect, and this extended to tying the box up with string so that it could be more easily carried.

Her task completed, Patricia handed the box to Mma Makutsi. "I'll give you the invoice some other time, Mma," she said. "I haven't got the book. I'll make it out to Mr. Radiphuti, if you like."

Mma Makutsi indicated that this would be exactly the right thing to do. She felt slightly awkward about having the invoice made out to Phuti, but she reasoned that this would be happening a great deal in the future and she might as well get used to it. Then, sitting down on one of the fitting stools, she slipped into the new shoes.

It was an incomparably pleasant experience. The leather of the linings was as soft and as smooth as silk; it caressed the feet. And yet at the same time there was that firmness, that confidence of construction that new shoes have. The leather would yield, of course, but for the moment it was a great pleasure for her feet to be supported in this way.

She said goodbye to Patricia and left the shop. She could not help but look down at her feet as she walked, noticing the sharp contrast between the pristine white leather and the well-worn concrete of the walkway. It was the white leather roses that made the shoes so undeniably beautiful, she thought. Beside them, other shoes, the shoes of passersby, looked mundane and shabby in their lack of adornment.

Yes, came a voice. *We're special. You look after us, you hear!*

It was the shoes talking—she was sure of it. She had, of course, heard enough from footwear as to be ready for this sort of thing, but what struck her about these shoes was their confident, almost cocky tone. It was not for shoes to tell their owners what to do, she felt, so she simply ignored them.

You hear us, hey?

She continued to ignore them, and the shoes fell silent.

She was now in the car park, and was heading over towards the Tlokweng Road, where she could flag down one of the crowded minibuses that plied their trade between the outlying suburbs and the centre of town. The lot was busy, and Mma Makutsi had to dodge several vehicles making their way out of parking places: a wide, gold-coloured Mercedes-Benz purred past her, its pampered occupants looking out on the world with that odd mix of disdain and boredom that seems to afflict the wealthy; a pickup truck heavily laden with crates of beer, two smiling men in the cabin; an elderly woman in a small and ancient car, her face slightly familiar—a client of Mr. J.L.B. Matekoni, she thought. And then, suddenly, a tiny white van.

Mma Makutsi stood quite still. The van, which had been manoeuvred out of a narrow corner, now turned and began to drive between two rows of parked cars. For a few moments Mma Makutsi stared in silence, paralysed in her astonishment. Then she snapped out of her inaction and waved wildly, trying to attract the driver's attention. There was no doubt in her mind that it was Mma Ramotswe's old van. That van had a dent at the back, just above the number plate, where Mma Ramotswe had once hit a post down at Mokolodi—the post, Mma Ramotswe arguing, being in the wrong place. This van had a dent in that precise position, and the odds against it being another van of similar appearance were therefore remote.

"Come back!" she called. "I want to speak to you!"

She was heard, but not by the driver of the van, who appeared to be unaware of the gesticulating figure behind him. A couple of shoppers, carrying their groceries out to their cars, looked at her and wondered what was going on, but there was no reaction from the driver.

"Please stop!" shouted Mma Makutsi, beginning to run after the van. "Please stop!"

The van was not travelling fast as the cars on either side of it were packed tight. This meant that it was easy enough for her to gain on it. Now she was only a couple of hundred yards behind, and was struggling to draw breath so she might shout out once more. But just as she opened her mouth, she felt something give beneath her, and she lurched forward, all but losing her balance, almost tumbling over. She saved herself, but not her shoes. The near-fall was caused by the breaking of the left heel of her new shoes, and her saving of herself was at the cost of its right counterpart, which snapped off under the sudden strain.

Mma Makutsi looked down at her new shoes with dismay. One of them felt loose, and she realised that not only had the heel broken, but so too had one of the cross-straps. She looked back up, and saw that the white van was in the course of disappearing round a corner; a moment later it was gone. Her effort, and the loss of her new shoes, had led to precisely nothing.

It was a moment at which one might simply throw up one's hands and weep, and for a minute or two Mma Makutsi was tempted to do just that. But then, taking a deep breath, she bent to remove her new shoes. She would not give up and cry; not Mma Makutsi, who had struggled so much to get where she had got in life, who carried on her shoulders all the hopes and prayers of that family back in Bobonong; not Mma Makutsi, graduate *summa cum laude* of the Botswana Secretarial College with ninety-seven per cent (a mark since equalled by nobody); not Mma Makutsi, the future Mrs. Phuti Radiphuti and associate detective of the No. 1 Ladies' Detective Agency.

Taking her old shoes out of the box into which Patricia had tucked them, she slipped them back on her feet and continued on her way to the Tlokweng Road. One or two people had witnessed the tragedy, or at least had seen part of it: a young man passing by, a boy on a bicycle, an old man standing in the shade of a tree. But they had only seen a woman racing after a white van and then stumbling; they had seen her bend down and change her footwear before walking off towards the main road. So might we fail to see the real sadness that lies behind the acts of others; so might we look at one of our fellow men going about his business and not know of the sorrow that he is feeling, the effort that he is making, the things that he has lost.

PHUTI RADIPHUTI called round for dinner that night, as was his habit. Mma Makutsi greeted him at the door and hung his jacket on the peg she had put up in the kitchen for just this purpose. She was proud of that peg, of the shining brass of which it was made, of the fact that she had positioned it in exactly the right place. She had an eye for decor, she felt, and she was looking forward to decorating their new home, when Phuti got round to acquiring it. Not much progress had been made in house-hunting—indeed, the search had not even begun yet, in spite of the steadily broadening hints she dropped in that direction.

That evening it was Phuti himself who brought up the subject of houses, although perhaps not with the intention of discussing their own situation.

"We sold a very large sofa today," he remarked, as Mma

Makutsi dished out the mashed potato. "It was every bit as wide as this room. I went to the customer's house with the delivery men."

"That must be a sofa for very wide people," said Mma Makutsi.

Phuti laughed. "Actually, they were very thin. He looked like a rake and his wife was not much more than a beanpole. I do not know why they need a sofa as big as that."

Mma Makutsi thought for a moment. "Perhaps they have very fat friends," she suggested. "Or perhaps they want a big sofa because they themselves are very small. Mma Ramotswe has a theory like that about men and cars."

"She has many theories," said Phuti. It was not a sarcastic or unkind remark, of the sort that one might make about an opinionated person; Mma Ramotswe did indeed have theories, and Phuti Radiphuti in general had a high regard for her views.

"Yes," continued Mma Makutsi. "She believes that men who buy big, powerful cars are making up for not feeling big and powerful inside."

Phuti Radiphuti considered this. He knew several people with such cars, and he thought that there was some truth in Mma Ramotswe's observation.

"I like going to see people's houses," Phuti said. "That is why I often go out with the delivery men. This house—the big sofa house—was very nice. Freshly painted. All yellow outside and green inside. It was a very pretty house."

Mma Makutsi seized her opportunity. "There are some very good houses," she said, and added, almost wistfully: "Some of them are for sale, I think."

Phuti nodded. "There are always houses for sale. Many houses."

Mma Makutsi looked down at the mashed potato on her plate. It made a small range of mountains, intersected by rivulets of dark brown gravy. An ant, she thought inconsequentially, might look on this and think it was a whole country.

She looked up. "Of course, when there are many houses for sale then that will be a good time to buy a house. That is what they call the law of supply and demand. We were taught about it at the Botswana Secretarial College. They mentioned it many times there."

Phuti nodded, but only vaguely. "And you?" he asked. "What did you do today?"

"I went—" she began, and stopped. She had been about to tell him about her trip to the shop to buy shoes, but she could not bring herself to confess to the disaster that had occurred. If she could get the shoes repaired, she could tell him then. But for now it was just too embarrassing—and too painful.

Phuti took a mouthful of potato, swallowed, and then wiped his mouth with the piece of paper towel Mma Makutsi had put by his plate. "Yes? You went . . . ?"

"I went to work," she said.

"Ah. And what happened there?"

"The usual thing."

"Nothing out of the ordinary, then?"

"No. As I said: the usual."

He nodded. "So it was a so-so day? Just so-so?"

"So-so," said Mma Makutsi.

There was a silence, and they both set to finishing their mashed potato and gravy. As she ate, Mma Makutsi could not help but remember what Mma Ramotswe had once said about telling the truth. "Not saying something can be exactly the same as telling a lie, Mma Makutsi," she had said. "There are lies you tell with your lips and lies you don't need your lips for. And once people start telling lies, then they become like spiders who weave their web about themselves. They become stuck—caught by the lies all about them. And then they can't get out of the web, no matter how hard they try." Mma Ramotswe had shaken her head in regret over these mendacious unfortunates, and then, as an afterthought, had added, "That is well known, Mma Makutsi. That is well known."

CHAPTER EIGHT

THE EVENTS OF AN EVENTFUL MORNING

HAVING BEEN the first to arrive in the office the next morning, Mma Ramotswe was one cup of tea ahead of Mma Makutsi. It was her second cup of red bush tea of the day, the first having been consumed in the garden of her house on Zebra Drive on her early morning walk-round. She did that walk every day, at exactly the same time, with the result that she was sure the birds she saw were those she had seen the day before, and the day before that. Some of them, she suspected, recognised her and understood that whatever dangers the day ahead held in store for them, this particular woman was not among them. And there were many dangers for birds— from snakes in the trees in which they made their nests to the hawks and eagles that could descend like arrows from the sky above. She remembered as a girl being called by her father to witness a noisy drama taking place in a tree on the edge of their fields near Mochudi. She had heard the birds before she had seen them, as they filled the midday air with strident, high-pitched squawking. And as she and Obed approached the tree, she saw a whole dancing flock of birds, dark little dots against the sky, dipping and darting above the canopy of a spreading acacia.

"Why are they dancing?" she had asked.

"Not dancing, Precious. They are defending their home."

Nearing the tree, they stopped, and he pointed to a dark shape that was the birds' nest. "Can you see it?" he asked. "There—just over there."

She had stared into the tangle of twigs and leaves. There was movement, but she was not sure what it was, until suddenly one of the twigs seemed to unwind itself and move sinuously between two neighbouring branches.

"Yes," said Obed. "That is the snake. And these poor birds can only shout and fly about. They cannot stop their enemy."

She had asked him to throw a stone, to deter the snake from its attack on the nest, but Obed had simply shaken his head. "We cannot do that," he said. "We cannot always stop the things we do not like."

She had been astonished. Everybody threw stones at snakes—it was what people did—and his refusal stuck in her mind. Later, much later, she remembered his words and pondered them. *We cannot always stop the things we do not like.* She knew now what he meant, of course—that nature had to be left to take its course—but she had realised that there was a far greater truth there too. There were some things that one could stop, or try to stop, but it was a mistake to go through life trying to interfere in things that were beyond your control, or which were going to happen anyway, no matter what you did. A certain amount of acceptance—which was not the same thing as cowardice, or indifference—was necessary or you would spend your life burning up with annoyance and rage.

Mma Makutsi might be gently reminded of this, she thought. Her assistant allowed herself to be annoyed by the apprentices—particularly Charlie—and by their feckless ways; it might be better, Mma Ramotswe felt, if she accepted that young men behaved fool-ishly no matter what anybody said to them, and that the only real cure for that was time and maturity. You could speak to them, of course, you could try to show them where they were going wrong, but you should not work yourself up into an impotent rage when they went off and behaved in exactly the same way as young men always had.

Charlie had come into her thoughts that morning as she walked about her garden. She wondered whether he would be at work that day. He had absented himself from the garage before on more than one occasion, but returned a day or two later, full of excuses, usually relating to family funerals or sick aunts or matters of that sort.

"Just how many grandfathers do you have, Charlie?" Mr. J.L.B. Matekoni had asked once. "If I remember correctly—and you must tell me if I am wrong—you went to the funeral of your grandfather ten months ago, and then again three months back. And now he has died again. This is very sad that he should be dying so much."

Mma Makutsi, who had overheard this reproach, joined in gleefully. "That is very unfortunate, Charlie," she said. "Most of us have to die only once. Once. You are making your poor grandfather die over and over. That is not very kind, Charlie."

On those occasions he had come back, and Mr. J.L.B. Matekoni, who was not only a fine mechanic but a good and generous employer too, had done nothing more than dock a small amount from the young man's pay—not even the proper amount that should have been forfeited, as Mma Makutsi had pointed out.

"Mr. J.L.B. Matekoni, you are too kind to that young man," she said. "He has to learn that no work means no pay. That is lesson number one, as they taught us at the Botswana Secretarial College. *Stay away, no pay; full day, can play.* That is what we were taught."

But Mr. J.L.B. Matekoni had just smiled. "When men are young, like Charlie, the brain is not quite right. It is like an engine that goes smoothly most of the time, but then backfires. That is what is happening. And it doesn't help to lose patience, you know."

Mma Ramotswe thought that Charlie's latest disappearance might be more serious. Although they had talked about the need for him to assume his responsibilities for his twins, she had her doubts as to the likelihood of this. It might have been unwise to put too much pressure on him, as he might just decide—as he probably already had done—simply to move away. There were jobs elsewhere to be had by young men with some mechanical skills, even if they were not fully qualified mechanics. Somebody had recently approached Fanwell with the offer of a well-paid post at a safari camp in the north, and had the young man not been reluctant to leave his family, he might well have seized the opportunity. If Fanwell, who was much quieter and less assertive than Charlie, could attract such offers, then Charlie could certainly do the same. The Okavango Delta, remote as it was, would be a good place for a young man seeking to avoid the demands of a girlfriend with twins.

She had finished her tea and walked back to the house. It was now that the day's work began: the rousing of Mr. J.L.B. Matekoni, who was quite capable of sleeping through his alarm clock; the waking up of the children and helping Motholeli to dress and get into her wheelchair; the preparation of breakfast—these were just the first of the many tasks that the day entailed. And then, of course, there was the office, and the . . .

. . . and the first cup of office tea, which she had almost finished by the time Mma Makutsi came in, put her bag down beside her desk, and started the day with a wail. "Oh, Mma Ramotswe, I am very, very upset. This is terrible. Oh, I do not know what to do— I do not."

Mma Ramotswe rose to her feet, crossed the room and put an arm round her assistant's shoulder. "Oh, Mma, what has happened?"

Mma Makutsi, feeling that perhaps she was being a trifle over-dramatic, tried to smile. "I'm sorry, Mma, I didn't mean to make you think the world is coming to an end. No, it is not that bad." She paused as Mma Ramotswe, looking relieved, returned to her desk. "But it is still bad. Very bad."

Mma Ramotswe did not have to prompt her assistant any further.

"I bought those shoes," Mma Makutsi began. "They were not quite the shoes that you saw, but they were like them. They were very beautiful, with white flowers on the front, made of leather, of course."

"Very suitable," muttered Mma Ramotswe.

"I have never seen such pretty shoes before," continued Mma Makutsi. "And they were comfortable too. They were very comfortable."

Mma Ramotswe noticed the ominous use of the past tense. The shoes had been stolen, perhaps, or left behind in a minibus. Anything left behind in a minibus would never be seen again, as Mma Potokwane had once discovered. She had taken a minibus back to Tlokweng one day after shopping in town for a new dress. The parcel containing the dress had been left under a back seat; a few days later she had seen her new dress being worn by a woman standing by the side of the road. She had tackled her about it, of course, but the woman had claimed to have been given the dress by a friend, and would certainly not be handing it over. And if Mma Potokwane wished to take the matter any further, she was perfectly welcome to raise the matter with the woman's brother, who was a policeman and did not take kindly to false accusations of crime being levelled against perfectly innocent persons . . .

Mma Makutsi sniffed. "I wore them out of the shop and I saw . . . well, I saw something and ran after it. And then I tripped and I broke both heels and a strap." She paused to sniff again. "And then I went home and Phuti came for dinner and I did not tell him what happened because I was so ashamed. And now I'm ashamed for not telling him. I am filled with shame, Mma Ramotswe—filled with shame."

Mma Ramotswe waited to see if Mma Makutsi had finished. She understood why anybody should feel upset about such a thing—particularly if shoes meant as much to you as they did to Mma Makutsi—but she had heard of considerably worse disasters than this. She knew, however, that it never helped to tell another that their troubles were eclipsed by the troubles of others, tempting though that might be. If you have a sore tooth, it does not help to be told that there are people with far more severe toothaches. Yet one thing in this story intrigued her: What had Mma Makutsi seen that made her want to run after it? People spoke of chasing a bargain: Had she seen something on sale in one of the shops? For a moment, she allowed an irreverent image to form in her mind of Mma Makutsi, her large glasses catching the sun, running towards a stall with a sign on it reading BIG SALE — HURRY! HURRY!

She banished the picture from her thoughts. "Tell me, Mma, what did you see that made you want to run?"

Mma Makutsi hesitated. "I will tell you in a moment, Mma. First, look at my poor shoes."

She extracted the damaged shoes from her bag to show Mma Ramotswe.

"See? See how beautiful they were, and now . . . Now, they are just rubbish."

Mma Ramotswe rose from her desk to examine the shoes. "This is very sad, Mma, but don't you think they could be fixed? These heels, they could be glued together, and this strap could be stitched. It should not be hard to stitch something like that."

She handed the shoes back to Mma Makutsi. "But what did you see, Mma? What made you run?"

Mma Makutsi replaced the shoes in her bag. "I think I saw a ghost," she said quietly.

There was silence. Then Mma Ramotswe spoke. "In broad daylight?"

Mma Makutsi examined her fingernails. "If ghosts exist, Mma—and I am not prepared to exclude that possibility—then why should they just appear at night? Where do they go during the day, might one ask?"

"I don't know," said Mma Ramotswe. "It would be interesting to find out."

Mma Makutsi agreed that it would. "In this case," she went on, "the ghost that I think I saw was the ghost that maybe you yourself saw only a few days ago—the ghost of your late van."

Mma Ramotswe gasped. "My van?"

"Yes, Mma. It was in the parking lot near the shops, on the Tlokweng Road side. I saw it reversing out of a parking place and I tried to stop it. But the driver did not hear me, and he just drove off."

Mma Ramotswe reflected on this. So the van really was running once more, in spite of Mr. J.L.B. Matekoni's conviction that it would not. And the driver was a man—that was an additional piece of information; as was the fact that he shopped at the River-walk shops—another piece of potentially useful knowledge. "I do not think it is a ghost," she said. "It is my van. I had heard that it had been bought by a young man up north somewhere, near the Tuli Block. I thought it had been bought for parts, but he must have changed his mind." She paused; perhaps something about the van had stayed his hand and he had been unable to end its life. "Yes," she continued. "That's what must have happened."

Mma Makutsi nodded. This seemed quite reasonable to her. "Well, you must be happy that it is back on the road, Mma."

Yes, thought Mma Ramotswe, I am. But in a curious way, if the knowledge that the tiny white van had been restored was reassuring, it was also saddening. Some other person—somebody who did not necessarily appreciate the white van—would be driving it while she, who loved it, was driving a new blue van of very little character. If only they were able to change places . . . She stopped herself. The thought had occurred to her on a whim, but now that she thought of it more seriously it seemed so obvious. The person who currently owned the white van would probably very much like to have a newer van. If she were to approach him and offer to exchange vans, he would no doubt leap at the chance.

The idea was a delicious one, and it brought a broad smile to her face.

"So you're happy, Mma Ramotswe," said Mma Makutsi. "You are smiling. That is very good."

Mma Ramotswe brought herself back to reality. It would be ridiculous to exchange a new van for an old one—far better to buy the tiny white van back. She now became aware that Mma Makutsi was speaking to her . . .

"I was thinking of something," she said quickly. "But we should really get back to work, Mma Makutsi, or we would spend our whole day talking and thinking about this and that."

"Yes, you're quite right," agreed Mma Makutsi. She knew, though, that talking and thinking about this and that was exactly what both she and Mma Ramotswe would love to do, but could not, as that brought in a great deal of happiness but no money, and a lack of money had a tendency to diminish happiness in the long run. It need not, of course, and she remembered that she had been happy enough when money had been tight. Now things were different, but she realised that she would have to remind herself of how life had been before. Those who had enough money, she thought, often forgot those who had none. Mma Ramotswe had once told her that, and she had remembered it. "Never forget, Mma," she had said, "that there are people who will be looking at you and wishing to be in your shoes. Because they have no shoes, you see." It was a puzzling comment, and a rather odd one, but now that she called it back to mind she found that she knew exactly what Mma Ramotswe had meant.

BY THE TIME of the mid-morning tea-break, Mma Ramotswe and Mma Makutsi had more or less completed the task of sending out the month's-end invoices. This was a pleasant task—the direct opposite of the business of paying bills, and now that the No. 1 Ladies' Detective Agency was reasonably well established, the invoices always added up to more than the bills to be paid. It had not always been so, especially in the early days of the agency, when there had been the merest trickle of clients and an even smaller number of invoices, given Mma Ramotswe's habit of taking on meritorious cases for no fee. She still did that, but there were plenty of cases that paid well enough to give them both a modest but adequate living.

"That's that then," said Mma Makutsi, as she stuck the last stamp on the final invoice. "Two thousand pula for knowing that your wife is a bad woman. I feel sorry for that man, Mma."

Mma Ramotswe glanced at the envelope. The Ditabonwe case. "Yes, that poor man does not deserve it. He should not have married that woman."

"Three boyfriends," said Mma Makutsi disapprovingly. "And all the time she was living in that expensive house and eating her husband's food."

"And where will the boyfriends be when they discover that she no longer has any money and has been thrown out of the house? Will they be at her side, Mma Makutsi?"

"They will not," said her assistant.

They were silent for a moment, both contemplating the foolishness of others—their bread and butter. Then Mma Ramotswe made a gesture of resignation. "People do not learn, Mma," she said. "But I suppose we must carry on hoping that they will. You never know." She paused, looking at the kettle. "And now, I think, it's time for tea. Would you mind switching on the kettle, Mma Makutsi?"

The tea was infusing in the pot when Mr. J.L.B. Matekoni came in, closely followed by Fanwell. Mma Makutsi, who was lining up the mugs on the filing cabinet, turned and looked the two men up and down. "No Charlie," she said.

At the mention of his fellow apprentice, Fanwell looked down at the floor.

"No," said Mr. J.L.B. Matekoni. "There is no Charlie, is there, Fanwell?"

Fanwell muttered something that none of them could make out.

"Well, Fanwell?" Mma Makutsi pressed. "I did not quite hear what you said. No Charlie, is there?"

"He is not here," said Fanwell. "I am here, but he is not. I am not his boss. I cannot answer for him."

Mma Makutsi glanced at Mma Ramotswe before turning again to the young man. "You know where he is, though, don't you?"

"I do not," muttered Fanwell.

Mma Makutsi shook her head. "I think you do, Fanwell."

Mr. J.L.B. Matekoni, pouring tea into his mug, made a gentle intervention. "I don't think we can expect Fanwell to know Charlie's whereabouts," he said. "You would tell us if you knew, wouldn't you, Fanwell?"

Fanwell thought for a moment. "He asked me not to tell you," he said.

"Ha!" exclaimed Mma Makutsi. "So he told you. You see? I was right. You cannot lie to me, Fanwell. You can't fool a detective."

Fanwell looked to Mr. J.L.B. Matekoni for help. Mma Ramotswe noticed this, and came to his rescue. "You mustn't worry, Fanwell," she said quietly. "Mma Makutsi is trying to be helpful, you see. We don't want to punish Charlie—we just want to make sure that he's all right."

"And make sure that he faces up to his responsibilities," interjected Mma Makutsi.

Mma Ramotswe made a calming gesture. "Mma Makutsi, please . . ."

"Justice," said Mma Makutsi. "That's what I believe in, Mma. Justice for wronged women, that's all."

Mma Ramotswe rose to her feet. "Fanwell, you come with me for a moment. Just come with me." She pointed to the door.

They went out through the garage, past the car on which the young man and Mr. J.L.B. Matekoni had been working.

"That poor car," remarked Mma Ramotswe. "It looks so sad with all its parts exposed like that. And yet you and Mr. J.L.B. Matekoni will put it all together again and it will be as good as new. It's a great skill you have, Rra."

Fanwell smiled with pleasure. "Thank you, Mma. It is easy when you know how."

It is easy when you know how. Yes, thought Mma Ramotswe. It was easy when you knew how, and right at that moment she was thinking of how Mma Makutsi most certainly did *not* know how, at least when it came to dealing with young men.

They went out from under the shade of the garage eaves, out into the warm morning sun; above them an empty sky, so high, so pale, and a bird, a speck of black, circling in a thermal current. Mma Ramotswe took Fanwell's arm and walked with him towards the acacia tree behind the garage. The young man, she noticed, was shivering, as if a cold breeze had suddenly blown up from somewhere; but the air was still.

"You're upset, Fanwell, aren't you? You're shivering."

He nodded almost imperceptibly.

"Why?" she asked. "Are you afraid of something?"

He did not answer immediately, but looked up into the sky. She followed his gaze. There was nothing; *or nothing I can see,* she thought.

"Charlie told me not to tell anybody," he said. "He has come to my place."

Mma Ramotswe nodded. That made sense.

"So he is staying at your place? With your grandmother and the children?"

"Eee, Mma." It was the way that people said yes, and it could be said through an exhalation of breath. It was an eloquent sound, capable of registering a range of emotions. The suggestion here was of regret, tinged with fear.

"It is not right that he should put you in this position," said Mma Ramotswe. "Charlie should not put his problems on your shoulders."

Fanwell turned to face her. "He said he would kill me."

Mma Ramotswe gasped. "Charlie said that?"

Fanwell inclined his head. "He said that if I told anybody where he was, he would kill me."

Mma Ramotswe snorted. "What nonsense! He didn't mean that, Fanwell. You know how Charlie is always talking nonsense. Big words that mean nothing—nothing at all."

Fanwell was not convinced. "He meant it, Mma. He put his fist in my face like this—shaking it about—and then he said that if I told anybody he would come at night when I was sleeping and pinch my nose so that I had no air. He showed me how he would do it."

"Pinch your nose!" exploded Mma Ramotswe. "That is complete, one hundred per cent nonsense, Fanwell. You cannot stop a person breathing like that. If you pinch somebody's nose, then they simply open their mouth and breathe that way. Charlie was joking— he must have been."

Fanwell listened to her, but still looked miserable. "Please do not come to fetch him," he said. "I do not want that. Even if he does not kill me, he will do something bad to me."

Mma Ramotswe reached out to touch him lightly on the forearm. "Very well," she said. "I will not come and look for him."

"And you won't tell Mma Makutsi?"

She assured him that she would not. "But you will have to do something for me," she said. "You must tell him that I have offered to help him. You must give him that message from me. You must tell him that he should come to my house—at night if he likes. He should come to see me and I can tell him how I shall be able to help him."

She waited for the young man to respond, and eventually he did. He would pass this message on to Charlie, he said, and he would try to persuade him.

They walked back to the garage, where Mma Ramotswe left him while she went back into the office.

"Where is he, then?" asked Mma Makutsi. "Did you get it out of him?"

Mma Ramotswe put a finger to her lips. "Subject closed, Mma," she said. "Closed until further notice."

She looked over her shoulder through the open door into the garage. Fanwell was standing next to Mr. J.L.B. Matekoni, looking down at the engine on which they were working. He seemed so slight beside the well-set figure of the older mechanic—not much more than a boy really, with all the vulnerability that boys have. The sight tugged at her heart and she turned away again. She knew that Fanwell supported his grandmother and several of his younger brothers and sisters on his tiny salary as an apprentice. Yet he never so much as mentioned this fact, nor complained about it. This made her think: those who have a great deal to complain about are so often silent in their suffering, while those who have little to be dissatisfied with are frequently highly vocal about it.

CHAPTER NINE

WITH REFERENCE TO THAT
PREVIOUS KISS

MMA RAMOTSWE liked to leave the concerns of the office where they belonged—in the office. But that evening, as she drove home from work, following the tree-lined route that she liked to take through the older area of town known simply as the Village, she found herself thinking of the Moeti case. She had done nothing about it that day—there had been other things to claim her attention—but now she found herself considering possibilities. As often happened, the words of Clovis Andersen came to mind. His general advice, applicable to almost all cases, was to talk to as many people as possible, or rather to get them to talk to you. *The more you listen, the more you learn,* he wrote in *The Principles of Private Detection,* and Mma Ramotswe had been particularly struck by the wisdom of these words, even on one occasion drawing them to the attention of Mr. J.L.B. Matekoni. He had frowned, inclined his head, and said, "Well, Mma, I think that is certainly true. You cannot learn anything if you close your ears. I think that is undoubtedly true."

She had gone so far as to work these words into a small needlework sampler that she had embarked upon, the words forming the centre part of the piece, with detailed pictures of Kalahari flowers around the edge, all executed in colourful thread. She had been pleased with the result, and had donated it to the sale of work in aid of the Anglican Hospice. It had sold well, she was told, to the wife of a hotel manager, a woman widely known to be something of a gossip. The humour of this had not escaped the ladies running the sale of work, who had all agreed that the woman in question was contemplating the listening being done by others rather than by herself.

Mma Ramotswe was certainly prepared to listen to anybody who had any light to shed on the unfortunate fate of Mr. Moeti's cattle, but she realised that it was going to be difficult to find that person or persons. It would be different if the case were in some suburb of Gaborone, or even in a village; one could always find somebody in the street with views to express—one of the neighbours usually. But this was in the country, where one's only company as often as not were the birds, or the small creatures that scurried through the bush. There was that boy, she recalled, and the woman who worked in the house. Mpho seemed to know something, but he was clearly frightened of Mr. Moeti—for whatever reason—and she doubted whether she would get anything out of him. Unless, of course, she were able to speak to the boy in private, if she could somehow get him on his own somewhere. Boys could be good informants, as she had discovered on a number of earlier occasions; boys saw things, and remembered them.

As she paused at a crossroads to allow a couple of trucks to lumber past, she considered the chances of a private conversation with Mpho. The boy was the son of the woman who worked in the house, the one she had met, so he presumably lived with his mother in the staff quarters behind the house. She was not sure how old he was, even if she was certain that he was under the age of legal employment; but that made no difference. There were plenty of children who worked on farms, unofficially, and there were even some who worked in towns. *Bobashi* were children whose parents were dead, or who had run away from home and who survived by their wits. They tended to be found in the towns rather than in the country; she had even come across one who lived in a storm-water drain, a scrap of a child with a face that had seemed so prematurely worldly-wise. She had tried to bring the child to the attention of Mma Potokwane, but when she had driven the matron to the place where she had spotted him, he was no-where to be seen. "They move about," said Mma Potokwane, sadly. "One day they live in a drain, the next day they are up a tree. There is no telling with that sort of child."

This boy was certainly not like that; he had a mother, and might even be in school. It was certainly not uncommon for children to attend school in the mornings and then work in the afternoons, especially now that the Government had made primary education compulsory. She wondered whether she would be able to speak to the mother. Botsalo Moeti had implied their relationship was a close one, but that meant very little. He would be using her, as likely as not, and she would no doubt be in awe of him—there were many such arrangements between strong men and vulnerable, desperate women. So, she thought, this woman, from her position of weakness, would not be what Clovis Andersen would call an "independent witness." *If somebody works under somebody,* the great authority wrote, *then do not expect that person to tell the truth about the person above him. He may either lie to protect his superior, lie because he is afraid of him, or lie in order to get revenge for some insult or slight.*

Mma Ramotswe decided that even if there would be no point in talking to the woman in the kitchen, it was still worth trying to seek out the boy; he knew something—she was sure of it. If he was in school, then perhaps she could speak to him there. That would involve finding the most likely village school for him to attend and then speaking to the teacher there. She would require some sort of pretext for this. Could she offer to give a talk to the school? "The Life of a Private Detective" by Mma Precious Ramotswe. They would be surprised, she thought, and might insist on her obtaining permission from the Ministry of Education or the local council or something like that. No, that would not work; it would be far better to use the tactic that she had employed on so many previous occasions when she needed something, and that was to ask for it directly. It was a rather obvious thing to do, but in her experience it was usually very effective. If you want to know the answer to something, then go and ask somebody. It was a simple but effective adage—one that perhaps should be embroidered on a sampler and sold at fundraising sales. Well, she would try it in this case, and see what happened. And if she drew a blank, then there was still another lead to follow: the key ring that had been found near the scene of the crime.

She had no idea what to make of that, but she was now getting closer to home, and she decided to concentrate on her driving and on the thought of the meal that she would shortly be preparing. There was a large chunk of fine Botswana beef waiting in the fridge, and as she turned into Zebra Drive she imagined that she could even smell it. It would gladden the heart of Mr. J.L.B. Matekoni, who loved beef, and it would be good for the children too, who loved all sorts of food, without any exception that she had yet discovered. She was of that school of thought too. Beef, pumpkin, potatoes, stringy green beans, melon—all of these things were loved by Mma Ramotswe; as were cakes, biscuits, doughnuts, and red bush tea. Life was very full.

MMA MAKUTSI also prepared a meal that evening, although she was cooking for two rather than four. Phuti had told her he would be late, as he had a meeting with a furniture supplier and would not be able to get away until almost seven o'clock. That meant that they would not sit down to eat for at least half an hour after their normal dinner-time. "Not that I mind waiting," he said over the telephone. "I'd wait for ten hours or more for your cooking, Grace. I'd wait all day."

It was a typical gallant remark by a man whose good manners stood out, even in a country noted for its politeness.

Mma Makutsi laughed. "I will not keep you waiting longer than is absolutely necessary," she said. "We shall sit down at the table the moment you come in the door."

"Yes," he said. "And then we can discuss the wedding. There are some details I must ask you about."

She hesitated. What details did he have in mind? She thought of her shoes—or, rather, the remnants of her shoes. If he asked her about those, then she would have to confess that they were already destroyed, and he might wonder why she had not spoken to him about that the previous day.

"I'd like that," she said blandly. "We have so much to plan."

Now, with the meal almost ready and the hands of the clock inching round to seven-fifteen, she took a deep breath and told herself not to worry. Phuti was a kind man, and he would understand if she told him about the shoe incident. She would tell him straight-away, she decided—the moment he came in through the door.

Shortly before seven-thirty she saw the beam of his car's head-lights swing past her paw-paw tree and come to rest on her front window. The lights threw the pattern of the bars on the window against her kitchen wall, and then she heard a car door slam. The car moved off. That would be his driver going away.

She was ready for him at the door. He smiled as she asked him in. "I am very hungry now," he said.

He sat down, his injured leg sticking out at an angle that she was only now getting used to. The prosthetic ankle and foot were concealed by a sock and a shoe, but every so often the unnatural angle they adopted reminded one that they were there. He was confident that they would work well, he had said; the prosthetic appliance people had done a remarkable job. "Of course I'm lucky," he pointed out. "There are people who cannot afford a leg. They cannot work. They lose their jobs. All for a leg." He paused, then added, "That is, in places like Malawi. Not here. We are lucky."

She had said, "Yes, we are lucky." And she had meant it. Mma Makutsi's memory of poverty was a recent one, and there were members of her family who, if they were to lose a leg, would never be able to afford an artificial one, were it not for the hospitals that the country's diamonds paid for.

She invited Phuti to the table and began to serve their dinner.

"This wedding of ours," he said. "It is getting closer and closer. We must make more plans."

Mma Makutsi nodded. "I have made a list. There is one column of things for you to do and one of things for me to do."

Phuti expressed satisfaction over this approach. "But before we go into that," he said, "you must tell me what you are wearing. What about those shoes? Have you bought them yet?"

Mma Makutsi looked down at her plate. It was a direct and unambiguous question—exactly what she had most feared. Had he simply made a general enquiry about her outfit, she could have talked at length and in great detail about her dress, or about the outfit she had planned for her bridesmaid. But this was a question that would be rather difficult to avoid.

"Those shoes?" she said faintly. "It's very important to get the right shoes. You know, I was looking at a picture of a bride the other day in *Drum*. And do you know, she was wearing a pink dress and bright yellow shoes. Bright yellow shoes, Phuti! She looked ridiculous. I laughed and laughed, and so did Mma Ramotswe."

Phuti Radiphuti smiled. "Yes, very silly. She should have worn pink shoes to go with her pink dress, or maybe a yellow dress to go with her yellow shoes." He took a forkful of food and then continued, his mouth half full, "But did you buy those shoes?"

Mma Makutsi looked vaguely into the middle distance. "Shoes? Oh, those shoes. They are very nice . . . You know, I've been wondering about your suit. Should we have it dry-cleaned now and put away in one of those plastic bags, or should we—"

"It has been dry-cleaned already," said Phuti. "It is in a bag and the bag is in a cupboard. It is very safe. But what about the shoes? Did you buy them?"

Mma Makutsi put down her fork and wiped her mouth carefully on a corner of her paper table napkin. "You are a very handsome man," she said.

Phuti looked surprised. "I am just an ordinary man . . ."

"No," said Mma Makutsi. "You are one of the most handsome men in Botswana. That is what people say, you know."

Phuti smiled nervously. "I think that there are many more handsome men than me. There definitely are."

Mma Makutsi edged her chair towards his, a curious manoeuvre that involved her folding the seat of the chair as she pushed it closer to Phuti. "I'd like to kiss you, Phuti," she said.

He dropped his knife onto his plate; there was a loud clatter.

"Do not be shy," said Mma Makutsi.

"I . . . I . . ." He had not stammered for a long time, but now it came back.

Mma Makutsi inclined herself forward and planted a kiss on his cheek.

"There," she said. "I am happy now that I have kissed you."

Phuti's lower jaw seemed to quiver. "Oh," he said.

"Yes," she said. "I am very happy."

He was silent for a moment. Then he said, "With reference to that previous kiss . . ."

"Yes?"

"Would it be possible to have another one?"

Mma Makutsi reached for his hand and squeezed it. "Of course," she said. "There are lots and lots of kisses."

There was no further discussion of shoes.

AFTER THEY HAD FINISHED DINNER and Puso and Motholeli had been put to bed, Mma Ramotswe and Mr. J.L.B. Matekoni sat together out on the verandah of their house on Zebra Drive. They often did this after a meal, savouring the slightly cooler breeze that sometimes moved between the trees, listening to the sounds of the night, so different from those of the day. Insects who were silent from dawn to dusk had their say once the sun went down, knowing, perhaps, that the birds were elsewhere. Those who lived in the Kalahari, or on its fringes, were told as children that these chirruping noises at night, these sounds that were like high-pitched clicks, were the stars in the sky calling their hunting dogs. And it sounded just like that, thought Mma Ramotswe, although all those things that sound so right were often just poetry, really—the gravy we put on reality to make it taste a bit better.

It was a good time for sitting together, Mma Ramotswe felt, and it was not necessary to say anything. That evening, the sky was all but white with stars, filled with acres and acres of constellations, right down to the horizon. She had learned the names of some of these clusters when she was younger, but had forgotten most of them now, apart from the Southern Cross, which could be seen hanging over the sky towards Lobatse, a pointer to the distant Cape and its cold waters. And the Milky Way was there too—she had always been able to identify that, like a swirl of milk in an ocean of dark tea. As a girl she had imagined the Milky Way was the curtain of heaven, a notion she had been sorry to abandon as she had grown up. But she would not abandon a belief in heaven itself, wherever that might be, because she felt that if she gave that up then there would be very little left. Heaven may not turn out to be the place of her imagining, she conceded—the place envisaged in the old Botswana stories, a place inhabited by gentle white cattle, with sweet breath—but it would surely be something not too unlike that, at least in the way it felt; a place where late people would be given all that they had lacked on this earth—a place of love for those who had not been loved, a place where those who had had nothing would find they had everything the human heart could desire.

She looked at Mr. J.L.B. Matekoni, sitting beside her, a mug of tea in his hands.

"Thinking of ?" she asked. "What do they say? I'll give you a thebe if you tell me your thoughts."

He laughed. "Some of my thoughts are not worth a thebe."

"I can be the judge of that."

"Charlie," he said. "I was thinking of Charlie. And you?"

He turned to her, and for a moment there was light in his eyes, a reflection of the half-lit doorway behind them.

"Me? I was thinking of the next thing I should be thinking of. I have a case that I need to deal with."

He nodded. "That Moeti business?"

"Yes."

"I do not know that man. I could ask around, though, if you want me to. There is a man at the automotive trades school whose brother lives down there, I think. Or cousin. Or somebody."

She smiled at the thought. It was like that in Botswana—people knew one another, or if they did not, they thought they did. And that was how she wanted it. There were places, she realised, where everybody was a stranger and where, when you saw somebody, you knew that you might never see them again in this life. She could not imagine Botswana being like that. Here there were no real strangers—even if you did not know a person, he was still the brother or cousin of somebody whom you might know, or whom somebody else would know. And people did not come from nowhere, as seemed to be the case in those distant big cities; everyone had a place to which they were anchored by ties of blood, by ties of land.

"Thank you," she said. "But don't bother to speak to your friend. I have had an idea." She told him about the boy, Mpho, who surely went to the local school. Teachers, she said, were helpful as long as you treated them with sufficient respect; she would have a word with the village teacher and see what came of that.

Mr. J.L.B. Matekoni thought for a moment. "I have a cousin who is a teacher in those parts," he said. "He is not the one you want to speak to, I'm afraid, but he will know that one. His school is on the other side of the Lobatse road, but roads are—"

"Nothing," said Mma Ramotswe. "Roads go through the land, not through people."

"Exactly," said Mr. J.L.B. Matekoni. I am a mechanic, he thought, and I cannot put it as well as Mma Ramotswe can. But what she said about roads was quite true, he decided, even if he felt that the matter would require further reflection. "Shall I ask him, then?"

Mma Ramotswe nodded. "Just an introduction, Rra. Just ask

him to tell the teacher that there will be a lady coming down from Gaborone who wants to talk to him. Or her, if the teacher is a lady. Say that this lady will not want to talk for long and will be no bother at all."

He could not imagine Mma Ramotswe ever being a bother to anybody at all, and he told her so. She thanked him, and then they went on to finish their tea.

CHAPTER TEN

THE TEACHER WAS A SMALL MAN

MR. J.L.B. MATEKONI was proved right. His cousin knew the teacher at the village school close to the Moeti farm. He would send a boy, he said, to let the other teacher know that Mma Ramotswe was coming; it was only ten miles there and back—nothing for a young boy who probably walked five miles to school every day anyway. He would do so immediately, first thing that morning.

"In that case," said Mma Ramotswe to Mma Makutsi, "I shall go down there straightaway, Mma. You will be in charge here. The office is in your hands."

"I am ready for that," said Mma Makutsi, adding, "I have often thought of what would happen if you had an accident, Mma."

Mma Ramotswe, who was retrieving the key for her van from its drawer, looked up in surprise. "An accident?"

Mma Makutsi was momentarily flustered. "Heaven forbid that it should happen, Mma. I was just thinking of what would happen to the business if you were to have an accident and . . ."

"Die?"

"No, no, Mma Ramotswe. Not die. Just be in hospital for a while. I wondered what would happen here in the agency. Would I need to get an assistant? Would I be able to handle all the important cases? Those are the things that I was thinking about." She paused. "But it is like thinking of what would happen if Botswana suddenly became a very wet country, or if cattle learned Setswana, or something equally unlikely. Just dreaming, really."

Mma Ramotswe straightened up. "Well, I'm sure that you would handle everything very well," she said. "Just as I hope I would, if you were ever to have an accident, which I very much hope never happens, Mma."

Mma Makutsi changed the subject, and talked about some correspondence that had been dictated by Mma Ramotswe but still had to be sent off. She would do that, she said, and do some filing, too, if she had the time. Mma Ramotswe thanked her, and left.

SHELL: the shell of an ostrich egg. Somebody had broken it and left the fragments by the side of the path that led to the school. It was a neatly kept path, one of those Mma Ramotswe would describe as a *government path*, marked on each side by a line of whitewashed stones. In the old days of the Protectorate, when the British still had their district commissioners, there were many such paths throughout Africa, and whitewashed tree trunks too. This habit of whitewashing had lingered in some places, where people thought of it as a way of holding disorder at bay: lines of white stones represented structure, a bulwark against the encroachment of the bush.

The ostrich shell was out of place; perhaps one of the children had brought it in to show the others and had dropped it, or there had been some childish fight that had led to its destruction. Mma Ramotswe reached down and pocketed a piece, feeling the thickness of the shell as she did so. Then, she continued on her way to the small cluster of buildings—no more than two or three—that made up the local primary school.

"Yes, Mma?"

A woman had emerged from the smaller of the two buildings and was staring at Mma Ramotswe.

Mma Ramotswe began the traditional greeting. Was this woman well? Had she slept well? And the woman asked the same questions of her, and then again said, "Yes, Mma?"

"I have come to speak to the teacher," said Mma Ramotswe. "My husband knows the teacher at the other school—the one over on that side. He is his cousin, and he said—"

The woman raised a hand to stop her. "Yes, you are that lady, Mma. We have heard that you would be coming. There was a message. You are welcome."

"Thank you. I will not take much of the teacher's time."

The woman indicated that this did not matter. "I am the school secretary. There is just me and the teacher. We are the staff, and we get very few visitors, Mma. We are very happy that you've come to see us."

Mma Ramotswe followed the woman into what she saw was a small office. The walls were plastered, but unpainted. There were no ceiling boards, just a criss-cross of wooden beams and the underside of a corrugated-iron roof above. In the centre of the room there stood a rectangular, three-drawered desk of the sort found in a thousand government offices up and down the country. Behind it there was a revolving chair covered in threadbare, greasy brown fabric. At the side of the room, pushed up against the wall, was another, smaller desk on which an unstable tower of box files had been built.

"This is the teacher's desk," said the secretary, pointing to the desk in the middle of the room. "And that one over there is mine. This is also the staff room." She smiled at her own joke. "When teachers come from bigger schools, they say, 'Where is your staff room?' And I say, 'You are in it right now!'"

She gestured to a spare chair that had been placed in front of the teacher's desk and invited Mma Ramotswe to sit down. "You sit there and I shall fetch the teacher."

While the secretary was out of the room, Mma Ramotswe looked about her. The walls were almost bare, apart from a small cluster of notices pinned to a square of discoloured soft board. There was a timetable of the hours from eight in the morning until one in the afternoon, with a subject noted after each: eight—roll-call and arithmetic; nine—Setswana and geography of Botswana; and so on through the day. Reading it brought a smile to Mma Ramotswe's face, as did a small notice addressed to "All Staff," setting out the dates of the school terms. It would be like putting up notices to herself and Mma Makutsi, she thought, although she could include notices about tea and the washing of teacups addressed to Mr. J.L.B. Matekoni and the apprentices.

A voice came from behind her: "Mma?"

She spun round. The teacher was standing in the doorway, the secretary behind him. She drew in her breath sharply; she had not expected this. The teacher was very short—a dwarf, in fact—and the secretary, who was a woman of barely average height, towered over him.

She recovered her poise quickly. "*Dumela,* Rra. I was just looking at the timetable. You must be very busy."

The teacher inclined his head. "There is just me," he said. "Me and this lady here, who you have already met."

He crossed the floor and extended a hand in greeting. Mma Ramotswe reached down; it seemed so strange to be bending to shake hands with a man. His handshake felt firm, almost too firm, as he gripped her.

"Please sit in that chair, Mma," he said. "I will go to my desk."

He walked round the desk, his head barely showing above its surface. "My name is Oreeditse Modise. And you, Mma, are . . . ?"

She gave her name, and he wrote it down solemnly on a pad of paper on his desk. That done, he looked up at her and smiled. There was something about the smile that touched her; it was as if he were reaching out to her.

"I am married to Mr. J.L.B. Matekoni," she said. "He is the cousin of your colleague at the other school."

Mr. Modise made a further note. "Cousin," he said. "That is very good."

"I am a detective," said Mma Ramotswe.

She expected him to note this down too, but he did not. This information had clearly surprised him, and he threw a glance in the direction of his secretary, who opened her mouth slightly in a silent *oh*.

"Not a police detective," said Mma Ramotswe quickly. "I am a person who works for people who have private problems. That sort of detective."

She saw him relax.

"Oh," he said. "I see."

"There has been a very unpleasant incident at a farm near here," she said. "There was—"

"I know all about that, Mma." Mr. Modise put down his pencil and leaned back in his chair. "There was a dastardly attack on some innocent cows over at Mr. Moeti's place. Very bad."

The secretary let out a wail. "Very bad! Cows! Cows!"

"So you're working on that, are you, Mma? Then I am very happy to assist in any way. We cannot have people attacking cattle in this country. We cannot."

"No, no!" shrieked the secretary.

Mma Ramotswe felt that the temperature in the room was rising rather higher than perhaps it should. "We must remain calm," she said quietly. "It is the sort of thing that makes anybody angry. But we must remain calm if we are to deal with this."

"Yes, indeed," said Mr. Modise, glancing at the secretary. "I am calm now. You need not worry, Mma. We are all calm."

Mma Ramotswe realised that her fears as to their cooperation were misplaced: these two, at least, were allies—the entire staff. She told them why she had come to see them. There was a boy called Mpho, whose mother worked in the Moeti house . . .

"Mpho?" said the teacher. "That boy is one of ours. He is in the classroom. He is there right now." He picked up his pencil and wrote the name on his pad of paper: MPHO, in capital letters.

Mma Ramotswe clasped her hands together involuntarily. It had worked.

"Does that boy know something?" asked Mr. Modise.

She explained about her meeting with the child on the Moeti farm. "I am sure that he knows what happened," she said. "But I am equally sure that he was frightened. So I need to speak to him."

"Yes, yes," said the teacher, making a signal to his secretary. "Fetch him straightaway. Then we can ask him about this thing. We shall get the truth out of him and he will tell us, or we shall give him a beating."

Mma Ramotswe gasped. "Please! Let's not beat anybody. And . . ." She paused. It would be impossible to speak to the boy in the teacher's presence, and yet she would need to be tactful. "If you wouldn't mind too much, I think it might be better for me to speak to him privately, Rra."

"Why? I am his teacher."

"Yes, and I'm sure that he respects you very much. But in my experience, Rra—and I have been a detective for a few years now—I find that some witnesses, and particularly children, do not speak freely if there is somebody they like and respect in the room. They say what they think that person will want them to say, Rra. It is very curious, but human nature is strange, and that is what I think."

He looked at her doubtfully for a moment, and then nodded his agreement. "You're the expert, Mma."

She thanked him for his understanding, and noticed how he beamed at the compliment. What compliments were paid to a teacher out in the bush, she wondered; and to a teacher like this, a small man who must be accustomed to the stares of others?

"It is nothing, Mma," he said. "Nothing at all. Would you like to speak to him in here, or outside?"

"Outside," she said quickly.

THE BOY MPHO, part-time herd boy, son of a domestic servant, a rather puny little boy who probably did not know who his father was—a boy with a running nose discharging mucus onto his upper lip—stood before her, shaking with fear.

They were under a tree a short distance from the schoolroom itself. It was hot, and the shade was welcome. From inside, through the open windows of the schoolroom, came the sound of the children reciting their tables. *Two fours make eight; three fours make twelve; four fours . . .*

"You remember me, Mpho?"

He looked up at her briefly, and then down at his feet. He was barefoot, and his feet were dusty. Such little toes, thought Mma Ramotswe.

"Yes, Mma. Yes."

She smiled at him. "You mustn't be afraid of me, Mpho. Look . . . look here." She reached into her pocket and took out the fragment of eggshell.

He glanced at the shell and said, "It's broken."

Mma Ramotswe handed it to him. "You can have it, if you like. There. Some people think that this brings good luck. Have you heard that before?"

He shook his head as he reached out to take the shell from her. She saw that he used both hands to receive the gift, as was proper. Somebody was still teaching children the right thing to do, even a poor little boy like this who could not have had much in his short life. She wondered whether he had ever been taken to Gaborone—probably not; or given a treat—almost certainly not. She remembered her first ice cream and the pleasure she had derived from that; how lucky she felt to have had a childhood in which she had been able to lay down good memories.

"When I saw you last time, Mpho," she said gently, "I thought you were a little bit frightened of something. I don't want you to be frightened now."

He continued to stare down at the ground. He was still shaking, she noticed.

"Sometimes, you know," she continued, "it's better to talk about something rather than to keep it inside you. Nobody is going to punish you for speaking to me, you see. And I won't tell anybody that you have spoken to me. I promise you that."

He remained silent. A shadow crossed the ground beside them, the shadow of a large bird, a buzzard perhaps, that was soaring between them and the sun.

"Rra Moeti won't know," she said quietly.

The effect of this was immediate. He looked up sharply, into her eyes; and she saw his fear.

"He cannot harm you," she said. "He is not allowed to harm you. There is . . ." What, she wondered, was there to stop Mr. Moeti harming this child? The law? As embodied by whom? A policeman in a police post fifteen miles away? An official in an office in Gaborone even further removed from the world inhabited by this boy? "It is not allowed," she said.

He stared at her. His lip was quivering, and then the tears came. She stepped forward and put her arms around the boy as he sobbed. She felt him shaking in her embrace, the shoulders so narrow, so vulnerable.

She did not say anything until his sobs had subsided and she was applying her handkerchief to his nose. "There, Mpho. That's better now."

"I'm sorry," he stuttered. "I'm sorry I did it, Mma. I'm very bad and they can send me to prison now."

Mma Ramotswe had not expected this. "You . . . you did it, Mpho? Those cattle? The cattle you looked after?"

He nodded silently.

"But why? Why would you harm the cattle?"

"Because Rra Moeti is a bad man, Mma. He has done bad things to my mother."

Mma Ramotswe drew in her breath. The inexplicable becomes explicable, she thought. Yes, it was more or less as she had imagined. The poor servant woman and the powerful farmer. It was nothing new; it would be happening up and down the country—up and down every country, no matter where it was. People with money and land treated those without either of those things as they wished. Poor people were at their mercy; it had always been like this, and, sadly, it would probably not ever change very much. Oh, there would be changes on the surface, with laws and regulations making it harder for people to take advantage of others, but there would always be places, places off the beaten track, that laws and regulations never reached. And there would always be men of the view that laws that protected women had nothing to do with them, or were not meant to be taken seriously.

She took stock of the situation. The boy must have seen his mother abused—beaten, perhaps, or made to cower—and decided to take matters into his own hands. He must have felt completely powerless in the face of his mother's tormentor, and then realised that there was a way in which he could strike back at Moeti. Every

Motswana loved his cattle, and Mr. Moeti was no exception. If one really wanted to hurt him, then what would be easier than to take a knife to the very cattle who knew and trusted one?

She was not sure what to say. Mpho had caused major loss and she could hardly ignore that, especially as it was her responsibility to find out what had happened. But how could she throw him on the mercy of Mr. Moeti—the very man who had been cruel to his mother? She remembered, too, that she had promised him that Mr. Moeti would never know that he had spoken to her.

She looked down at the boy. "Listen to me, Mpho. What you did was terrible—one of the worst things anybody can do. You must never do anything like that again, Mpho. Never. Do you understand?"

"You are going to beat me, Mma?"

She tried not to smile. "Of course not. What I'm saying is this: I can see how you felt very angry when you saw your mother being harmed. But you can't go and do something like that, even if you think that man deserved it. It is not the way we do things here in Botswana. Do you understand?"

He had stopped shaking, she noticed, and she thought that his voice sounded stronger.

"I understand, Mma."

She looked at him. She suspected that this boy knew all about punishment, and children who knew about punishment often did not need to learn any more.

"All right," she said. "You remember what I said. You remember it. Now, let's go back to the classroom."

She walked him back to the schoolroom, her hand in his. As they crossed the short expanse of hot red earth she asked him whether he enjoyed being at the school. "And Mr. Modise?" she said. "Do you like your teacher?"

Mpho nodded. "I like him, Mma, even if he is too small, Mma."

"Yes, he is small," she said. "But you must always remember: small people are often big inside—and that is what matters."

"Maybe," muttered Mpho.

SHE DROVE BACK to Gaborone deep in thought. There were some enquiries that fizzled out remarkably quickly, when a well-placed question led to the rapid unravelling of what had seemed to be a tangled and opaque skein of confusing facts and half-truths. She had not expected the solution in this case to come quite so quickly, and so simply; but that, she reminded herself, was how many problems in this life sorted themselves out—quickly and simply.

She found herself thinking of Mpho's mother—the woman she had met in the Moeti house; of her subservient manner in the presence of her employer; of his dismissive manner towards her. She wished that she could do something about that—could release the woman in some way from the near-servitude in which she must live her life. But what could she do? This sort of oppression was nothing new; men did that to women everywhere, all the time, and there were some cases, less common perhaps, where women did it to men. Things had become better, of course, with the achievement by women of greater equality, but the news of all that would hardly have penetrated out there. A farm could be a little world, a law unto itself; even a house could be that too.

And then she thought of the boy. Her first reaction had been to believe him. His distress had clearly been genuine, and the words of his confession had come tumbling out unrehearsed. But children made things up, including confessions.

For the time being, though, she would act on the assumption that he had been telling the truth. One thing was clear: the confession did not put the matter to rest. She had her duty to Mr. Moeti to consider; she might not like him, but he was, after all, her client, and she could hardly keep the truth from him. At the same time she realised that she could not go to him and reveal that Mpho was responsible for the attack. Not only was there her promise to the boy, but if she did identify him as having been responsible for the incident, then she would be accountable for whatever harm came to him, or indeed to his mother. Could she tell Mr. Moeti that she had discovered the culprit but that she would punish him herself? Mr. Moeti would hardly accept that, and he would have a point.

When she arrived back at the office, while Mma Makutsi made tea, Mma Ramotswe gave her an account of her visit to the school. She told her assistant about Mr. Modise, which interested Mma Makutsi a great deal; she had a cousin who was very short, she said, and had fallen into an anteater's burrow. "He was too short to get out," she explained. "And so he had to stay there until somebody came that way and pulled him out. But before that the anteater came back and was very cross that there was this short person in his burrow. Apparently he growled and tried to bite my cousin. It was a very dangerous situation."

Mma Makutsi had several more stories to tell about this cousin, but Mma Ramotswe gently interrupted her after the second story—a rather long-winded and unfortunate tale about the cousin's marriage to an unusually tall young woman. "Perhaps you could tell me the rest of the story some other time, Mma," she said. "I need to talk to you about this Moeti business."

"But it was very funny," persisted Mma Makutsi. "You see, when a very short man marries a tall woman—"

"I can imagine," said Mma Ramotswe. "But I really have to make some sort of decision, Mma, and it would be helpful if you could advise me."

Mma Makutsi put aside thoughts of short men and tall women and gave Mma Ramotswe her attention. She listened intently as Mma Ramotswe described the boy's sudden confession, clicking her tongue in disapproval. "Children do very bad things these days," she said, "because they see television. If you turn on the television, what do you see, Mma? You see people being violent—that is all that there is. And if you were a child watching that, what would you think? You'd think that this is how we should behave—breaking things, breaking people."

Mma Ramotswe understood that, but she wondered whether it applied in this case. "I doubt if that boy sees television," she said. "He is a herd boy and his mother is a kitchen servant, second-class. I doubt if he has seen television."

"Then he will have heard about these things, Mma. That is how it happens. And remember that all those violent television signals are all around us, in the air. How do you know that violence doesn't spread that way?"

Mma Ramotswe did not wish to argue about this novel, and in her view highly dubious, theory. What she wanted to find out was what Mma Makutsi would *do* about this. "But what would you do, Mma?" she pressed.

Mma Makutsi thought for a moment. "I would tell Moeti that you have heard that he has brought this upon himself by behaving badly. Then I would tell him that it was unlikely to happen again. If you have stopped it, then I think that you have done him a good service."

Mma Ramotswe was doubtful. "I don't know if he'll look on it that way," she said.

"Well I don't see how it would help him to punish that boy," said Mma Makutsi.

"You're right," said Mma Ramotswe.

"You could go to the police," said Mma Makutsi. "The police are always there."

Mma Ramotswe sighed. "I promised the boy that I wouldn't speak to anybody about what he said. Perhaps I shouldn't have made that promise, but I did. At that point I was thinking of him as a witness, you see, not as the person who did it."

"But, why didn't Moeti go to the police himself?" asked Mma Makutsi. "It's up to him if he wants to make it a police matter. He didn't—he came to you. So in fact it is not for you to go to the police, Mma. No."

"Perhaps not," said Mma Ramotswe.

"Well then," said Mma Makutsi, in a certain tone of satisfaction. "Well then, that solves that, doesn't it? QED—as we were taught to say at the Botswana Secretarial College."

"QED?" asked Mma Ramotswe. "What does that stand for?"

Mma Makutsi looked uncomfortable. "QED? I'm not one hundred per cent sure. I think it might mean *There you are,* or maybe *I told you so . . ."*

Mma Ramotswe came to her rescue; she understood Mma Makutsi's sensitivity, and she did not want to show her up. "You may not be one hundred per cent sure," she said. "But I imagine that you'll be at least ninety-seven per cent sure!"

It was a very good joke, and it enabled them both to leave the issue of the Moeti attack and start thinking of something else. But Mma Ramotswe remained less than satisfied. She felt vaguely guilty, as if she had embarked upon a plan to conceal a major crime. And that, she suddenly realised, was what she had almost done; it was not for her to decide whether or not to disclose what had happened. A crime had been committed, even if it was a crime by a child—something that should normally be dealt with by a stern talking-to and promises by parents. No, she would have to go and see the boy's mother and hand the affair over to her. She would plead for the boy, but she could not protect him, nor his mother, completely; the world was not as she would like it to be, but there was very little she could do to change that. Withholding the truth from Mr. Moeti was wrong, but it was also wrong to break a promise to a small, vulnerable child, who would never forget that an adult he trusted had let him down. So here she was faced with two evils, and the lesser one, she was sure, was unquestionably the one to choose.

CHAPTER ELEVEN

CHARLIE COMES TO ZEBRA DRIVE,
BY NIGHT

THAT EVENING Charlie came to the house on Zebra Drive. He came quietly, appearing at the back door like a wraith, startling Mma Ramotswe, who was washing up after dinner. She had been standing at the sink, her hands immersed in soapy water, when she noticed the movement outside, half in the darkness, half in the square of light thrown out from the window.

"Charlie!"

He did not hear her; he was staring in through the window now, as if searching the room. She waved a hand, signalling to him, and he glanced at her.

"I'll let you in," she mouthed.

He did not look as if he wanted to come in, as he now seemed to retreat back into the shadows.

"Wait. Don't go away."

She dried her hands perfunctorily before opening the door that led from the kitchen to the yard outside. The open door cast an oblong of light in the yard outside, revealing the figure of Charlie, standing awkwardly by one of the struggling shrubs that Mma

Ramotswe had planted in that difficult, rather sandy part of her garden.

She made an effort to appear natural, as if the arrival by night of an unannounced visitor lurking in the darkness was nothing unusual.

"So, Fanwell passed on my message," she said. "I'm glad that you've come."

He mumbled something that she did not catch.

"Why don't you come into the kitchen?" she asked. "I can give you something to eat, if you like."

He shook his head. "I'm not hungry. And I don't want to see the boss."

She made a gesture of acceptance. "You don't have to see him. We can talk out here." She moved towards him, taking his hand. "I often like to come out into the garden at night, you know. It's a good time to smell the plants. They smell different at night, you see. They—"

"I cannot stay long," he said.

"You don't have to. You can go any time. But it would be better, don't you think, to talk about this."

She drew him towards the side of the house, to two old iron chairs they kept outside and rarely sat in, but he resisted.

"It is my business," he said sullenly. "I am not a child."

She squeezed his hand. "Of course it's your business, Charlie. Of course it is."

"Then why does she shout at me, that woman? Why does she—"

"Mma Makutsi?"

He sniffed. "She is like a cow. She is always talking like a cow."

Mma Ramotswe shook her head. "You two don't see eye to eye, do you?" It was, she felt, putting it mildly; Mma Makutsi and Charlie had sparred for as long as they had known each other—a personality thing, Mr. J.L.B. Matekoni had said. Petrol and diesel, he had added; they don't mix.

"She cannot tell me what to do," continued Charlie. "Those babies . . ."

Mma Ramotswe waited for him to finish the sentence, but he fell silent. "Those babies," she said gently. "Your children."

"I did not tell her to have them," he said. "It is her fault. She is a stupid girl."

Mma Ramotswe bit her lip. Mma Makutsi, she felt, might have a point; she kept her voice from rising. "Nobody has to marry somebody they don't want to marry," she said evenly. "It is not a good idea to make people do that—they will only feel unhappy."

"I don't want to get married yet," said Charlie.

"Then don't," said Mma Ramotswe. "And she may not want you to, anyway. Have you spoken to her about it?"

He had not, he said. He had not seen Prudence since she had told him that she was pregnant.

Mma Ramotswe was still trying to be gentle, but her question slipped out. "Why? Why did you do something like that, Charlie?"

She saw the effect of her question: there was pain in his expression; she could see that, even in the faint light from the window.

"What could I do, Mma? I cannot look after her children."

"*Your* children, Charlie."

He opened his mouth to say something, but she stopped him. "But let's not speak about that, Charlie. Would you like me to talk to her?"

She saw his eyes open wide.

"You, Mma?"

She sighed. "Yes, Charlie. I can go. Sometimes it is easier if you get somebody to talk to somebody else for you. They can explain.

They can tell the other person how you're feeling. That makes it easier."

She could tell that he was torn, and she pressed her advantage. "I could tell her that you feel you can't get married, but that you would like to do something—even if it is not very much—to help with the babies. It's not money, I think—not in this case. It's maybe just enough for you to visit the babies so that as they grow up they have a father."

He was listening, she thought.

"But what if she makes me marry her?"

"I don't think she will. And I can tell her not to talk about that—if she'll listen to me."

Charlie was silent. "And Mma Makutsi?"

Mma Ramotswe did not hesitate. "I'll talk to her too. I don't think she will say anything." She hesitated. "Remember, I am her boss, after all. And I know that she can be a bit . . . a bit forceful at times."

She had not anticipated it, but this remark seemed to change everything.

"You can tell her to shut up, Mma?" Charlie said. "That is very good. All the time I thought that everyone agreed with her. There were all these women. You. Her. Mma Potokwane too. All against me."

"Well, I'm not against you, Charlie. I promise you that." She paused. "And you'll come back to work tomorrow? If you do, I'll tell Mr. J.L.B. Matekoni. He won't say anything."

"Nothing?"

"I'll talk to him too. He'll understand."

Charlie considered this. "He's a good man."

"Of course he is, Charlie, and so are you, you know."

Had it not been quite so dark, Mma Ramotswe would have seen the effect of her words. Charlie, who had been slouching, as if expecting some sort of physical blow, seemed to grow in stature. The furtiveness with which he had acted disappeared, and he stepped forward, as if putting the shadows, real and otherwise, behind him. "Thank you, Mma. Thank you . . ." His voice became choked.

She looked at her watch. "It's getting late, Charlie. Would you like me to run you home in my van?"

"I am at Fanwell's place."

"I can take you there. Go to the van. I'll fetch the key."

They drove across town to Old Naledi, where Fanwell lived with his grandmother. It was a poor neighbourhood—the poorest in town—and the lighting was non-existent. At one point they took a wrong turning and drove up an unfamiliar road. Charlie thought that they would be able to get back to where they wanted to be if they took the next road on the right, and told Mma Ramotswe to continue.

"You could get really lost in here," she said. "Even in daytime."

"There are too many houses," said Charlie. "They shouldn't let people put these things up." He peered into the night. "Turn here, Mma. This road goes round the back there."

Mma Ramotswe swung the wheel of the van. The beam of the headlights moved across a makeshift fence and the walls of a house behind it, then back to illuminate the surface of a road that was not much more than an urban track, unpaved and bumpy. A struggling tree beside it and then a gate, another house, a bit larger this one and painted an indeterminate colour—in that light it was difficult to make out just what—and on the edge of the road a bit further along, half on the track, half off, parked carelessly as every vehicle seemed to be in this ramshackle place, a small van, and in this case there was no mistaking its colour, which was white.

She saw it a few seconds before Charlie did, and put her foot firmly on the brake.

"No," he said. "This is the right way. Carry on."

"Charlie," she stuttered.

And then he saw it too. "Oh," he said. "That looks like your old van, Mma."

Mma Ramotswe engaged gear and drove forward slowly, stopping just short of the other van. In the glare of the headlights, the white was bright, almost shiny. She switched off the engine, but left the lights on.

"It's my van, Charlie. I know it."

"There are many such vans, Mma. White is a popular colour."

"This one is mine," she said. "I'm going to check. There is a place where a post hit me."

She got out of the van and was followed by Charlie. Bending down, floodlit in the darkness, she examined the place on the bodywork where she had encountered the errant post. It was there, in exactly the right place. She straightened up and moved towards the front, peering in the window on the driver's side. Yes. It was there—the large scratch on the metal dashboard that Puso as a small boy had made with a knitting needle.

She turned to Charlie. The lights were shining directly into her eyes, two great suns in the darkness, and she could not make out his face. "It is definitely my van, Charlie. There is that dent, and the scratch that Puso made. This is my tiny white van."

He had been persuaded. "Well," he said, touching the bodywork affectionately. "So here it is, Mma. Our old friend. Still going."

She looked about her. The house outside which the van was parked was slightly better than many around it—there was a well-kept yard with a small chicken coop, a lean-to latrine with a tap on the outer wall, a path on the side of which small stones had been lined. The house itself was in darkness, although lights were on in neighbouring homes.

"So, Mma," said Charlie. "It is good to see this van still going. It must have cost a bit to fix up. Or maybe it was done by somebody with a lot of time on his hands."

"Like me."

They both spun round. The voice had come from behind them, from the roadside rather than the yard. A man was standing in the middle of the road, a shape in the darkness.

"That is my van," he said, addressing himself to Charlie. "What are you doing, Rra? Why are you looking at my van?"

Mma Ramotswe answered. "We are not doing anything wrong, Rra," she said. "I used to own this van. We were driving past and I saw it. That is all."

The man came closer; now they could see him properly in the headlights. He was of stocky build, somewhere in his thirties, wearing neat khaki trousers and a white shirt. As he looked at them, they saw him relax.

"I put some work into it," he said. "But most of it was done by the man up north who bought it before me. He didn't have the time to finish, and so I did the rest."

"You are a mechanic, Rra?" asked Charlie.

"No," said the man. "I am not a mechanic. Not a proper one."

"I am," said Charlie. "Tlokweng Road Speedy Motors."

"I know the place," said the man. "That woman detective place."

"And that is me," said Mma Ramotswe. "I am that woman."

The man nodded at her. "You drove the van, Mma?"

She reached out to touch it. "For many years, Rra. Many years."

"And now? Now this nice new vehicle here?" He gestured towards the blue van. "Lucky you."

Mma Ramotswe agreed that the new van was comfortable, indeed smart. But she still loved the old van, she confessed. It had been a friend.

"I know what you mean," said the man. "You get used to a car, I think. It is like an old pair of shoes."

"It grows to fit you," said Mma Ramotswe.

The man nodded. "Well . . ."

Mma Ramotswe drew in her breath. There were moments in life when something had to be said, or be left unsaid forever. It was ridiculous—she knew it was—but she had to speak.

"Tell me, Rra, would you consider selling this van if you were given a good price—and I mean a *really* good price?"

Charlie glanced at her and frowned. She touched him on the wrist—a gesture to tell him to leave it to her.

"A really good price?"

"Yes, Rra. What if somebody paid you enough for you to buy a newer van? Not a really new one, of course, but one that had much less mileage. Much less."

The man did not hesitate. "I would say yes," he said. "Anybody with any sense would say yes if such a person came along."

"I am that person," said Mma Ramotswe quietly.

Charlie tried to intervene. "Mma, what would Mr. J.L.B. Matekoni say?"

Mma Ramotswe answered curtly. "It is my money, Charlie. Mine. And if I wish to spend it on a van, then—"

"All right," said Charlie. "But let me ask what has been done to the van."

Mma Ramotswe turned to the man. "You have already answered that, Rra, haven't you?"

The man now appeared to scent an opportunity. "Everything has been done, Mma! Everything. New this, new that, new the other thing. Yes, everything."

"There," said Mma Ramotswe to Charlie. "You heard him."

Charlie shook his head. "What is a *this*? What is a *that*? Those are not mechanical terms, Mma."

The man defended himself. "She is a lady, Rra. You do not want to burden ladies with talk about big-ends and rebores. You should know that—as a mechanic."

"That is right," said Mma Ramotswe. "There is no point in making ladies unhappy with mechanical details." She touched the car again. "Can we talk tomorrow, Rra?"

The man nodded eagerly. "I work at that electrical store at Riverwalk. You know the one?"

"I do," said Mma Ramotswe. "Can I come to see you some time soon to discuss the price?"

"Yes," agreed the man. "When you get there, you ask for Daniel. That is me. I am not always in the front, and they may have to fetch me from the back office. I am assistant manager, you see."

"Then that is what I shall do, Daniel," said Mma Ramotswe.

They said goodnight and returned to the blue van. As they drove away, Daniel waved cheerfully before opening his gate and disappearing up the path lined with stones.

"I do not think this is a good idea, Mma," said Charlie. "This van is very good. It was very expensive. What are you going to do?"

"I am going to sell it, Charlie."

He whistled. "You can't. You can't sell this good van and buy back your old van. You can't do that sort of thing, Mma."

"Can't I?" said Mma Ramotswe. "Why not? Can you tell me why not?"

SHE DROPPED CHARLIE at Fanwell's house, which was in darkness. He had become silent again, but she did not have the impression that he had changed his mind about returning. She took his hand briefly before he got out of the car and squeezed it. "You can sleep well tonight, Charlie," she said. "No need to worry."

On the way back home, she thought about what she had done. She had acted impulsively—she recognised that—but there were times when that was what you had to do. And did it matter, did it really matter that she would probably lose money in the sale of this blue van? Mr. J.L.B. Matekoni had bought it for her, but he had used the money in their joint bank account to do so, and she had put that money there from the profits of the No. 1 Ladies' Detective Agency. She and Mr. J.L.B. Matekoni shared everything and normally did not even think about who earned what, but if he were to call her to account for the sale of the blue van, she could always point out that she had effectively paid for it.

Would he understand why she felt she had to have her tiny white van back? She did not think that he would: men didn't love things in the same way as women did. They were fond of some things, of course, but she did not think that they *loved* things in that way. The heart of a man was different—every woman knew that.

That was what she thought, but then, as she drove round the roundabout near the Anglican cathedral she thought of her father, the late Obed Ramotswe, and of how he had loved his battered old hat. That was where it came from, perhaps—her love of the white van was love of exactly the same sort that her father had had for his hat. So maybe she was wrong about men; maybe they did love things in the same way as women; maybe they had just as many tears to shed for the things they had lost.

She arrived back at the house to find Mr. J.L.B. Matekoni waiting anxiously in the kitchen.

"Where have you been, Mma? I was worried."

She put the van key down on the table. "Charlie," she said. "He came to see me."

He looked incredulous. "Charlie?"

She told him of her encounter with the young man, and about his promise to return to work. "Just pretend that nothing has happened," she said. "Don't say anything. Just carry on as normal."

"But it has happened," he said.

"Yes, but there are times when something that has happened has to be treated as if it hasn't. This is one of those times, I think."

He shrugged. "I do not always understand you, Mma Ramotswe."

She laughed. "And another thing, Rra. What would you do if I did something that you thought was a very bad idea, but that I really wanted to do? What if that thing was a thing that made me very happy, but looked ridiculous to you?"

He frowned. "Something your heart was set on?"

"Yes," she said. "Something that my heart said I just had to do."

"In that case, I would say to myself: It is an odd thing that Mma Ramotswe has done, but if that is what makes her happy, then I am happy too."

She looked at him fondly; that he had been sent to her, when there were so many other, lesser men who might have been sent, was a source of constant gratitude. That we have the people we have in this life, rather than others, is miraculous, she thought; a miraculous gift.

CHAPTER TWELVE

CARBOLIC SOAP AND LIES

THE NEXT FEW DAYS were marked by the fact that virtually nothing happened. Such spells in otherwise busy lives are like breaks in bad weather: we know that they will not last, and our knowledge of their impermanence makes them seem all the more precious. But although throughout this time scarcely a soul crossed the threshold of the No. 1 Ladies' Detective Agency, both Mma Makutsi and Mma Ramotswe had more than enough to occupy their thoughts. For Mma Makutsi, the main concern was her impending wedding; the date was fast approaching, and the invitations had already been posted. Her long list of preparations was now marked by rows of ticks as task after task was completed with all the efficiency one would expect of one who, after all, had achieved a hitherto unheard-of ninety-seven per cent in her final examinations. But there were still things to do, and things to worry about, or to worry that Phuti was not worrying about enough.

An example of the latter was the cattle that would be used for the wedding feast. A very large cow and three well-fed goats had been identified for this purpose, and Phuti was meant to have arranged for them to be brought in from his family's cattle post.

Had this been done? And what about the cow he had promised her people for their feast up in Bobonong? Was this going to be purchased up there, or would it be taken up from the Radiphuti cattle post? These were important questions, and Mma Makutsi was not entirely satisfied that Phuti was on top of them. It was all very well for men; they assumed that weddings *happened,* and they often enjoyed themselves conspicuously at such events, but did they know *how* these things went off smoothly? Did men make lists, she wondered; and concluded that they did not. She had never seen a man with a list—not once—although she often saw men in the supermarket struggling to read the lists made for them by their wives. Mma Makutsi had, in fact, once helped such a man to interpret his wife's instructions and had ended up doing his entire shopping for him, consequently making herself late for an appointment at the hair-braiding salon.

While Mma Makutsi sat at her desk and thought about the wedding, Mma Ramotswe sat in her place, her mind filled with thoughts of a rather different nature. She had more than enough on her plate, she reflected, and several things that were concerning her seemed to be without obvious and immediate solution. There was Charlie, of course. He had returned to work and appeared to be coping; Mr. J.L.B. Matekoni had been tact itself, and had not even docked his wages for the missing days. But there was still the issue of Prudence, and the visit that Mma Ramotswe had promised to pay to the wronged young woman. Charlie, she suspected, had assumed that a few words to Prudence from her would solve the whole issue; they would not, thought Mma Ramotswe. He would have to make some effort, and she was not sure whether he had the staying power for that. Time would tell, as Mma Potokwane sometimes said; *time will tell, Mma Ramotswe.* Yes, Mma Potokwane, but what if time tells us what we don't want to hear?

At least with the Charlie affair she knew what she had to do. It was not that simple when she turned her attention to the other difficult problem with which she was confronted—the Moeti case. Her heart sank even as she started once again to think about it. She had decided that she could not let Mpho's deeds go unreported, but she remained deeply concerned about the small boy's safety if Mr. Moeti were to hear, even indirectly, that he was responsible for the attack on his cattle. Terrible things happened out in the country, and a person like Moeti would, as likely as not, take a sjambok to the errant herd boy. Sjamboks, those cruel cattle-hide whips, would do real damage to a small boy; she could not allow that. But how could she deal with the problem and yet keep it from Mr. Moeti? The obvious thing to do would be to speak to the boy's mother and ask her to do something about disciplining or watching the boy. But could she be sure that the information would not somehow leak out? People talked. If she went to the police and told them what had happened, they would be bound to let Mr. Moeti know who was responsible for the outrage; that was how the police operated. They had their rules, of course—it was not their fault— and one of those rules would probably state that the owner of damaged property had to be informed of who had done the damage if that fact were to emerge. Well, it had emerged—if, of course, Mpho were to be believed.

And then there was the van. That at least had been a positive development, but she had done nothing about going to see Daniel because that would involve negotiations and she was in no mood for negotiations at present. So the only thing to do, she decided, was to wait at her desk and see if anything happened. Which it did—not that day, nor the next, but the day afterwards, when everything seemed to happen at once, as is often the case.

"There is a man parking his car under the tree," said Mma

Makutsi. From her vantage point on the other side of the room, she could see through the window that Mma Ramotswe could not really look through unless she craned her neck uncomfortably.

"Coming to see us?" asked Mma Ramotswe.

"I think so. If he was going to the garage I think he would have parked his car there rather than under the tree. That is what I think, Mma." There was a note of reproach in Mma Makutsi's voice, almost as if she was suggesting that Mma Ramotswe's powers of deduction were failing. Mma Ramotswe just smiled; brides-to-be could be testy—that was a well-known fact.

Mma Ramotswe rose to her feet. "Perhaps we have a new client, Mma," she said. "And about time, I think."

"Or an old one come in to see you," said Mma Makutsi. "That is equally possible, don't you think, Mma?"

Again, Mma Ramotswe said nothing. Mma Makutsi had a lot on her mind, and once she was married these comments would surely stop.

She opened the door and saw Mr. Moeti speaking to Mr. J.L.B. Matekoni, who was directing him to the office door.

"Moeti," she whispered to Mma Makutsi. "This is him."

Mma Makutsi glanced out of the door. "I shall put on the kettle, Mma," she said. "And I am right here if you need me."

Moeti approached, holding out his hand in greeting. "So this is your place, Mma Ramotswe. It is a very nice office, I think. And very handy for that garage, too, if your car breaks down."

Mma Ramotswe smiled. "That mechanic is my husband, Rra."

"Very good," said Mr. Moeti. "And this lady is your secretary?"

"Associate detective," corrected Mma Makutsi.

Mr. Moeti made a show of apologising. "Oh, very sorry, Mma. Big mistake on my part. Very sorry."

"That is all right," said Mma Makutsi primly. "There are two detectives here. Mma Ramotswe, who is the proprietor, and myself. Would you like some tea, Rra? These mornings are so hot these days, aren't they?"

Mr. Moeti looked about the room. "Tea would be very nice, Mma. Three spoons of sugar, please." He turned to Mma Ramotswe, who was offering him the client's chair. "Yes, a very good office, Mma."

Mma Ramotswe acknowledged the compliment. She had been surprised by Mr. Moeti's appearance, and a little concerned. He would ask her for a progress report, no doubt, and that would be tricky, as she would be unable to reveal what had happened. So she would have to watch her words carefully, weighing each one to ensure that she told him nothing without telling any outright lies. *Never, ever lie to your client,* Clovis Andersen had written. *That's Rule No. 3, right up there with Rules 1 and 2. Don't lie.*

As she sat down at her desk and faced her client, the thought occurred to her that something about Mr. Moeti's visit was not quite right. When he had first contacted her, he had been careful to arrange a meeting elsewhere, wanting to avoid being seen coming to the detective agency. He had appeared frightened, and jumpy in his manner. Now, by contrast, he seemed cheerful and unconcerned about visiting her quite openly at the No. 1 Ladies' Detective Agency. It was strange.

"It is good to see you, Rra," she said. "And I'm happy to see you here in the office. Last time, you seemed unwilling . . ."

Mr. Moeti looked at her suspiciously. "What last time? What unwilling?"

Mma Ramotswe watched him carefully. Her remark had wrong-footed him, she thought. That was interesting; had he forgotten? Actors forget; people who are not acting never do.

"Last time you consulted me," she said. "You didn't want to come to the office. And forgive me if I say this, Rra, but you seemed very anxious then. Are you no longer worried?"

For a moment or two he said nothing. He's thinking, she said to herself; thinking what to say.

He looked over his shoulder—an exaggerated glance. "I am still worried, Mma. And wouldn't you be, if you knew that somebody was trying to harm you? Even during the day, things can happen . . ."

He transferred his gaze to the window, looking out as if to identify any threat lurking outside. From where she was sitting, if she half turned in her seat, Mma Ramotswe could not see a great deal, but she had a good view of the sky, which was empty, innocent. A shadow passed over his face, though; she could see its effect in his eyes.

"You have reminded me, Mma Ramotswe," he said quietly. "I had almost forgotten, and I was happy. But you have reminded me."

She had not expected this, and his comment made her catch her breath. Perhaps he really was frightened, and perhaps she had tactlessly spoiled things for him. *He is my client,* she reminded herself. *He is not a suspect.*

"I'm very sorry, Rra," she said. "It is not my business to tell you how you're feeling."

The apology was accepted with a quick movement of the hands. "That's all right, Mma. No damage. It's best to be positive, I find, and that's what I'm trying to do. We cannot let wicked people spoil our lives for us, can we?"

Mma Ramotswe indicated that she agreed with this sentiment. And she did; stopping wicked people from spoiling the lives of the non-wicked was, after all, what she and Mma Makutsi did in their working lives.

"So," went on Mr. Moeti, "tell me, Mma: What have you found out? Have you any . . . what do you people call them? Any *leads*?"

Mr. Moeti's use of the word *lead* was a godsend to Mma Ramotswe. She had an answer, not a lead, so she replied, "No leads as such, Rra."

He did not seem unduly disappointed. "Well, I have."

She looked at him politely. "Oh yes, Rra? What have you found out?"

He sat back in his chair. "You remember that thing we found? The key ring?"

She nodded: the cheap metal map of Botswana.

"I have found out where it is from."

"Who dropped it?"

He hesitated. "No, not directly, but I have found out which firm gives them to its business clients. There is a firm of livestock-feed manufacturers in Lobatse. They make that lick that you give to cattle."

Mma Ramotswe knew the lick in question. She used it herself out at her cattle post. Cattle loved the salt it contained, and it gave them all sorts of other things too. Of course humans were rather like cattle these days, she thought—always taking extra vitamin pills. Perhaps they should make a vitamin lick for people, which they could put on people's floors, and they would get down on all fours and lick away, just like cattle.

"So, Rra," she said. "You have found out who gives the key ring away. But you have not found out who owned this particular key ring, have you? Is that correct?"

Mr. Moeti reached forward and tapped the desk lightly. "No, I have not done that because that would be impossible, Mma Ramotswe. Nobody, not even the best detective in the world, could look at a key ring and say that it belonged to this person or that person. But . . ."

He was looking at her with a curious intensity; she held his gaze. "Yes?"

"But I can tell you something about this key ring, Mma—something that will make you sit up straight in your chair."

Mma Ramotswe shifted slightly. Had she been slouching? Perhaps it was just the impression that her chair gave—it had always sagged in the middle, for some reason.

"Yes," continued Mr. Moeti. "I know that the firm that gives away this key ring is in Lobatse. I know that it makes cattle-lick. And I know who owns it."

Mma Ramotswe nodded politely. "That is a lot to know, Rra. But what has it got to do with our inquiry?"

"It is the person who owns that firm that will interest you. He is my neighbour."

Mma Ramotswe digested this information. "So are you saying that he must have dropped it?"

There was a look of undisguised triumph on Mr. Moeti's face. "Exactly. That is exactly what I am saying. This thing—this attack on my cattle—was carried out by my neighbour."

He paused, watching the effect of his disclosure. From the other side of the office there came a muttered comment: "Neighbour! It is always the neighbour!"

Mr. Moeti turned in his seat and stared at Mma Makutsi.

"My assistant," said Mma Ramotswe. "As she told you, she is an—"

"Associate detective," supplied Mma Makutsi.

Mr. Moeti nodded. "Very good," he said. "And you are right, Mma Makutsi. It is always the neighbour who is the problem."

"Except sometimes," Mma Ramotswe said gently, "some neighbours are no trouble at all. Many, in fact."

"That may be true," said Mr. Moeti. "But not in this case. This neighbour of mine is big trouble. Big trouble. It should have been obvious to me that he was suspect number one. I don't know why I didn't think of it."

The way he said that he did not know why he had not thought of it struck Mma Ramotswe as very strange. It was said flatly, as a bad actor will deliver a line in an unaccented monotone.

"But we need a motive, Rra," she said.

This, by contrast, brought an energetic reply. "Motive? He is a bad man, Mma. Bad men always have motives—plenty of motives, I think."

She wanted to find out in what respects this neighbour—still nameless—was bad. "You must tell me about him, Rra," she said. "His name first, and then why you have this low opinion of him."

"He is called Fortitude Seleo," Mr. Moeti began.

He uttered the name with an expression of disgust, or as one might talk if one were obliged to speak with a slice of bitter lemon in one's mouth. Or carbolic soap. Carbolic soap had been administered to children who used bad language when Mma Ramotswe had been young. The miscreant's mouth had been opened and a sliver of soap applied to the tongue and palate while others looked on. And the punished child would pull a face and run off to the taps to rinse out the offending mouth. It had been effective, she remembered, and although one could never do such a thing today, she could not help but notice that people used bad language casually and with no regard to the feelings of others. There would not be carbolic soap enough, she thought, to clean up the language used in films, where people found it necessary to curse and swear with utter abandon. Mma Potokwane would have views on this, she imagined; none of the children at the orphan farm used such language. Love, not punishment—that was the solution; the sort of love that Mma Potokwane could dispense to scores of children: a brisk, understanding love; a love that made them want to do their best and make the most of a world that had treated them badly at the start of their young lives.

"Fortitude Seleo," she said.

"Yes, that is the man, Mma. He owns that factory and he thinks that because he is a big manufacturer of cattle-lick he can have the whole country for his own cattle." He paused. "And so when his fences fall down he doesn't bother to fix them, but lets them wander wherever they like. They could go into the middle of Gaborone and start grazing on the lawn of the Grand Palms Hotel for all he cared!

"But do his cattle catch a bus and ride into Gaborone for their breakfast? No, they do not, Mma. They just wander onto his neighbour's land—that is me, by the way—and eat and eat there until all the grass is eaten up. Then they go back and are sent down to Lobatse for slaughter with their stomachs full of my grass! That is what happens, Mma. It has happened four times, five times, one hundred times maybe.

"And what does he do when I phone him and tell him that his cattle are on my land? He says, 'Are you sure, Rra? Because I do not think any of my cattle are missing. Maybe you should get your herd boy to check. Maybe he is just making these things up.' That is what he has the cheek to say to me, Mma Ramotswe. He thinks I am just some ignorant man who doesn't know what's going on. He thinks that he can fob me off with this nonsense."

The diatribe continued. "I took him to the broken fence one day and pointed out where it was lying on the ground like some old fence from the Protectorate days. Some old British fence maybe. And I said to him, 'Look here, what is this? Is this not your fence?' And he said, 'That fence is your fence, Rra. That fence is your responsibility and you should be fixing it rather than me. Do not tell me to fix a fence that is not mine or anything to do with me.' Those were his actual words, Mma. That is what he said. And I had to take a big breath because I was so angry that I had forgotten to breathe and all my oxygen was gone. He is a man who makes you use up all your oxygen when you are with him, Mma. It is not just me, I assure you. There are many people who have run out of oxygen when arguing with that man. Maybe that is the way he wants it—maybe that is his technique. He makes people run out of oxygen, and then they fall over and he has won. There are people like that, Mma—I'm sure you know that as well as I do."

Mma Ramotswe sat quite still. There was an eloquence to this denunciation that was as alarming as it was impressive. And even if Mr. Moeti had almost run out of oxygen when arguing with Fortitude Seleo, there seemed to be no danger of that happening now.

"He would not accept," Mr. Moeti went on, "that the fences were his. I said that I would look at the title to the land and check up on what it said about fences, and he said that titles were drawn up by lawyers and what did lawyers know about fences? How can you argue with a man like that, Mma? I couldn't, and so I just had to chase his cattle off my land and wait until it happened again. And again after that.

"He is a greedy man, that man. Very large, Mma. Not that there is anything wrong in being large, I must say. It is a good thing to be large; it shows that the country is prosperous. I am just saying that sometimes people can be a little bit too large because they have eaten a bit too much beef. That is the case with Seleo, I think. The country is not big enough for him, he thinks, Mma. There really need to be two Botswanas—one for Mr. Fortitude Seleo and one for the rest of us Batswana. Two whole countries. And then his cattle would start wandering out of his private Botswana and coming over to eat the grass in our Botswana. That would happen, Mma, I have absolutely no doubt about it. It is definite. His cattle have got a very bad temperament, Mma. They are like their owner. They are arrogant. Arrogant man, arrogant cattle. That is definite, Mma. Definite."

He sat back in his chair and folded his arms with the air of one who has proved his case. Mma Ramotswe waited for a few moments to see if he had anything further to say, but he had not.

"So, Rra," she began. "You do not like this Mr. Seleo."

Mr. Moeti shook his head, but remained mute.

"Well," continued Mma Ramotswe, "it sounds to me as if he is not the best of neighbours, but that does not mean that he—"

"Of course he did it," interrupted Mr. Moeti. "We found his key ring at the scene. That is big proof."

Mma Ramotswe was tactful, but felt that she had to spell out just what was meant by real proof. "You have to ask yourself what a clue means," she said. "What does it say to you? That is the question you must ask."

"It says to me: this man Seleo attacked my cattle. That's what it says to me."

Mma Makutsi, who had been following this exchange with rapt attention, now intervened. "It says: somebody has dropped a key ring. That is all it says. It does not say whose key ring has been dropped. It could be anybody's."

Mr. Moeti did not turn to face Mma Makutsi, but addressed her while still looking at Mma Ramotswe. "Seleo makes that key ring. It is his key ring. He does not like me, or my cattle. He drops his key ring after he has done his wicked deed. Anybody can tell that."

It was clear that Mma Makutsi was irritated by being addressed by one facing the other way. "I hope you can hear me, Rra," she said. "I think sometimes that when you talk to the back of somebody's head they do not hear you because their ears are facing the other way."

Mma Ramotswe raised a cautionary finger, but Mma Makutsi continued undaunted. "That is why it is not only polite, but also wise to face the person who is talking to you—that way you don't miss anything. That is just one view, of course, but it is significant, I think, that it is the view held by all polite people in Botswana." She paused. There was more to come. "Of course, there may be countries where things are done quite differently. I do not know, for instance, whether it is customary to talk to the back of people's heads in China. For all I know that might be considered quite polite and normal; but I do know that this is not the case in Botswana."

Mma Ramotswe looked down at the desk. It was hard to stop Mma Makutsi once she had started, and it was particularly difficult to do so now that she was about to become Mrs. Phuti Radiphuti and would shortly have no financial need of the job, even if she had indicated that she wanted to continue working.

Mr. Moeti had now turned, slowly and awkwardly, so that he was facing Mma Makutsi. He looked embarrassed.

"So the point is this, Rra," Mma Makutsi went on. "There will be many key rings of that sort. The fact is that we cannot link *that* key ring to Mr. Seleo. So we have nothing against him, other than that he and you are not friends."

Mr. Moeti turned round again to face Mma Ramotswe. "So you and that lady behind me, Mma, have nothing to report."

"We will be looking very carefully into the whole thing," said Mma Ramotswe. "We shall consider every aspect of the situation." She spread her hands. "At present, we do not really have anything concrete, but I shall certainly look into your suggestion that it is this Seleo man who has done this dreadful thing."

This seemed to satisfy Mr. Moeti, who nodded enthusiastically. "Good," he said. "And then, when we catch him, Mma, we can tell the world what sort of man he is and how I have been putting up with his nonsense for such a long time. That will be very good."

Mr. Moeti departed, taking great care to say an elaborate farewell to Mma Makutsi as he left. Once they were alone, Mma Ramotswe and Mma Makutsi exchanged glances across the room.

"A very rude man," said Mma Makutsi. "But what can we expect these days? The world has forgotten about manners."

"Yes, sometimes it seems like that, Mma, and then you suddenly come across somebody with good manners and you realise that there are still people who believe in these things." She paused. "Like your Phuti. He has very good manners—old Botswana manners."

Mma Makutsi beamed at her employer. "Oh, Mma, thank you. I think you are quite right."

"Yes, I am," said Mma Ramotswe. "I think Phuti would have got on very well with my Daddy. I am sure of it, in fact. They would have been very good friends, I believe."

Mma Makutsi knew that this was the highest possible praise from Mma Ramotswe. "It is a shame that they cannot meet," she said. "Since your father is late, that will no longer be possible, but it would have been a very good thing had it been able to happen."

They sat in silence for a moment, both imagining the scene of that meeting: Obed Ramotswe, with his battered old hat and his face that had such understanding and kindness etched into every line of it; Phuti Radiphuti, with his slightly ill-fitting suit and his artificial foot, but with his polite and gentle manner. It would, thought Mma Ramotswe, have been an embodiment, an affirmation, of everything that Botswana stood for: decency and the things that decency brought with it.

Mma Ramotswe brought the spell to an end. "There's something odd going on, Mma Makutsi," she said.

"Very odd, Mma Ramotswe. And in my opinion it is that man who is odd. He is lying, if you ask me."

Mma Ramotswe said that she, too, had the impression that Mr.

Moeti was not being truthful, but what exactly was he lying about? Was he lying about his neighbour? Was he inventing the story of the fence, which would, of course, be a gross defamation of his neighbour's cattle? "I just can't work it out, Mma Makutsi," she said. "But one thing I think is very clear: that man was never frightened. He had been pretending to be frightened, but his fear was not real."

"You are right," said Mma Makutsi. "He was not a frightened man. A rude man, yes, but not a frightened one."

"And that Fortitude Seleo?"

Mma Makutsi thought for a moment. "I would like to think he is an ordinary man who has the misfortune to have a farm next to Moeti's farm. That is what I'd like to think, Mma. But what I actually think is quite different."

Mma Ramotswe looked expectantly at her assistant. "Yes, Mma. What do you think?"

"I think that he's probably very rude too," said Mma Makutsi. "So put two cats in a box and what do they do, Mma? They fight."

_____

CHAPTER THIRTEEN

WAS PRUDENCE PRUDENT?

PRUDENCE RAMKHWANE lived with her parents, Leonard and Mercy, in a large house behind the shopping centre at the beginning of the Lobatse road. It was not a good place to live, thought Mma Ramotswe, who did not like the clutter and noise of that particular conglomeration of shops, but there were those who did, she had to remind herself, and there must also be those who did not mind living close to such places.

As she parked her car outside the Ramkhwane gate, Mma Ramotswe found herself looking at the house with her detective's eye. This was a special way of looking at things that she had developed over the years, not without some assistance from the relevant chapter of Clovis Andersen's _The Principles of Private Detection._ The author of that seminal work had sound advice in this regard. _Always remember that things are where they are because somebody has put them there,_ he wrote. _So if there is a kennel in a yard it is there because the owner of the yard put it there, and that means that he has a dog. If there is a boat in the yard, then you may conclude that he likes fishing. Things are always there for a reason. I learned this les-_

son myself from Mrs. Andersen, who always accuses me of moving things that she needs!

It was a lovely, intimate glimpse into the home life of the great authority, and Mma Ramotswe had read the passage aloud to Mma Makutsi, who had enjoyed it a great deal.

"How interesting to hear about his wife," Mma Makutsi said. "I would not have guessed that he was married, but there you are."

"She must be very proud of him," said Mma Ramotswe. "It must be strange to be married to such a famous man."

"I expect she's used to it," said Mma Makutsi. "And she probably talks to him like any wife, telling him to be careful and to watch what he does and so on."

Mma Ramotswe had smiled at this. "Is that how you think wives talk, Mma?" she asked. "If so, you should be careful when you and Phuti get married. Men don't like being told to watch what they do."

"But if we let them do what they wanted, then what would happen?" asked Mma Makutsi. "It would be chaos. Big chaos."

Mma Ramotswe had agreed that it would not be a good idea to allow men to do as they pleased, but she felt that there were tactful ways of achieving the desired result. "Rather than telling a man directly what to do," she said, "a wife should make the man think that he is doing what *he* wants to do. There are ways of making this happen, Mma—tactful ways."

There had then followed a certain amount of instruction on how to handle husbands, during which Mma Makutsi made the occasional note.

"This will be very useful for when I am married," she told Mma Ramotswe, and then added, "And I think you should possibly write a book, Mma. It could be called *How to Handle Husbands and Keep Them Under Control.* Or something like that. It would be a very successful book, Mma, as there are many ladies who would rush to buy a book like that."

Now, standing in front of the Ramkhwane house, Mma Ramotswe looked about the yard to determine what it said about the Ramkhwane family. The yard was well swept, which was a good sign—indeed, the most important message that a householder could send out was that based on the neatness, or otherwise, of the yard. Then there was the car: that spoke to modesty—a modest person drives a modest car, a pushy person drives a pushy car. The Ramkhwane car was unostentatious, she was pleased to note: a medium-sized vehicle painted white—a traditional Botswana colour for a car and completely unobjectionable for that. And at the back of the yard, a vegetable patch and a hen coop—both good signs of traditional Botswana values.

Good manners would have required that she call out from the gate and await an invitation before entering the yard. That was difficult to do, though, when the gate was some distance from the house as this one was, so she made her way towards the front door, a large, red-painted affair with an elaborate brass knocker fixed to its central panel.

A maid answered—a thin, rather lethargic woman in a faded print smock. Unhappy, thought Mma Ramotswe. There would be a hundred possible reasons for her unhappiness, but it was probably something to do with poverty and the bad behaviour of some man somewhere—just as was the case with the maid at Mr. Moeti's place.

"I have come to see Prudence, Mma," said Mma Ramotswe. "I think this is her house."

The woman gave a reply that sounded like a sigh. "Yes, Mma. This is her place."

The maid gestured to Mma Ramotswe that she should follow

her. They went along a corridor and into a room at the side of the house. It was a sparsely furnished bedroom with a large cot. Two babies under a year old were sleeping in the cot, one at each end, their small rounded stomachs exposed. In a chair by the window, reading a magazine, was a young woman in jeans and T-shirt. This was Prudence.

Prudence looked up in surprise.

"I have come to see you," said Mma Ramotswe. "My name is Precious Ramotswe. I know . . ." She glanced at the babies. Should she say, *I know their father?* She decided to say, "I know Charlie."

Prudence looked away. She had not got up when Mma Ramotswe had entered, in spite of the difference in their ages. "Oh yes," she said flatly. "Charlie. How is he?"

"He is very well," said Mma Ramotswe.

There was a silence. Then Mma Ramotswe spoke again: "I think you must be cross with him."

Prudence looked up sharply. "Cross with Charlie? Why should I be cross with Charlie?"

Mma Ramotswe glanced at the twins. "The babies . . ."

Prudence stared at her. "What have they got to do with it?"

Mma Ramotswe was perplexed. "I thought . . . I heard that Charlie was the father. That is what I heard."

Prudence frowned. "Charlie? Oh no, Charlie is not the father. No, it is not him."

"Some other man then?"

Prudence flicked a page of her magazine. "Yes, some other man. He is a pilot. He flies up in Maun—those small planes that go to the safari camps. He is Kenyan. We're going to get married in a few months—at long last."

"Does Charlie know this?" asked Mma Ramotswe.

"About me getting married?"

"Yes. About the twins . . . and this other man, this Kenyan."

Prudence shrugged. "He doesn't think he's the father of the babies, does he?"

Mma Ramotswe explained that Charlie had drawn that conclusion, and that was why there had been a rather sudden termination of the relationship.

Prudence listened to her with interest, but without any great show of emotion. "Well, he's wrong," she said once Mma Ramotswe had finished. "I never told him he was the father. I told him I was pregnant—that's all." She looked at Mma Ramotswe to see if she had grasped the distinction. "Listen, Mma, the point is that I had more than one boyfriend then. I know you shouldn't, but it's difficult sometimes when there are all these men knocking on the door. What are you expected to do?"

Mma Ramotswe was about to say, *You choose one and you stick to him,* but she judged it best not to engage. There would be no point in getting into an argument about faithfulness with Prudence; it was too late for her to change, she thought. And there were other people who should tackle her about that.

But she could not let the matter pass altogether. "But you told your parents that Charlie was the father?"

Prudence looked away sulkily. "I didn't say that, Mma. Not exactly. Maybe they thought it themselves—because I was seeing Charlie at the time."

"And they didn't know about the other man . . . or men?"

Prudence shrugged. "Maybe not."

Mma Ramotswe stared at her. She found it hard to imagine such callousness. She sighed. "I don't think you behaved very well, Mma," she said gently.

Prudence looked at her blankly. Perhaps she simply does not understand, thought Mma Ramotswe. Something was missing.

"Oh well, Mma," she said, "I think that I should be on my way. Charlie says hello, by the way."

"Tell him hello," said Prudence. "Tell him that I think of him a lot. Tell him to come and see me some time, but to phone first."

"I shall," said Mma Ramotswe.

"And if you'd like something to eat," Prudence went on, "I can get you something."

Mma Ramotswe raised an eyebrow. "Thank you, Mma, but I am not hungry." She paused. One of the babies had stirred, but only to move an arm. "They are very fine babies, Mma. You must be proud of them."

"They eat a lot," said Prudence. "And I'm having another one, you know."

Mma Ramotswe looked at her watch. "I really must go, Mma. I have a lot of work to do." She did not, but she wanted to leave the house; she wanted to be away from this silly young woman with her casual ways and her utter indifference. How could anybody be so *bored* with life, she wondered, when all about one there were all these *things* happening?

The maid showed her out. As they approached the front door, Mma Ramotswe leaned over and whispered, "Mma, that girl, Prudence, doesn't seem to care very much about things, does she?"

There was a flicker across the maid's otherwise impassive face. "She is seeing two men. Two men, Mma! One is the man who is going to marry her, the other is another man altogether. I know these things; I see them."

Mma Ramotswe shook her head. "It is very bad."

"She is a bad girl," said the maid. "It is very unfair, Mma. She has all this—she has her good parents and she has their money, their food. And all the time she is bad. It is unfair, Mma."

Mma Ramotswe reached out and took the maid's hand. "Do

not feel too sad about it, my sister," she said. "I know what you mean."

The maid looked down at the floor. "Sometimes I think that God has forgotten about me," she said.

Mma Ramotswe shook her head. "He hasn't, Mma," she whispered. "You must never think that. His love is always there, Mma, always there. And it doesn't matter who we are—if we are poor people or people who have been badly treated—we are every bit as important in God's eyes as anybody else. Every bit."

The maid listened, but said nothing.

"You heard me, did you, Mma?" asked Mma Ramotswe.

The other woman nodded. "I heard you, Mma."

Mma Ramotswe reached into the pocket of her skirt. Fifty pula—not a small sum. "This is a present, Mma," she said, pressing the banknote into the woman's hand. "No, you must take it. I want you to have it."

The maid tucked the note away. "I have a little boy," she said.

"Then tonight he will have a very good meal, I think," said Mma Ramotswe.

For the first time, the maid smiled.

SHE RETURNED DIRECTLY to the No. 1 Ladies' Detective Agency. Parking her van under the tree, she went not into the office but into the garage, where Mr. J.L.B. Matekoni's legs, together with two other sets of legs, all clad in blue overalls, protruded from under a large green truck. She called out to her husband, who answered from below the vehicle.

"This is a very tricky repair, Mma," he shouted out, his voice sounding distant under the truck. "I am doing my best, but it is very, very tricky."

"I do not want to disturb you, Rra," she shouted back. "I need to talk to Charlie."

"I am watching Mr. J.L.B. Matekoni, Mma," Charlie called out.

"You can go, Charlie," said Mr. J.L.B. Matekoni. "Fanwell and I can manage all right."

She watched as Charlie wiggled out from under the truck. He had, she noticed, a large fresh oil stain on the bib of his overalls. She tut-tutted. "You will have to put those in the wash, Charlie. Oil is a very difficult thing. Soak them first, then put them in the wash."

He looked down unconcernedly at the stain. "Oil is nothing, Mma. I do not mind." He looked at her inquisitively. "What do you want, Mma?"

She drew him aside. "I offered to help you, Charlie. Remember?"

He became nervous. His hands shook slightly; you would have to be looking for it, but she noticed it.

"Yes, Mma, you did."

"And I have done that," she went on. "I have been to see Prudence."

She saw his lip was now quivering.

"Yes, Mma?"

"Let me tell you this straightaway, Charlie. You are not the father of those twins. It is another man."

He stared at her wide-eyed. "I am not . . ."

"No," said Mma Ramotswe. "You see, that girl, Prudence, is very friendly with men. She should watch out."

Charlie started to smile. "I am not the father? Is this true?"

"She thinks it is," said Mma Ramotswe. "And what the mother thinks tends to be the most important thing, I think."

The news seemed to be sinking in slowly. "I do not have twins?"

"You do not."

Charlie shook his head in disbelief. "I am going to be different from now on, Mma Ramotswe. You'll see. I'm going to be different."

"In what way, Charlie?"

"In every way, Mma. I am going to be a different man. More careful. Just one girlfriend. That's all. A better mechanic too."

She looked at him. For all his faults—and she had to admit they were manifold—he was a well-meaning young man. And much as he could be frustrating, he could also be amusing and generous and attractive.

"Don't change too much," she said gently. "We like you the way you are, Charlie."

He stared at her incredulously, and she realised that he might not have heard many people say that. So she repeated herself: "We like you, Charlie; you just remember that."

She looked down. He had clasped his hands together, his fingers interlaced. It was a gesture, she thought, of unequivocal pleasure—pleasure at hearing what all of us wanted to hear at least occasionally: that there was somebody who liked us, whatever our faults, and liked us sufficiently to say so.

CHAPTER FOURTEEN

A GOOD MAN, A KIND MAN

WHAT, Mma Ramotswe asked herself, did she know about Mr. Fortitude Seleo?

The answer to this question was brief. She knew that he had a factory that made cattle-lick; she knew that this factory was in Lobatse; and she knew that he was the neighbour of her client, Mr. Botsalo Moeti. That was all that she actually *knew*. The rest was all gossip and allegations from a single source—Mr. Moeti himself, who did not like Mr. Seleo, and, more significantly, did not like his cattle. That thought itself led to further surmise: if Moeti did not like Seleo's cattle, then it was odd, was it not, that Moeti's cattle had been attacked, rather than the other way round. There would have been a clear motive had that happened: Seleo's cattle had a habit of trespassing on Moeti's land; if Seleo's cattle were attacked, then the finger of suspicion would surely point at Moeti.

But what if the truth were rather different from the story as told by Moeti? What if Moeti's cattle had been every bit as lawless as Seleo's cattle and had themselves crossed over onto Seleo's land? Then Seleo would have had a clear motive to wreak his revenge on the poor beasts. That made sense of what had happened. Seleo had been angry over the incursions and had taken action. Moeti knew why his neighbour had done this, but had kept this knowledge from Mma Ramotswe—presumably to appear more of the innocent victim.

Then a disturbing possibility suggested itself: she had been treating Mr. Moeti as the victim, but it was possible that he was, in fact, the perpetrator. That would mean, of course, that he had attacked his own cattle, something that no farmer would dream of doing—unless he did not know that they *were* his cattle.

She pictured it. Night-time, and the herd boy, young Mpho, knocks urgently on the door of the farmhouse. "Who is it?" calls Moeti. "His cattle have broken through the fence, Rra. You must come." Moeti comes to the door, belting his trousers, cursing under his breath. He runs to his truck; Mpho, shivering, sits in the back. They drive along the bumpy track; the stars are bright overhead, the moon nowhere to be seen; the headlamps cut into the darkness, and then there is just the dark hump of the hills in the distance. The cattle eyes are yellow points caught in the lights; they lift their heads and move off into the darkness. Two stragglers. Moeti shouts and there is bellowing. The blood cannot be seen because of the dark. He shouts at the boy again and returns to the truck and they are gone and do not hear the crying of the injured beasts.

And in the morning he discovers that his own cattle were mixed up with the neighbour's herd, and he has maimed his own beast, and he vents his fury on the boy, and beats him. "You are not to say anything about this, understand? Nothing!" The idea occurs to him that he should blame somebody else—his neighbour, whose fault this really was. Let old scores be settled; put somebody on to him—not the police, because he would talk his way out of that and was friendly with the local policeman, but get somebody from outside, somebody accepting Moeti's money and answerable to him alone.

Of course, all of this implied that Mpho's confession was false, and of that she was simply unsure. One moment she thought that the boy was probably telling the truth, the next she found herself inclined to think that he had made it up too quickly, or was lying to protect somebody else. And would a small boy, she wondered, have thought up something so devilish as to attack cattle in this way? Surely not.

She was driving to see Fortitude Seleo when she thought this, and the train of thought was so compelling that she almost stopped her van in order to sit still and think the matter through. But then, as is often the case with good ideas, the obvious flaw appeared, and so she continued with her drive. The flaw arose from what Mr. Moeti had said to her of the events. There had been two attacks, he said—the second one just a week before their first meeting. This ruled out the possibility that he had mistakenly attacked one of his own animals: he would never have made the same mistake twice. That was unlikely, she had to admit—unless, of course, the second attack had never occurred and had simply been invented to make the situation seem more serious.

She made an effort to stop thinking about it. Sometimes, she found, it was better to defer deliberations of that sort until the end of a case, when you had to hand all the information you were going to get and could put the jigsaw together without suddenly finding fresh pieces. And she had almost reached her destination—the premises of the not very imaginatively named Botswana Cattle Food Company, from the chimneys of which emanated wisps of steam, rising up in short-lived spouts and clouds. A large truck, painted with the name of the company, was reversing towards a loading bay and a security guard, bespectacled and officious, was approaching the van.

The guard told her where to park before directing her to the front office. He noted her name on his clipboard and smiled at her. "You have many cattle, Mma?" he asked.

She nodded. "I have a cattle post. My father—he is late now—was good with them. He was a fine judge of cattle."

"I have cattle too," he said. "Not many. Three. Out there." He waved a hand in the direction of the Kalahari.

She hesitated. She did not like to miss opportunities to talk to people, as this was the way one found things out. This guard must know Mr. Seleo; if she wanted to find out about his employer, then she should chat to him. Security guards, cleaners, porters—these were the ones who often knew what people were really like.

"I have come to see Rra Seleo," she said.

The guard beamed. "Yes. If you go to the office, you will find him. He is always there."

"You must know him well," she said. "I have never met him."

"Yes. You will meet him, Mma. He will be there."

She tried again. "What's he like?"

"You will see, Mma. If you ask at the office, they will take you to him. He is over there."

It was not working. "Thank you, Rra. I'll go there."

He began to walk with her. "So you haven't met him, Mma?"

"No."

"He is a good man. A kind man."

"Kind? Why do you say he's kind, Rra? Usually these business-men are tough, aren't they? You do not find many kind people run-ning businesses these days, I think."

The guard considered this gravely before replying. "I don't know about that, Mma. Perhaps you are right; I am just an ordinary man and do not know about these things. But I can tell you about Mr. Seleo. He never shouts. He never fires people if they are late for work. You don't see him chasing after the young secretaries—there is none of that here."

Mma Ramotswe smiled. "I am glad to hear that, Rra. There is too much of those things going on in Gaborone. I'm glad that it is not happening here."

"Yes, Mma. I'm glad too."

They had reached the door to the office, and the guard opened it for her before he went back to his post at the gate. Mma Ramotswe thanked him and made her way over to a reception desk. A young woman took her name and lifted the telephone. She spoke briefly, and then pointed to a door on the other side of the room.

"That is where he is," she said. "In there."

MR. FORTITUDE SELEO was a tall, well-built man somewhere in his mid-fifties, or a bit beyond. His hair was greying and his face was lined about the eyes and mouth. When he stood up to greet Mma Ramotswe, she immediately saw the reason for the lines: a broad smile spread across his face.

"Mma Ramotswe," he said. "I am very happy to meet you, Mma. You are well, I hope."

It was an effusive greeting, and it took Mma Ramotswe slightly aback. But she recovered quickly and returned the smile.

"I am very well, Rra. Thank you. And you are well?"

"Very well too, Mma Ramotswe. Very well. And glad that winter is over."

"I am glad too, Rra."

He indicated the chair in front of his desk, and she sat down.

"So, Mma, you are the great detective, aren't you? I have heard about you—even down here."

Mma Ramotswe's embarrassment was unfeigned. "I didn't think that people knew about me, Rra. I am not famous."

"No, perhaps not famous, Mma. But people driving along the Tlokweng Road see your sign. What is it, Mma? The No Ladies Detective Agency? That makes them think: Who are these no ladies?"

"It is the No. 1 Ladies' Detective Agency, Rra."

Mr. Seleo laughed. "Oh, I see. But that is how people know about you." He paused, watching her, his smile still broad. "So why have you come to see me, Mma? Is it something to do with my friend Botsalo Moeti? Something to do with a dead cow?"

Clovis Andersen was quite clear on this: do not let your reactions show. Control your feelings. Do not look excessively surprised or dismayed.

Mma Ramotswe felt both of these emotions. "Oh," she said lamely. "So, you know."

He seemed concerned about the effect of his words. "I'm sorry, Mma," he said quickly, his smile fading. "I did not mean to take you by surprise."

"I did not think that you knew," Mma Ramotswe said.

"Knew what?"

"That you knew that I was interested in this affair."

Mr. Seleo leaned back in his chair. The smile and jovial manner had both returned. "Oh, I knew all right," he said. "In the country we all know what's going on, Mma. I heard about your visit. The bush has eyes, you know."

"And those eyes were watching me," said Mma Ramotswe.

"They were."

He looked at her with complete affability and equability; the security guard, she thought, must be absolutely right.

"I'm afraid," continued Mr. Seleo, "that relations between me and my neighbour are not all that I would wish them to be. It is so important, Mma, to get on with your neighbours—as I'm sure you are very well aware."

"It is very important indeed," agreed Mma Ramotswe. "A fight with a neighbour is like a fight in your own home. Almost as bad."

He considered this. "Yes, I think I'd agree. And for this reason I did my best to get on with Botsalo Moeti. I really did. But his cattle kept coming onto my land, and I had to take the matter up with him. I did so as gently as possible—I invited him round for a meal, and my wife made a great big stew and lots of trimmings. I raised the issue as tactfully as I could, but he flew off the handle, Mma. He went off like a firework."

It was exactly as she had imagined in the car; or at least this part of it was. And there was no question in her mind now as to whom she believed and as to whose cattle had wandered.

"There has been a whole lot of things since then," Mr. Seleo explained. "It seems that he's a man who just has to settle scores. If he thinks that you've done something to him, then he will attempt to get back at you. It's quite extraordinary, Mma Ramotswe. So along comes this business with the cow—somebody does something nasty to one of his cows and he gets the idea that this is his chance to even things up with me. I'm not at all surprised that he's trying to pin the attack on me—that's the way he is, I'm afraid."

She sat in silence once he had finished. Mma Ramotswe was usually positive in her outlook, but now she felt somewhat bleak. There were some people who would never change—they seemed irredeemably malevolent. Fortunately there were few of these, but you did come across them from time to time, and then you felt strangely dirtied by the contact.

After a while she spoke. "I am very sorry, Rra," she said. "I am very sorry that I even thought that you might be responsible for such a thing."

Mr. Seleo shrugged. "You were only doing your job, Mma. I don't hold anything against you."

"So what do we do about Mr. Moeti?"

The smile did not slip. "We have to live with him, Mma. What else can we do?"

She could not think of anything else to say, so she brought the conversation round to cattle-lick. She had used his lick and her cattle loved it. They could not say thank you, of course, but she could on their behalf. This made Mr. Seleo burst into peals of laughter.

"Oh, Mma," he said, "that is extremely amusing. You are the spokesman for the cattle of Botswana! And have the cattle got anything further to say? Are they happy with conditions in general?"

She thought for a moment. Were the cattle of Botswana happy? "I think they are," she said. And then she became more definite. "Yes, they certainly are." She hesitated. "Or most of them."

An idea had occurred to her. It was not the most obvious idea, and she was not sure whether it would work. Happiness, she thought, is a healer, and could sometimes shift a log-jam in the most seemingly impossible circumstances. In every human heart, even the most forbidding, there was a place that could be touched. The difficulty was finding it; there were people who concealed that place with dogged determination. Sometimes, though, their guard slipped for a moment or two, and the way to a heart lay open.

Mr. Seleo showed her out, saying that he would walk her to her van.

"Tell me, Rra," she said. "Would you do something to end this dispute with your neighbour?"

"Of course," he said. "But what can I do? The fences that he complains of are his, not mine. His cattle keep coming over onto my land. It's not my fault."

"But what if that were to stop?"

"Then I wouldn't have to talk to him about it. It would not be a problem."

"And do you have to talk to him about it often?"

He thought for a moment. "Every few days I have to telephone him. Or I go over to see him at his place." He paused. "But I am always polite, Mma."

She told him that she was sure he was. But then she thought: How easy would it be to get annoyed by a neighbour—even a smiling, agreeable one like this—who kept raising an issue with you, day after day? Very easy, she thought.

"Perhaps you should think of stopping that, Rra. Just for a while. Perhaps that would help."

There was a sudden and very obvious change in Mr. Seleo's demeanour. The smile was still there, of course, but the light had gone from it; it was frozen. "Why should I, Mma? I am in the right here, you know."

"I don't doubt that, Rra, but I think . . ."

He waited for her to finish. What did she think, and how should she put it? They were standing outside the main building of the factory, now, and she turned to face the building, looking up at the hissing steam pipes. There was a pleasant smell in the air—rather like the smell of baking cakes.

"I think we could sort this out," she said. "But it will require you to swallow your pride."

He looked at her intently. "I am not a proud man, Mma."

"Good," she said. "So, Rra, would you like me to tell you what I think you should do? You may not like it, but I think it may be the solution to this problem you have. But I need first to ask you something. Does Mr. Moeti look after his cattle well?"

He raised an eyebrow. "That's a difficult question for me, Mma."

"Why? Do you not know?"

"No, I know perfectly well. It's just that I do not like to speak ill of people, Mma, especially when it comes to the way they treat their cattle."

There was no doubt in her mind that he meant it. This man, she thought, really is a good man. "You are very right about that, Rra," she said. "We should not speak badly about people—except where we have to. And this is one of those occasions. I have to know."

"Terribly," he blurted out. "He's hopeless—a hopeless farmer. He has no idea how to look after cattle. He thinks he does, but he doesn't, I'm afraid. Just look at the condition of his herd."

It was the answer for which she had hoped. "So that's why they wander?"

He nodded. "Yes, and if I were one of his cows I would move on. I'd emigrate to Namibia, maybe."

Mma Ramotswe laughed, and then asked a further question. "Your cattle, of course, are happy, I imagine."

"Yes. They are in very good condition."

"They get plenty of healthy cattle-lick? Cattle-lick with all the right things? Vitamins, magnesium, salt—all those other things that cattle need?"

This broadened his smile. "Yes, as you can imagine."

"And his cattle get none?"

He shrugged. "I don't think they get anything extra at all. Just look at them. He probably doesn't know that they need it."

She sniffed at the air. "There's plenty of cattle-lick round here, Rra, isn't there?"

The smile grew proud. "Naturally. This is cattle-lick headquarters, you might say."

She took his arm and began to walk to her van. She had something to explain to him, and she did this as they walked together. When they reached the van, they stood for a while longer. He nodded from time to time, with the air of one to whom something was becoming clear. Then she drove off and Mr. Seleo returned to his office.

In her van, Mma Ramotswe started to smile. It's infectious, she thought.

CHAPTER FIFTEEN

_____

AN OFFER OF HELP

ONE WEEK ONLY!" exclaimed Mma Potokwane. "My, my! In
one week you will be Mma Grace Radiphuti! Just think of that!"

Mma Potokwane had dropped in on the offices of the No. 1
Ladies' Detective Agency ostensibly to share a cup of tea with her
old friend Mma Ramotswe, but in reality with the ulterior motive
of asking Mr. J.L.B. Matekoni to fix the orphan farm tractor. This
tractor, an ancient grey machine, had been nursed by Mr. J.L.B.
Matekoni over the years—all at no cost—and could generally be
persuaded to do what was asked of it; now, however, the wheel on
one side appeared to be turning at a different speed from its counterpart on the other, resulting in the tractor's refusal to travel in a
straight line without vigorous correction by the driver. "Could Mr.
J.L.B. Matekoni possibly come out and take a look at it?" Mma
Potokwane had asked as Mma Ramotswe came to meet her outside
the office.

"I'm sure he can," said Mma Ramotswe. And he would; her
soft-hearted husband, she knew, would never turn down a request
from the orphan farm.

"I shall bake him a cake," said Mma Potokwane, who knew of

the mechanic's soft spot for the heavy and immensely rich fruit cake for which she was so well known throughout southern Botswana. In her view, it was a fair exchange of the sort that kept the orphan farm running: a whole list of skills of one sort or another could be called upon in return for her cake. This was how the accountant was paid (ten cakes a year); how the painter and decorator was rewarded (three cakes per room); and, in the case of Mr. J.L.B. Matekoni, two large slices of cake for attention to a small mechanical or electrical problem, and a complete cake for each larger or more time-consuming chore.

Mr. J.L.B. Matekoni's services having been booked, Mma Potokwane and Mma Ramotswe had made their way into the office, where Mma Makutsi was sitting at her desk contemplating one of her to-do lists. It was her last day at work before going off on four days' pre-wedding leave, and her filing, accounts, and typing tasks were all up-to-date.

When Mma Potokwane made her remark about only a week being left, Mma Makutsi beamed with pleasure. She and Mma Potokwane did not enjoy the closest of relationships, but this was not a time to be on difficult terms with anybody. Besides, Mma Potokwane had been treating Mma Makutsi with more consideration recently, owing, Mma Ramotswe thought, to the impending change of Mma Makutsi's status. It was nothing to do with Mma Makutsi's origins—Mma Potokwane was completely indifferent to such matters, but she showed the tendency that many women of her generation had not to take unmarried women completely seriously. *That's what you may think now,* such an attitude implied, *but just wait until you're married—you'll think differently then.* That view was not intended unkindly or cuttingly, but of course there was nothing more annoying for those at whom such condescension was directed, and this went some way to explaining the tension between the orphan-farm matron and Mma Makutsi.

"Yes, it's on Saturday," Mma Makutsi said. "And there is still a lot to do."

Mma Potokwane settled herself into the client's chair. "There is always so much to do when you're getting ready for a wedding," she said. "There's so much that can go wrong—and it usually does."

Mma Ramotswe, who was busy switching on the kettle, pointed out that Mma Makutsi was very well organised. "I don't think anything will go wrong with this wedding," she said reassuringly.

"I hope not," said Mma Potokwane. "But there is always something. There is always something unforeseeable."

Mma Makutsi was listening to this attentively. "Such as, Mma? What unforeseeable things?"

Mma Potokwane smiled. "I cannot answer that," she said. "And that is because unforeseeable things cannot be foreseen. So I do not know what they are."

Mma Makutsi glanced at her list. "What sort of thing, though, Mma? To do with guests? To do with food?"

"Both of these," said Mma Potokwane.

"It will be a very big wedding, this one," interjected Mma Ramotswe. She did not want Mma Makutsi to be unsettled just when she seemed to be getting on top of all the arrangements.

"That is very nice," said Mma Potokwane, in a slightly strained tone. She and her husband had not been invited to the wedding; lines had had to be drawn, and they were on the wrong side. "I like large weddings. It is so kind of the people getting married to invite all their friends—that way nobody feels left out, Mma."

"It is very difficult," said Mma Ramotswe quickly. "Often the couple want to invite everybody, but cannot do so because there simply is not enough room. Everybody understands that, of course."

"I'm sure they do," said Mma Potokwane, in the same rather pinched voice.

Mma Makutsi looked up from her list. "What sort of unforeseeable things, Mma? Can you give me examples?"

"Certainly," said Mma Potokwane. "Guests. How do you know that family members travelling down from wherever will not bring extra relatives with them? Then where do you put these people? You may have arranged for places to stay for everybody on the list, but what about those who are not? That can be a big problem."

Mma Makutsi sat quite still. She had arranged accommodation for forty people from Bobonong—staying with friends of the Radiphuti family, or with distant relatives on the Makutsi side. It had been a major feat of calculation and persuasion, and she did not know what she could do if any more people turned up unannounced, expecting a bed to be found for them for three or four days.

Mma Potokwane noticed the other woman's uncertainty. "Yes," she continued. "There's that problem. And then there's another one. Problems come in threes, I find, Mma. So the next one—problem number two, so to speak—is the cooking of food. You know what I find, Mma, it is this: the people doing the cooking *never* have enough pots. They say they do, but they do not. And right at the last moment they discover that there are not enough pots or, more likely, the pots they have are too small. A pot may be big enough to cook your meat and pap at home, just for a family, but do not imagine that it will be big enough to cook for a couple of hundred people. You need big, catering-size pots for that."

She was now warming to her theme. "And the third problem is the food itself. You may think that you have enough for the feast, and you may be right when it comes to the meat. People usually have enough meat—often rather too much, in fact. But they forget that after their guests have eaten a lot of meat, they need something sweet, and often they have made no arrangements for that. A wedding cake? Yes, but there will only be one small piece of that for each guest—usually not enough. So people find themselves wishing that they had had the foresight to get a supply of ordinary cake for the guests to eat with their tea. And where is this cake? Not there, Mma."

Mma Ramotswe glanced at Mma Makutsi; this was not the way to speak to a nervous bride, she thought. "I'm sure that everything will work out well," she said reassuringly. "And if there are any problems, they will surely just be small ones—nothing to worry about."

Mma Potokwane looked doubtful. "I hope so," she said. "But in my experience it never works out like that. I think it's better to be realistic about these things."

Mma Makutsi picked up her pencil to add something to her list. "You said something about pots, Mma. Where would I be able to get these big, catering-size pots?"

Mma Potokwane examined her fingernails. "Well, we have them at the orphan farm. Each of the house-mothers has a very large pot. I'm sure that we could do something . . ."

Mma Makutsi seized her chance. "Oh, would you, Mma?"

"I'll see what I can do," Mma Potokwane said. "And I wondered if I could help out with cake. There are many people, I believe, who like my cake."

Mma Makutsi made a mental calculation. "You're very kind, Mma," she said. "And I was wondering—I know it's short notice— but I was wondering whether you would care to come to the wedding too? You and your husband, of course."

Mma Potokwane waited a decent interval of time before replying. "Come to the wedding? Well, I hadn't thought of that, but yes, I think that we might be free."

"Well, that's settled, then," said Mma Makutsi.

Mma Potokwane gave Mma Ramotswe a triumphant look. She suspected that her friend thought that she was occasionally a little bit too pushy, but there were times when pushiness was the only way to get what you wanted. Mma Ramotswe needed to learn that, and if she asked in the right way, Mma Potokwane would be prepared to teach her.

The conversation now moved to other topics, including the forthcoming by-election.

"It will be the same result as before," said Mma Potokwane. "It always is. Some will vote for the Government, and others will not. There will be many speeches made, and we all know exactly what will be in these speeches."

Mma Ramotswe laughed. "You never know, Mma. There may be some surprises."

She poured the tea and handed her guest a cup before giving one to Mma Makutsi.

"But there is a big threat in this election," Mma Makutsi said. "One of the candidates . . ."

Mma Ramotswe remembered. "Oh, of course." She turned to Mma Potokwane. "Violet Sephotho is standing. Do you know her, Mma?"

Mma Potokwane put down her cup so quickly that she spilled half her tea. "Violet Sephotho? That woman?"

Mma Makutsi nodded sadly. "Yes. I knew her at the Botswana Secretarial College, you know. We were contemporaries."

"She is a danger to Botswana," said Mma Potokwane. "If she gets anywhere near power, then we are—"

"Finished," supplied Mma Makutsi.

Mma Potokwane asked which constituency Violet was standing in, and was told that it was the constituency next to her own. She groaned. "That is a big tragedy," she said. "We must stop her."

Mma Makutsi needed no persuading. "Yes, we must. I was saying the same thing to Patricia at the clothing shop a few days ago." She frowned. "But how do you stop a political candidate from standing? We are a democracy. You cannot stop somebody from standing for election."

"You can stop them winning," suggested Mma Ramotswe. "You can tell people about them and hope that they'll make the right decision."

"Too late for that," said Mma Potokwane. "No, something else is needed." She looked thoughtful. "Do you think that she wants to get into parliament because she thinks she would like the work?"

Mma Makutsi snorted. "Violet, work? She is not one of these people who are made for work," she said. "She did no work at the Botswana Secretarial College and she hasn't done any since. No, it is not the work."

"Then what is it?" asked Mma Potokwane.

Mma Makutsi said that she thought it was the power, and possibly the glamour, that had attracted Violet to politics.

"It's not all power and glamour, though, is it?" said Mma Potokwane. "It's a lot of hard work—answering letters from constituents, dealing with complaints and so on. That's not the sort of thing that Violet likes, I think."

"I knew a politician once," said Mma Ramotswe. "He used to complain about having to deal with letters from members of the public. He said they expected him to solve all their problems, even to arrange rainfall during a dry spell. It very nearly drove him mad, he said."

Mma Potokwane picked up her cup again and took a sip of tea. "It would be interesting," she mused, "to see what would happen if Violet were to receive a lot of letters *before* the election—letters from her future constituents asking her to deal with all their problems." She paused, watching the effect of her words on the others. "Not small problems—big, difficult problems."

A smile began to cross Mma Makutsi's face. "You don't happen to know people in her constituency, do you, Mma Potokwane?"

Mma Potokwane took a further sip of tea. "I might," she said. "Let me think about it."

She thought for only a few moments.

"It can be done," she said. "I think that we'll be able to persuade Violet that being a politician is no fun."

THAT NIGHT, Mma Ramotswe had a vivid dream. She was with Mma Potokwane and they were searching for cooking pots in a dark storeroom. Mma Potokwane was singing a strange, rather haunting song, but Mma Ramotswe was having difficulty in making out the words. *There are many pots,* the song began; thereafter the sounds became indistinct. *Potokwane, Pots, Potokwane, Pots*—these words suggested themselves, but she could not be sure. *Poto, Poto, Potokwane.* It was a very strange song.

Mma Potokwane disappeared, as people in dreams so seamlessly do. Now she found herself in a landscape at the same time both familiar and unfamiliar; it was Mochudi, or a place just outside it—a place where there is a great jacaranda tree, its spreading boughs weighed down by age, a tree she knew well from her childhood. Beneath this tree were two chairs, traditional Botswana chairs made of hardwood trunks, decorations—animals and people—carved into the wood; not far away, a traditional house with murals of brown and blue daub, the work of a grandmother, now sitting on a stool by the front door. It was the Botswana of the past, even if it still survived here and there in places where the modern world had now come barging in and destroyed it; and her father was somewhere nearby, she thought; she heard his voice and knew that he was with her. *Our country, Precious,* he said to her. *Our Botswana.*

She looked for him, but could not see him, because she knew, even in the dream, that he was dead. Sometimes people in our dreams are dead but not quite dead, yet still talk to us. *Late people can be loved too.* Yes, of course they can, she thought; and the dream dissolved, faded, and she saw not the landscape of Mochudi but the ceiling above her in the house on Zebra Drive and the first rays of the sun through the window.

She turned in her bed—she had been lying on her right arm and it felt numb, as if it belonged to somebody else who had carelessly left it in her bed. She noticed that she was alone in bed, that Mr. J.L.B. Matekoni, who usually got up after she did, was not in his accustomed position. She sat up and looked about her, half expecting to see him standing in the room somewhere—by the wardrobe, perhaps, dressing himself in his daily khakis—but there was no sign of him.

Mma Ramotswe felt a twinge of alarm. He had been in the bed, had he not, when she drifted off to sleep the previous night? He had. There were, she assumed, marriages where wives did not notice whether or not their husband was in bed with them, but her marriage was not like that. She had said goodnight to Mr. J.L.B. Matekoni before going to sleep—she did that every night, and she would have noticed if she had said goodnight to an empty bed or to a pillow on which no head was resting.

She put on her dressing gown and made her way out of the bedroom into the corridor outside. The children's doors were closed—they would still be asleep, as she always awoke well before they did. The bathroom? She put her head round the door: he was not there.

She went into the kitchen and switched on the kettle. Every so often, when some car needed to be fixed urgently, Mr. J.L.B. Matekoni had to make an unusually early start at the garage. When this happened, though, he usually told her first and she would get up early herself to make his breakfast before he left. Had he said something about this last night and had she forgotten about it? She did not think so.

She looked out of the window. The seasons had changed, but in this period, when the memory of winter was still alive, there were times when the morning air still had a nip in it, and this was one such. A wisp of mist, just detectable, hung over the tree-tops; it would not last, she knew, but seeing it made her want to go out-side, to stand under those trees and look up at the sky through their lattice-work of leaves. Mr. J.L.B. Matekoni must have slipped away to the garage and forgotten to tell her; she would make him a large bacon sandwich and take it to him when she herself went into work in an hour or so.

A steaming mug of red bush tea in her hand, she went outside. The doves who had taken up residence in her large acacia were preening themselves on their bough—to all intents and purposes a contented married couple preparing for an ordinary day of what-ever work the world had in mind for doves. She smiled at them; they looked down at her for a second or two, fluffing up their neck feathers, and then returned to their task of grooming. She turned the corner of the house.

Then she saw it. In the place where she had parked her blue van the previous evening was her old van. She stood quite still, closing her eyes and then reopening them, fully expecting the hal-lucination to have corrected itself. But it did not; it was there, as real and substantial as the house, as the garden about it, as the ground upon which she, and the van itself, stood.

She stepped forward, half stumbling in her confusion. As she did so, Mr. J.L.B. Matekoni and Charlie came round the corner of the house. Both were beaming with pleasure, seemingly delighting in the surprise they had created.

Her hand rose to her mouth. "What is this . . . ?"

"It's what you wanted, I think," said Mr. J.L.B. Matekoni. "Or it's what Charlie told me you wanted."

"That's right, Boss," said Charlie.

"So I decided that there was no point in trying to make you love that blue van," Mr. J.L.B. Matekoni went on. "You cannot make somebody love something. They must have love in their heart first."

"That's right, Boss," repeated Charlie.

Mma Ramotswe walked up to the van and opened the driver's door.

"He made a very good job of the restoration," said Mr. J.L.B. Matekoni. "I thought it would be impossible, but it just goes to show that you can do these things if you really set out to. Charlie and I had a really good look at it. It's a very nice job."

"And the blue van?" asked Mma Ramotswe. "What about that?"

"We need a new vehicle for the garage," said Mr. J.L.B. Matekoni. "We can use it for there—if you're happy enough with that. We can sort out the money."

"It is not the money," said Mma Ramotswe. "It has never been the money. No, I am very happy indeed."

She lowered herself into the driver's seat, caressing the steering wheel as she did so. Then she bent forward and kissed the wheel, as tenderly as one might kiss a much-loved child.

"Thank you," she said. "I am very happy now."

"Then I am happy as well," said Mr. J.L.B. Matekoni.

"And me too," said Charlie.

Mma Ramotswe got out of the van. "Have you had breakfast yet, Charlie?" she asked.

He shook his head. "Not yet, Mma. I will have a piece of bread when I get into work."

She shook her head. "No, you will not. You come in right now and I shall make you a couple of eggs and some bacon."

"Oh, Mma," said Charlie. "That sounds very good."

The two of them went inside to watch Mma Ramotswe cooking breakfast. Charlie ate enthusiastically and was served a further two eggs after his initial helping. Then Mma Ramotswe went off to wake the children and begin her day in earnest, starting with the drive to the agency in her tiny white van, just as she had always done in the past, year in and year out, and just as she had never really lost hope of doing once more. She cried a little, out of sheer joy, and stopped for a minute or two at the corner of Zebra Drive to compose herself, so that tears should not interfere with her driving, with her triumphal journey, her proud return.

CHAPTER SIXTEEN

THE MOTHER OF MPHO

WITH MMA MAKUTSI out of the office now, on leave for the final preparations for her wedding, Mma Ramotswe had no excuse for putting off that which she knew she had to do. It was not that Mma Makutsi made it impossible for her to get on with her work; it was really just that if she and her assistant were in the office together, then there always seemed to be something to talk about, some office chore that could be tackled together, or a letter that needed to be dictated.

She thought about dictation. Mma Makutsi was, of course, proud of her skills in this respect, having learned shorthand at the Botswana Secretarial College, where her average speed was one hundred and twenty-eight words per minute.

"I cannot speak at that rate," Mma Ramotswe had said when Mma Makutsi revealed this fact to her. "One hundred and twenty-eight words per minute is very fast, Mma. I am not sure if I can even think at that speed."

Mma Makutsi laughed—the relaxed laugh of one who knows that her secretarial skills are beyond question. "It's true, Mma, that most people cannot write shorthand at even one hundred words per minute. Take Violet Sephotho, for example: she managed forty-two words per minute, and probably couldn't even do that these days. Forty-two words, Mma! It would take all day to write one letter at that rate." She paused; there are some remarks, like some temptations, that simply cannot be resisted—at least by those of us who are made of ordinary human stuff. "Of course, Violet was always much faster in some other matters . . ."

Mma Ramotswe smiled. "I see," she said. "Well, there we are. There are all sorts of people, aren't there?"

It was not a remark with which one could disagree, but Mma Makutsi felt that it did not *convey* very much. Of course there were all sorts of people—surely that went without saying. If there were not all sorts of people then life would be remarkably dull, and indeed she felt that she and Mma Ramotswe would be out of a job. But she did not wish to say anything further about Violet Sephotho: her point had been made, and it was clear enough.

"Typing speed is important too," Mma Makutsi had continued. "I have been known to type at just under one hundred words per minute, Mma. There are some typists who are quicker than that, but I have not met one yet—personally, that is. I have read about these people, but have not met them."

"They will type many pages, those people," said Mma Ramotswe.

"I think so, Mma."

That sort of conversation could go on for hours, and sometimes did. That meant tasks which had been put off would remain undone, and that was exactly what had happened with the Moeti case. Mma Ramotswe knew what she had to do: she had to make a journey out to Mr. Moeti's place and speak to Mpho's mother. This woman, she felt, somehow held the key to what had happened. She was now inclined to discount Mpho's confession, but she would still have to raise with his mother the possibility that the boy was responsible for the attack. She was not looking forward to this, as no mother likes to hear of the delinquency of her son, especially when, as Mma Ramotswe imagined would be the case here, the son was one of the few things she had in this world. People lived for their children, and she could imagine how difficult must be the realisation that your child has done something terrible. What would you do if you discovered that a member of your family—a husband or a son, perhaps—was wanted by the police? Would you have to give him up? Surely no mother would do that.

Her mind wandered. What if she were to discover that Mr. J.L.B. Matekoni were a car thief—that all those cars sitting around the garage were in fact stolen? But that was something she found it impossible to contemplate: Mr. J.L.B. Matekoni was incapable of doing anything underhand or unkind, and if anybody were ever to accuse him of such a thing, she would simply not believe it. And that, she thought, might be how Mpho's mother would react. She remembered now how she had looked when she first met her at Mr. Moeti's house. She looked guilty, and Mma Ramotswe had thought that she might well have been responsible for the attack on the cattle. Now, of course, that guilt made sense: a mother who knows that her son has something to answer for will of course look guilty.

She decided that she would go out to the Moeti farm in the late afternoon. She wanted to speak to Mpho's mother without Mr. Moeti himself being present, and she felt that her best chance of doing that would be when she had finished her work for the day. A domestic helper might return later on to make dinner, serve it, and then wash up, but round about five or six she would probably be allowed to be in her own quarters. She would go there, talk to the woman, and then go to Mr. Moeti and speak to him. She was not yet sure what she would say; there were still matters needing to be resolved, and what she said to him would be dependent on how these worked out.

The trip itself was an unalloyed pleasure. The white van was running quietly and contentedly; the terrible knocking sound was nowhere to be heard, the brakes were responsive and silent, and the suspension was comfortable and evenly balanced. That could change, of course, and the van could resume its list to starboard, but that would be a minor irritation and one that traditionally built people were well accustomed to. The old van, of course, was slower than the new one, but that did not bother Mma Ramotswe in the slightest; she was not the sort of detective—or person, indeed—who needed to get anywhere fast. In her experience, the places one set off for were usually still there no matter when one arrived; it would be different, naturally enough, if towns, villages, houses *moved*—then one might have a real reason to hurry—but they did not. Nor did people themselves move very much, in Mma Ramotswe's experience; she remembered how in Mochudi, in what people fondly called the old days, there were people who could be seen standing or sitting in one place for days on end. If one wanted to see a certain man—an expert in goats—then it was well known that he could be found sitting under a particular tree, and that was where advice on goats could always be obtained. Her father told her that this man had once been accused of stock theft by somebody from a neighbouring village. The police at Mochudi had listened to the complaint but had dismissed it out of hand—and quite rightly too. They had explained that the man in question never went anywhere, as everybody knew very well, and that it was quite out of the question that he could have participated in a stock theft elsewhere. "That shows, Precious," Obed Ramotswe had said, "that if you do one thing all the time, then people will know that is what you do."

The old days: people sometimes laughed at those who talked about the old days, but Mma Ramotswe was not one of them. She knew that all of us, even the youngest, had some old days to remember. Children of ten remember how it was when they were five, just as men or women of fifty remember the way things were when they were twenty; and if those distant pasts are coated with sweetness and longing, then that might be because people indeed felt happier then. She did not think that people now were any *worse* than they used to be, but it was very clear to her that they had less time. In the old days Botswana people were rarely in a rush to get somewhere else—why should they be? Nowadays, people were always thinking of getting somewhere—they travelled around far more, rushing from here to there and then back again. She would never let her life go that way; she would always take the time to drink tea, to look at the sky, and to talk. What else was there to do? Make money? Why? Did money bring any greater happiness than that furnished by a well-made cup of red bush tea and a moment or two with a good friend? She thought not.

I'M SORRY, Mmampho. You never told me your name."

Mma Ramotswe felt that it was her fault. People ignored domestic helpers—presences in the background—and rarely asked their names. She usually did, but had forgotten to do so when she first met this woman; addressing her as *Mother of Mpho* was perfectly polite in such circumstances, of course, but using her real name would be even better.

The courtesy had its effect. "I am Pelenomi, Mma. Thank you."

Mma Ramotswe held out her hands in greeting. She was pleased that she had found the woman at home, as she had hoped to do, and that Mpho did not appear to be there.

"Your little boy?" she asked. "Is he looking after the cattle?"

Pelenomi nodded. "He must count them each night before it gets dark. Then he comes home for his food."

"He has a busy day," said Mma Ramotswe. "School, and then the cattle."

"Yes. He is a good boy, Mma. He works hard." She looked at her visitor. "You have children yourself, Mma?"

Mma Ramotswe explained about the fostering of Puso and Motholeli. "I am their mother now," she said. "Their own mother is late." She paused. "And I have a late baby, Mma. It is a long time ago now."

"But it is never long ago when that happens," said Pelenomi. "I have a late child too, Mma. Mpho had a sister. She was never well. God took her back."

There was a silence—a moment of shared loss. Then Pelenomi asked why Mma Ramotswe had come to see her. "It is something to do with that cattle business?" she asked.

Mma Ramotswe nodded. "It is very difficult, Mma. I am not sure how to talk to you about this."

They were standing outside the entrance to her single-roomed servants' quarters—not much more than a whitewashed shack. Pelenomi now invited Mma Ramotswe inside and sat down—with the natural grace of one accustomed to sitting on the floor. Mma Ramotswe lowered herself to the ground. One should not forget how to sit on the floor, she thought—never, no matter what happened in one's life, no matter where one's life journey took one. A president, she believed, should be able to sit on the floor with as much ease as the humblest herdsman.

"What have you found, Mma?" asked Pelenomi.

"I was at the school, Mma."

Pelenomi stiffened. "At the school? Why?"

"I wanted to speak to Mpho. I didn't want adults to be around him when we spoke. I'm sorry, Mma, I didn't ask your permission— I hope you don't mind. I thought he was a witness, you see."

"He did not see anything. He is just a boy."

Mma Ramotswe said nothing for a moment. Then she said, "He told me that he did it, Mma."

There was no mistaking Pelenomi's surprise. "Mpho told you that, Mma? Oh, that is just a child speaking, Mma. A child says the first thing that comes into his mind. You should not listen to a child. My son did not do anything, Mma. Nothing."

Her voice had risen towards the end of this, as her indignation grew. It was as Mma Ramotswe had imagined—the loyal mother refusing to accept that her son could have done something like that. But what was said next was less than expected.

"No, it is not my son, Mma. It is . . . it is another person altogether." She paused. "I know who it is, Mma. I know."

Mma Ramotswe watched her carefully. This woman was not lying.

"Who then, Mma? Mr. Fortitude Seleo?"

Pelenomi's lip curled. "Not that man. He could not do a thing like that. He is too busy walking around smiling at people."

There was bitterness in this last remark.

"That is better than scowling at them, I think, Mma. But that is neither here nor there. If it is not Seleo, then who is it?"

"It is another man altogether. I cannot name him, Mma. I'm sorry."

"But why did Mpho say that it was him? I saw his face when he told me, Mma. I could tell that he was very upset. A child does not make these things up."

The answer came quickly. "Because he thought it was me, Mma. He thought that his mother had done it. He was frightened for his mother. That is why he told you it was him. A child does not want his mother to go to prison."

"Why did he think it was you?"

"Because he saw something. And I told him. I had to tell him something."

"What did he see?"

Pelenomi was now becoming flustered, and was clearly regretting allowing herself to be pushed into a corner by Mma Ramotswe's questions. "There are some things that children see . . ."

"What did he see, Mma?"

"He saw some blood. He saw a handkerchief with blood on it."

A small insect moved slowly across the floor, a spider perhaps, making Mma Ramotswe move her legs slightly. Pelenomi watched the movement.

"I keep this house clean, Mma," she muttered.

"I'm sure you do. There are ants everywhere. It is not your fault. But what about this handkerchief, Mma?"

The misery came through Pelenomi's voice. "It was the handkerchief of the man who had done that thing to the cattle. He was in this house after he had done it. Mpho was asleep—he never wakes up. He saw the cloth in the morning."

"And he thought it was yours?"

Pelenomi nodded. "I told him it was mine. I told him that Moeti had done some bad thing to me and that I had taken my revenge on his cattle. That is why he lied to protect me."

Unless, thought Mma Ramotswe, *you are lying to protect him.*

There was a knock on the door, a voice muttering *Ko! Ko!*

Pelenomi looked up in alarm and began to scramble to her feet. *Moeti?* wondered Mma Ramotswe. The door opened before she could reach it and a man stepped into the room. He stood for a moment, confused by the unexpected presence. It was not Moeti. Oreeditse Modise, the teacher at the school.

He'd come in with the confidence of one entering the house of his lover. And that, Mma Ramotswe decided at that moment, was exactly what he was. She did not have to think about it: the dwarf was the lover of Mpho's mother. And more than that: he was the man who had attacked the cattle. Of course he was; why else had he and his secretary exclaimed their outrage over the incident with such forcefulness? That had been an act: he was the perpetrator, and the secretary must somehow have come into that information. But why had he done it? Pelenomi had given a clue to that in saying that she had made up a story about her being a victim of Moeti. Well, she had not made it up; she was. And Modise had avenged her in the way they knew would cause maximum distress to Moeti.

They looked at each other wordlessly. Then Mma Ramotswe rose to her feet and dusted off her skirt. "I mustn't stay, Mma," she said. "Now that you have another visitor."

The teacher was staring at her. She met his gaze.

"I have been looking into this cattle problem," Mma Ramotswe said quietly. "Now I must go. But there are a few questions I would like an answer to. Please think carefully before you give me your reply."

Pelenomi and Modise exchanged glances. Then Modise nodded. "What are these questions, Mma?"

"My questions," began Mma Ramotswe, "are these ones, Rra. Would I be right in thinking that this very bad thing that has happened here will not happen again? Would I be right in thinking that if I were to tell Moeti that everything is over, that not one more of his cattle will suffer, then there would be no more of this sort of thing happening? Would I be right in thinking that the person who did this would realise that I could go to the police if I wanted to and insist that they sorted it all out? Would that person—whoever he might be—also understand that there is no excuse for settling one wrong with another?"

There was a further exchange of glances between Modise and

Pelenomi. Then he spoke: "I think you would be right, Mma. I am sure of it."

"Good," said Mma Ramotswe. "Then that is the end of that, I think."

SHE LEFT THE VAN where it was and walked over to the Moeti farmhouse. She found him in his living room, listening to the Radio Botswana news. He greeted her cheerfully and offered her a cold beer, which she declined.

"I hoped that you might have celebrated with me, Mma Ramotswe," he said. "But I can drink your beer too! A bigger celebration for me."

She was puzzled. "Celebrating, Rra?"

"Yes. Celebrating your solving the issue of my poor cattle." He reached for a beer from a tray on his side table. "Here goes, Mma Ramotswe. Here's to the top detective who sorts everything out one hundred per cent. Here's to you!"

"You are happy, Rra?" she said lamely.

"Happy? Yes, of course I am. Seleo came to see me. Not to complain this time but to tell me that he had arranged for the fencing work to start on Tuesday. So no more trespassing by his cattle. But he did something else—to make up for all my inconvenience. He has given me six months' supply of cattle-lick for my cattle."

Mma Ramotswe was at a loss as to what to say.

"I think what happened was that you must have put the fear of God into him, Mma. Once he realised that the country's top detective was on to him, he must have caved in and decided to apologise. And there's another thing, Mma. He gave me the cash value of the cattle he did that terrible thing to. A good price. So I am happy now to say that it is all over. We can be good neighbours again. That is the Botswana way, and that is what I want."

Mma Ramotswe looked up at the ceiling. She had no idea what to make of this, but she knew that whichever way one looked at it, this was an entirely satisfactory outcome. She might not be completely certain who carried out the attack on the cattle, but the issue was well and truly put to bed. It was not Mpho, she thought; and although until a few moments ago she had thought it was the teacher, that conclusion had now been called into question. Pelenomi had effectively blamed Modise, but if he had done it, why had Seleo acted as he had? She had advised him to make some sort of friendly approach to Moeti and to give him a gift of cattle-lick. He had then gone further than that—much further—and had more or less acknowledged his guilt by compensating his neighbour for the loss of his cattle. Why would he do that? Unless, of course, he was trying to protect the real culprit—the teacher? But what possible reason could he have to do that?

She continued to stare up at the ceiling. Perhaps everybody is lying, she thought. And as she thought this, she remembered a passage from Clovis Andersen. *There are some cases where everybody tells lies,* he wrote. *In these cases you will never know the truth. The more you try to find out what happened, the more lies you uncover. My advice is: do not lose sleep over such matters. Move on, ladies and gentlemen: move on.*

She continued to think about it as she drove home. She was now inclined to acquit Mr. Seleo, who was exactly as the security guard had described him. He was a good man who had decided to see whether a generous approach to his neighbour would heal their rift. And it had. No, it was not him. It was the teacher, then—the jealous lover who resented the way Mr. Moeti had treated the woman he loved. Or—and she kept coming back to this possibility—it really had been Mpho, that poor little boy who was desperate for attention and filled with anger at the man who had harmed his mother in some unspoken way. And the mother had then so engineered things that Mma Ramotswe would think it was the teacher, in order to cover for her son . . . or for herself.

These questions occupied her mind all the way back to Gaborone. She was sure that it was one of the three: Mpho, his mother, or the teacher. The mother had been genuinely surprised at Mpho's confession, and that pointed to his innocence. If it was not the boy, then, it was the mother, or the teacher. Of the two, she favoured the teacher as the culprit; the attack itself did not seem to be the work of a woman. She was not sure why she felt that; she just did. A woman knows what another woman will do, she thought.

But then, as she reached the edge of the city, she suddenly smiled and said to herself: "Does it really matter? The milk is spilled. It will not be spilled again." There would be no further attacks—that was clear, and the damage had been set right by one who was not responsible for it. All that was lacking was the punishment of the one responsible. But punishment often did not do what we wanted it to do. If the teacher were to be denounced, he could lose his job and then Mpho and his mother could lose the man who was their one chance of something better. There was no reason for her to bring that about.

This thought of milk brought tea to her mind. She needed tea—a large cup of it—and that was what she would make when she returned home to Zebra Drive. She would say to Mr. J.L.B. Matekoni: "A dreadfully difficult case, Rra, all sorted out now. But don't ask me to explain how it worked out, Rra. There are some things that are just too hard to explain, and I think that this is one of them."

Perhaps she would say that. Perhaps. But she was not sure whether she would *think* that, as she was now reaching a firmer conclusion. The teacher did it. It *was* him. Yes, definitely. Or perhaps . . .

CHAPTER SEVENTEEN

SHE CRIED FOR JOY

WHEN HE READ ALOUD the wedding invitation Mr. J.L.B. Matekoni had said, "At long last the elder Mr. Radiphuti and the late Mrs. Radiphuti have pleasure in inviting you to the wedding of their beloved Phuti Edgar Radiphuti, to Grace Makutsi, Dip. Sec. RSVP."

He had corrected himself immediately. "It doesn't actually say *at long last,* Mma Ramotswe. That was me. It just says *The elder Mr. Radiphuti,* and so on."

Mma Ramotswe smiled. "I see that the invitation is also from the late mother," she said. "I'm not sure whether that wording is quite right, but that does not matter. The important thing is, as you say, that at long last those two are getting married." She also had some doubt about putting RSVP so close to Dip. Sec. as some people—perhaps some of the older country guests—might interpret RSVP as a qualification and wonder what it was.

These were little things, though, as Mma Ramotswe pointed out. What counted was that on that particular Saturday, Mma Makutsi was to become Mrs. Phuti Radiphuti; that the weather was behaving itself, with no unexpected storm to disrupt proceedings; that the bus bringing the Makutsi guests down from Bobo-nong had made the journey with no greater disaster than a flat tyre just outside Mahalapye; and that all the arrangements for the wedding feast had gone as smoothly as could possibly be hoped for.

This last achievement was partly to the credit of Mma Poto-kwane, who had interpreted Mma Makutsi's acceptance of help with the pots and with cake as a green light to take over control of all aspects of the feast. Nobody had objected to this, not even Mma Makutsi, who, although she had in the past been irritated by Mma Potokwane's controlling tendencies, found them a great reassurance now.

"She is like a hurricane," Mma Makutsi whispered to Mma Ramotswe on Friday morning when Mma Ramotswe phoned her to check that all was well. "She is in the next room right now, and there is a lot of banging of pots and some big thumping sounds that I cannot make out."

"Cakes," suggested Mma Ramotswe. "That is the sound of her cakes being taken out of their tins."

"Maybe, Mma. Now I think they are chopping something, but I do not know what it is."

"She will make sure that everything is all right," said Mma Ramotswe. "I remember what she did at my own wedding. She got all the house-mothers at the orphan farm to do the cooking. She was like a general telling the Botswana Defence Force what to do. March this way, march that way—that sort of thing."

"I don't think she will let anything go wrong," said Mma Makutsi, not without relief.

In this, she proved to be right. With the same efficiency and determination with which she organised the affairs of the orphan farm, Mma Potokwane ensured that everything was cooked and ready well before the guests began to file into the church where the ceremony was to be held. So while the guests waited in their pews, craning their necks to look at and admire the fine outfits that every-body had donned for the occasion—the bright traditional print dresses of the women, the smartly pressed blue suits of the men, the colourful voile frocks of the little girls—back in the grounds of the Radiphuti house the tables along the sides of the tent were already stacked with pots of meat, with large bowls of gravy, with pumpkin and peas, with every sort of dish that anybody present might wish for. Mma Potokwane had left nothing to chance, and had been delighted to discover the generosity of the catering budget that the Radiphuti family had made available. If anybody came to the feast hungry or undernourished, she felt, then they would not go away in that state. Belts could be loosened if necessary, collars unbuttoned; it would be a memorable feast.

Mma Ramotswe had been allocated a seat in the front row, alongside Mr. J.L.B. Matekoni. Puso and Motholeli were in the row immediately behind them, seated beside two other children from Bobonong, with whom they had formed those instant friendships that children seem to manage so effortlessly. A little further behind, Charlie and Fanwell, both wearing shiny suits and bright ties, studied their hymn sheets conscientiously. When the time came to sing, as the bride entered on the arm of her uncle, the two young men proved to be enthusiastic singers, even if in different keys from each other.

As Mma Makutsi entered the church, a ripple of applause broke out at the back and spread through the congregation. Children waved, and some of the women ululated—a traditional sign of pleasure, pride, and congratulation. Mma Makutsi's eyes were moist behind her large glasses; it had been so long a journey for her, and now she was at its culmination, in the presence of her family and those whom she loved. She saw their faces—the aunt who had helped her financially, in every small way that she could, who had paid for that first bus journey that she made to Gaborone all those years ago; the cousins who had written to her regularly and had so generously congratulated her on each small triumph; and there, halfway down the church, in an aisle seat and turned to face her as she took those few steps to the altar, was the retired Principal of the Botswana Secretarial College, smiling with pride at her own, indirect role in bringing about the career that had led to all this.

Mma Ramotswe's eyes, and the eyes of every woman present, were on the dress. It was magnificent: a floor-length creation of ivory satin, with large puffed sleeves and a sash round the waist. At the back, this sash was tied in a giant bow, like the wings of a butterfly. The bodice was trimmed with white lace, and around her neck Mma Makutsi wore a delicate gold chain with a pendant cross, a gift from Phuti Radiphuti, the groom who now awaited her at the altar.

There would be many speeches in the wedding tent later on. Now, as Phuti Radiphuti stepped forward to take his bride from the uncle, and as the congregation finished the opening hymn, the minister cleared his throat.

"Dearly beloved," he began, "we are gathered here in this place to bring together in marriage two people, our brother and our sister, Phuti and Grace. They are being married here because they love one another and they declare that love now before you, this congregation, and before all Botswana. If there is any person who knows of any reason why these two people cannot be joined together in marriage by the laws of this country, then that person must now speak."

There was silence. Charlie glanced at Fanwell, and winked.

The minister continued, "And so I shall now ask them to exchange their vows. Phuti, please take Grace's hand. That is right. Now then . . ."

The marriage was solemnised. Mma Ramotswe watched, and from her position so close to the front heard every word of the vows.

She had so many memories: of her first meeting with Mma Makutsi, who had presented herself for interview with such confidence and determination; of her initial difficulties in coming to terms with her new assistant's rather prickly behaviour; of her growing appreciation for her many fine qualities; of her pleasure when eventually she had found Phuti Radiphuti and her delight in their engagement. Mma Makutsi had been fortunate in finding Phuti, but fortune had also smiled on Mma Ramotswe, who now glanced tenderly at Mr. J.L.B. Matekoni at her side. He noticed her glance, and touched the sleeve of her dress lightly, a small gesture that conveyed so much.

Mma Ramotswe cried, privately and unseen. She, the only begetter of the No. 1 Ladies' Detective Agency, cried. She cried for joy.

AFTERWARDS, they left the church and went to the wedding tent at the Radiphuti house. Now the sound of voices rose, and there were children and dogs, and even one or two interested birds circling overhead. The uncle with the broken nose—the greedy one from Bobonong—made the main speech on Mma Makutsi's side. Mma Ramotswe tried to follow what he had to say, but it seemed to her that it was hopelessly confused—some story of a cow that had run off to another field but who never forgot the cows back in the first field. It was a message of some sort, she assumed, but nobody seemed to be very interested in it. It was not very tactful, she thought, to use cow metaphors when one was talking about a bride, but Mma Makutsi herself did not seem to mind, and clapped as loudly as everybody else did when the uncle eventually sat down.

Mma Makutsi moved from table to table, from chair to chair, talking to the guests, accepting good wishes, showing her bouquet of flowers to the children, and doing her duty as hostess, as the new Mma Radiphuti. When she reached Mma Ramotswe's table, at first she did not say anything, but leaned forward and embraced the woman who had given her her one great chance in life, who had been such a good friend to her.

Then she spoke. "I am still going to be coming into the No. 1 Ladies' Detective Agency, Mma," she said. "This will not change things. I shall still be working."

"I will be waiting for you," said Mma Ramotswe. "After your honeymoon, of course."

She looked at the bride. She saw the shoes.

"The shoes you gave me, Mma," Mma Makutsi said. "They are very beautiful."

Mma Ramotswe smiled. "Charlie did his best, didn't he?"

Mma Makutsi inclined her head graciously. "He did. It was very good of him to try."

They both laughed. Charlie had tried to fix the original pair of broken shoes, and had not done too bad a job. He had done it discreetly, unasked, taking the shoes from a cupboard in the office and returning them a couple of days later. Mma Makutsi had been touched by this, even if his repair had in the end been inadequate. It was a peace offering, and she accepted it, for her part apologising for jumping to unwarranted conclusions in the affair of the twins. And that brought forth an apology from him. "You are not a warthog," he said. "I am very sorry, Mma, for saying that."

Mma Ramotswe had then slipped out and bought a new pair of shoes for Mma Makutsi—ones that she thought would be suitable for the wedding. These had proved perfect, and Mma Makutsi had shown them to Phuti Radiphuti at the same time as she confessed to the destruction of their predecessors. He had not minded in the least. "The important thing is that you didn't hurt your ankle," he said. "That is what counts."

212 Alexander McCall Smith

THERE WERE MANY SPEECHES, mostly by relatives on either side. Weddings and speeches went together, and the guests listened patiently, knowing that there would be more food later on. That food kept the guests busy for the best part of two hours. Then there was music, provided by the Big Time Kalahari Jazz Band. This led to dancing, with Mma Makutsi and Phuti Radiphuti taking to the floor to general applause and whistles. The dance lessons they had both taken all that time ago came in useful, and Phuti, who had not been a particularly good dancer to begin with, proved competent enough now, even with his artificial foot. After that first dance, Mma Makutsi danced with Mr. J.L.B. Matekoni, and Mma Ramotswe was invited to dance with the uncle with the broken nose. She put on a brave face over this, managing to control her winces as the uncle trod heavily on her toes and pushed her clumsily about the floor of the tent. It was a great relief to her when the band stopped and she was able to make her way back to her chair.

Eventually it was time to leave, and Mma Ramotswe and Mr. J.L.B. Matekoni drove home in the white van, with Mma Ramotswe at the wheel. It was early evening now, and Mr. J.L.B. Matekoni, who was feeling tired, went off to have his somewhat delayed Saturday afternoon nap. After the feast there would be no question of dinner, so she had no cooking to do. The children had gone to a friend's house for the night; Mma Ramotswe was alone.

She went out into the garden. The sun had set, but there was still a faint glow in the west, above the Kalahari—enough to provide that half-light that makes everything seem so rounded, so perfect. She stood in her garden and looked about her. Against the gradually darkening sky, the branches of the trees traced a pattern of twigs and leaves—a pattern of such intricacy and delicacy that those standing below might look up and wonder why the world can be so beautiful and yet break the heart.

She stood still for a while, thinking about marriage. A wedding was a strange ceremony, she thought, with all those formal words, those solemn vows made by one to another; whereas the real question that should be put to the two people involved was a very simple one. *Are you happy with each other?* was the only question that should be asked; to which they both should reply, preferably in unison, *Yes.* Simple questions—and simple answers— were what we needed in life. That was what Mma Ramotswe believed. Yes.

She went back into the house, as night had come over the town, the sky suddenly going from deep blue into black—and stars had appeared over Africa. She gave one last glance towards the horizon, to check whether the Southern Cross was where it should be. It was.

africa
africa africa
africa africa africa
africa africa
africa

ABOUT THE AUTHOR

Alexander McCall Smith is the author of the No. 1 Ladies' Detective Agency series, the Isabel Dalhousie series, the Portuguese Irregular Verbs series, and the 44 Scotland Street series. He is professor emeritus of medical law at the University of Edinburgh and has served on many national and international bodies concerned with bioethics. He was born in what is now known as Zimbabwe and taught law at the University of Botswana. He lives in Scotland.